# The RoutledgeFalmer Reader in Inclusive Education

## What is 'Inclusion'?

This invaluable text draws together an impressive and wide-ranging selection of articles on inclusion to bring clarity and lucidity to a complex subject. While the majority of texts deal with inclusive education within narrow parameters, this book aims to extend our understanding of inclusion by connecting issues of race, social disadvantage, gender and other factors. It successfully integrates rigorous theorising and sound empirical research with clear, accessible and practical guidance for professionals.

The book has 18 chapters divided into key areas such as:

- concepts and contexts
- gender, race, disability, poverty and social class
- exclusion from school
- action in school
- inclusion post-school
- promoting and managing systematic change.

Each chapter ends with questions and issues for reflection. The book also includes an annotated list of further reading. It is designed to encourage readers to conduct their own research. This is an important and useful text for practitioner, postgraduate students, researchers, academics and policy-makers in education.

**Keith Topping** is Professor of Educational and Social Research in the Faculty of Education and Social Work at the University of Dundee, Scotland.

**Sheelagh Maloney** worked as a teacher, manager and senior psychologist before starting her own company The Inclusion Consultancy Ltd in 2003.

# Readers in education

**The RoutledgeFalmer Reader in Higher Education**
*Edited by Malcolm Tight*

**The RoutledgeFalmer Reader in Inclusive Education**
*Edited by Keith Topping and Sheelagh Maloney*

**The RoutledgeFalmer Reader in Language and Literacy**
*Edited by Teresa Grainger*

**The RoutledgeFalmer Reader in Multicultural Education**
*Edited by Gloria Ladson-Billings and David Gillborn*

**The RoutledgeFalmer Reader in Psychology of Education**
*Edited by Harry Daniels and Anne Edwards*

**The RoutledgeFalmer Reader in Science Education**
*Edited by John Gilbert*

**The RoutledgeFalmer Reader in Sociology of Education**
*Edited by Stephen J. Ball*

**The RoutledgeFalmer Reader in Teaching and Learning**
*Edited by E. C. Wragg*

# The RoutledgeFalmer Reader in Inclusive Education

Edited by
**Keith Topping and
Sheelagh Maloney**

RoutledgeFalmer
Taylor & Francis Group

LONDON AND NEW YORK

First published 2005
by RoutledgeFalmer
2 Park Square, Milton Park, Abingdon, Oxon OX14 4RN

Simultaneously published in the USA and Canada
By RoutledgeFalmer
270 Madison Ave, New York, NY 10016

*RoutledgeFalmer is an imprint of the Taylor and Francis Group*

Typeset in Sabon by
Newgen Imaging Systems (P) Ltd, Chennai, India
Printed and bound in Great Britain by
The Cromwell Press, Trowbridge, Wiltshire

*British Library Cataloguing in Publication Data*
A catalogue record for this book is available from the British Library

*Library of Congress Cataloging in Publication Data*
A catalog record for this book has been requested

ISBN 0–415–33664–3 (hbk)
ISBN 0–415–33665–1 (pbk)

# CONTENTS

# ILLUSTRATIONS

## Figures

## Tables

## Boxes

# PREFACE

This book aims to integrate and bridge theorising and empirical research with accessible and clear evidence-based practical guidance for workers in all educational contexts at all systemic levels. It seeks to bring some clarity to what is often a muddy area, while sustaining balance and avoiding reinforcing singular perceptions or espousing particular value judgements. It raises many questions that await a clear answer or invite alternative answers – but tries to raise these questions clearly so that the challenges for the future are evident to all.

The book seeks to offer students, lecturers and researchers some of the best material in the area, saving time and effort in developing their own collections of relevant papers and chapters, as well as offering a consistent high quality of material from a systematic rather than opportunistic search. It incorporates prompts to onward reading and reflection designed to add continuing value to the reader.

The main readership is expected to be those engaged in pre-service or in-service education and training in education and related welfare professions (as learners, module designers, deliverers, directors or inspectors). This would include postgraduate students (PGCEs, masters and doctorates) and undergraduates. As teachers are encouraged to undertake research as part of their professional development and progress to Chartered Teacher status, this book should prove essential reading.

The book will also appeal to other professionals engaged in self-managed continuous professional development (e.g. educational psychologists), and to academic staff interested in applied and interdisciplinary research. It should also appeal to policy-makers and administrators charged with translating the inclusion rhetoric into reality.

Keith Topping and Sheelagh Maloney

# INTRODUCTION

## K. Topping and S. Maloney

'The act of embracing as a member of a whole.'

(Oxford English Dictionary)

'We, being many, are one body – and every one, members one of another – having gifts differing according to the grace that is given to us...'

(Romans 12: 5–6)

'Inclusion' – a word much more used in this century than in the last. It has to do with people and society valuing diversity and overcoming barriers. But what exactly does it mean? Do different people mean different things by it? Would you recognise it if you walked past it? Where would you find it? How do you create it? How do you know when you have created it? This book hopes to illuminate the way to some of the answers to some of these questions. You will not find all the answers here, but the editors hope that you will emerge asking more intelligent and challenging questions. Like learning, inclusion is a dynamic process, not a static condition – a journey, not a destination.

So, welcome to the debate! This introductory chapter aims to offer a broad overview of the field, but be warned that it also aims to provoke and challenge. The chapters that follow offer more specific detail connected directly to relevant evidence. Critical analysis features throughout, but this is not intended to be negative and destructive or designed to shatter naïve optimism. On the contrary, the aim is to better equip the reader to deal with the realities of everyday life, while moving towards a more selective, effective and robust form of inclusive practice which is founded solidly on clear conceptualisation and good evidence.

## Focus

This book addresses that subset of the social inclusion agenda that is within educational contexts, including early years provision, primary and secondary education, further and higher education, and community education. It addresses inclusion issues arising from special educational needs and disability, but goes far beyond that to consider those arising from social class, socio-economic disadvantage, race, gender and other factors. One practical reason for this wide scope is that these factors often interact, and consideration of only one factor in isolation can lead to faulty conclusions.

## Definitions and historical changes

Exploring some of the main concepts and boundaries of the territory of inclusion can prove a tricky business. A brief overview is offered here, and the first ensuing section of this volume (Concepts and Context) explores these issues in greater detail.

### Special education and disability

It all started with 'special educational needs' (as we now call them – in the past much more offensive terms were used). In the previous century, concern about pupils with serious learning difficulties led to the development of whole industries providing 'special education' in 'special schools'. This development of provision was paralleled by feeder industries categorising children into 'special' or otherwise. Much of this segregation into 'special schools' proceeded without reference to any evidence as to whether such pupils learned more effectively in such settings. However, once the 'special education' industries were well established, professional vested interest in the status quo tended to resist any changes. And once a child was in a special school, few ever returned to the mainstream.

In fact, it is difficult to find convincing evidence that pupils do better in special schools. However, much of the subsequent movement in political and public opinion towards the 'integration' or 'reintegration' of pupils with learning difficulties into 'mainstream' schools stemmed more from ethical arguments than from any functional rationale. Many educationalists came to talk about 'integration', but rather fewer of them were actually doing it. Even before 'integration' became widespread in practice, the rhetoric moved on and 'Inclusion' became the new buzzword.

### Social inclusion and political agendas

The concept of educational inclusion was now set in the much wider context of 'social inclusion', implying concern about all those of all ages who were marginalised, unproductive and non-participative in society. If 'society' operates in family, friendships, the community, education, the workplace and leisure activities, social inclusion in some or perhaps all these contexts was presumed desirable. This does not mean that everybody should be the same. Social exclusion is associated with a combination of problems such as poor skills, unemployment, low incomes, poor housing, high crime environments, bad health and family breakdowns. It should not be assumed that these are purely urban phenomena (Shucksmith, 2000). Economic, political and cultural inclusion should also be considered. Section two of this volume explores issues of gender, race, disability, poverty and social class.

Margaret Thatcher (erstwhile UK right-wing Prime Minister) famously stated that there was no such thing as society, and therefore presumably no such thing as social inclusion. Concerns about social inclusion articulated much more with the traditional agenda of left-wing government, and in the United Kingdom were associated with the Labour Party assuming and sustaining governmental office. Such concerns were not new, and might previously have been debated in the context of the 'Equal Opportunities' agenda. Of course, equal opportunities did not mean simply treating everyone equally, since that would merely reinforce pre-existing differences – rather, it implied treating different people differently so that they would have equal opportunities to maximise their potential.

## Human rights

The concepts of 'equal opportunities' and inclusion incorporated notions of human rights and entitlements – grand ethical ideas which can prove difficult to translate into effective practice on the ground. The rights and entitlements of children (in particular) have received increasing attention in recent years (e.g. Alaimo and Klug, 2002), being for example strongly endorsed by the UN Convention on the Rights of the Child, by UNESCO in the Salamanca Statement, and reflected in the United Nations' call for 'Education for All'. This has been coupled with developments in practical methods to promote pupil involvement and participation in their own schooling (e.g. Beresford, 2003).

## Conceptual and legislative change – and unintended consequences

As these definitional changes unfolded, previous ways of understanding the world (and educational needs) were challenged. Within special education, the old system of categorisation of children located the problem within the child, conceptualising it as a deficit or defect in the individual, and applying a medical, diagnostic model – as if learning difficulties were some kind of disease. Pseudo-diagnostic labels such as 'educationally subnormal' were used. Sometimes this medical way of thinking was extended further, as in talk of 'social pathology' in families or communities.

From 1980 onwards, such categorisation of children (which implied a permanent condition and that they were labelled for life) was made illegal in the United Kingdom (although in the United States such categorisation carried on). Political pressure from disability groups and parental advocacy had begun to change societal values, with consequent effects on legislation. Instead, the emphasis in assessment was to be on specifying the needs of the child – what kind of teaching and resources were most likely to effect educational progress.

Unfortunately, this apparently positive development degenerated all too rapidly into a welter of wasteful bureaucracy, with statutory assessments conducted by highly qualified professionals used by various stakeholders as a tool to unlock resources. However, the total pool of resources available did not grow rapidly enough to meet the increased demand, so these expensive levers often yielded rather small movement. Also, a postcode lottery operated, some local authorities maintaining statements or records of special educational needs on over twice as many children as other authorities with very similar demographic characteristics (although whether volume of paperwork related to actual meeting of needs is another issue). Additionally, the articulate and assertive middle classes who could play the system tended to do disproportionately well out of it, diverting resources from more needy children from socio-economically disadvantaged families.

Nonetheless, the emphasis on needs did result in a movement away from medical models of disability, and towards social and educational models of disability, which acknowledged that educational difficulties are dependent upon the educational context in which the child is situated, and the type and quality of the teaching they receive – in other words, factors outside the child as well as inside (Mittler, 2000). Subsequently, assessment of children became even broader, with increasing emphasis on a range of contexts or ecologies in which the child operated in different ways at different systemic levels – ecosystemic assessment. It followed that if the micro-ecology changed, the child's performance and behaviour was likely to change.

Government thinking was also becoming more ecosystemic, acknowledging the interaction of a multiplicity of variables. Traditionally, various central and local government services for children and families had been delivered by separate agencies, sometimes characterised not only by a lack of coordination but at times by active enmity and obstruction. Central government increasingly called for 'joined up' or integrated services. Some local government authorities introduced developments such as 'community' or 'full-service' schools as vehicles for this (at times while remaining patently un-joined-up themselves). Others combined education and social services for children into a notionally integrated 'Children's Services' department.

However, other government policies had unintended consequences which hampered inclusion. For example, the emphasis on reaching attainment targets, free parental choice of school and the publication of league tables of raw scores on high stakes tests of questionable reliability and validity created powerful disincentives for head teachers to open their doors to pupils whose performance might in any way damage the reputation and consequently the viability of the school. At the same time, these factors created a pressure on existing school populations to achieve the new targets, doubling the barriers to Inclusion.

Despite this, national policy-making continued undeterred. One strand of the government's Skills Strategy relates to the vision of Learning Communities as a means of tackling educational disadvantage. Alongside the Regional Skills Partnerships that focus on linking skills, business support and economic development to drive up regional and local productivity, the government is interested in promoting and applying 'the capability of local councils to develop their collective base of skills and learning as "learning communities"', to raise aspirations and build the confidence and skills of local people. Indices of 'community cohesion' encompassing eight domains of 'social capital' have been developed (Forrest and Kearns, 1999; Cantle, 2001), not least in response to concern in places about community unrest and racially motivated rioting.

Beyond this, there is a growing critical mass of thinking that the term SEN is becoming redundant, and may actually be unhelpful (given its overtones of bipolar categorisation rather than continuous dimension). Legislative change in education often tends to follow operational change rather than lead it. Consequently, legislation in the United Kingdom is only just beginning to emerge from the conceptual constraints of SEN terminology, by incorporating the notion of 'Reasonable Adjustment', which places an obligation on the school to create a suitable learning environment for all children. It will be interesting to see how this is addressed by the legal profession as case law develops, and whether this will lead to more inclusive practice. As it becomes accepted that every child has a right to learn differently and teaching has to take account of these differences, then Inclusion should truly become a school improvement issue, with quality assurance at its core.

## Conceptual confusion and behavioural divergence

However, this plethora of conceptions has led to considerable semantic confusion. The different implicit definitions of 'inclusion' espoused by different workers might not be immediately evident in their conversations related to the topic – worsening later confusion. Catlett and Osher (1994) undertook a content analysis of various policy and position statements from national organisations in the United States on the inclusion of students with disabilities. Less than half of these actually offered a definition of inclusion, and no two definitions were alike. Small wonder that teachers and parents can become confused.

Rhetoric also often departs from reality. Croll and Moses (2003) tracked a number of local authorities (all of whom had policy statements committing them to the fullest possible 'inclusion') over a period of years, during which time some of these authorities actually increased the number of pupils in segregated special provision. Indeed, the move towards actual inclusion of pupils with special educational needs has been characterised as 'painfully slow' (Gold, 2003). Based on statistics analysed by Norwich (2003), the Centre for Studies on Inclusive Education (www.csie.org) calculated that at current rates of change it would take the average local education authority 55 years to reach the inclusion levels already achieved by the London Borough of Newham – and the worst performing local authority well over 100 years (Gold names these authorities). Between 1997 and 2001, 41 local authorities actually increased the numbers of children in segregated special schools.

## Expanding concepts of inclusion

All commentators now agree that inclusion should mean much more than the mere physical presence of pupils with special educational needs in mainstream schools (e.g. Nind *et al.*, 2003). Such pupils should also be able to access the mainstream curriculum successfully, which may need supporting, individualising or differentiating in some way. Indeed, in the United Kingdom and the United States there is a legal obligation on schools to provide curricular and physical access for **all** pupils. Apart from issues of learning, they should feel, behave as, and be treated as full members or citizens of the school community. Farrell and Ainscow (2002) have described this as the Presence–Acceptance–Participation–Achievement cycle. Beyond this, inclusion implies celebrating the diversity and supporting the achievement and participation of **all** pupils who face learning and/or behaviour challenges of any kind, in terms of socio-economic circumstances, ethnic origin, cultural heritage, religion, linguistic heritage, gender, sexual preference and so on. However, ideally inclusion should go even further, and schools should engage **all** families and the community as well as **all** children, seeking effective intergenerational learning across the lifespan, which might occur inside schools or outside or through a combination of these. These expanding notions of inclusion are illustrated in the four levels of Figure 0.1.

However, the area of social and educational inclusion remains chronically under-theorised, limiting attempts to bring consistency and cohesiveness to the field, (despite the courageous efforts of such as Clough and Corbett, 2000; Dyson and Millward, 2000; Norwich, 2000).

It is also worth noting that little of this might be completely new. Thus, Brendtro *et al.*, (1990) asserted that inclusion is not a new concept, but rather something that operated very effectively before cultures were economically and culturally driven by 'things material' and social mobility led to the decline of family and community life. If it 'takes a whole village to raise a child', it is likely to take a bundle of resources to raise a child with special challenges if the community and family have disintegrated.

## Perceptions of inclusion

Legislation in the UK has tended to be based upon epidemiological surveys suggesting that 20 per cent of the child population might be construed as having some degree of special educational need, and of these 2 per cent have such substantial special needs as to merit detailed assessment and special provision enshrined in statutory

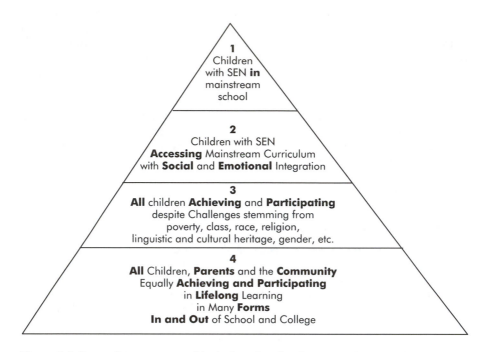

*Figure 0.1* Expanding concepts of inclusion: four levels

documentation accessible to parents and other professionals. Of course, in the continuous dimension of need, divisions are inevitably arbitrary and lines could be drawn anywhere. Over the last 20 years in the United Kingdom teachers have tended to perceive an increase in the number of children with special needs in mainstream classes, but this perception does not match with other data, since the decline in the special school population has actually been quite small (Croll and Moses, 2003).

The biggest increase in mainstreaming has actually occurred for children with learning difficulties. However, teachers tend to express greatest concern about pupils with emotional and behaviour difficulties – perhaps because such children are perceived as most likely to damage the education of their classmates as well as being most stressful for the teacher (Scruggs and Mastropieri, 1996; Hastings and Oakford, 2003). The third section of this volume explores the exclusion of such children from schools.

It is also clear that some children who are seen as having special educational needs in one classroom are not seen as having them in another. Many more boys than girls are perceived as having special needs (especially in the predominantly female environment of the primary school). Also, teachers tend to perceive learning difficulties more readily in children of South Asian origin, and behaviour difficulties more readily in male children of African-Caribbean origin, although both tendencies have become less strong in recent years. Children with physical and/or sensory impairments tend to be perceived as less of a problem in mainstream environments, although presumably their presence occasions considerable problems of access to buildings and to specialist ancillary services.

Teacher belief systems and attributions are likely to have a significant effect on the implementation of 'inclusion' within educational systems. Teachers with and without experience and training with pupils with various levels and types of special educational need might have very different perceptions and expectations, self-confidence and self-efficacy, resulting in very different effectiveness in teaching and learning. However, these relationships might not be simple or in the expected direction. Thus while contact with pupils with special needs tends to make teacher attitudes more positive, there is some evidence that teachers with more years of teaching experience tend to express more negative attitudes to inclusion.

Additionally, special educational needs legislation has typically ignored interaction with socio-economic disadvantage. The correlation between poverty and attainment at the age of 11 is $-0.7$ (Croll, 2002), suggesting that half of the variance in attainment between schools (and children) could be accounted for by poverty.

## Does inclusion work?

Much of the discourse of inclusion takes it for granted that inclusion is a 'good thing', like motherhood and apple pie. Some of this comes from the human rights agenda. Of course, human rights can be viewed from another angle – if a parent or child prefers a segregated special school (as some do), should they have a human right to have it? Others might take a more pragmatic view, and wish to look at the evidence for the relative effectiveness of inclusive and segregated educational placements on a variety of relevant indicators.

There is some research concerning the effectiveness of different kinds of provision for pupils with special educational needs at Inclusion Levels 1 and 2. If this shows that there is not much difference in outcomes between the different types of provision, the question of what is the default circumstance becomes relevant. If you are already in mainstream provision and there is no evidence that special provision is more effective, you might as well stay where you are. If you are already in special provision, and there is no evidence that mainstream provision is more effective, you might as well stay where you are. However, the question of what is the normal default circumstance is relevant for all children newly assessed and to be placed in the future.

In fact, the evidence suggests that any differences in outcomes for children with special needs between special and mainstream schools are small, but tend to favour mainstream school, in terms of both educational attainments and social integration. Socially, children with special needs in mainstream school tend not to be as well accepted as 'normal' children, but they nevertheless enjoy a fair degree of social integration, while learning to cope in a situation more akin to the outside post-school world than the protective environment of a special school.

In a seminal review, Madden and Slavin (1983) concluded that there was no evidence that segregated placements enhanced either academic or social progress compared to mainstream placements. Baker *et al.* (1994–5) synthesised three meta-analyses of inclusion, but found very small average effect sizes for both academic and social outcomes. Staub and Peck (1994) reviewed many studies of mainstreaming, and found no evidence of deleterious effects for pupils with special needs or their classmates. Manset and Semmel (1997) reviewed learning outcomes for mainstreamed and segregated pupils, finding no difference in mathematics but a small advantage for mainstreamed pupils in literacy. These authors also found that 'normal' pupils in mainstreamed environments were actually advantaged in terms of attainment by the presence of pupils with special educational needs – perhaps because their teachers were sensitised to the different learning needs of others in the class with challenges.

Special educational provision is hardly likely to be effective on a one-size-fits-all basis, so presumably it is important to place pupils in learning environments specifically designed and resourced to meet their own specific individual needs. But there is more to it than this. Salend and Garrick Duhaney (1999) found little difference in outcomes between mainstream and special placements overall – commenting that some students did better in one environment and some in another, they asserted that the quality of the programme was the critical variable, rather than its location. Assuming that all pupils are placed in environments thought most likely to meet their specific personal needs (a risky assumption), this implies that there should be less emphasis on inclusion and more on quality assurance. Peetsma *et al.* (2001) conducted a 4-year longitudinal study of matched pairs of pupils, one in special and one in mainstream placement. The mainstream pupils academically outperformed the special school pupils over the period.

Perhaps surprisingly, few studies address issues of cost-effectiveness. If special and mainstream placements are equally effective, it would seem to make sense to place children in the environment which costs less. Such a placement would release resources to help other children. Crowther *et al.* (1998) conducted one of the few studies in this area, finding that special schools for pupils with learning difficulties in the United Kingdom were consistently higher in cost than mainstream placements. However, mainstreaming might be fraught with paradox, systems sometimes seeming to reward schools with additional resources for demonstrating persistent lack of pupil achievement. There should be no assumption that mainstreaming is automatically less costly and more cost-effective, when all the real costs incurred are accounted.

At Inclusion Levels 3 and 4, evidence of effectiveness is more scattered as interventions are much more numerous, and in more diverse and disconnected bodies of literature. Also, as such research is conducted in much more complex environments, the quality of research and the security of the conclusions are sometimes less robust. However, such research does exist. Examples would include studies of the effectiveness of family literacy programmes. Questions of cost-effectiveness are also important at these Levels.

## Action for inclusion

So, if we have decided we want inclusion (for whatever reason and at whatever Level), how do we get there? Dyson *et al.* (2002), in a systematic review of the effectiveness of school-level actions for promoting participation by all students, implied a broad definition of inclusion in their research question: 'What evidence is there that mainstream schools can act in ways which enable them to respond to student diversity so as to facilitate participation by all students in the cultures, curricula and communities of those schools?'

They concluded that:

1   'Some schools are characterised by an "inclusive culture." Within such schools, there is some degree of consensus amongst adults around values of respect for difference and a commitment to offering all students access to learning opportunities. This consensus may not be total and may not necessarily remove all tensions or contradictions in practice. On the other hand, there is likely to be a high level of staff collaboration and joint problem-solving, and similar values and commitments may extend into the student body and into parent and other community stakeholders in the school.

2 The extent to which such "inclusive cultures" lead directly to enhanced student participation is not clear from the research evidence. Schools characterised by such cultures are likely to be characterised by forms of organisation (such as specialist provision being made in the ordinary classroom rather than by withdrawal) and practice (such as constructivist approaches to teaching and learning) which could be regarded as participatory by definition.

3 Schools with "inclusive cultures" are likely to be characterised by the presence of leaders who are committed to inclusive values and to a leadership style which encourages a range of individuals to participate in leadership functions.

4 Such schools are likely to have good links with parents and with their communities.

5 The local and national policy environment can act to support or to undermine the realisation of schools' inclusive values.'

A number of publications offer advice about creating inclusive educational environments. The fourth section in this book considers Action in Schools and the fifth section Promoting and Managing Systemic Change in schools. Advocates such as Ainscow (1999), Allan (1999), Cheminais (2001) and Lorenz (2002) give broad guidelines. Other authors suggest quite specific practical strategies, not only in the special needs area (e.g. Tilstone and Rose, 2003), but also in other areas such as gender equity (e.g. Horgan, 1995; Noble *et al.*, 2001) and bilingualism (Gardner, 2002; Smyth, 2003). Continuing Professional Development (in-service training) for relevant staff (not only teachers) is obviously important (Hopkins, 2002). Gross and White (2003) (among others) propose a whole-school inclusion audit leading to consideration of arrangements to train, deploy, support and effectively manage relevant staff. Daniels *et al.* (1997) propose the development of teacher support teams in both primary and secondary schools to facilitate peer support at the local level. Developing an inclusive school can be firmly set in wider issues of overall school effectiveness and school improvement.

However, moving towards inclusion can be a slow process, testing the frustration tolerance of the most patient individual. As Table 0.1 shows, many factors need to come together for successful systemic change, and the absence of only one can thwart progress.

Adoption of ideas in theory is a start, but adoption of those ideas in practice can take much longer. The speed of adoption in theory depends partially upon clarity of conceptualisation and exemplification and the absence of overt conflict with ruling cultural value judgements, leading to gradual initial acceptance of the idea, which then begins to permeate prevailing public opinion and eventually becomes enshrined in regulation or legislation (statutory legitimation).

*Table 0.1* Managing complex change

| ? | + | Skills | + | Incentives | + | Resources | + | Action plan | = | Confusion |
|---|---|---|---|---|---|---|---|---|---|---|
| Vision | + | ? | + | Incentives | + | Resources | + | Action plan | = | Anxiety |
| Vision | + | Skills | + | ? | + | Resources | + | Action plan | = | Resistance |
| Vision | + | Skills | + | Incentives | + | ? | + | Action plan | = | Frustration |
| Vision | + | Skills | + | Incentives | + | Resources | + | ? | = | Treadmill |
| Vision | + | Skills | + | Incentives | + | Resources | + | Action plan | = | Change |

*Source*: Originally adapted by Knoster from Enterprise Group Ltd

These developments might be more or less influenced by empirical research. Rationally, the evidence on the positive effects and unintended consequences of any policy or practice shift should be explored in pilot research projects before any widespread implementation. However, this happens relatively rarely in education, and policy and practice often change because of shifts in opinion rather than the evidence base, sometimes because of political decisions taken thoughtlessly on the run or evangelistic campaigns operated by those with a drum to beat, a career to make or a product to sell.

Adoption in practice is likely to be much slower, and will depend upon the quantity and quality of content and delivery of continuing professional development made available to practitioners. Of course, big national initiatives create a need to find many expert trainers all at the same time – almost by definition impossible. Adoption in practice will also depend upon prioritisation among competing pressures for time and resources, both at the level of the individual practitioner and at larger systemic levels. New initiatives tend to be seen as additional burdens, for which by definition no time is available since all the available time is already being used. Practitioners are rarely told what to leave out in order to make space for a new initiative.

Also, practitioners may be more comfortable doing what they have always done rather than exploring more challenging and difficult areas in which they are likely to make mistakes. If senior management is punitive and blaming rather than encouraging and supportive, practitioners have very little incentive to do other than plod along in the same old rut – the 'factory mentality'. Belief and motivation also play a large part. Practical professionals might never believe something is possible until they have seen someone else do it. Concrete exemplars of good practice – positive models of possibility – tend to be more effective than evangelistic exhortation. However, the resistant practitioner might still argue that the positive model is insufficiently proximate to their own context to be credible – 'well, it might work with that class, but it could never work with mine ...'.

Eventually, however, islands of good practice become more numerous, sooner or later every practitioner has contact with at least one, and the small islands begin to join up into larger islands – implementation becomes more widespread. Unfortunately, another cycle can then begin to operate. The initial examples of good practice might have emanated from especially innovative, energetic and well-organised teachers, who made them work by virtue of their general capability as much as by the intrinsic benefits of the initiative. Later replications might suffer from dilution of the initiative in content as well as in quality of delivery. If there have been early empirical studies of effectiveness, these might overestimate later effectiveness when the initiative is delivered by more ordinary professionals in less favoured contexts. Consequently, as an initiative becomes widespread and institutionalised, so overall quality can begin to suffer. Then a backlash can set in, with the antagonistic 'I told you so' camp re-finding their voice.

There are a number of barriers to change at a systems level, many of them embedded in particular conceptions of teaching and learning. Teacher training in the United Kingdom remains highly focused on curricular subjects, rather than generic pedagogical skills. The teacher's role is still often seen as that of intergenerational transmitter of received wisdom and cultural heritage – the 'sage on the stage'. Such a role is not readily adaptable to pupil diversity. The information technology revolution has yielded a world in which knowledge is both vast and transient, and accessible from anywhere in a host of ways. Given this, transferable skills such as the capacity for critical thinking and creativity seem likely to prove more useful in an accelerating future. Additionally, social and communication skills seem likely to be increasingly important as learning becomes ever more peer and computer mediated.

Teachers often cite a 'lack of resources' as a barrier to mainstreaming pupils with special needs. Adequate appropriately expert practitioner time, adequate appropriate physical space, and adequate appropriate learning and teaching materials are certainly essential. 'Main-dumping' (placing pupils with special needs in mainstream environments without consideration of and/or meeting their specific additional support needs) is not to be condoned (Thomas *et al.*, 1999). However, 'lack of resources' is often cited as a barrier without any clarity about exactly what resources are needed and why. Correspondingly, pumping the wrong type of resources into a mainstream environment without a specific action plan may worsen the situation rather than improve it.

However, forewarned and forearmed with this book, readers will doubtless be able to avoid such mistakes. Some consideration of its structure and use might be timely at this point.

## Structure and use of the book

Most readers will dip into the book strategically for a variety of purposes (rather than reading it in a linear way), and the structure is intended to facilitate such an approach. After this Introduction, the book has 17 chapters, divided into subsections:

A   Concepts and Context (definitions, terminology, history, legislation, stake-holders, ideals and reality).
B   Gender, Race, Disability, Poverty and Social Class (cultural, class and gender differences, their interaction and how they impact on achievement, and the importance of pupil involvement).
C   Exclusion from School: Problems and Challenges (including truancy, absenteeism, exclusion from school).
D   Action in Schools (examples of various types of intervention and their effectiveness, including curriculum differentiation and adaptation, positive behaviour management, and peer mediated learning).
E   Promoting and Managing Systemic Change in Schools (positive action for inclusion at whole-school and local authority level, including organisational, political and financial choices).
F   Post-school (transition from school to further/higher education or 'life', and the special challenges facing those with disabilities.

Each chapter ends with questions and issues for onward reflection. The book ends with an annotated list of further reading (including items considered for inclusion in the book but eventually not prioritised).

The editors have tried to avoid material that will rapidly date or is deeply embedded in the current legislation, procedures and jargon of one country. However, readers will nevertheless note some emphasis on England. The editors have chosen not to provide a glossary for the terminology and acronyms particular to any one country, since cross-referring to this would create endless distraction for the reader. Readers are encouraged to read over and around acronyms with a focus on extracting issues of general importance which will endure over time and location.

Owing to constraints of space, many groups at risk of educational and social exclusion have not been discussed in detail in this book – for example 'looked after' (in care) children, gypsy and travelling children, gay and lesbian youth and many more. Even some of the chapters included have been shortened by the editors. There is much more to be read. Why not start with Frederickson and Cline (2002), which takes full account of linguistic, cultural and ethnic diversity as well as special educational needs. And there is much more to be done. In the spirit of inclusion, the editors encourage readers to think towards writing up their own professional practice and action research in this area, and making this available more widely to colleagues.

After delving into the book, it will be evident to the reader that the chapters mostly deal with inclusion at Levels 1, 2 and 3. A next edition of this book might hope to include more chapters, taking the ambit more firmly up to Level 4. However, this would be a very thick book.

## Reflective questions

1   '... teachers have tended to perceive an increase in the number of children with special needs in mainstream classes, but this perception does not match with other data, since the decline in the special school population has actually been quite small (Croll and Moses 2003)'.

   What might be happening here? Are there really more children in mainstream classes with additional needs, or is the curriculum becoming increasingly matched to fewer children, with the latter being driven by tighter curricular prescription, high stakes testing, attainment targets and league table pressures?

2   '... teachers tend to express greatest concern about pupils with emotional and behavioural difficulties.... (Scruggs and Mastropieri, 1996; Hastings and Oakford, 2003)'.

   Any conflict or confrontation in any system is usually seen as creating undesirable turbulence. But can any system change without some pressure to change, some problem to solve? Would encapsulating or removing the problem remove any press for systemic change? Can behaviourally problematic pupils be seen as an opportunity to promote systemic change, rather than a problem?

## References

Ainscow, M. (1999). *Understanding the development of inclusive schools*. London: Falmer.

Alaimo, K. and Klug, B. (eds) (2002). *Children as equals: exploring the rights of the child*. Lanham, MD: Rowman & Littlefield.

Allan, J. (1999). *Actively seeking inclusion*. London: Falmer.

Baker, E. T., Wang, M. C. and Walberg, H. J. (1994–5). The effects of inclusion on learning. *Educational Leadership*, 52 (4), 36–40.

Beresford, J. (2003). *Creating the conditions to involve pupils in their learning*. London: Falmer.

Brendtro, L. K., Brokenleg, M. and Van Bockern, S. (1990). The circle of courage. In *Reclaiming youth at risk: our hope for the future*. Bloomington, IN: National Educational Service.

Cantle, T. (2001). *Community cohesion: Report of the independent review team*. London: Home Office.

Catlett, S. M. and Osher, T. W. (1994). *What is inclusion, anyway? An analysis of organizational position statements*. Eric Document Reproduction Service No. ED369234.

Cheminais, R. (2001). *Developing inclusive school practice*. London: Fulton.

Clough, P. and Corbett, J. (2000). *Theories of inclusive education*. London: Chapman.

Croll, P. (2002). Social deprivation, school-level achievement and special educational needs. *Educational Research*, 44, 43–53.

Croll, P. and Moses, D. (2003). Special educational needs across two decades: Survey evidence from English primary schools. *British Educational Research Journal*, 29 (5), 731–47.

Crowther, D., Dyson, A. and Millward, A. (1998). *Costs and outcomes for pupils with moderate learning difficulties in special and mainstream schools*. (Research report RR89). London: Department for Education and Employment. (www.dfes.gov.uk/research/data/uploadfiles/RB89.doc).

Daniels, H., Norwich, B. and Creese, A. (1997). *Teacher support teams in primary and secondary schools*. London: Fulton.

Dyson, A. and Millward, A. (2000). *Schools and special needs: Issues of innovation and inclusion*. London: Chapman.

Dyson, A., Howes, A. and Roberts, B. (2002). *A systematic review of the effectiveness of school-level actions for promoting participation by all students* (EPPI-Centre Review). London: Research Evidence in Education Library, EPPI-Centre, Social Science Research Unit, Institute of Education, University of London.

Farrell, P. and Ainscow, M. (2002). Making special education inclusive: mapping the issues. In P. Farrell and M. Ainscow (eds), *Making special education inclusive*. London: Fulton.

Forrest, R. and Kearns, A. (1999). *Joined-up places? Social cohesion and neighbourhood regeneration*. York: Joseph Rowntree Foundation.

Frederickson, N. and Cline, T. (2002). *Special educational needs: inclusion and diversity*. Milton Keynes: Open University Press.

Gardner, P. (2002). *Strategies and resources for teaching and learning in inclusive classrooms*. London: Fulton.

Gold, K. (2003). *Give us inclusion . . . but not yet*. Times Educational Supplement, May 23, 2003, 19.

Gross, J. and White, A. (2003). *Special educational needs and school improvement*. London: Fulton.

Hastings, R. P. and Oakford, S. (2003). Student teachers' attitudes towards the inclusion of children with special needs. *Educational Psychology*, 23 (1), 87–94.

Hopkins, D. (2002). *Improving the quality of education for all* (second edition). London: Fulton.

Horgan, D. D. (1995). *Achieving gender equity: Strategies for the classroom*. Boston and London: Allyn and Bacon.

Lorenz, S. (2002). *First steps in inclusion: a handbook for parents, teachers, governors and local education authorities*. London: Fulton.

Madden, N. A. and Slavin, R. E. (1983). Mainstreaming students with mild handicaps: Academic and social outcomes. *Review of Educational Research*, 52 (4), 519–69.

Manset, G. and Semmel, M. I. (1997). Are inclusive programs for students with mild disabilities effective? *Journal of Special Education*, 31 (2), 155–80.

Mittler, P. (2000). *Working towards inclusive education: social contexts*. London: Fulton.

Nind, M., Sheehy, K., Simmons, K. and Rix, J. (eds) (2003). *Inclusive education: diverse perspectives*. London: Fulton.

Noble, C., Brown, J. and Murphy, J. (2001). *How to raise boys' achievement*. London: Fulton.

Norwich, B. (2000). Inclusion in education: from concepts, values and critique to practice. In H. Daniels (ed.) *Special education reformed: beyond rhetoric?* London: Falmer.

Norwich, B. (2003). *LEA inclusion trends in England 1997–2001*. Bristol: Centre for Studies in Inclusive Education.

Peetsma, T., Vergeer, M., Roeleveld, J. and Karsten, S. (2001). Inclusion in education: Comparing pupils' development in special and regular education. *Educational Review*, 53 (2), 125–35.

Salend, S. J. and Garrick Duhaney, L. M. (1999). The impact of inclusion on students with or without disabilities and their educators. *Remedial and Special Education*, 20 (2), 114–26.

Scruggs, T. E. and Mastropieri, M. A. (1996). Teacher perceptions of mainstreaming/inclusion, 1958–1995. A research synthesis. *Exceptional Children*, 63, 59–74.

Shucksmith, M. (2000). *Exclusive countryside? social inclusion and regeneration in rural Britain*. York: Joseph Rowntree Trust.

Smyth, G. (2003). *Helping bilingual pupils to access the curriculum*. London: Fulton.

Staub, D. and Peck, C. A. (1994). What are the outcomes for non-disabled students? *Educational Leadership*, 52 (4), 36–40.

Thomas, G., Walker, D. and Webb, J. (1998). *The making of the inclusive school*. London: Routledge.

Tilstone, C. and Rose, R. (2003). *Strategies to promote inclusive practice*. London: RoutledgeFalmer.

# PART I

# CONCEPTS AND CONTEXTS

# CHAPTER 1

# INCLUSIVE EDUCATION
## The ideals and the practice

### G. Thomas, D. Walker and J. Webb

*The Making of the Inclusive School* (1998), London and New York: RoutledgeFalmer, pp. 3–25

## From segregation to inclusion

Inclusion is not a new idea. Although recent concern about inclusion can be traced to the civil rights movements of the 1960s, the ideals behind inclusive education have much deeper roots in liberal and progressive thought. If we research the shaping of the current school system a century earlier, we can see that two avenues were then open. One was inclusive, the other segregative.

A significant body of opinion at the turn of the century – perhaps exemplified best in the work of the child welfare pioneer Elizabeth Burgwin – saw neither purpose nor virtue in segregation. Those who shared these views did not even seriously consider segregated schooling. Instead, in thinking about the needs of children with disabilities, they thought automatically of adaptations that could be made to ordinary schools. It is quite possible that this inclusive thought might have prospered and provided the philosophical and organisational foundation for the school system of the twentieth century.

Another body of opinion, however, considered that children could be categorised according to their difficulties and suggested that different, 'special' schools be established to cater for children who, in the words of the School Board for London (1904), could not be taught 'in ordinary standards or by ordinary methods'. (The origins of the special system are discussed in detail by Potts, 1982; Copeland, 1995, 1996; Scott, 1996.)

It is possible that this segregative body of opinion might have lost the argument against the progressive opinion of the day. However, the segregative conviction was reinforced greatly by the burgeoning 'science' of psychometrics and associated ideas on eugenics. These suggested that 'misfits' should be removed from the genetic pool; it needed only a minor extension of this logic to propose that defectives and degenerates be removed from society's mainstream institutions, notably schools. When Cyril Burt was appointed the first psychologist for London in 1911 further momentum was added to this body of opinion. His growing reputation, his fondness for psychometrics and his commitment to the idea that intelligence was inherited and more or less immutable all combined to give great stimulus to a segregative education system based on the categorisation of the child. This was especially so as Burt was one of the principal architects of the 1944 Education Act insofar as it related to special education. The 1944 Act constructed a highly seg-regative post-war education system with its ten categories of handicap for which special schools would cater.

It became received opinion that special schools provided a sensible way of meeting the needs of a minority of children, at the same time as safe-guarding the efficient education of the majority in the mainstream. Indeed, it seemed more than just sensible: it was self-evident fact that special schools were appropriate. Pijl and Meijer (1994) go so far as to suggest that the system of special schools was widely accepted throughout western Europe. They even suggest that it was one of which society as a whole was proud. Since the facts as to its utility were plain, evidence to support it was unnecessary. This orthodoxy became so firmly embedded in the individual and institutional consciousness that no serious challenges were made to the idea until the mid-1960s.

It took the world-wide push for civil rights to begin to challenge this orthodoxy. The changing world-view liberated people with disabilities to give voice to their anger about the stigma, degradation and curricular and social limits imposed by the segregated education to which they had been subjected. Simultaneously, evi-dence about the surprising lack of success of the segregated system (surprising, that is, given the generous resources allocated to it) began to accumulate with such con-sistency that it could not be ignored (e.g. Christophos and Renz, 1969; Galloway and Goodwin, 1979; Lipsky and Gartner, 1987; Reynolds *et al.*, 1987; Reynolds, 1988; Anderson and Pellicer, 1990). All this built on evidence (e.g. Dunn, 1968; Birch *et al.*, 1970; Mercer, 1970) which showed that the special system selected children disproportionately from ethnic minorities and children from lower socio-economic groups. Moral arguments and empirical evidence came together to result, towards the end of the twentieth century, in a consensus which sees inclu-sion as an appropriate philosophy and a relevant framework for restructuring education.

Looking back on this history, however, one realises that the seeds of an integra-tive philosophy existed many years ago. The segregated system, which a few years ago seemed so manifestly right (and still seems natural to some), can be seen as simply one possible method of organising the education system. It succeeded in providing the blueprint for the school system for the great part of this century because of the psychometric and eugenic views that prevailed before the Second World War. However, it is now recognised that segregation by no means offers a common sense or natural way of organising education.

An inclusive philosophy has ultimately risen again and prospered. It has been able to succeed because it chimes with the philosophy of a liberal political system and a pluralistic culture – one that celebrates diversity and promotes fraternity and equality of opportunity. Inclusion must be at the heart of any society which cherishes these values and at the heart of a truly comprehensive education system.

## Evidence for inclusion?

So, although inclusion has won partly because of evidence from educational research showing that special schools are not as effective as one would expect or wish, it has won mainly because it is *right* that it should have done so. Arguments for inclusion are principled ones, stemming from concern for human rights. As Fulcher (1993) points out, these principles drive policy. Now, this creates problems for evaluation, for values cannot be evaluated. Fulcher goes on to say that value-driven policy 'cannot be evaluated by an ecological-systems model, nor by rich databases, nor by looking at the interdependence of elements of the system' (Flucher, 1993: 128).

Newman and Roberts (1996) support Fulcher's case. They point out that many pioneering developments in welfare for children (such as the shipping of children to Australia for a 'new life' at the turn of the century) seemed right and proper at the time. However, it is now recognised that these were often disastrous in their consequences. There are indeed several contemporary detractors who pick up this theme and warn that an inclusive philosophy is an inappropriate and misleading one to follow. Within the deaf community, for example, Mason (1994) suggests that inclusive dialogue has stressed political, economic, bureaucratic, professional and administrative issues, rather than the effects of inclusive education on individual children. Gerber argues that special education should be valued because it has always been subversive. It has ever striven, he suggests, to accommodate children with 'extreme individual differences' (Gerber, 1996: 156) within a wider educational system which tacitly seeks to exclude them entirely. And Dorn *et al.* (1996) warn that by focusing on inclusion the positive action accumulated over decades in favour of children with disabilities and learning difficulties may evaporate.

They have a point. The move to inclusion must be monitored to ensure continuity of services. Special provision in special schools has always been made on the axiom that resources should be provided in direct ratio to need, heeding (albeit unconsciously) Rawls's (1971) advice on the redistribution of resources to achieve social justice. But a gradual attrition of provision is possible if the critical mass of the special school does not exist to ensure the survival of advantageous provision. And if principles cannot be evaluated for their veracity nor ethics for their truth, it is crucial that the consequences of the principled policy decision to provide inclusive education are rigorously monitored, especially as recent evidence concerning the academic, social and emotional benefits of integrative programmes are nowhere near as clear-cut as earlier evidence promised. For instance, Hegarty, in summarising a major international review of the literature on integration for the Organisation for Economic Cooperation and Development (OECD), suggests that 'research has failed to establish a clear-cut advantage in either direction' (OECD, 1994: 197), partly due to the methodological problems of comparing non-comparable groups receiving different kinds of education. He emphasises that integration and segregation are not sharply defined and that integration can take numerous forms, some of them overlapping with segregation. These problems in definition make comparison extremely difficult. Moreover, there are important differences between organisational structures of schools and integration schemes which exaggerate the difficulties of comparative research. Further, any matching of variables in the comparisons of groups do not (presumably because of the small numbers generally involved) extend beyond age, sex and IQ. The corollary of all this, Hegarty says, is that 'the body of research comparing integration and segregation has a limited validity' (OECD, 1994).

Steinberg and Tovey (1996), reporting mainly on American research, concur with Hegarty, pointing to the heterogeneity of disabling conditions which make matching difficult or impossible for control grouping. They also emphasise the difficulty of comparing outcomes of inclusion versus special education where there is bound to be selection bias – that is, the tendency to select 'harder to teach' children for special class placement and 'easier' children for inclusion programmes. Despite the difficulties of comparison, many researchers feel able to offer their findings. Baker *et al.* (1995), for instance, report from three meta-analyses that there is a small-to-moderate beneficial effect of inclusive education on social and academic outcomes of students with special needs. And Lipsky and Gartner (1996) summarise over 20 recent studies which report academic and social benefits arising from inclusion.

The problems of selection bias do, however, remain and are even present in the largest longitudinal study of outcomes for students placed in mainstream schools (the US National Longitudinal Transition Study of Special Education Students), which is tracking the post-school progress of 8000 young people. This shows that students with physical disabilities who had received mainstream education were 43 per cent more likely to be employed post-school than counterparts who had attended special placements. Although selection bias must have existed, it is reassuring to note that children with different disabilities were separated in the analysis and that the analysis was sensitive enough to show better outcomes for certain of these groups, notably those with physical disabilities (see Woronov, 1996, for a report).

As Hegarty concludes from the existing research, 'While [the inadequacies of comparative research] means that any inferences drawn must be tentative, the absence of a clear-cut balance of advantage supports integration' (Hegarty, 1993: 198). Hegarty appears to be saying that unless evidence relating to children's progress and happiness at school is unequivocally unsupportive of integration, then the principles we have used to guide the current practice toward inclusion should be used to determine the direction of policy.

More than this, given that the move to inclusion is a principled one, it is important also that research should focus on ways of making inclusion work. It should illuminate good practice and investigate problems in such a way that obstacles can be recognised and overcome.

## Inclusion in society

Most educational discussion on inclusion concentrates on curriculum, pastoral systems, attitudes and teaching methods, but there is a further dimension to inclusion which goes beyond these narrowly school-based considerations. It is the wider notion of inclusion in society – for the notion of inclusion is not unique to education. Indeed, the recent popularity of inclusion as an idea in education probably rests at least in part on its consonance with this wider notion of inclusivity in society – of a society in which each member has a stake. Commentators (e.g. Hutton, 1995; Kay, 1996; Plender, 1997a) have begun to discuss the meaning of this new inclusiveness. There is an interesting notion of reciprocity in their discussion – a recognition of *mutual* obligations and expectations between the community and institutions such as schools, in such a way that these institutions are reminded of their responsibilities and public duties.

To illustrate the point, Kay notes from etymological research that many ideas which seem unrelated to us now – for example, the notions of owing and owning – share a root which reveals that there was once a bond between the notions. The bond between *owe* and *own* rests in an expectation of duty, sharing and a concern for others who are weaker. Thus, *owning* always carried with it some implication of *owing* – some bearing of obligations. Only relatively recent usage has separated the two. The ethic of a stakeholding, inclusive society implies a renewed bonding of these ideas.

Now, while Kay draws this distinction in the context of large companies and their obligations to their employees and their customers, the lessons learned from this analysis are surely valid also in relation to schools in their willingness to become inclusive. For there is an injunction in the inclusive, stakeholding ethic, says Plender (1997b), to take account of social costs and benefits that are not explicitly priced in the market. In this process the role of state and individual are downplayed while the role of intermediate institutions (companies, unions, schools, etc.) is reinforced. In an inclusive society, entrustment to governors and headteachers of large amounts of capital and the futures of many children must be accompanied by an obligation to find ways of making inclusion happen. And these obligations must not merely be to the parents of high-achieving children.

So, aside from the curricular and social principles which educationists may wish to see embodied in the policy and practice of a school which claims to be inclusive, one might also include a broader set of principles, imposed not only by the direct stakeholders in the school (teachers, parents and students), but also by those in the local community and society at large and recognised by politicians and the legislature. If this were the case, some further inclusive principles for schools might therefore incorporate, in Mason's (1995) term, the 'intentional building of community'. Such intentional building might include (to paraphrase Hutton (1995) and Kay (1996)) the following expectations:

- governors and school managers, being entrusted by local communities to run schools, have obligations to run those schools inclusively;
- an effective school is recognised to be one where all members are included and have a stake, not simply one which achieves high scores on academic criteria.

This notion of inclusivity now emerging is in contrast to the individual, instrumental ethic of the 1980s, which was legitimised by the political rhetoric of the time and given academic credence by the economic doctrine of Hayek and others. It was acceptable, fashionable even, to be selfish. Writing at the beginning of the 1980s, Hargreaves (1982) saw this as the efflorescence of *egoism*, which – as Durkheim noted – has deep roots in northern European thought. The aggressively meritocratic, individualistic and competitive thought associated with that tradition clearly provides ample rhetorical justification for segregation. By contrast, in the new philosophy which sees all members of society as stakeholders it is natural to see schools as places where all are welcomed – and duty is felt to all.

It is worth at the outset examining what is meant specifically by 'inclusion', and in particular how inclusion may differ from 'integration', a term which has been used – and is still used – to describe the process of transfer of children and young people from special to mainstream schools.

Ten years ago the term 'inclusive education' was not used. It is only since the late 1980s that 'inclusion' has come to supersede 'integration'. Whether the two words can be said to describe different processes in schools is open to question, and has been discussed by a number of commentators (e.g. Booth, 1995, 1996; Sebba and Ainscow, 1996).

## Inclusion versus exclusion

Most discussion about inclusion stresses its contrast with *segregation* – in exactly the same way that distinctions are drawn between integration and segregation. But an important distinction between integration and inclusion concerns inclusion's status as the opposite of *exclusion* (as separate from segregation), as Booth (1995) notes. Segregation and exclusion are currently thought of as somewhat different processes: segregation is usually associated with children with learning difficulties, sensory impairments or physical disabilities, whereas exclusion is usually of children whose behaviour is found difficult. Integration – perhaps because of its focus on the child – does not define what is to be done instead of segregation, as Flynn (1993) notes, and thus it has been possible for the processes of segregation and exclusion to continue to be thought of separately. Using *inclusion*, however, specifically shifts the focus onto the school rather than the child when thinking about excluded pupils.

Many of the unashamedly market-oriented education policies implemented by national governments in recent years (e.g. the publication of 'league tables' of examination results) have had clear consequences in the reduced willingness of schools to accept children regardless of ability or background. Schools are now wary of accepting children who might, through their own low attainment or through their effects on others, depress mean exam or standard assessment task (SAT) scores. This has a potential effect not merely on admissions policies but also on exclusions. The significant increase in exclusions in recent years (see OFSTED, 1996) testifies that this is the case. One hopes that the greater acceptance of the ideas embodied in an inclusive, stakeholding society augurs a reversal of this trend.

## Inclusion as international descriptor

Another feature of 'inclusion' is its present status as an international descriptor of a particular marriage of ethos and practice. This is a further reason to prefer its use to that of 'integration'. While 'integration' was used in the United Kingdom, Australia and New Zealand, the preferred term in the United States and Canada was 'mainstreaming' (e.g. Strain and Kerr, 1981). The understanding of inclusion, however, is international.

The new notion central to inclusion is that exceptional students belong in the mainstream; mainstream classteachers must believe this and have confidence that these young people will learn there (Table 1.1). A central aspect of an inclusion project must therefore lie in the deconstruction of the idea that only special people are equipped and qualified to teach special children. It must convince mainstream staff of their competence. This presents quite a task, of course, since for the last one hundred years special educators have been saying the opposite – that there is a set of teaching procedures which is especially appropriate for a segment of the child population. The system built around this idea has been reinforced and buttressed by a whole range of investments, from school buildings to professional careers.

*Table 1.1* Walker's (1995) contrast of inclusion and integration

| Integration emphasises | Inclusion emphasises |
| --- | --- |
| Needs of 'special' students | Rights of all students |
| Changing/remedying the subject | Changing the school |
| Benefits to the student with special needs of being integrated | Benefits to all students of including all |
| Professionals, specialist expertise and formal support | Informal support and the expertise of mainstream teachers |
| Technical interventions (special teaching, therapy) | Good teaching for all |

## Key aspects of inclusion in practice

Many definitions have been written of inclusion. One of the least prescriptive is provided by the Centre for Studies on Inclusive Education (CSIE, 1996). This suggests that an inclusive school contains the following elements:

- it is *community based*: an inclusive school reflects the community as a whole. Membership of the school community is open, positive and diverse. It is not selective, exclusive or rejecting;
- it is *barrier-free*: an inclusive school is accessible to all who become members – physically in terms of the buildings and grounds and educationally in terms of curricula, support systems and methods of communication;
- it promotes *collaboration*: an inclusive school works with, rather than competitively against, other schools;
- it promotes *equality*: an inclusive school is a democracy where all members have rights and responsibilities, with the same opportunity to benefit from and take part in the education provided by the school both within and beyond its premises.

The Council for Exceptional Children (CEC, 1994) has a list of 12 principles for successful inclusive schools, and many of these are similar to the CSIE's list. However, it also states that the inclusive school has the following:

- a *vision* of equality and inclusion, publicly articulated;
- *leadership* which publicly espouses inclusion and equal opportunities;
- an *array of services* that are co-ordinated across and among education and agency personnel;
- *systems for co-operation* within the school: inclusive schools foster natural support networks across students and staff. Strategies are implemented such as peer tutoring, buddy systems, circles of friends, co-operative learning and other ways of connecting students in natural, ongoing and supportive relationships. In addition, all school personnel work together and support each other through professional collaboration, team teaching, co-teaching, teacher and student assistance teams and other collaborative arrangements;
- *flexible roles* and responsibilities: there will be changed staff roles and responsibilities arising from inclusion;
- *partnerships with parents*: parents are involved in the planning and implementation of inclusive school strategies.

## Self-advocacy and inclusion

Children with disabilities have been (and still are) particularly susceptible to benevolent, but often misguided, attempts to plan for them, as noted by Newman and Roberts (1996, discussed earlier). But in an education system which aspires to be inclusive, it is important that discourse does not exclude the perspectives and interpretations of children, particularly the perspectives of those children with disabilities. If planning is informed by stereotypical images of disability or outdated models of childhood the risk is that marginalisation and exclusion will continue.

For children – and particularly children with disabilities – have habitually been excluded from discussion about their education (or, indeed, other aspects of their lives). The results of this exclusion are seen in the anger of adults with disabilities over the education that was planned for them when they were children. The tacit assumption has been that children will be neither sufficiently well informed nor sufficiently articulate or rational to contribute to such discussion. It has been assumed that it is somehow illegitimate to seek or to accept the views of children. And where children are disabled, discussion has predominantly taken place about disabled children by professionals and academics (see, e.g. the critique offered by Rieser and Mason, 1990).

To be both a child and disabled therefore conjoins characteristics which are doubly disadvantaging as far as having one's voice heard is concerned. Disabled children are people for whom it has seemed only too self-evident that rights about self-determination should have been taken away and important life decisions taken instead by someone else who 'knows better'. And these others who know better are guided by models of childhood which elevate adult rationality, diminish child rationality and relegate the child to the status of onlooker.

Some local authorities are, in effect, implementing only *re-placement* policies (where a child is moved from special school to the mainstream, perhaps with the support of a learning support assistant). The term 'main-dumping' has been used in the United States (see, e.g. Stainback and Stainback, 1990) to describe the worst examples of this process – wherein children are moved from special schools to mainstream schools with inadequate preparation or resourcing. Many schools, in fact, have accepted disabled children only on the basis of 'assimilation' – that is, children are welcome only if they can benefit from what is already on offer.

Other local authorities have more sophisticated schemes in which 'outreach' support is provided by specialist teachers who visit mainstream schools. Sometimes, under the guidance of a forward-thinking headteacher, a special school has decamped from its special location and reformed on the premises of its local neighbourhood school. There are a few published accounts of such developments: in *Bishopswood* (CSIE, 1992) there is an account of a school for children with severe learning difficulties which moved in its entirety to mainstream institutions.

One forward-thinking local authority, Newham, has planned the closure of all its special schools. This has involved the integration of all children in mainstream schools with varying degrees of support, as described by Jordan and Goodey (1996). A controversial aspect of the programme of closure has been (at least in the short term) the placement of the transferred children to 'resourced schools' – that is, schools which are especially resourced to take a group of former special school pupils. The consequence of this compromise policy is that children do not necessarily attend their neighbourhood schools. Staff of the special schools were offered transfers to the resourced schools or to the authority's learning support service.

Some of the forms of organisation and reorganisation taken by the move to inclusion are summarised below:

- *re-placement*: moving individual children to the mainstream with varying degrees of support, and varying levels of success for the children involved;
- *de-camping*: moving a special school, with its students and staff, into the mainstream;
- closing special schools and providing *resourced schools* – that is, schools which are especially resourced to take a group of former special school pupils;
- closing special schools and providing a *support service* – comprising support teachers and learning support assistants, usually from the former special schools;

- providing an *inclusion service* – that is, converting a special school to a service, whereby ex-special school staff restructure and work in neighbourhood schools.

The various changes outlined can be contrasted with integration, wherein the emphasis is only on 're-placement'.

## Financing and implementing inclusion

The Audit Commission (1992) also found in the United Kingdom that inclusion was being held back by the financial systems operating in local government. The commission found that local authorities were reluctant to delegate more money to schools to enable inclusion because, the authorities said, they could not be confident that the delegated money would be used wisely or correctly. However, the local authorities at that time had no way of monitoring how well schools were performing with special pupils, so they would not know whether this assertion was true or not. There was also a problem, the commission found, in that an authority – knowing that an inclusive placement would be expensive – would have 'an incentive...not to specify what is to be provided because they thereby avoid a long-term financial commitment' (Audit Commission/HMI, 1992: 25).

Of the four underlying causes for a slower-than-acceptable move to inclusion identified by the commission, three concerned financial matters surrounding the organisation of the school system by the local authority. These were:

1   'the LEA is legally in the position of the person representing the child's educational interests. However, it is also the provider of education through special schools. There is no separation of the role of the client, who purchases services, and the contractor, who delivers them. Hence the LEA is in the position of monitoring itself' (1992: 31). In this situation, decisions about possible school transfer would usually be left to the special school headteacher, who would rarely advise on a transfer, due to (3), below;
2   there is a 'financial disincentive' for authorities to move pupils from special schools to the mainstream as they then have to fund the ordinary school place as well as an empty special school place;
3   there is no incentive for special school heads to pursue programmes of transfer of pupils to mainstream schools, since the consequence could be a loss of viability for their own schools.

Even though the number of pupils with special needs being educated in ordinary schools is rising, the number of teachers employed in special schools has not declined in line with that trend. The commission found that if special schools had indeed reduced in size (or if they had restructured themselves in some way, through, for example, enabling teaching and support staff to do outreach work), £53 million would have been released to support special pupils in mainstream schools over the period 1986–1991. This, however, is an underestimate of the potential redirection of funds, since it includes the redirection made only through the reduction in numbers of teachers; it does not allow for redirection of the substantial fixed costs of maintaining and running the special school. The commission found that different authorities, and different schools within one authority, varied greatly in their success in 'releasing' teachers to work in the mainstream, and the ability to release teachers did not seem to relate to the size or type of special school.

The correct policy will not magically induce inclusive practice. Many case studies and analyses (e.g. those of Weatherley and Lipsky, 1977; Fulcher, 1989; Loxley and Thomas, 1997) show that the best intentions can be subverted at local level if the conditions are not right – if people are not prepared for and committed to the change at the 'chalk-face'. Fullan (1993) says that school reform efforts have often failed because they have been imposed from the top without input from and part- nership with those who do the work. In words which are strikingly similar to those of Weatherley and Lipsky (1977), who indicated the problems which come from initiatives in special education emerging from 'street-level bureaucrats', Fullan says that the assumptions behind reform efforts often simply express a desire by some politicians to want to be seen carrying out a reform agenda.

As Fullan says, both bottom-up and top-down strategies are necessary. Initiatives must come from the bottom – from the schools – but legal and financial structures must be in place to support the initiatives and enable them to succeed. The message, then, is that change to inclusion will have to be a partnership among those at national, regional and school levels. At the national level legislation has to provide the ground-rules and at regional level there have to be real money-follows- child accounting systems available to those groups of schools who wish to move to inclusive practice. But ideas and initiatives for change must come from those who do the work in the schools.

## Reflective questions

1   To what extent were educational psychologists and other 'experts' to blame for segregation? Are they still?
2   What is 'special' about 'special schools'?
3   To what extent does an inclusive perspective inevitably shift the focus from the individual to the system?
4   Is the main barrier to inclusion a lack of resources?

## References

Anderson, L.W. and Pellicer, L.O. (1990) 'Synthesis of research on compensatory and remedial education', *Educational Leadership*, 48, 1, 10–16.
Audit Commission/HMI (1992) *Getting in on the Act: Provision for Pupils with Special Educational Needs: The National Picture*, London: HMSO.
Baker, E.T., Wang, M.C. and Walberg, H.J. (1995) 'The effects of inclusion on learning', *Educational Leadership*, 52, 4, 33–5.
Birch, H.G., Richardson, S.A., Baird, D., Horobin, G. and Illsley, R. (1970) *Mental Subnormality in the Community: A Clinical and Epidemiological Survey*, Baltimore: Williams and Wilkins.
Booth, T. (1995) 'Mapping inclusion and exclusion: concepts for all', in C. Clarke, A. Dyson and A. Millward (eds) *Towards Inclusive Schools*, London: David Fulton.
——(1996) 'A perspective on inclusion from England', *Cambridge Journal of Education*, 26, 1, 87–98.
CEC (1994) '12 Principles for Successful Inclusive Schools', *CEC Today Newsletter (Council for Exceptional Children)*, May.
Christophos, F. and Renz, P. (1969) 'A critical examination of special education programs', *Journal of Special Education*, 3, 4, 371–80.
Copeland, I. (1995) 'The establishment of models of education for disabled children', *British Journal of Educational Studies*, 43, 2, 179–200.
——(1996) 'Integration versus segregation: the early struggle', paper presented to the Annual Conference of the British Educational Research Association, Lancaster.

CSIE (1992) *Bishopswood: Good Practice Transferred*, Bristol: Centre for Studies on Inclusive Education.

Dorn, S., Fuchs, D. and Fuchs, L.S, (1996) 'A historical perspective on special education reform', *Theory into Practice*, 35, 1, 12–19.

Dunn, L.M. (1968) 'Special education for the mildly mentally retarded: is much of it justifiable?', *Exceptional Children*, September, 5–22.

Flynn, G. (1993) 'Leadership forum; inclusion, reform and restructuring in practice', paper presented to the Annual Convention of the Council for Exceptional Children, April 5–9, San Antonio, CA.

Fulcher, G. (1989) *Disabling Policies*, London: Falmer.

——(1993) 'Schools and contests: a reframing of the effective schools debate?' in R. Slee (ed.) *Is there a Desk with my Name on it? The Politics of Integration*, London: Falmer.

Fullan, M. (1993) *Change Forces*, London: Falmer.

Galloway, D.M, and Goodwin, C. (1979) *Educating Slow Learning and Maladjusted Children: Integration or Segregation?*, Harlow: Longman.

Garner, P. and Sandow, S. (eds) (1995) *Advocacy, Self-advocacy and Special Needs*, London: David Fulton.

Gerber, M.M. (1996) 'Reforming special education: beyond "inclusion" ', in C. Christensen and F. Rizvi (eds) *Disability and the Dilemmas of Education and Justice*, Buckingham: Open University Press.

Hargreaves, D.H. (1982) *The Challenge for the Comprehensive School*, London: Routledge and Kegan Paul.

Hegarty, S.(1993) 'Reviewing the literature on integration', *European Journal of Special Needs Education*, 8, 3, 194–200.

Hutton, W. (1995) *The State We're In*, London: Jonathan Cape.

Jordan, L. and Goodey, C. (1996) *Human Rights and School Change; The Newham Story*, Bristol: CSIE.

Kay, J. (1996) *The Business of Economics*, Oxford: Oxford University Press.

Lipsky, D. and Gartner, A. (1987) 'Capable of achievement and worthy of respect', *Exceptional Children*, 54, 1, 69–74.

——(1996) 'Inclusion, school restructuring and the remaking of American Society', *Harvard Educational Review*, 66, 4, 762–96.

Loxley, A. and Thomas, G. (1997) 'From policy to the real world: an international comparison of special needs administration', *Disability and Society*, 12, 2, 273–91.

Mason, D. (1994) 'Inclusive education leaves deaf children outsiders', *WFD (World Federation of the Deaf, Helsinki) News*, 4 (December), 22.

Mason, M. (1995) *Invisible Children: Report of the Joint Conference on Children, Images and Disability*, London: Save the Children and the Integration Alliance.

Mercer, J.R. (1970) 'Sociological perspectives on mild mental retardation', in H.C. Haywood (ed.) *Sociocultural Aspects of Mental Retardation*, Englewood Cliffs, NJ: Prentice-Hall.

Newman, T. and Roberts, H. (1996) 'Meaning well and doing good: interventions in children's lives', in P. Alderson, S. Brill, I. Chalmers, R. Fuller, P. Hinkley-Smith, G. Macdonald, T. Newman, A. Oakley, H. Roberts and H. Ward (eds), *What Works? Effective Social Interventions in Child Welfare*, London: Barnardos.

OECD (1994) *The Integration of Disabled Children into Mainstream Education: Ambitions, Theories and Practices*, Paris: Organisation for Economic Co-operation and Development.

OFSTED (1996) *Exclusions from Secondary Schools*, London: The Stationery Office.

Piji, S.J., and Meijer, C.J.W. (1994) 'Introduction', in C.J.W. Meijer, S.J. Pijl and S. Hegarty (eds) *New Perspectives in Special Education*, London: Routledge.

Plender, J. (1997a) *A Stake in the Future: The Stakeholding Solution*, London: Nicholas Brealey Publishing.

——(1997b) 'A stake of one's own', *Prospect*, February, 20–4.

Potts, P. (1982) *Origins*, Milton Keynes: The Open University Press.

Rawls, J. (1971) *A Theory of Justice*, Oxford: Clarendon Press.

Reynolds, M.C. (1988) 'A reaction to the JLD special series on the Regular Education Initiative', *Journal of Learning Disabilities*, 21, 6, 352–6.

Reynolds, M.C., Wang, M. and Walberg, H. (1987) The necessary restructuring of special and general education', *Exceptional Children*, 53, 1, 391–7.

Rieser, R. and Mason, M. (1990) *Disability Equality in the Classroom: A Human Rights Issue*, London: Inner London Education Authority.

Scott, P. (1996) 'LEAs and the development of the special education system in the UK', unpublished PhD thesis, Milton Keynes: Open University.

Sebba, J. and Ainscow, M. (1996) 'International developments in inclusive schooling: mapping the issues', *Cambridge Journal of Education*, 26, 1, 5–18.

Stainback, S. and Stainback, W. (1990) 'Inclusive schooling', in W. Stainback and S. Stainback (eds) *Support Networks for Inclusive Schooling; Interdependent Integrated Education*, Baltimore: Paul H. Brookes.

Steinberg, A. and Tovey, R. (1996) ' "Research says . . . ": a cautionary note', in E. Miller and R. Tovey (eds) *Inclusion and Special Education*, HEL Focus Series No. 1, Cambridge, MA: Harvard Educational Publishing.

Strain, P.S. and Kerr, M.M. (1981) *Mainstreaming of Children in Schools: Research and Programmatic Issues*, London: Academic Press.

Weatherley, R. and Lipsky, M. (1977) 'Street level bureaucrats and institutional innovation: implementing special educational reform', *Harvard Educational Review*, 47, 171–97.

Woronov, T. (1996) 'New research supports inclusion for physically disabled: vocational ed prevents dropping out', in E. Miller and R. Tovey (eds) *Inclusion and Special Education*, HEL Focus Series No. 1, Cambridge, MA: Harvard Educational Publishing.

# CHAPTER 2

# INCLUSIVE PRACTICE
## What, why and how?

### L. Florian

In C. Tilstone, L. Florian and R. Rose (eds) *Promoting Inclusive Practice (1998),*
London and New York: RoutledgeFalmer, pp. 13–26

The concept of inclusive education enjoys a high profile around the world by virtue
of its incorporation into the policy documents of numerous international organisations, most notably the United Nations. Standards of UN policies such as those
embodied in the UN Convention on the Rights of the Child (1989), the UN Standard
Rules on the Equalisation of Opportunities for Persons with Disabilities (1993) and
the 1994 UNESCO Report on the education of children with disabilities (Salamanca
Statement) all affirm the rights of all children to equal education without discrimination within the mainstream education system. Although this means different things
in different places there is a universality to the underlying human rights philosophy
of inclusion which suggests that the concept is destined to persist rather than represent the latest educational fad or bandwagon. For this reason, the study of the education of pupils with learning difficulties is rightfully placed in a context of inclusion.

Within special education, the term inclusive education has come to refer to
a philosophy of education that promotes the education of all pupils in mainstream
schools. The Centre for Studies of Inclusive Education articulated the principles of
this philosophy as follows:

- all children have the right to learn and play together;
- children should not be devalued or discriminated against by being excluded
  or sent away because of their disability or learning difficulty;
- there are no legitimate reasons to separate children for the duration of their
  schooling. They belong together rather than need to be protected from one
  another.

(CSIE, 1996, p. 10)

However, there is a gap between policy and implementation which must be
acknowledged and addressed. How it is that there can be so much philosophical
agreement on rights and yet so much divergence in practice is not well understood.
Culture explains some but not all of the differences as many of the differences
between policy and implementation are as much *within* as *across* cultures. The
acknowledgement of rights embodied in policy and the practical implementation
of that policy is confounded by many variables such as other competing policies,
the struggle over limited resources, and the prescriptive and centralised nature of

special education. Indeed, in an international review, Loxley and Thomas (1997) identified these among eight common themes which characterise current special education policy.

Initially in education circles, ideas about the inclusion of pupils with disabilities in mainstream classrooms began to emerge from North America in the mid to late 1980s when Canadian provinces started to develop programmes which focused on including all children with disabilities in mainstream class settings (Aefsky, 1995). In the United States, a growing awareness of the variability among states and local education authorities in their interpretation of the legal mandate to provide educational opportunities for pupils with disabilities in the least restrictive environment (i.e. the mainstream classroom) led to calls for greater understanding and generalisation of the conditions that enabled some states to educate more pupils in these settings (Danielson and Bellamy, 1989). Over the past ten years, the concept of inclusive education has been gaining momentum. The term was introduced in the United Kingdom around 1990 with the launch of annual inclusion conferences aimed at extending and refining ideas about integration (Hall, 1996).

## From integration to inclusion: more than a change in terminology

Lewis (1995) suggested two reasons why ideas about integration were in need of refinement in the United Kingdom. One is that, over time, the term integration had become too narrowly interpreted as a placement without any regard to the quality of that placement. The second and more complex reason has to do with a critique of the concept of normalisation, a key influence on integration polices throughout the world. The influential Warnock Report (DES, 1978) described the process of integration as locational, social or functional. These qualifying terms referred to the sharing of the same site by special/ordinary school provision (locational integration); shared out-of-classroom activities (social integration); and joint participation in educational programmes (functional integration). Here, the task of integration has been about how to join in the mainstream, how to become like others. How to become like others is at the heart of the concept of normalisation. Normalisation is widely understood as 'making available to all persons with disabilities, patterns of life and conditions of everyday living which are as close as possible to or indeed the same as the regular circumstances and ways of life of society' (Nirje, 1985). For many years advocates believed that the concept of normalisation could be achieved by the process of integration. The problem was that integration, by virtue of being a process of joining, first assumed that the exclusion of people with disabilities from ordinary life was acceptable. Although a key influence on special education, the concept of normalisation has not been without critics (Jenkinson, 1997). Criticisms include the claim that the concept involves a 'denial of differentness' and asks whether the concept itself has contributed to a devaluing of people who are different (Peters, 1995).

When the International League of Societies for Persons with Mental Handicap (ILSMH) announced in April 1996 that it had adopted a new name, Inclusion International, the organisation noted: 'This new name expresses a hope for the future. It is a hope that goes beyond the hope of the past of simply integrating people.... The word inclusion acknowledges a history of exclusion that we have to overcome' (Inclusion International, 1996, p. 1). Two phrases confirm Lewis's observations about dissatisfaction with the term integration and provide a rationale for the new term, inclusion. These are: (1) that the term inclusion 'goes beyond simply integrating people', and (2) that it 'acknowledges a history of exclusion that must be overcome'. Overcoming a history of exclusion requires fundamental changes in thinking about 'patterns of life and conditions of everyday living'. The task for inclusion is to redefine these things so that people with disabilities are valued for who they are because of rather than despite difference.

## A definition

Many definitions of inclusive education have been advanced. A selection of these definitions, presented in Table 2.1, range from 'extending the scope of ordinary schools so they can include a greater diversity of children' (Clark *et al.*, 1995, p. v) to 'a set of principles which ensures that the student with a disability is viewed as a valued and needed member of the community in every respect' (Uditsky, 1993, p. 88). Some definitions focus on human interaction: for example, Forest and Pearpoint (1992) see inclusion as a way of dealing with difference while Uditsky emphasises valuing all children as members of the school community. Others (i.e. Ballard, 1995; Clark *et al.*, 1995; Rouse and Florian, 1996) adopt an institutional perspective and focus on organisational arrangements and school improvement. To date, none of the proposed definitions have gained currency in the field suggesting that a truly satisfactory definition has yet to emerge.

Recently, it has been suggested that inclusion is 'the process of increasing participation in and decreasing exclusion from mainstream social settings'

*Table 2.1* Definitions of inclusion

Being with one another...How we deal with diversity, How we deal with difference (Forest and Pearpoint, 1992).

Inclusive schools are diverse problem solving organisations with a common mission that emphasises learning for all students (Rouse and Florian, 1996).

Being a full member of an age-appropriate class in your local school doing the same lessons as the other pupils and it mattering if you are not there. Plus you have friends who spend time with you outside of school (Hall, 1996).

A set of principles which ensures that the student with a disability is viewed as a valued and needed member of the school community in every respect (Uditsky, 1993).

Inclusion can be understood as a move towards extending the scope of 'ordinary' schools so they can include a greater diversity of children (Clark *et al.*, 1995).

Inclusive schools deliver a curriculum to students through organisational arrangements that are different from those used in schools that exclude some students from their regular classrooms (Ballard, 1995).

Increasing participation and decreasing exclusion from mainstream social settings (Potts, 1997).

Inclusion describes the process by which a school attempts to respond to all pupils as individuals by reconsidering its curricula organisation and provision (Sebba, 1996).

An inclusive school is one which is accepting of all children (Thomas, 1997).

(Booth *et al.*, 1997; Potts, 1997, p. 4). This is consistent with Inclusion International's more specific 1996 definition which we have adopted:

> Inclusion refers to the opportunity for persons with a disability to participate fully in all of the educational, employment, consumer, recreational, community, and domestic activities that typify everyday society.

This definition is the only one we are aware of to transcend the concept of normalisation. It does so by using language that emphasises participation over normalcy. The opportunity to participate is quite different from making available patterns of life and conditions of everyday living. Opportunity to participate implies active involvement and choice as opposed to the passive receipt of a pattern or condition that has been made available. Locational, social and functional integration are things that are made available. They are easily contrasted with inclusion, which cannot be made available because by definition it requires participation. As advocate Micheline Mason noted: 'inclusion is not something that can be done to us. It is something we have to participate in for it to be real' (Pugh and Macrae, 1995).

For pupils with learning difficulties, the full opportunity to participate in the educational activities that typify everyday society will ultimately require education reform policies that do not treat them as members of a minority group. Unfortunately, the movement for inclusive education will not change the underlying reality of an education system unable or unwilling to meet the needs of all children. To the extent that children are labelled, special education will not change as a social construction. In the meantime, teachers will have to satisfy themselves with the knowledge that a philosophy of inclusive education can be applied in mainstream schools and classrooms. Research has demonstrated that under the right conditions, positive outcomes, though difficult to achieve, are possible for all pupils.

## If inclusion cannot be made available, how can it be achieved? A summary of current research and a review of reviews

Research on inclusive education (Katsiyannis *et al.*, 1995; O'Hanlon, 1995) suggests that its meaning may be contextual. In other words, the meaning will take different forms in various places depending on the situation. Differences in context result in different pictures of inclusive education despite the fact that many jurisdictions base arguments for inclusive education on human rights. However, despite these differences, there is a great deal of agreement in the literature about practice.

Giangreco (1997) identified common features of schools where inclusive education is reported to be thriving. These features are:

- collaborative teamwork;
- a shared framework;
- family involvement;
- general educator ownership;
- clear role relationships among professionals;
- effective use of support staff;

- meaningful Individual Education Plans (IEPs);
- procedures for evaluating effectiveness.

This is consistent with other research (i.e. Hopkins *et al.*, 1996; Lipsky and Gartner, 1997; Rouse and Florian, 1996; Sebba, 1996) which links inclusive education to the development of effective schools. The emphasis is on changing school structures so that schools are able to accommodate a greater range of pupils.

In general, the research on inclusive education does not differentiate effects among different groups of pupils. Pupils with learning difficulties may be included in studies of inclusive practice but less frequently are they the focus of the study. Two reviews summarising research on integration and inclusion for pupils with severe learning difficulties appeared in the special education literature. One (Farrell, 1997) involved a wide-ranging review of research on the effects of integration on children with severe learning difficulties (SLD). The second (Hunt and Goetz, 1997) was more narrowly focused on research investigations that included the full-time placement of children with severe disabilities in mainstream schools. Obviously, the parameters the reviewers set themselves resulted in the identification of different sets of studies for review but, surprisingly, there was no overlap on references between the two reviews.

Both Farrell and Hunt and Goetz found a diversity of methodologies utilised in the studies; however, the focus of the reviews was different. Hunt and Goetz were interested in evaluating the state of research on inclusion and pupils with severe disabilities. Farrell wanted to examine selected areas of the research literature because they were thought to be relevant to inclusive education. He reviewed the research on:

- the role of support workers in facilitating integration;
- effect of integration on communication and linguistic interaction;
- relevance of curriculum differentiation;
- effects of integration on children without disabilities;
- attitudes of mainstream teachers and LEA staff toward integration.

Hunt and Goetz identified practices which emerged from triangulation across studies. These were:

- parent perceptions of the pursuit and impact of inclusive educational placement;
- issues and practices in inclusive schools and classrooms;
- educational achievement outcomes in inclusive classrooms;
- social relationships and friendships in inclusive settings;
- the cost of inclusive educational placement.

It is interesting to note the agreement on areas of practice across the two reviews. The ways in which people work together to adapt the curriculum, their attitudes toward pupils with learning difficulties and concern about social and academic outcomes for all pupils emerge in both reviews as critical features of inclusive education.

Although Farrell did not review research on the effects of parental involvement, Hunt and Goetz found it to be a major force in the development of inclusive options for pupils with SLD. They reviewed several studies which found the willingness of parents to 'take on the system' as leading to the establishment of inclusive education as a placement option.

Interesting issues and practices in inclusive schools and classrooms emerged from the reviews. Hunt and Goetz found these centred on the development of positive attitudes among staff, a positive identity among pupils and staff consensus on the value that all children belong in mainstream schools. Farrell's review suggested there may be a relationship between the severity of the disability and attitude although teachers who had experience working with pupils with SLD tended to be more positive.

Another common practice identified by Hunt and Goetz involves a reconceptualisation of teaching roles and responsibilities to enable collaborative teaming for curriculum development and instruction. To accept the idea that inclusion represents the opportunity to participate rather than something that can be made available requires changes in professional thinking and practice. Just as disabled people are asking philosophical questions about why they should accept definitions developed and imposed on them by others, professionals must begin the process of examining their own role in imposing limits on the ways people with disabilities exist in the world. Clarity about professional identity and future mission requires a consideration of the extent to which the separate system of special education itself has disabling effects. John has argued that it

> is one of the main channels for disseminating the predominant able-bodied/minded perception of the world and ensuring that disabled school leavers are socially immature and isolated. This isolation results in passive acceptance of social discrimination, lack of skills in facing the tasks of adulthood and ignorance about the main social issues of the times. All this reinforces the 'eternal children' myth and ensures at the same time disabled school leavers lack the skills for overcoming the myth.
>
> (cited in Oliver, 1988, p. 24)

Clearly, it is the reconceptualisation of teaching roles and responsibilities that is directly relevant to the idea of inclusion as an opportunity to participate for pupils with learning difficulties. Farrell found the role of support staff to be key.

> The role of support staff is both complex and crucial...if support workers devote their time to the delivery of a carefully planned individual programme...opportunities for social interaction with their peer group become reduced.... However, if the support worker devotes time to foster social interaction, this may leave less time for individual teaching...If the child with SLD is simply placed with a group of mainstream children, he or she may be ignored, if the support worker 'joins in', this can influence the 'naturalness' of the interaction.
>
> (Farrell, 1997, p. 10)

When teachers and other support staff are able to work together, for example in co-teaching situations, problems associated with the severity of the learning difficulty and the relevance of the curriculum are diminished. But, as Farrell pointed out, school staff need training and support to take on these new roles and responsibilities.

The scant literature on the effects of inclusive education for pupils with learning difficulties on their educational achievement is equivocal. Though it is not possible to generalise from the research to date, a 'no-difference' finding seems to characterise it. The reported 'no-difference' outcome of the Hunt and Goetz review is consistent with Hegarty's (1993) international review of the research on academic and social benefits of integration. He also found no clear-out academic advantage for mainstream education. However, it is important to bear in mind that the research base is small and it is not yet possible to rule out the effects of confounding variables which have not been subject to analysis. Thus far, no-difference findings have been interpreted as pro inclusion since the impetus for the movement is grounded in human rights. As a result, the absence of differences in educational achievement for pupils with learning difficulties who are placed in inclusive classrooms when compared with the achievement of those in traditional special education programmes is considered supportive of inclusive education.

The social relationships and friendships of pupils with SLD in inclusive settings has received more attention from researchers. Farrell found a majority of studies reported some degree of social acceptance by non-disabled peers. An even more positive picture emerged from the Hunt and Goetz review. Through case study analyses of friendship, researchers reported that when parents of pupils without disabilities and their teachers were supportive of inclusive education, friendships based on reciprocity (as opposed to the 'tutorial' relationship) were possible. Studies using ratings of social competence reported that levels of acceptance of pupils with SLD varied despite the level of social competence, suggesting that some children with disabilities are more popular than others. Farrell found younger and more able children were more likely to be successfully included. However, the Hunt and Goetz review revealed certain interventions appear promising in their power to increase social interaction and friendship among pupils with SLD and their peers without disabilities. This is an important finding because Farrell's review concluded that the 'degree of social and linguistic interaction between the children with SLD and their peers in integrated settings is limited and tends to be didactic and one way in nature' (Farrell, 1997, p. 10). Interventions which enhance participation are essential.

The cost of inclusive education is an important and difficult area to research. Hunt and Goetz argue that any analysis of cost should include a consideration of effects on pupils. In other words, if, as it is possible to argue from this review, children with SLD are, at the very least, no worse off academically, and have the opportunity to participate in mutually satisfying interpersonal relationships with peers, then the cost of inclusive education represents good value for money.

Although Farrell concluded that some form of segregated provision would always be necessary, a careful reading of his review shows that he is referring specifically to limitations on the extent to which a curriculum can be differentiated and relevant. He does not argue for the continued segregation of children in special schools. Rather, he says '*full functional integration* can never be a viable option for all children with SLD throughout their school lives' (Farrell, 1997, p. 11). Farrell argues that a relevant curriculum for a child with profound and multiple learning difficulties (PMLD), for example, will necessarily emphasise subjects not included in the National Curriculum. The segregated provision that Farrell refers to is with respect to the curriculum and not the location in which the curriculum is delivered. Indeed, he concludes with a plea for resource-based models of integration as part of what mainstream schools offer to enable 'full-time integration for some children while providing segregated education with opportunities for social integration for children with profound and multiple difficulties' (Farrell, 1997, p. 11). McInnes (1988) concurs. He argues that the local school can be a viable option for pupils with multisensory impairments if the right support system is established. In his examples, support systems depend on access to specialist teachers who understand the effects of multisensory deprivation on learning and can develop interventions. The extent to which the environmental conditions of the ordinary classroom must be adjusted for these pupils may not be possible at all times. Environments which facilitate communication, and promote cognitive development and concept formation, must also be available.

## Conditions

The teaching methods and practices associated with the provision of inclusive education are easier to identify than to implement on a wide scale. Despite a great deal of agreement about the practice of inclusive education difficulties in doing so remain. Giangreco (1997) has noted that the criticisms of inclusive education are often criticisms of poor quality or partial implementation efforts. It is also possible that the teaching methods available to support inclusive education are neither sufficiently refined nor understood to overcome the variability in implementation efforts. For example, it is possible to interpret some of Farrell's findings in terms of a failure properly to implement inclusive education practices. Though 'effective use of support staff' was identified as a commonly agreed practice in inclusive education Farrell concluded this was a difficult area particularly with respect to fostering interaction with non-disabled peers. In his example quoted earlier, it is clear that if the support worker lacks skill in facilitating interaction then the 'naturalness' of the interaction between the children will be contaminated. It is the lack of skill on the part of the support worker rather than his or her role that results in a misplaced criticism about inclusive education.

Thus, it may be possible that there are a set of conditions which form the basis of inclusive education for pupils with learning difficulties. Such conditions might include:

- an opportunity for pupil participation in the decision-making process;
- a positive attitude about the learning abilities of all pupils;
- teacher knowledge about learning difficulties;
- skilled application of specific instructional methods;
- parent and teacher support.

This review suggests that each of these conditions is necessary but not solely sufficient for inclusive education. All must be in place to avoid implementation failure. For example, a positive attitude alone is not sufficient to achieve inclusive education, though it is a necessary condition. An unskilled teacher, however open minded and willing to try, will fail to provide an appropriate education for pupils with learning difficulties or other special educational needs if he or she is not supported by more experienced colleagues. Likewise, skill in the use of various teaching methods is insufficient without knowledge of pupils' learning difficulties and the belief that such pupils can learn.

Programmes that meet only some of these conditions run the risk of partial implementation and possible failure. Of course, it is possible that programmes that do meet these conditions may also fail, but if the lessons from the research can be applied, the chances are far more in favour of success.

Accepting the idea that inclusion is about participation requires the development of methods which ensure the meaningful participation of people with learning difficulties in the decision-making process. It also requires that the process emphasises participation over placement.

A fundamental respect for the individual must underlie any intervention. As people with disabilities challenge the definitions developed and imposed on them by others, professionals must be prepared for choices that may not be their own. A pupil with learning difficulty may choose to associate with other pupils with learning difficulties. It is not uncommon for people, as they get older, to identify with others like themselves. It is the acceptance of difference that is the hallmark of inclusive practice.

The relationship between identification with a group and inclusion has been documented by Campbell and Oliver (1996) in their history of the disabled people's movement in Britain. The achievement of inclusive schooling for pupils with learning difficulties has been greatly assisted by the momentum generated by the movement as it becomes increasingly better organised and sophisticated. Although the movement has been criticised for failing to include people with learning difficulties, efforts are being made to address this:

> Through their very open and blunt criticisms about the ways in which we can be exclusive, about the way we run our organisation and the ways we can be quite cliquey, People First are challenging us to continue to open up. We started very exclusively and perhaps we needed to be exclusive at that time. Some people find this opening up very hard, but this is the process of inclusion; it's the process of becoming a mass democratic movement of all disabled people, and not just a bunch of white wheelchair users!
>
> (Campbell and Oliver, 1996, p. 203)

## Conclusion

The critique of the concept of normalisation provides a challenge to the status quo requiring changes in thinking and practice. This chapter has explored this challenge by clarifying the difference between integration and inclusion; elaborating on the meaning of 'opportunity to participate'; and reviewing what is known about the provision of inclusive education for pupils with learning difficulties. A set of conditions necessary to promote inclusive practice were identified to aid implementation efforts and help to bridge the gap between the acceptance of equal rights for all as embodied in policy and the actual achievement of inclusive education.

The literature reviewed here suggests a set of necessary but not sufficient conditions must be in place for the successful implementation of inclusive education policies. These are: an opportunity for pupil participation in the decision-making process, a positive attitude about the learning abilities of all pupils, teacher knowledge about learning difficulties, skilled application of specific instructional methods, and parent and teacher support. To the extent that barriers such as other education laws are incompatible with the establishment of these conditions in mainstream schools (Rouse and Florian, 1997), the range of provision currently available will continue to provide educational opportunity for pupils with learning difficulties. Though it is easy to understand how the separate system of special education evolved in response to the exclusionary practices of schooling, it is much harder to see how current practice depends on a set of practices which require another form of exclusion. To understand this it is necessary to remember that the creation of special education as a separate system was in part a response to the exclusion of pupils with disabilities from mainstream schools. Thus, special education as an exclusive field of study originated in an act of discrimination which now supports a profession. Acknowledging this is a fundamental requirement in moving the debate about inclusive education forward. Consideration of the extent to which special education policy itself leads to possible pupil exclusion, may be useful in illuminating the assumptions underlying and defining the way services are delivered. Practice can then be re-examined in light of the knowledge produced by this line of investigation.

In this way, the development of practice can become a vehicle for change. Thirty years ago innovative professionals were able to demonstrate that all pupils could learn despite policies excluding certain children from school. Though the methods that were developed adhered to a behavioural model emphasising a structural, teacher-directed approach to instruction (Rosenberg and Jackson, 1988), the contribution of special education to the development of instructional methods with applicability to all learners represented a significant advance in extending the right to education for all. Today the same level of innovation is required to demonstrate how all children can learn together. Ainscow (1997) has called upon the profession to develop new ways of working so as to enhance the capacity of mainstream schools to accommodate successfully increasing levels of student diversity.

## Reflective questions

1   How can there be so much agreement about the desirability of inclusion and yet so much difficulty and diversity in putting it into practice?
2   Is an agreed definition of inclusion necessary? Is it desirable? Agreed by whom?
3   By what criteria should the effectiveness of inclusion be measured? Whose criteria?

## References

Aefsky, F. (1995) *Inclusion Confusion*, Thousand Oaks, CA: Corwin Press.
Ainscow, M. (1997) 'Towards inclusive schooling', *British Journal of Special Education*, 24(1): 3–6.
Ballard, K. (1995) 'Inclusion, paradigms, power and participation', in C. Clark, A. Dyson and A. Milward (eds) *Towards Inclusive Schools?*, London: David Fulton.
Booth, T., Ainscow, M. and Dyson, A. (1997) 'Understanding inclusion and exclusion in the English competitive education system', *International Journal of Inclusive Education*, 1(4): 337–55.
Campbell, J. and Oliver, M. (1996) *Disability Politics: Understanding Our Past, Changing Our Future*, London: Routledge.
Centre for the Study of Inclusive Education (1996) *Developing an Inclusive Policy for Your School: A CSIE Guide*, London: CSIE.
Clark, C., Dyson, A. and Millward, A. (1995) *Towards Inclusive Schools?*, London: David Fulton.

Danielson, L. C. and Bellamy, G. T. (1989) 'State variation in placement of children with handicaps in segregated environments', *Exceptional Children*, 55: 448–55.

Department for Education and Science (1978) *Special Educational Needs. Report of the Committee of Enquiry into the Education of Handicapped Children and Young People (The Warnock Report)*, London: HMSO.

Farrell, P. (1997) 'The integration of children with severe learning difficulties: a review of the recent literature', *Journal of Applied Research in Intellectual Disabilities*, 10(1): 1–14.

Forest, M. and Pearpoint, J. (1992) 'Putting all kids on the MAP', *Educational Leadership*, 50(2): 26–31.

Giangreco, M. F. (1997) 'Key lessons learned about inclusive education: summary of the 1996 Schonell Memorial Lecture', *International Journal of Disability, Development and Education*, 44(3): 193–206.

Hall, J. (1996) 'Integration, inclusion, – what does it all mean?', in J. Coupe O'Kane and J. Goldbart (eds) *Whose Choice? Contentious Issues for Those Working with People with Learning Difficulties*, London: David Fulton.

Hegarty, S. (1993) 'Reviewing the literature on integration', *European Journal of Special Needs Education*, 8(3): 194–200.

Hopkins, D., West, M. and Ainscow, M. (1996) *Improving the Quality of Education for All: Progress and Challenge*, London: David Fulton.

Hunt, P. and Goetz, L. (1997) 'Research on inclusive educational programs, practices and outcomes for students with severe disabilities', *The Journal of Special Education*, 31(1): 3–29.

Inclusion International (1996, April) *Inclusion: News from Inclusion International*, Brussels: Inclusion International.

Katsiyannis, A., Conderman, G. and Franks, D. J. (1995) 'State practices on inclusion: a national review', *Remedial and Special Education*, 16(5): 279–87.

Lewis, A. (1995) *Children's Understanding of Disability*, London: Routledge.

Lipsky, D. K. and Gartner, A. (1997) *Inclusion and School Reform: Transforming America's Classrooms*, Baltimore: Paul H. Brookes.

Loxley, A. and Thomas, G. (1997) 'From inclusive policy to the exclusive real world: an international review', *Disability and Society*, 12(2): 273–91.

McInnes, J. (1988) *Integration*, Deaf–Blind Education (Jan–Jun), 7–12.

Nirje, B. (1985) 'The basis and logic of the normalisation principle', *Australia and New Zealand Journal of Developmental Disabilities*, 11: 65–8.

O'Hanlon, C. (1995) *Inclusive Education in Europe*, London: David Fulton.

Oliver, M. (1988) 'The social and political context of educational policy: the case of special needs', in L. Barton (ed.) *The Politics of Special Educational Needs*, London: Falmer Press.

Peters, S. (1995) 'Disability baggage: changing the educational research terrain', in P. Clough and L. Barton (eds) *Making Difficulties: Research and the Construction of SEN*, London: Paul Chapman.

Potts, P. (1997) 'Developing a collaborative approach to the study of inclusive education in more than one country', paper presented to the European Conference on Educational Research, Frankfurt am Main, September.

Pugh, A. (Producer) and Macrae, I. (Series Editor) (1995) *Old School Ties* [Film], London: BBC Disability Programmes Unit.

Rouse, M. and Florian, L. (1996) 'Effective inclusive schools: a study in two countries', *Cambridge Journal of Education*, 26(1): 71–85.

Rouse, M. and Florian, L. (1997) 'Inclusive education in the marketplace', *International Journal of Inclusive Education*, 1(4): 323–36.

Sebba, J. (1996, Spring/Summer) *Developing Inclusive Schools*, University of Cambridge Institute of Education, No.31, p. 3.

Thomas, G. (1997) 'Inclusive schools for an inclusive society', *British Journal of Special Education*, 24(3): 103–7.

Uditsky, B. (1993) 'From integration to inclusion: the Canadian experience', in R. Slee (ed.) *Is There a Desk with My Name on It? The Politics of Integration*, London: Falmer Press.

United Nations (1989) *Convention on the Rights of the Child*, New York: UN.
United Nations (1993) *Standard Rules on the Equalisation of Opportunities for Persons with Disabilities*, New York: UN.
United Nations Educational, Scientific and Cultural Organisation (1994) *The Salamanca Statement and Framework for Action on Special Needs Education*, Paris: UNESCO.

# CHAPTER 3

# INCLUSIVE EDUCATION
## Are there limits?

### J. Evans and I. Lunt

*European Journal of Special Needs Education* (2002), 17(1), pp. 1–14

## Introduction

Over the past ten years, there has been a growing impetus worldwide towards 'full inclusion', stimulated in part by the Salamanca Statement of 1994 (UNESCO, 1994), and in the United Kingdom at least, by a 'rights' agenda promoted by those who believe that inclusion is a matter of human rights and a liberal society (e.g. Thomas, 1997), or a matter of 'effectiveness' (e.g. Ainscow, 1997). At the same time, there have been moves towards what has been described as a more 'cautious' or 'responsible' form of inclusion (e.g. Vaughn and Schumm, 1995), whose proponents argue that individual pupils have an overriding right to appropriate education, and that there is a small minority of pupils with severe and complex needs who policy-makers in most countries agree are very difficult to include in mainstream schools (e.g. Pijl and Meijer, 1991).

There are strongly held views on both sides. Further, there is a wide range of different conceptualizations and definitions of 'inclusion', which encompass a number of confusions (Hornby, 2001) and contradictory elements in thinking and discourse between a principled and ideological stance, as compared with a more pragmatic orientation (Skidmore, 1999; Croll and Moses, 2000; Farrell, 2001). In this chapter, we argue that the contradictions inherent in the current policy context make full inclusion problematic, and impose limits which it is important to recognize and to plan for. We also present the results of focus group interviews carried out with education professionals, which explored the question of whether they considered that there are limits to 'inclusion'.

## The policy and legislative context

Inclusion is a buzz-word in social and educational policy in the United Kingdom and the European Union, and also in the United States and further afield. Increasingly, politicians stress their commitment to inclusion and social justice. All European Union countries now have legislation firmly in place to promote or require inclusion, while the United States effectively has led the way with its PL 94–142 of 1975, the Education for All Handicapped Children Act, amended in 1990 as the Individuals with Disabilities Act (IDEA) and, again, in 1997, to promote 'whole-school' approaches to inclusion.

The legislative context in the United Kingdom is provided by the 1996 Education Act which promotes a weak, or provisional, form of integration or inclusion; the 1988 Education Act (the Education Reform Act), which promotes competition, parental choice and a quasi-market for the education system; and the 1998 Act, which promotes standards (and competition). The legislation promotes a broad agenda of standards, to be raised by competition and league tables, consumer choice and cost effectiveness. The policy framework has been set by the UK government White Paper (DfEE, 1997a); the Green Paper (DfEE, 1997b), which asserts the right of the pupil with special educational needs (SEN) to be educated in mainstream schools 'wherever possible'; and documents such as the original version and revision of the Code of Practice (DfEE, 1994) and the government Programme of Action (DfEE, 1998), which promotes inclusion 'where parents want it and where appropriate support can be provided'. These words show an acknowledgement by the government that there are limits to inclusion; as indeed do the provisos of the 1996 Act, which replicate the provisional form of integration of the original 1981 Education Act, and that continue to let schools and local education authorities (LEAs) 'off the hook' when it comes to full inclusion. It is evident that recent legislative changes have seen a 'shift from legislation and policies based upon principles of equity, social progress and altruism, to new legislation underpinned by a market-place philosophy based upon principles of academic excellence, choice and competition' (Rouse and Florian, 1997, p. 324; and see Evans and Lunt, 1994), and further, that there is a tension between pressures for effectiveness and pressures for inclusiveness (see Lunt and Norwich, 1999). The legislative and policy framework in the United Kingdom clearly provides for limits to full inclusion; the question of interest in this study was to explore the nature and extent of these limits.

## Inclusion

The term 'inclusion' replaced 'integration' and is often contrasted with 'exclusion', thus having a welcome wider significance (see Pijl *et al.*, 1997), frequently embracing social disadvantage as well as SEN (cf. the government's social exclusion unit, and widespread concerns over the exclusion of pupils whose behaviour is causing concern). While 'integration' was largely a 'disability' or SEN issue, inclusion is usually promoted from a wider principled and idealistic, or even ideological, perspective, as demonstrated by the Salamanca Statement:

> Regular schools with this inclusive orientation are the most effective means of combating discriminatory attitudes, creating welcoming communities, building an inclusive society and achieving education for all; moreover, they provide an effective education to the majority of children and improve the efficiency and ultimately the cost-effectiveness of the entire education system.
> (UNESCO, 1994: ix)

This principled perspective is promoted by Thomas (1997), who suggests that 'inclusion must be at the heart of any society which cherishes...a liberal political system and a pluralistic culture: one that celebrates diversity and promotes fraternity and equality of opportunity' (p. 106). A government-supported initiative within the United Kingdom, the *Index for Inclusion* (Booth *et al.*, 2000), which was distributed to all schools, attempted to facilitate inclusion at the school level.

Some of the complexity of the field has been captured in a number of publications (e.g. Ainscow, 1999; Daniels and Garner, 1999; Clough and Corbett, 2000; Mittler, 2000; Norwich, 2000b).

Nevertheless, there are critics of what have been perceived as ideological approaches, for example, Bailey (1998), who is critical of the 'fervent crusade promoting inclusive schooling'; Wilson (2000), who disparages 'passionate intuitions, which we then translate uncritically into practice' (p. 297); and Low (1997), who suggests that 'the quest for full inclusion contains a measure of expressive zeal which denies some of the realities of disability' (p. 76). He urges a recognition of both the commonalities and the differences between disabled and non-disabled people which lead to 'instances where the requisite support is most effectively mobilized through separate systems' (p. 78). This has led some to call for the replacement of the rhetoric of 'full inclusion' with the promotion of 'responsible inclusion' (Vaughn and Schumm, 1995; Hornby, 1999) or 'cautious inclusion' (Fuchs and Fuchs, 1994; Kauffman, 1995), while Farrell (2000) has pointed out 'the very real difficulties one can get into if arguments about inclusive education are pursued solely in terms of human rights'. In a recent volume focusing on 'enabling inclusion', O'Brien (2001) suggests that 'we have to answer, with integrity, the questions about where and how a pupil learns best' (p. 49).

Norwich has pointed out that the field of special needs education demands the balancing of multiple values such as those of equality, individuality, social inclusion and practicability, and the tolerance of 'ideological impurity' (Norwich, 1996, 2000b). The tension between ideology and logic has been highlighted by Wilson (1999, 2000), who suggests that it is more appropriate to ask what sorts of learning activities actually suit what types of pupils than to attempt to make one school fit all pupils.

But what does inclusion mean in practice? Does it mean that the local school should provide for 100 per cent of its local pupils, for 99 or 98 per cent, or some other proportion? Does it mean that all pupils should be educated together in the same class or in the same school, and with the same teacher? Should particular schools include particular pupils, thus enabling pupils to attend mainstream though not their local school? Does it include on-site or off-site units? Pijl and Meijer (1991) concluded from an OECD study that 'the countries seem to agree that at least 1.5 per cent of the students are difficult to integrate on a curricular level in regular education'.

Inclusive education is about values and principles, about the kind of society that we want and the kind of education that we value. In the current educational climate, what do the policy-makers and practitioners see as the limits to inclusive education?

## Trends towards inclusion in England and Wales

The Centre for Studies in Inclusive Education (CSIE) has published six analyses of trends in the percentage of pupils in special schools in England since 1982. According to the sixth analysis carried out by Brahm Norwich, the special school population had fallen in 1998 to 1.35 per cent of all five- to 15-year-olds, the lowest ever for England (Norwich, 1997, 2000a). However, this needs to be set against the considerable increase in the numbers of pupils being permanently excluded from school for disciplinary reasons in the three years up to 1998, and the establishment of pupil referral units for pupils whom schools find hard to teach

(OFSTED, 1995). The DfEE statistics for 1998 show that exclusions in the year 1998/99 totalled 10,400, compared to the previous three years, in which exclusions totalled over 12,000.

Fundamental to the implementation of a strategy of greater inclusion of pupils with SEN in mainstream schools is the willingness and ability of LEAs and schools to change. Indeed, as Thomas *et al.* (1998) suggested in their study, when asking the question: 'why, given the moral imperative for inclusive schools, and the empirical evidence in their favour, inclusion had not caught on faster. The answer surely lies in a mixture of conservatism, inertia and fear of the unknown' (Thomas *et al.* p. 198). This study evaluated the implementation of a planned and resourced programme of inclusion, and the transformation of a special school into an inclusion service.

The numbers of pupils excluded from school, mainly for unacceptable behaviour, have steadily increased (Parsons, 2000). A high proportion of those pupils who are excluded also have SEN. An analysis by Hayden (2000) suggests that children with statements of SEN are six times more likely than other children to be excluded. She states that children identified with some level of SEN accounted for 67.2 per cent of all exclusions and 79.1 per cent of permanent exclusions from school. The current regime of inspection and testing has led to a situation where there is less room for flexibility or innovation in teaching approaches to encompass the needs of a wide range of pupils.

## The research

We were interested to gauge the situation in schools and LEAs as perceived by a range of professionals from education, health services and social services and the challenges they saw for schools and LEAs wishing to promote greater inclusion. We used two methods to collect our data:

1   A national questionnaire distributed to all Principal Educational Psychologists in England and Wales at the end of 1998.
2   Four focus group discussions, with a range of professionals, to explore the topic of inclusion. Each group contained eight participants, comprising a mixed group drawn from teachers, health professionals and social workers and covered those working in a range of integrated and segregated settings for children with special educational needs. Each of the focus group discussions was facilitated by one of the researchers who 'moderated' the discussion, ensured that all participants were able to express views, but did not contribute substantively to the discussion. The discussion was based around the following set of stimulus questions:

   –   What do we mean by inclusion?
   –   What could be the advantages and/or disadvantages of inclusion for professionals and pupils?
   –   What would help schools to be more inclusive?
   –   How do parents view inclusive settings?

The focus group discussion was tape recorded and transcribed for subsequent analysis.

## Findings from the questionnaire survey

A total of 60 questionnaires were returned, a response rate of 37.5 per cent. The respondents covered the range of LEAs in England and Wales, including the newly created unitary authorities. About half of the responses were from LEAs in rural areas, and half in urban areas, and there was a mixture of very large and tiny LEAs.

The questionnaire asked for basic data on the number of pupils with statements of SEN in the LEA; the number and types of special schools provided by the LEA; the percentage of pupils in special schools; and the numbers of pupils permanently excluded from school in the current year and the provision available for excluded pupils. It also asked questions designed to elicit the LEA's policies and readiness to promote inclusion.

The overall rate of statements in the sample LEAs was 3.45 per cent. This is higher than the reported national average, but may reflect the more up-to-date figures which the respondents had access to, compared with DfEE figures. The latter are at least one year out of date, due to the method of compiling them from annual returns submitted by LEAs. If there is an upward trend in provision of statements, which these data seem to indicate, then it appears that the goal of reducing the statement rate, expressed in the Green Paper, will be difficult to achieve. However, since students with statements are being educated, to a large extent, in mainstream schools, a high statement rate does not of itself indicate that greater inclusion is not possible. Over half of the students with statements in our sample were being educated in mainstream schools. The proportion of pupils in special provision (i.e. not in mainstream) in the LEAs in the sample was 1.37 per cent, which is about the national average calculated from published figures (Norwich, 2000a). This proportion has changed very little over the past ten years, indicating a lack of policy development for inclusion in most LEAs. There have been one or two notable exceptions to this, but, on the whole, the proportion of children in segregated settings has remained fairly constant.

However, a growing concern among educationists and policy-makers is the number of children who are being permanently excluded from schools, mainly for disruptive behaviour. There is evidence (Spencer, 1998) that children excluded from school are more likely to be socially marginalized and to commit crimes. The number of permanent exclusions from school has grown dramatically in the past few years, according to Parsons and Castle (1998); in their survey, the number of pupils permanently excluded from school in England was 13,581. Among our sample, 49 respondents could give the number of excluded pupils for their LEA; the total for these 49 was 4,396 permanent exclusions. Extrapolating that figure to the total LEA population of England and Wales would give a national figure of 14,653 for 1996/97.

Thus, as well as children educated outside the mainstream because they have been assessed as having SEN that cannot be met in regular schools, there is another group of children outside mainstream because they have been excluded for reasons of their behaviour. These students are catered for in a variety of ways. Under legislation passed in 1993, LEAs are mandated to set up Pupil Referral Units (PRUs), which are specifically designed to provide education for children whose behaviour or other circumstances (such as pregnancy) might make it difficult for mainstream schools to cope with them. Such units are generally small schools and provide education for only a small proportion of excluded pupils. An inspection report published in 1995 criticized PRUs for failing to provide an acceptable standard of education (OFSTED, 1995). Other alternatives for such pupils are home tuition (i.e. individual teaching in the child's home), which might amount to 5 hours per week, or other alternative placements such as (for older pupils) in a Further Education college.

The respondents to our survey gave details of the arrangements made for excluded pupils in their LEAs. Most (78 per cent) had one or more pupil referral units. These were more likely to be available for older pupils. Less than half (41 per cent) offered home tuition to excluded pupils. A range of other alternatives, including part-time placement, placement in FE colleges and support for reintegration into school from a Behaviour Support Team, were also offered by 33 per cent of the LEAs in the sample. A further 10 per cent offered placement in a special school or unit for pupils with behaviour problems. On the whole, it appears therefore that this group of disaffected and disruptive pupils is at risk of being marginalized and excluded from the mainstream on a long-term basis. When 'inclusive education' is discussed, this group of children is not at the top of the agenda as candidates for inclusion.

When asked if the LEA had a policy for inclusion, the responses from the Principal Psychologists were mixed. Half the LEAs had no specific policy regarding inclusion; and 37 per cent had a policy sometimes contained within its general policy statements regarding SEN. Eight LEAs (13 per cent) had a draft policy on inclusion. It must be concluded therefore that, in English and Welsh LEAs, there is not a strong push towards a more inclusive system of schooling. The majority of the LEAs in the sample (68 per cent) had not attempted to ascertain the cost of inclusion – a further indication that it is not, a policy priority.

All the LEAs in the sample could give examples of the various forms of inclusion currently practised. These were:

1    Part-time placements in special and in mainstream schools. (78 per cent)
2    Outreach support from special school to integrated pupils. (60 per cent)
3    Units or centres on the site of a mainstream school. (92 per cent)
4    Modifications to mainstream facilities. (76 per cent)
5    Additionally resourced mainstream schools. (80 per cent)
6    Supported placements in mainstream schools. (96 per cent)

Other forms of inclusion reported were: special school-run 'satellites' on mainstream sites; an inclusion project within a mainstream high school; and early entry to further education.

Most of these are what might be termed 'weak' forms of inclusion (i.e. pupils with SEN are identified individually, given statements and then placed on an individual basis with extra funding to meet their specific needs). In this type of situation, the mainstream school does not have to adapt in any major way to the needs of the pupils – these are catered for by expertise coming from outside (in the case of outreach support or units placed on the site of mainstream schools), or by the use of individual support allocated through statements.

When asked if the outcomes of inclusion were evaluated, most respondents said that this was done on an individual basis, through the Annual Review process for pupils with statements. There was no overall strategic evaluation of inclusion as a policy in the majority of LEAs which responded to the survey.

A wide range of responses was given to the question: 'What do you perceive to be the difficulties in moving towards greater inclusion in your LEA?' These may be categorized as involving (1) attitudes and beliefs held by staff in schools,

(2) resourcing difficulties, (3) LEA structures, (4) parental choice and decisions of tribunals, (5) social reasons and (6) limitations of school provision.

1    Attitudes and beliefs held by staff in schools:

   – resistance of mainstream schools, with reference to children with emotional and behavioural difficulties, and children with learning difficulties who might lower the school's score in competitive national tests;
   – belief that the needs of some children are too complex to be supported in mainstream;
   – attitudes of mainstream schools, and reluctance to take responsibility for SEN;
   – fears about careers of teachers in special schools;
   – lack of evaluated practices to demonstrate the value of inclusion.

2    Resourcing difficulties:

   – loss of economies of scale which operate when children are grouped in special schools;
   – inadequate funding;
   – the policy of providing a statement as a method of funding SEN;
   – the investment tied up in special school buildings.

3    LEA structures:

   – the management and organization of support services;
   – reluctance of health services to organize to support inclusion;
   – lack of clear policy direction from senior management.

4    Parental choice and decisions of tribunals:

   – parental choice (parents who prefer segregated provision);
   – decisions of SEN tribunals.

5    Social reasons:

   – lack of a peer group for pupils;
   – change in 'culture' required;
   – social marginalization of pupils with SEN.

6    Limitations of school provision:

   – unsuitable physical environment in mainstream schools (e.g. for pupils with hearing problems);
   – poor curriculum differentiation/flexibility;
   – lack of training for staff.

There is a mixture here of reasons connected to a positive view of what special schools can provide and a lack of confidence in the capability of mainstream schools to replicate this, together with views about inertia in the system, vested interests and the costs of change. A lack of strategic leadership was evident, since local politicians were often driven by the need to please certain sections of the population and would not take the lead in promoting controversial policies.

When asked which types of special needs were most difficult to accommodate in mainstream schools, a majority of respondents cited emotional and behavioural difficulties as the most difficult, followed by severe learning difficulties. The table below gives a breakdown of the 'easy' and 'difficult' SEN to be accommodated in mainstream schools:

| Easy to include | Difficult to include |
|---|---|
| Physical difficulties | Emotional and behavioural difficulties |
| Sensory difficulties | Low-incidence SEN needing high levels of expertise |
| Speech and language difficulties | Profound and multiple difficulties |
| Moderate or general learning difficulties | Severe learning difficulties |
| Autistic spectrum disorders | Autism |
| Specific learning difficulties | Those needing health service input |

There was unanimity among the respondents that the most difficult children to include in mainstream schools were those with challenging behaviour. There were several comments made about this:

> Schools are more ready to accept children with learning or physical difficulties, rather than behaviour difficulties.

> Most can be accommodated, except EBD (Emotional and Behavioural Difficulties).

> All types can be accommodated, except EBD and PD.

> Difficulties [in inclusion] mainly due to the culture set of schools, hence EBD and SLD are more difficult [to accommodate].

> You've guessed it...EBD and SLD [are more difficult to accommodate].

There were one or two respondents who dissented from the commonly held view about the difficulty of providing for pupils with severe learning problems. One respondent argued that:

> Paradoxically, schools sometimes seem to cope better with apparently more severe problems (e.g. autism or SLD) than with pupils with problems similar to their own, but needier than their neediest groups.

And another echoed this:

> SLD, because so clearly different from other pupils [is easier to accommodate].

The questionnaire replies gave a hint of the complex array of factors which might set limits to the extent of inclusion possible within the framework of legislation and local circumstances in England and Wales. These were explored in more depth in the focus group interviews reported later.

## Findings from the focus group interviews

### What is meant by inclusion?

The groups were asked to explore the differences denoted between the old term 'integration' and the new term 'inclusion'. For many in the groups, the term inclusion denoted a much wider concept than integration, which appeared to have been ignored in the Green Paper, and which they felt had focused on placement in the mainstream or what the Warnock Report (1978) termed 'locational' integration:

> having read the Green Paper in quite some detail, I think they've missed the whole thing of the informal side of school. They don't talk about the playgrounds and the refectory and the sports field or wherever else. I think it's incomplete ... and whether or not they mean it, they have certainly missed it ...

> what we've always seen is that, with integration, the onus of responsibility for integration is on the shoulders of the parents, the young people themselves that are being integrated ... I think inclusion is about the practice and is irrespective of whether or not anybody with special needs or disabilities is actually attending. Inclusion says the practice will be inclusive of everybody, irrespective of who's there. To me, that's a clear shift because it's not talking about 'Let's set up an integrated classroom, whereby we'll invite in some child with learning difficulties'. We're saying 'The classroom will be accessible generally'. So that's a shift.

> you need to alter the whole situation rather than fit the child to the situation; it needs a radical reframing of the way that schools work.

It was acknowledged that this was idealistic and inclusion was fundamentally a question of ethos and attitude. A child could be in a mainstream class, yet still be excluded because of the attitude of teachers or other children in the class. Most respondents felt that inclusion was *more* than integration, that it had an emotional content and involved the whole community of the school: 'That the children [are] part of it, they [are] in a community.'

It was felt that it is much harder to generate an inclusive atmosphere than an integrated one. Many respondents felt that the presence of learning support assistants (LSAs) to support children with SEN in mainstream classrooms tended to work against inclusion:

> One thing that needs to change is the idea, in integration, that you had to have an LSA or a teacher and that had to be part of the package. I think in inclusion it's more of a feeling of ownership of the whole community and what can we do ... rather than we've got to have somebody else to sit next to that child .... We've got to reassess, re-evaluate how we're using LSAs because they exclude children. You know: 'Your LSA's not here so you can't come' or 'Your LSA's doing your work for you'. Rather than: 'What is the class doing, what is the teacher doing to exclude the child?'

## The advantages and/or disadvantages of inclusion for professionals and pupils

It was acknowledged that there were problems involved for some children in providing more inclusive settings. These focused on the delivery of some specialist services, such as speech therapy, which is normally provided by the health service. It was felt that such services are more difficult to provide intensively outside a specialist setting, such as a unit or special school. It was also felt that it might be difficult to include some children who need a specialized environment (such as soundproofing for children with severe hearing problems):

> there could be advantages for individual children with SEN, and teachers can learn from the challenge if given the support and training.

> for parents the advantages are that it is normality and not stigmatization, and ordinary school provides role models for children.

> but there is a segregationist legacy in some areas because of good special schools and a culture of parents expecting this kind of provision.

Again, there seemed to be some problems with the idea of including pupils with EBD in mainstream schools:

> there could be real disadvantages for children with EBD as they are returned to the kind of school where they have failed and are not loved.

## What would help schools be more inclusive?

It was felt that more preventive, multidisciplinary support might enable schools to keep more of the children who cause them problems. If help and support were available to troubled and troubling children before it got to the stage where they might be excluded, then schools would be able to create a supportive environment within the school:

> it is not just an education problem, there should be a mandate from government, so that health services work together to provide the support needed.

Some respondents considered that there was a need to overcome fear and ignorance:

> schools need to develop the confidence...really they are afraid of the unknown; if they can experience some success, then they will develop more confidence.

Others believed that a system of incentives would help schools to become more inclusive:

> there ought to be incentives or rewards for inclusion, and a system of rewarding success, so that schools see that there is something in it for them.

## How parents view inclusive settings

Some respondents felt that parents fought hard for what they saw as their children's rights, which was sometimes seen to be special school placement. Parents wanted what they saw as the best provision for their child, and when a child had failed in ordinary school, it was sometimes perceived as impossible for them to succeed. There was a general feeling that parents wanted first to try mainstream school and would prefer to see more possibilities of movement between ordinary and special school. However, most respondents perceived parental views to play a significant role in the maintenance of special school provision:

> obviously parents want what they see to be the best for their child, and often they see that this is a special school, and so they stick out for this. This means that parental choice prevents us from becoming more inclusive.

## Discussion

On the whole, respondents felt that total inclusion of all children was idealistic and unrealistic, given the current circumstances of lack of resources and lack of an inclusive attitude on the part of schools; however, a minority took an idealistic stance, considering that full inclusion was possible in a longer time-frame.

The government Green Paper gives a deadline of 2002 for the implementation of its proposals. But as mentioned earlier, the government target is simply 'greater inclusion wherever possible'. As has been pointed out, the move towards integration over the past 20 years has been slow, although very many more pupils in mainstream schools have been identified with SEN. Such individual identification can of itself be exclusionary, creating the impression that children identified and placed on a register of SEN are no longer the responsibility of the class teacher, but are 'someone else's problem'. Fulcher (1989) has argued that SEN policies in the United Kingdom have created a culture where teachers feel that they are responsible only for the learning outcomes of 80 per cent of the children in their classes, the remaining 20 per cent being the responsibility of the SEN teacher. Such a culture is also evident in the United States, where up to 10 per cent of children in mainstream schools are taught separately in resource rooms (OECD, 1997). Many of these children have emotional and behavioural problems; for example, in 1992/93, 35 per cent of pupils with Emotional and Behavioural Difficulties (EBD) were educated in special classes and 14 per cent in special schools (Whelan, 1998).

It should also be noted that nationally in England and Wales the inclusion rate varies considerably between LEAs from less that 0.5 to over 2 per cent in segregated special provision. Although Pijl and Meijer (1991), in their comparative study of integration in eight countries, argued that England which segregated 1.4 per cent of its pupil population, was one of the less segregated countries, its education reform policies of the 1980s were in danger of pushing it towards more segregation. Although this does not appear to have happened, in terms of where children with SEN are educated, the trend for increased numbers of pupils with emotional and behavioural difficulties to be excluded reveals the reduced tolerance of schools for this group of pupils produced, in part, by the tension between the 'standards agenda' and the 'inclusion agenda'. The current system, which emphasizes parental choice and school competition, together with the maintenance of a 'dual' system of provision for pupils with SEN, has a tendency to produce social and academic segregation, by sifting the pupil population and enabling popular schools to select the academically most able children and reject those with learning and behaviour difficulties.

Skrtic (1991) has argued that the current organization of schools as 'machine bureaucracies', focused on following prescribed curricula to achieve pre-set targets, makes them inflexible to the point where they cannot adapt to meet the needs of pupils with difficulties. Overwhelmingly, our respondents suggested that, while schools might be able to accept pupils with sensory or physical difficulties, they were more likely to reject those with behaviour problems. Thus inclusion is possible for some pupils with SEN, but not for those whose behaviour presents a challenge to the current culture and system of schooling, with its emphasis on conformity and academic excellence.

## Conclusion

Our analysis of the contradictions in government policy and the ambivalence of practitioners leads us to conclude that progress towards a fully inclusive educational system in England and Wales will be slow, and that its end-point may never be achieved. In order for a fully inclusive system to evolve, there would need to be a huge shift in the culture, organization and expectations of schooling. The current emphasis on conformity, improving results and league tables, and the lack of recognition among policy-makers of the inappropriateness of the curriculum for many young people at risk from social disadvantage, poverty and minority status, create and sustain SEN. Exclusion and segregation are key elements in protecting an educational system which does not sufficiently recognize and cater for individual difference.

## Reflective questions

1   This chapter clarifies the perceived problems that form barriers to Inclusion. The resulting question is 'So what do you do about them?' Explore your own limits by asking, 'What do you mean by Inclusion?' and 'What could you do to support a school in becoming more inclusive?'
2   What could you do to change negative attitudes and beliefs held by staff in schools?
3   What incentives are there from central government to encourage schools to become more inclusive?

## References

Ainscow, M.(1997). 'Towards inclusive schooling', *British Journal of Special Education*, 24, 1, 3–6.

Ainscow, M. (1999). *Understanding the Development of Inclusive Schools*. London: Falmer Press.

Bailey, J. (1998). 'Australia: inclusion through categorisation'. In: Booth, T. and Ainscow, M. (eds) *From Them to Us: An International Study of Inclusion in Education*. London: Routledge.

Booth, T., Ainscow, M., Black-Hawkins, K., Vaughan, M. and Shaw, L. (2000). *Index for Inclusion*. Bristol: Centre for Inclusive Studies in Education.

Clough, P. and Corbett, J. (2000). *Theories of Inclusive Education*. London: Paul Chapman.

Croll, P. and Moses, D. (2000). 'Ideologies and utopias: education professionals' views of inclusion', *European Journal of Special Needs Education*, 15, 1, 1–12.

Daniels, H. and Garner, P. (eds) (1999). *Inclusive Education: Supporting Inclusion in Education Systems. World Yearbook of Education*. London: Kogan Page.

Department for Education (1994). *Code of Practice on the Identification and Assessment of Special Educational Needs*. London: DfE.

Department for Education and Employment (1997a). *Excellence in Schools* (Cm 3681). London: The Stationery Office.

Department for Education and Employment (1997b). *Excellence for All Children: Meeting Special Educational Needs* (Cm. 3785). London: The Stationery Office.

Department for Education and Employment (1998). *Meeting Special Educational Needs: A programme of Action*. London: DfEE.

Evans, J. and Lunt, I. (1994). *Markets, Competition and Vulnerability: Some Effects of Recent Legislation on Children with Special Needs*. London: Institute of Education.

Farrell, P. (2000). 'The impact of research on developments in inclusive education', *International Journal of Inclusive Education*, 4, 2, 153–62.

Farrell, P. (2001). 'Special education in the last twenty years: have things really got better?', *British Journal of Special Education*, 28, 1, 3–9.

Fuchs, D. and Fuchs, L. (1994). 'Inclusive schools movement and the radicalisation of special education reform', *Exceptional Children*, 60, 4, 294–309.

Fulcher, G. (1989). *Disabling Policies: A Comparative Approach to Education and Disability.* London: David Fulton.

Hayden, C. (2000). 'Exclusion from school in England: the generation and maintenance of social exclusion'. 'In: Walraven, G., Parsons, C., Van Veen, D. and Day, C. (eds) *Combating Social Exclusion through Education.* Leuven: Garant.

Hornby, G. (1999). 'Inclusion or delusion: can one size fit all?', *Support for Learning,* 14, 4, 152–57.

Hornby, G. (2001). 'Promoting responsible inclusion: quality education for all'. In: O'brien, T. (ed.) *Enabling Inclusion: Blue Skies … Dark Clouds?* London: The Stationery Office.

Kauffmann, J. M. (1995). 'The Regular Education Initiative as Reagan–Bush education policy: a trickle down theory of education of the hard-to-teach'. In: Kauffmann, J. M. and Hallahan, D. P. (1995) (eds) *The Illusion: of Full Inclusion: A Comprehensive Critique of a Current Special Education Bandwagon.* Austin, Tex.: PRO-ED.

Low, C. (1997). 'Is inclusivism possible?', *European Journal of Special Needs Education,* 12, 1, 71–79.

Lunt, I. and Norwich, B. (1999). *Can Effective Schools Be Inclusive Schools?* London: Institute of Education.

Mittler, P. (2000). *Working Towards Inclusive Education: Social Contexts.* London: David Fulton.

Norwich, B. (1996). 'Special needs education or education for all: connective specialisation and ideological impurity', *British Journal of Special Education,* 23, 2, 100–04.

Norwich, B. (1997). *A Trend Towards Inclusion: Statistics on Special School Placements and Pupils with Statements in Ordinary Schools, England 1992–96.* Bristol: CSIE.

Norwich, B. (2000a). 'The withdrawal of inclusion, 1996–1998: a continuing trend, by the Centre for Studies in Inclusive Education (CSIE)', *British Journal of Special Education,* 27, 1, 39–40.

Norwich, B. (2000b). 'Inclusion in education: from concepts, values and critique to practice'. In: Daniels, H. (ed.) *Special Education Reformed: Beyond Rhetoric?* London: Falmer Press.

O'Brien, T. (2001). *Enabling Inclusion: Blue Skies … Dark Clouds?* London: The Stationery Office.

OECD (1997). *Implementing Inclusive Education.* Paris: OECD.

Office for Standards in Education (1995). *Pupil Referral Units: The First Twelve Inspections.* London: Ofsted.

Parsons, C. (2000). 'The third way to educational and social exclusion'. In: Walraven, G., Parsons, C., Van Veen, D. and Day, C. (eds) *Combating Social Exclusion through Education.* Leuven: Garant.

Parsons, C. and Castle, F. (1998). 'Trends in exclusions from school – New Labour, new approaches?' *Forum,* 40, 1, 11–14.

Pijl, S. and Meijer, C. (1991). 'Does integration count for much? An analysis of the practices of integration in eight countries', *European Journal of Special Needs Education,* 6, 2, 100–11.

Pijl, S., Meijer, C. and Hegarty, S. (1997). *Inclusive Education: A Global Agenda.* London: Routledge.

Rouse, M. and Florian, L. (1997). 'Inclusive education in the market place', *International Journal of Inclusive Education,* 1, 4, 323–36.

Skidmore, D. (1999). 'Relationships between contracting discourses of learning difficulty', *European Journal of Special Needs Education,* 14, 1, 12–20.

Skrtic, T. (1991). 'Students with disabilities: artifacts of the traditional curriculum'. In: Ainscow, M. (ed.) *Effective Schools for All.* London: David Fulton.

Spencer, D. (1998). 'The excluded progress to crime', *Times Educ. Suppl.,* December 11, 4302, 2. TES Archive, 11/12/1998. Available at: http://www.tes.co.uk

Thomas, G. (1997). 'Inclusive schools for an inclusive society', *British Journal of Special Education,* 24, 3, 103–07.

Thomas, G., Walker, D. and Webb, J. (1998). *The Making of the Inclusive School.* London: Routledge.

UNESCO (1994). *The Salamanca Statement and Framework on Special Needs Education.* Paris: UNESCO.

Vaughn, S. and Schumm, J. (1995). 'Responsible inclusion for students with learning disabilities', *Journal of Learning Disabilities*, 28, 264–70.

Warnock Report. Department of Education and Science (1978). *Special Educational Needs*. London: HMSO.

Whelan, R. (1998). *Emotional and Behavioral Disorders: A 25-year Focus*. Denver, Colo: Love.

Wilson, J. (1999). 'Some conceptual difficulties about inclusion', *Support for Learning*, 14, 3, 110–13.

Wilson, J. (2000). 'Doing justice to inclusion', *European Journal of Special Needs Education*, 15, 3, 297–304.

# PART II

# GENDER, RACE, DISABILITY, POVERTY AND SOCIAL CLASS

# CHAPTER 4

# PUPILS' PERSPECTIVES ON THEIR EDUCATION

T. Cox

*Combating Educational Disadvantage: Meeting the Needs of Vulnerable Children* (2000), London and New York: Falmer Press, pp. 136–55

## Introduction

The present government's vigorous campaign to raise the general standards of school attainment, particularly in the basic skills, is laudable but less emphasis seems to be placed upon the development of positive attitudes towards learning in all pupils, but especially those from disadvantaged backgrounds. The statutory national curriculum subject orders are predominantly concerned with skills and knowledge and even the 'Desirable Outcomes' for children's learning on entry to compulsory education (SCAA, 1996) includes only one reference to attitudes to learning. This is under the heading of personal and social development and refers to children '... being eager to explore new learning and show the ability to initiate ideas and to solve simple practical problems' (SCAA, 1996, p. 9).

Although, as discussed later in this chapter, there is an important distinction between pupils' attitudes to school and learning and their actual behaviour and application in school, it is surely desirable as an educational goal that all pupils should be helped to develop a positive attitude to learning which will sustain their motivation both at school and in life beyond. This is certainly a central tenet of the philosophy of play-based learning espoused by many early years educators. It is equally important for children to be helped to develop positive attitudes to themselves as learners, that is, in terms of their self-concepts, self-esteem, and their levels of aspiration in learning, so that they can approach the challenges of learning with confidence.

On the premise that the development of positive attitudes to learning and to the self as learner are vitally important in the education of children it is incumbent on all those involved in the education process to monitor the development of such attitudes. Equally it is important for them to be aware of pupils' views on a range of educational topics and questions which directly concern them, particularly within the context of school improvement programmes. As Davie and Galloway (1996) point out, the pragmatic benefits of listening to children, such as their greater readiness to cooperate in situations where they feel that they have a voice, should not obscure the moral and educational arguments for doing so. The United Nations Convention on the Rights of the Child (Article 12) states the right of children to express their views upon all matters affecting them and for their views to be given due weight in accordance with their age and maturity. In the view of Davie and Galloway the educational service has, to date, been relatively slow to provide the necessary opportunities and contexts in which children can exercise these rights, particularly in comparison with the Social Services, following the 1989 Children Act, which explicitly embodied the principle of listening to children.

More recently the Education White Paper produced by the government (DfEE, 1997a) makes virtually no reference to the importance of seeking pupils' views on various aspects of education covered in the proposed reforms. The topics on which it would have been highly relevant to have sought pupils' views include:

> home-school contracts;
> information on pupils' reports, school prospectuses and annual reports;
> a national framework for motivating pupils outside the classroom; and
> programmes for citizenship and parenting skills, including teenage pregnancies,
> smoking and drug/alcohol abuse.

Rudduck *et al.* (1997) discuss the traditional exclusion of young people from the consultative process, which they argue is founded upon an outmoded view of childhood which fails to acknowledge children's capacity to reflect on issues concerning their lives. They go on to assert that teachers and researchers find that 'Young people *are* observant, *are* often capable of analytic and constructive comment, and usually respond well to the responsibility, seriously entrusted to them, of helping to identify aspects of schooling that strengthen and that get in the way of their learning (Rudduck *et al.*, 1997, p. 4). Rudduck's own pioneering work on eliciting the views of secondary school pupils upon aspects of their educational experiences is described in the second part of this chapter. The first part examines the research on the pupils' attitudes to school and learning.

## Pupils' attitudes to learning

The *Concise Oxford Dictionary* provides several definitions of attitude, one of which is 'a settled opinion or way of thinking'. It is useful to make at least a relative distinction between generalized attitudes on the one hand, and views or opinions on the other. In relation to attitudes, opinions or views tend to be expressed with regard to fairly narrow or specific points or questions, and a person's expressed opinions on a number of related questions may allow us to infer the existence of a more general underlying attitude (Oppenheim, 1992). For this reason the measurement of attitudes for research purposes, ideally, makes use of composite attitude scales which sample the respondent's views/opinions on a range of related matters, but, in practice, as we shall see, some studies rely upon the use of only one or two specific questions or statements in order to measure attitudes. In this part of the chapter research studies on the attitudes of pupils towards school and learning are presented, particularly those of pupils from disadvantaged backgrounds.

### The attitudes to school/learning of socially disadvantaged pupils

Given the well-researched link between social class and social disadvantage and educational attainment, it might be predicted that a similar correlation would exist between these factors and pupil attitudes to school and learning. In fact the association is somewhat weaker. As part of the National Child Development Study

(NCDS) (1958 Cohort), in 1974, a sample of over 8,000, 16-year-old pupils were asked to respond to the question 'I feel school is largely a waste of time.' Eighty per cent of the pupils rejected this view but a breakdown of the responses by social class showed that a higher proportion of pupils from non-manual (professional) backgrounds (84–89 per cent) did so, compared with pupils from manual (working-class) backgrounds (70–77 per cent). It was also found that pupils who were doing well in school, as judged by their reading test scores, were more likely to take a positive view of school whatever their social background (Fogelman, 1983).

The NCDS finding was in line with the results of a longitudinal study of disadvantaged pupils carried out by the present writer. This followed the school progress of approximately 50 children from homes judged to be disadvantaged on a number of related measures, and compared it with that of a group of children chosen to be comparable in age, sex and non-verbal reasoning ability, and who attended the same schools as their disadvantaged peers but came from homes judged to be more favourable to their educational progress. All of the schools in the study were judged to be serving socially disadvantaged areas in England and Wales. In a second follow-up phase of the study, the pupils, who were then aged 15+ years, were asked to complete a written attitude to school scale, as well as scales designed to measure their self-concepts and self-esteem. The disadvantaged pupils scored significantly lower as a group on all of these measures than their more advantaged peers but the differences between the mean scores of the two groups were not as pronounced as on the measures of the pupils' academic attainments in reading, writing and mathematics. Thus the disadvantaged children in this study showed less positive general attitudes to school and learning, and lower levels of academic self-concept and self-esteem than their more advantaged peers, but these between-group differences were not as great as might have been expected on the basis of the achievement gap between the two groups at age 16 (Cox, 1983).

In another longitudinal study the school attitudes and views of pupils attending schools serving inner city, largely working-class areas in the former Inner London Education Authority were explored by Blatchford (1996). No attempt was made to assess the home backgrounds of these pupils but the author describes the catchment areas they lived in as predominantly disadvantaged. The sample comprised British black (Afro-Caribbean) and white pupils, who were interviewed about their views on the value and interest of school work and related matters. At age 16 the pupils were also asked to complete a short attitude to school scale and a self-description scale. At ages 11 and 16 almost all pupils felt that it was important to do well at school but there was a trend for the number of pupils who claimed to find school work interesting to decline between the two ages. Despite this broad endorsement of the importance of schooling, at age 16 years, white pupils had lower scores on the attitude to school scale than black pupils. For example, they were more likely to agree with the statement that school work was a waste of time, and to agree that they did not want to come to school, and fewer of them judged that their parents thought it was important for them to come to school. They also had lower scores than black pupils on the measures of general and academic self-concepts, being more likely to agree that they were too stupid to go to university and stupid at most subjects. In contrast to these marked ethnic differences, however, the study found few significant differences between boys and girls in their school views and attitudes. Also there were few significant associations between the pupils' attitudes and their school attainments, for example, between how interesting they found school, mathematics or reading at age 7 years and their attainments in English at age 16 years.

In discussing possible reasons for the markedly less positive attitudes to school and school work of white pupils at age 16, compared with those of black pupils, Blatchford suggests that one might be that the attitudes to school work of white working-class parents may be less positive than those of other parents. Linked with this is the possibility that white working-class parents in this study may have offered less active support to their children during their learning of the basic skills during their early years, compared to that received by children of the black parents. A similar difference in favour of ethnic minority pupils was found in a survey of school attitudes carried out in the London Borough of Tower Hamlets (Tower Hamlets Education Strategy Group, undated). Over one thousand pupils aged 13 to 17 years completed a questionnaire concerning their views on a range of educational questions. The majority of the sample were Bangladeshi or white pupils, with a small proportion of black pupils. While the majority of all pupils expressed satisfaction with their education, Bangladeshi pupils, especially girls, expressed greater satisfaction than white pupils and white UK boys had the lowest positive response rate on this question. These ethnic minority pupils also reported better attendance records than their white peers, and were more likely to report finding homework useful for their studies.

As in Blatchford's study, no attempt was made to assess the socio-economic level of the homes and the level of educational support they provided, but it is well known that there is a relatively very high level of social and material disadvantage in this particular borough. Here also it may have been the case that the ethnic minority parents in this sample provided a higher level of support for their children than did the parents of the white pupils. In support of this interpretation the study found very marked differences between the ethnic minority and white pupils in their use of public libraries and also in their reported reading habits, with three quarters of Bangladeshi girls and half of the Bangladeshi boys claiming to read regularly, compared to only 1 in 5 white boys and 2 in 5 white girls. As with all surveys of this type one makes the assumption that respondents are providing honest answers to the questions, but if these reported differences in reading habits were valid, it seems very likely that they were at least an indirect reflection of the degree of parental support received by the different groups of children.

A major national study of the school attitudes of secondary school pupils in Year 7 (11–12) and Year 9 (13–14) age groups provides only qualified support for the association between social disadvantage and attitudes to school and learning (Keys and Fernandes, 1993). This survey was commissioned by the National Commission on Education and carried out in 1992. There were approximately 1,000 students in each age group which constituted a nationally representative sample. A major aim of the study was to identify factors associated with motivation towards school and school learning and to hypothesize causes for hostility towards school. The inquiry was based on written attitude questionaires completed by the pupils. It was found that the majority of students in both age groups, but particularly in the younger group, expressed positive attitudes towards the value of school and school learning, with lower proportions of pupils expressing a liking for school or judging school work to be interesting. Most of the pupils appeared to believe that their parents were interested in their schooling.

The only home background measure used in this study was an estimate by the pupils themselves of the number of books in their homes. The results of statistical analyses carried out on the data showed that factors significantly associated with positive attitudes to school included a high level of perceived parental support by the pupils in the sample. The cultural level of the home, based upon the pupils' estimates of the number of books at home, was only weakly related to measured school attitude, as was the type of catchment area served by the school, that is, pupils in schools serving disadvantaged areas did not show markedly less positive school attitudes than those in schools serving more favoured areas. In fact most of the variation in measured school attitudes was due to differences between pupils *within* schools, with only a small amount attributable to differences between schools. This finding of limited between-school variation was in line with previous research reviewed by these authors.

The evidence from the studies reviewed earlier appears to show that pupils from socially disadvantaged backgrounds may not have markedly poorer attitudes to school and learning than those from more favoured backgrounds and this is encouraging. On the other hand a MORI survey of attitudes to learning amongst a nationally representative sample of over 1,000 adults and young people, aged 16 years and above, in England and Wales, found that those from lower social class households, the retired, and those with no qualifications were less likely to be currently involved in learning, or to express a desire to be involved in learning in the future. They were also less likely to feel that learning was important or enjoyable (Campaign for Learning, 1998). This is a worrying finding since it does suggest a clear link between social disadvantage and attitudes to learning among adults from as young as age 16. This survey also sampled the views about learning of over 4,000 pupils in England and Wales and, while they found that, encouragingly, only a minority of them found learning at school unenjoyable (22 per cent), their enquiry did not enable them to break down the responses by social class or any other home background measure. Had they been able to do so it is possible that social group differences might have emerged, as in their adult sample.

Although the research evidence for a link between social disadvantage and attitude to learning is inconclusive at this stage, there is strong evidence that the school behaviour and academic attainment of these pupils is related strongly to socio-economic factors. This was also clearly shown in the present writer's own study of disadvantaged pupils (Cox, 1982), whose GCSE examination performance and school attendance in their fourth and fifth secondary school years were markedly poorer than those of their more advantaged peers. This raises the question of how attitudes to school relate to academic achievement and motivation and to school behaviour. These relationships may be complex. Blatchford (1996), for example, found no significant association between certain school attainments and pupils' feelings about school and concluded that the lack of any clear-cut relationship between the two still left open the possibility of an indirect influence of attitudes on academic performance (and probably vice versa). On the basis of reviewing the research literature, Keys and Fernandes (1993) argue that the direction and strength of the relationship depends on the attitude dimension under consideration. Liking for school, for example, shows only a weak relationship with attainment, but attitude to school work, educational aspirations and self-esteem show low but significant associations. In a survey of secondary school pupils' attitudes carried out at Keele University it was found that, while over 90 per cent of pupils appeared to regard school work as important, as many as 40 per cent showed a general lack of school motivation (Barber, 1996).

More research needs to be done to clarify the interplay between attitude, motivation and performance. Even so there is already enough evidence to show that attitudes to learning, or certain aspects of them, do have some bearing upon academic achievement, quite apart from their importance in the personal development of pupils.

## Disaffected pupils

Although the evidence reviewed here suggests that, in general, social disadvantage may not be strongly related to attitudes to learning among children, studies of selected groups of disaffected and underachieving pupils show a much clearer link between negative school attitudes and disadvantaging factors, including a lack of educational support at home. Keys and Fernandes (1993), for example, list the following student-home related factors which tend to be associated with early school leaving and drop out, based on their review of the literature:

> disillusionment with and dislike of school;
> belief that school would not improve their career prospects;
> low educational aspirations;
> lack of interest and effort in class and less time spent on homework;
> disruptive behaviour and resentment of rules;
> poor academic achievement;
> poor attendance and truancy;
> lack of parental interest and support; and
> low socio-economic status.
>
> (Keys and Fernandes, 1993, pp. II–5)

In their own attitude survey Keys and Fernandes found that pupils expressing negative attitudes to school were more likely than other pupils to have negative views of their own abilities and perseverance, to behave badly in school and to judge that they received lower levels of support from their parents. In their exploration of the school views of 12- to 14-year-old-pupils Rudduck et al. (1996) found that, compared with other pupils, students who were judged by their teachers to be disengaged from their school work differed in the way they perceived themselves as learners and in the way they tackled their work. In particular they showed lower self-esteem and poor self-concepts, poor strategies for coping with school work and poorer relations with their teachers and their peers. Despite this they still expressed the desire to do well in school.

Rudduck et al.'s exploration of the views on their education of a sample of pupils aged from 12 to 16 years offers insights into the additional factors which may lead particular pupils downwards on the path to disaffection with school. One of these is a failure to realise how learning in the early secondary school years provides the foundation for more advanced, examination-oriented work in Years 10 and 11. In consequence, such pupils may fail to establish the skills, knowledge and ways of working that would equip them to cope with the multiple demands of the later school years. Rudduck et al. (1997) describe how some pupils, who had not worked steadily in their early secondary school years, looked back from Year 11 'with regret and a sad sense of powerlessness'.

A second disadvantaging factor mentioned by Rudduck is that of peer labelling, particularly during Year 8. Pupils showing a strong academic motivation may be castigated by their less committed peers as 'swots, boffs or keenos'. In contrast other pupils may come to be labelled as non-academic 'thickos', partly perhaps as a result of policies of grouping by ability within the school which can lead to such negative labelling by other pupils and even teachers. As Rudduck *et al.* (1997) points out, such pupils may come to identify themselves with their negative labels since, for a time at least, they accord them a certain status with their peers. However, once such self-accepted labelling becomes fixed, unproductive behaviours are reinforced and it becomes very difficult for these pupils to escape from their stereotypes, with the result that they may reject school and its values.

## Intercultural comparisons

The studies by Blatchford (1996) and Tower Hamlets (undated) described earlier found that the attitudes to school and learning of ethnic minority children in their research samples were distinctly more positive than those of white children. There is also supporting evidence for this from a more recent MORI survey of the attitudes to learning of a sample of British school children, carried out on behalf of the Campaign for Learning (1998). This found that black and minority ethnic group pupils were more likely to express an enjoyment of learning than white boys.

On the basis of these studies at least, it seems that ethnic minority group children in Britain tend to have more positive attitudes to school and learning than their white British peers. It also appears that French primary pupils have more positive attitudes than their British counterparts, according to an ongoing cross-cultural study being carried out at Bristol University and Christ College Canterbury, entitled 'Quality in Experiences of Schooling Transnationally' (QUEST). As part of a larger study written questionnaires were given to 800 children in the top two years of primary school in England and France during 1996. The sample schools were chosen to represent a geographic and socio-economic mix and were drawn from two contrasting regions in each country, a socially disadvantaged and a more affluent area, respectively. On the basis of their written responses the French pupils appeared to be more highly motivated to learn and to succeed than their English peers, 86 per cent, compared with only 66 per cent expressing the strong desire to do well in school. The authors concluded that the importance of hard work and the work ethic was more firmly entrenched in French schools and was accepted as necessary by the pupils (Osborn *et al.*, 1997, 1998).

The QUEST study found few significant differences in attitude between high and low social status pupils within England and France respectively but, in contrast, large differences between French and English pupils in their attitude to teachers and to being at school, regardless of social status, in favour of the former. After studying their data the authors concluded that there were important differences between the educational cultures of England and France. In their view, in England, a culture unsupportive to the notion of intrinsic and lifelong learning appears to be thriving more strongly, both inside school from the existence of pupil counter cultures, and outside school from an emphasis on instrumental, rather than intrinsic reasons for learning (Osborn *et al.*, 1997). They surmise that the combination of school ethos and wider familial and cultural values are more mutually supportive of positive attitudes to education and academic motivation in French society, in comparison with that in England. This cultural difference appears to extend even to socially disadvantaged children, for the study found that the low socio-economic status French children showed significantly more positive school attitudes and motivation than the equivalent English children. The authors attributed this difference to the French system's ideological emphasis on equal entitlement, in contrast with the English system's emphasis upon differentiation of curriculum and task according to ability.

Support for the QUEST findings comes from an international comparison of the educational attitudes, motivation and school behaviour of samples of pupils from Russia (St Petersburg), the United States (Kentucky), and Britain (Sunderland) by Elliott *et al.* (1999). They found that the British and American pupils showed less positive attitudes than their Russian peers and held a more instrumental view of their education. The authors concluded that the academic motivation of the British and American students was negatively influenced by an anti-work climate in many classrooms.

## Gender differences

Without citing any supporting evidence, the annual report of HM Chief Inspector of Schools for England for 1996–1997 (OFSTED, 1998), reporting the poorer academic achievement of boys than girls, particularly in GCSE examinations, comments that this is often linked to weaknesses in their basic skills and their lack of commitment to school. The report urges secondary schools to make every effort to combat the 'anti-achievement culture' which can develop at Key Stage 3, alienating some boys from academic work. The research evidence for gender differences in pupils' attitudes to learning is, however, not conclusive.

In their review of the previous literature on pupil attitudes Keys and Fernandes (1993) state that many studies found that girls tend to hold more positive attitudes to school than boys, although boys, on average tend to show higher self-esteem. Despite this however their own major study of the attitudes of Year 7 and Year 9 pupils found only a slight tendency for girls to show more positive attitudes than boys. Similarly Blatchford's (1996) study of the attitudes of secondary aged, mainly working-class pupils in inner London found relatively few differences between the sexes in their attitudes to school and school work, in contrast with their finding of marked ethnic differences. As against this, a large study of secondary school pupils' school attitudes carried out at Keele University found that girls showed more positive attitudes than boys and appeared to be better motivated (Barber, 1996). Also a MORI survey of 4,000 pupils aged 11 to 16 found that boys had significantly more negative attitudes to learning than girls, with over a quarter of them finding learning 'boring', compared with fewer than 1 in 6 girls. This difference was more pronounced among the older age groups. However, this study, which was commissioned by the Campaign for Learning (1998), did not make use of specially constructed attitude scales, unlike the studies by Keys and Fernandes and Blatchford, but relied upon the pupils' responses to specific questions such as 'School is boring'.

## Pupils' views on their education and how it can be improved

As well as assessing and monitoring children's general attitudes towards school and learning, it is equally important to listen to their views on particular aspects of their education so that these can be taken into account when improvements are planned, whether at a national, local authority or school level. The views of pupils drawn from a selection of research studies will be presented under the headings 'Purposes of Schooling' and 'Teaching and Learning in School'.

## Purposes of schooling

A number of studies have explored pupils' views on the goals of school education. In the present author's own study of disadvantaged children, carried out at the second follow-up stage, when aged 15 plus years, the pupils were asked to assess the importance of 20 selected possible objectives of school education. These were then ranked in order of their perceived importance according to the number of pupils endorsing each one as 'very important'. The resulting sets of rankings for the disadvantaged pupils and their more advantaged peers respectively were so close that they were combined into one composite set, as shown in Figure 4.1 (Cox, 1983).

It is clear from Figure 4.1 that the children overwhelmingly endorsed the importance of schools preparing them for examinations, and a correspondingly low rating to the importance of developing an interest in non-examination subjects. It is equally clear that the children accorded the highest importance to career-related objectives, including the passing of examinations. Objectives relating to the teaching of everyday skills, including numeracy, literacy and oracy, and the fostering of personal development received middle rankings, while those concerning general interest and awareness received the lowest rankings on the whole. Perhaps surprisingly the objective that school should 'make sure that you have an education so interesting, useful and enjoyable that you will be keen to continue it into adult life' received only a middle ranking of importance, supporting the proposition, discussed earlier in this chapter, that British pupils may have a strongly, extrinsic, instrumental view of the purposes of schooling.

This general pattern of results showed some concordance with the attitude survey carried out by Keys and Fernandes (1993) with Year 7 and Year 9 pupils. As part of this study five statements which focused on the students' perceptions of the purposes of school were presented. It was found that all of them appeared to believe in the utilitarian purposes of school. The vast majority (around 90 per cent in both groups) strongly agreed or agreed that schools should help them to do well in exams, teach them things which would be useful when they got jobs, and to be independent. Although couched in a different way the MORI survey of pupils' views on learning commissioned by the Campaign for Learning (1998) produced a similar finding. Ninety six per cent of the sample agreed that 'learning will help me to get a good job'. On the other hand only 39 per cent of them agreed with the view that 'I only learn in order to get qualifications', with a further 24 per cent neither agreeing nor disagreeing. Blatchford's (1996) study of mainly working-class pupils in disadvantaged areas of London provided further evidence of pupils' utilitarian views. It found that the vast majority of pupils at age 11 and 16 years judged that it was important to do well at school, the main reasons for this, at age 16, being 'in order to get a good job' (52 per cent), 'to get good grades' (31 per cent), and 'to do well in life' (23 per cent). Blatchford emphasized the constant concern shown by these pupils, even at entry into their secondary schools, with future employment and careers, and their awareness of the importance of school work in getting a job. In this they may of course simply be reflecting an emphasis upon such instrumental goals by both their teachers and their parents.

## Teaching and learning

Teachers' behaviour and attitudes towards their pupils, and their expectations regarding them, are likely to have a powerful influence upon children's academic

Rank                                                                        %

1. Help you to do as well as possible in external exams

2. Tell you about different jobs and careers

3. Make sure you are able to read and study
   on your own

4. Make sure that you can speak well and put
   what you want to say into words easily

5. Teach you things that will be of direct use to you
   when you start work in your job/career

6. Encourage you to be independent and able to
   stand on your own feet

7. Help you to think out what you really want to
   achieve in life

8. Make sure that you feel confident and at ease
   when dealing with figures and numbers

9. Make sure that you can express yourself clearly
   in writing

10. Make sure that you have an education so interesting,
    useful and enjoyable that you will be keen to continue
    it into adult life

11. Help you to have opinions of your own

12. Teach you about what is right and wrong

13. Give you experience of taking responsibility

14. Make sure that you really enjoy lessons

15. Help you to take an interest and to understand what
    is going on in the world now

16. Help you to get on with other people

17. Run clubs and societies for pupils out of school hours

18. Teach you about bringing up children, home repairs,
    decorating, etc.

19. Help you to develop an interest in subjects other than
    those studied for exams

20. Encourage you to have a sense of duty towards the
    community

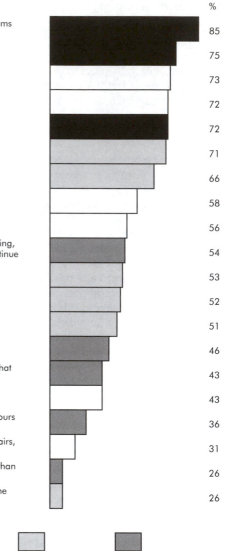

85

75

73

72

72

71

66

58

56

54

53

52

51

46

43

43

36

31

26

26

Key    Careers    Everyday life    Self-development    Interest and
                                                       awareness

*Figure 4.1* Percentages of children saying that various school objectives were very
          important (control and disadvantaged groups combined) (*n* = 92)
*Source*: Cox (1983, p. 75)

motivation and progress. Given the salience of teachers in their lives at school it
is not surprising to find that pupils are very ready to articulate their views on
what makes for good teachers and good teaching. Rudduck's interviews with
secondary school pupils yielded a range of teacher behaviours judged by their
pupils to be most likely to increase their commitment to learning. These included

teachers who:

> enjoy teaching their subject;
> enjoy teaching their students;
> make their lessons interesting and link them to life outside school;
> will have a laugh but know how to keep order;
> are fair;
> explain things and go through things students don't understand without making them feel small; and
> don't give up on students.
>
> (Rudduck et al., 1997)

The students aged 15 plus in the present writer's own study of disadvantaged pupils referred to a similar range of desired qualities or behaviour in their teachers to these, including:

> approachability, so that pupils do not feel scared to ask for help;
> helpfulness, e.g. 'He helps us with our work if we are stuck and if we are falling behind he will drive us until we catch up.';
> treating pupils with respect, e.g. 'Teachers who treat you more like adults than children.'

Conversely pupils were critical of teachers who failed to keep discipline, with the consequent disruption of learning. Other sources of dissatisfaction from pupils in this study were favouritism and unfairness on the part of teachers. One pupil, for example, criticized the tendency of teachers to favour compliant, well-performing students:

> If you are the type who has 100 for this and 100 for that they love you. They say it's a pleasure to teach you. They don't think about the girl in the back years who wants to learn but got a problem and can't.

Also the understandable desire of students for acknowledgement of their work and effort was reflected in the finding of Keys and Fernandes (1993) that only half of the sample of pupils said that teachers praised them for good work. Their further finding that nearly one-quarter of the pupils felt that their teachers were easily satisfied with their work suggests that pupils probably appreciate work which challenges them appropriately.

As part of the MORI attitude survey of 11- to 16-year-old pupils commissioned by the Campaign for Learning (1998), the pupils were asked to identify, from a list, factors which impeded their learning. A high proportion, particularly of older pupils, selected poor teaching, feeling unhappy, and 'having teachers who do not understand how children learn' as such factors. They were also asked questions relating to their preferred learning styles. Over half of them expressed a preference for learning in groups, but there were gender differences, with boys preferring to learn by doing practical things, by using computers, and also by learning alone. The most frequently endorsed changes they wished to see made to their schools were more visits to places of interest, being allowed to concentrate on things they were good at, more work experience placements, and being helped to plan for their own futures.

Although pupils appear to be well aware of teacher behaviours which either facilitate or impede their learning they also show a readiness to acknowledge their own responsibilities in the learning process. A large majority of the 16-year-old students in Blatchford's (1996) study of pupil attitudes felt that they were not doing as well as they would like academically. (These pupils were drawn from working-class area schools whose GCSE results were well below average.) The main reasons they offered for their self-perceived underperformance were that they were lazy or made no effort, that they could work harder and that there was too much pressure of work. There were no ethnic or gender differences in this respect. When asked how teachers and pupils could help in this situation they emphasized pupil strategies such as doing more work and applying themselves more to home-work and revision, and organizing themselves to work better, for example, through meeting deadlines and pacing their work better. The main ways that teachers could help were by giving more help and attention, by pushing and encouraging them more, explaining things better and making work more challenging and interesting.

Blatchford concluded that, at 16, these pupils took the prime responsibility for their school progress themselves and that, apart from their own level of ability, the internal factors bearing upon their academic performance which they identified were ones over which they had some control. However, he questioned the extent to which the pupils were being truly objective in their self-appraisal since, during adolescence, they may have been more inclined to blame themselves when they did badly. Moreover, as Blatchford points out, the analysis of external factors influencing their performance relating to school organization and structure requires a certain maturity (which, by implication, they may not have achieved at that stage).

Rudduck's study of pupils making their way through secondary school identified a number of these school-related factors. The study was conducted in three English secondary comprehensive schools and followed a core group of pupils in each school from ages 12 to 16, using interviews supplemented with data gathered from teachers and from analyses of school documents and records. One of the schools served a predominantly disadvantaged, ethnically mixed community. On the basis of this study Rudduck et al. (1997) offered a number of suggestions for school improvement, including the following:

Giving each year of secondary schooling a distinct identity that might motivate students as they look ahead and that offers progress in terms of autonomy and responsibility.

Creating time for dialogue about learning so that students develop a language for thinking about learning and about themselves as learners.

Making time for teachers to talk to individual students about problems with school work and legitimizing such discussion so that students do not feel that talking about their work is not 'cool'.

Helping students to manage the multiple demands of homework, course work and revision.

Formalizing opportunities to support one another in learning.

Responding to the problem of catching up for students who have missed work.

An interesting study by de Pear (1997) illustrates the apparent benefits for some pupils of one or more of the strategies recommended earlier. She interviewed a sample of secondary aged pupils who had been excluded from their mainstream schools and placed in one of two special schools. Prior to exclusion they had all been identified as having special educational needs (SEN). The author hypothesized that these pupils wanted to be accepted socially in school and wanted to take some responsibility for their own learning, but, as a result of having been labelled and marginalized by their learning difficulties, their inherent fear of failure kept them distanced from others and induced in them a feeling of incompetence as pupils. She speculated that these pupils might have been helped, prior to their exclusion, if they had been given a chance to express their views regarding their preferred learning style and the teaching style that would best serve their needs. The Code of Practice for special educational needs (DfE, 1994) allows pupil advocacy as part of the review strategy and, in the context of her work as a secondary school special educational needs co-ordinator (SENCO), de Pear observed how much more the pupils with SEN were achieving after they were brought into the process of negotiating their learning targets and discussing barriers to learning. She concluded that these vulnerable pupils need to feel valued, that what they have to say about their learning is important, and that future planning of their education should be a negotiated process in which they feel some ownership. These principles surely apply to students in general.

## Conclusions

Although, like their more advantaged peers, socially disadvantaged pupils, in general, endorse the value of school education in principle, and acknowledge the importance of doing well in school examinations in order to get a good job, this awareness is not, in many cases, translated into a personal commitment to learning which can sustain these pupils' effort and motivation during their secondary school careers. The more disadvantaged the pupil's personal circumstances, within home, school and community, the greater the risk that she/he will become steadily more disillusioned with school learning and will then opt out of it either actively or passively. Even among the wider population of British secondary aged pupils surveys have shown that attitudes towards school learning become more negative between the ages of 11 and 16, particularly among boys, and it also appears that white pupils, again, especially boys, tend to have less positive attitudes and motivation to learn than ethnic minority children in Britain. There is some limited evidence too that, compared with French and Russian pupils, British primary pupils have a more instrumental attitude to learning, regarding it as more of a means to an end than as an inherently worthwhile and fulfilling experience. Such a view, if coupled with a peer group culture which is antithetical to learning, will act as a real barrier to the development of a personal commitment to learning.

On the positive side, the evidence from the limited research available to date suggests that, on the whole, the attitudes of many socially disadvantaged children in Britain do not appear to be markedly poorer than those of their more advantaged peers, and this gives grounds for hope that, if we take the right measures, these pupils can be helped to become more highly motivated to learn, not only within school but beyond it.

Certainly more research is needed into the process by which attitudes to learning develop through the school years, and into the influences which most powerfully shape their development. More research is also needed into the evidently complex and indirect relationships between attitudes to learning and motivation and scholastic achievement. Given the urgency of the challenge posed by the under-achievement of many socially disadvantaged pupils, however, we cannot afford simply to wait upon the future outcome of such research, important though it is. A multi-pronged strategy is urgently needed if the attitudes and academic motivation of disadvantaged pupils are to be significantly improved. Such a strategy, based upon our existing research knowledge and good practice should include the following aims:

to raise the status of learning among disadvantaged children;
to raise the level of involvement of parents in their children's learning and their perception of the importance of education; and
to raise the level of involvement of pupils in the shaping of their school education.

## Raising the status of learning

The more that our society proclaims its belief in the importance of learning and gives a tangible demonstration of that belief, the more likely it will be that children will maintain throughout their lives the drive and enthusiasm for learning which characterizes their early years. In its Education White Paper the present British Government states its goal of achieving a greater awareness across society of the importance of education and increased expectations of what can be achieved (DfEE, 1997a). Osborn et al. (1998), in discussing how British pupils can be helped to develop a more intrinsic form of learning motivation, proposes that the media should be harnessed in a concerted effort to combat negative peer group attitudes to learning and to improve attitudes to learning in wider society. The latter is precisely the aim of the Campaign for Learning, a sponsored charity whose vision is of 'an inclusive society in which learning is valued, understood and widely available; a society in which every individual and every organisation is actively involved in learning' (Campaign for Learning, 1998, back cover). This campaign is targeted particularly upon those in our society who have negative experiences of learning in the past and may even have developed a deep-rooted hostility to it. Further suggestions as to how the national status of learning could be enhanced are made by Barber (1996).

## Raising the level of involvement of parents in their children's education

If a nationwide campaign to raise the status of learning in Britain does succeed this will positively influence both parents and children, especially the disadvantaged. Nevertheless, given their key role in their children's education, such parents need to be directly informed, encouraged and supported in their exercise of this role. In their survey of secondary pupils' attitudes to learning Keys and Fernandes (1993) reported that most of the students believed that their parents were interested in their educational progress, were supportive and held high aspirations for them. These authors stated their belief that there was a pool of parental interest waiting to be tapped but more research was needed to map the extent and type of such interest and to yield recommendations on ways in which secondary schools can involve parents more fully and effectively.

## Raising the level of involvement of pupils in the shaping of their education

Rudduck and her co-workers (1996, 1997) have consistently argued that the views of pupils themselves should be seriously and systematically taken into account by schools and teachers in the general drive to improve the quality of their education and learning. Their work, referred to earlier in this chapter, has yielded practical suggestions for school improvement based upon pupils' views and experiences. They engaged in an action research project entitled 'Improving Learning: the Pupils' Agenda', based jointly at the universities of Cambridge and Keele, and supported by the Nuffield Foundation. The project aims to support both primary and secondary schools in enhancing pupils' achievement by documenting and disseminating good educational practice in relation to three themes: 'Creating a Learning Culture', 'Catching Up and Keeping Up' and 'Pupils Helping Other Pupils in their Learning'.

Under the first of these themes the project has sought schools which have changed the pupils' attitudes to learning in significant ways, particularly where teachers have successfully combated a strong anti-work culture among peer groups. It is hoped that the project studies will help teachers to understand and take account of pupils' views about factors which either help or hinder their learning.

In addition to the work of Rudduck and her co-workers (1996, 1997) there have been a number of other significant developments in the provision of structured opportunities for students' voices to be heard on relevant educational matters. MacBeath *et al.* (1998) describe a European project involving 101 schools in 18 countries entitled 'Evaluating Quality in School Education'. Each participating school completes a self-evaluation profile following a rigorous analytic process involving pupils, teachers, parents and governing bodies, all coming to the exercise as equal partners with an equal right to be heard. Also the Government's Advisory Group for Citizenship and Democracy in Schools, under the chairmanship of Professor Bernard Crick, pressed strongly for pupils to be given meaningful opportunities to contribute to discussions concerning their lives within their schools and their local communities (TES, 1998).

## Reflective questions

1 It has been argued that inclusion is not done to somebody; it is a process in which they participate. Is this possible without listening to the voices of the pupils – and responding to those voices? How might such listening be done cost-effectively in practice?
2 Might the very act of listening enhance motivation and self-efficacy among the learners?
3 What should be done when the preference of the learner (and/or their parents) is for segregated provision?
4 What positive effects can engagement with the peer group culture have – in schools and in the community? What negative effects? To what extent is this true for teachers as well as pupils?

## References

Barber, M. (1996) *The Learning Game: Arguments for an Education Revolution*, London: Victor Gollanz.

Blatchford, P. (1996) 'Pupils' views on school work and school from 7 to 16 years', *Research Papers in Education*, 11, pp. 263–88.

Campaign for Learning (1998) *Attitudes to Learning 98. MORI State of the Nation Survey: Summary Report*, London: Campaign for Learning.

Cox, T. (1982) 'Disadvantaged fifteen-year-olds: initial findings from a longitudinal study', *Educational Studies*, 8, pp. 1–13.

Cox, T. (1983) 'The educational attitudes and views about school of a sample of disadvantaged fifteen-year-olds', *Educational Studies*, 9, pp. 69–79.

Davie, R. and Galloway, D. (1996) *Listening to the Voice of the Child in Education*, London: David Fulton.

Department for Education (DfE) (1994) *Code of Practice on the Identification and Assessment of Special Educational Needs*, London: DfE.

Department for Education and Employment (DfEE) (1997a) *Excellence in Schools* (Education White Paper), London: The Stationery Office.

Department for Education and Employment (DfEE) (1997b) *Education Action Zones: An Introduction*, London: DfEE.

Elliott, J., Hutton, N., Hildreth, A. and Illusin, L. (1999) 'Factors influencing educational motivation: a study of attitudes, expectations and behaviour of children in Sunderland, Kentucky, and St Petersburg', *British Educational Research Journal*, 25, pp. 75–94.

Fogelman, K. (ed.) (1983) *Growing Up in Great Britain: Collected Papers from the National Child Development Study*, London: Macmillan.

Keys W. and Fernandes, C. (1993) *What Do Students Think About School? Research into Factors Associated with Positive and Negative Attitudes Towards School and Education*, Slough: National Foundation for Educational Research.

MacBeath, J., Meuret, D., Jakobsen, L. and Schratz, M. (1998) 'Evaluating quality in school education', *Paper Delivered at the American Educational Research Association*, San Diego, April 1998.

Office for Standards in Education (OFSTED) (1998) *The Annual Report of Her Majesty's Chief Inspector of Schools in England. Standards and Quality in Education 1996/97*, London: The Stationery Office.

Oppenheim, A.N. (1992) *Questionnaire Design and Attitude Measurement*, 2nd edn, London: Pinter.

Osborn, M., Broadfoot, P., Planel, C. and Pollard, A. (1997) 'Social class, educational opportunity and equal entitlement: dilemmas of schooling in England and France', *Comparative Education*, 33, pp. 375–93.

Osborn, M., Broadfoot, P., Planel, C., Sharpe, K. and Ward, B. (1998) 'Being a pupil in England and France: Findings from a Comparative Study', in Kazamias, A.M. and Spillane, M.G. (eds) *Education and the Structuring of the European Space*, Seirios Editions, Athens, Greece and the Greek Comparative Education Society, for the Comparative Education Society in Europe (CESE).

Pear, S. de (1997) 'Excluded pupils' views of their educational needs and experiences', *Support for Learning*, 12, pp. 19–22.

Rudduck, J., Chaplain, R. and Wallace, G. (1996) *School Improvement: What can Pupils tell us?*, London: David Fulton.

Rudduck, J., Wallace, G. and Day, J. (1997) 'Students' perspectives on school improvement', in Hargreaves, A. (ed.) *Rethinking Educational Change with Heart and Mind. ASCD Yearbook*, Vancouver: ASCD.

School Curriculum and Assessment Authority (SCAA) (1996) *Nursery Education: Desirable Outcomes of Children's Learning on Entering Compulsory Education*, London: SCAA.

*Times Educational Supplement* (TES) (1998) 27 March, p. 17.

Tower Hamlets Education Strategy Group (undated) *Living in Tower Hamlets: A survey of the attitudes of secondary school pupils*, London: Tower Hamlets Education Strategy Group.

# CHAPTER 5

# SOCIAL BACKGROUND AND ACHIEVEMENT

## A. West and H. Pennell

*Underachievement in Schools* (2003), London and New York: RoutledgeFalmer, pp. 27–50

In this chapter we examine three related issues that are associated with achievement in schools, namely social class, poverty and parental educational levels.

## Social class and achievement

Some might argue that social class nowadays is relatively unimportant, given societal changes, social mobility and universal primary and secondary education. However, there is clear evidence that social class is still an important and persistent issue. Indeed, the British educational research literature contains strong evidence of differences in outcomes of pupils from different social backgrounds (e.g. Bramley 1989; Sammons 1999). As noted by Bramley: 'The literature has not produced completely consistent results, but it does present a general picture where outcomes are dominated by the socio-economic background of pupils/area' (1989: 55).

### Social class and cognitive attainment in the early years

At the very earliest stage of education, differences have been found in terms of the relationship between socio-economic background and cognitive development. The Effective Provision of Pre-school Education project (Sammons *et al.* 1999) involved 'in its early stages' an examination of the associations between a range of personal, family and home environment characteristics and cognitive attainment of children aged around 3 years at entry to pre-school. Sammons *et al.* (1999) found that socio-economic background was highly significant even at 3 years of age: children whose fathers were in professional or managerial work had higher scores than those whose fathers were in partly or unskilled manual work.

### Social class and achievement in the primary school

*Pupils' academic attainment and progress*

One of the most important studies carried out in recent decades that has explored social class and its effect on attainment was undertaken by Mortimore *et al.* (1988). The 'Junior School Project' was carried out in inner-London schools during the 1980s and involved 50 primary schools. The study found that both mothers' and fathers' occupations were strongly associated with reading and mathematics achievement on entry to junior school (age 7), having taken account of a wide range of other factors, including, amongst others, the child's age, sex, ethnic background, fluency in English, family size and the child's known eligibility for free school meals – all of which had an impact on attainment. For reading, a gap in reading age emerged between children with fathers in non-manual occupations and those with fathers in partly and unskilled manual occupations; the difference between children with fathers in 'professional' or 'intermediate' non-manual occupations and those with fathers in unskilled work was equivalent to nearly 10 months in terms of reading age. For mathematics it was also found that pupils whose fathers were in non-manual occupations had significantly higher attainment than those with fathers in unskilled manual work.

As the research study was longitudinal, it was possible to analyse the effects of social class on reading and mathematics *progress* as well as attainment. The results indicated that reading attainment at entry to junior school accounted for most of the variation in test performance 3 years later. The father's social class was statistically significantly related to progress, although the mother's occupation was not related in this way; this, the researchers suggest, is likely to be because a high proportion of the mothers were not in paid employment. Overall, children whose fathers were in non-manual occupations made significantly more progress than those in other groups. Similar class differences in writing attainment and progress in terms of a judgement both of quality and length were also found. In contrast to reading, *progress* in mathematics was not statistically significantly related to social class when account was taken of the effects of initial attainment and other background factors; in short, although the gap in achievement remained marked it did not increase (Mortimore *et al.* 1988).

## Social class and teachers' assessments

Mortimore *et al.* (1988) also examined teachers' assessments of pupils' ability and once again they found clear differences. They found that a higher proportion of children from non-manual backgrounds were rated as being of above average ability whilst a higher proportion of pupils from manual backgrounds were rated as being of below average ability. Even when account was taken of reading, mathematics and writing attainment, social class background was still related to teachers' ratings of pupils' abilities, with teachers tending to have a slightly more favourable view of those from non-manual backgrounds. The researchers concluded that higher teacher expectations may be one factor that contributes to the greater progress in reading and writing made by the non-manual compared with the manual pupils during junior school. The same study also found that socio-economic factors were highly related to teachers' assessments of pupils' behaviour at entry to junior school, with children from semi-skilled and unskilled backgrounds being reported to have a higher incidence of behaviour problems at school.

## Social class and pupils' attendance

Mortimore *et al.* (1988) also found that attendance was significantly related to social class. Children with fathers in non-manual occupations were absent from school for the least time, whilst those with fathers who were unemployed, economically inactive or not present were absent the most in the first year of junior school.

Interestingly, the mother's occupation was also related to attendance. There was a tendency for children whose mothers were economically inactive or unemployed to be absent for a higher proportion of time than was the case for children whose mothers were employed. Mortimore *et al.* note: 'This may reflect the difficulties working mothers have in obtaining time off work, which could explain why they were less likely than non-working mothers to keep children at home' (1988: 139).

## Social class and achievement at the end of compulsory education

### Social class and achievement

Whilst the studies described earlier were based on samples of pupils – which may not be nationally representative – national data relating to attainment and destinations post-16 of young people from different socio-economic groups are available from the Youth Cohort Study (YCS) in England and Wales.

Data from the Youth Cohort Study (DfES 2001a) reveal that parents' socio-economic group is related to the number of General Certificate of Secondary Education examination passes that are achieved at the end of Year 11. In the spring of 2000, the ninth cohort survey of 16-year-olds was carried out, around 8 months after the young people had completed compulsory secondary education.

Overall, fewer young people from manual backgrounds reported five or more high-grade GCSEs than those from non-manual backgrounds. This is particularly obvious with young people from unskilled manual backgrounds, more of whom reported no GCSEs or General National Vocational Qualification examination passes. In general, young people from manual socio-economic groups achieved either fewer GCSEs and/or lower grades than those from non-manual backgrounds.

Notwithstanding these differences the YCS shows a rise since the 1989 survey in the proportion of young people gaining five or more GCSEs (or equivalent GNVQs) at grades A* to C amongst all young people of all family backgrounds. Thus, the percentage of 16-year-olds with parents in unskilled manual occupations achieving this level more than doubled between 1989 and 2000. However, large differences remained in 2000, with nearly seven out of ten of those with parents in managerial or professional backgrounds gaining five or more GCSEs at grades A* to C in Year 11 compared with three out of ten of those with parents in unskilled manual occupations.

The YCS also enables us to examine young people's main activity at 16 years. Young people have been classified as being in full-time education, government-supported training, in employment or out of work.

Young people from non-manual backgrounds were more likely to be in full-time education post-16 than those from manual backgrounds. Government training was more common amongst those from manual backgrounds. Reflecting at least in part differences in Year 11 attainment, those with parents in manual occupations were more likely to be outside education, training or employment than those with parents in non-manual occupations.

### Social class and progress

Some research has also been carried out on social class and progress at the end of compulsory education. Sammons (1995) followed up the children who had been part of the Inner London Education Authority's (ILEA) Junior-School Project. She found that the impact of socio-economic factors on attainment at the end of compulsory schooling (age 16) mirrored patterns apparent in junior school. In terms of progress there was evidence of socio-economic effects during secondary education. Taking account of attainment at the age of 11 years, girls and pupils from non-manual backgrounds and those not on low incomes obtained higher GCSE scores than other groups.

Payne (2000) used data from the YCS to examine the progress of low achievers after the age of 16. She found that having parents in higher level occupations increased the likelihood of staying in full-time education after the age of 16. The pervasive effects of social class are thus apparent even amongst pupils who are not high achievers.

## Social class and entry to higher education

Social class is also important when it comes to entry to higher education. Blackburn and Jarman (1993) report that before the Second World War, university education was very much a privilege for a small elite with less than 2 per cent of the relevant age group entering university in 1938. In the post-war period access to higher education was still very limited and was structured in terms of social class and gender. Social class differences were striking (see Blackburn and Jarman 1993); between 1928 and 1947, an estimated 8.9 per cent of all boys from non-manual backgrounds attended university courses compared with 1.4 per cent of all boys with fathers who were manual workers.

Today university education is open to more students than ever before and participation in terms of the Age Participation Index has increased from 2 per cent in 1940 (House of Commons Education and Employment Committee Eighth Report 1999) to 33 per cent in 2000/1 (DfES and OFSTED 2002). In 1940, 2 per cent of young people from the three lowest social groups (skilled manual, partly skilled and unskilled) experienced university education compared with 8 per cent of those from the highest social groups (professional, intermediate and skilled non-manual) (House of Commons Education and Employment Committee 1999). By 1998 these percentages were 17 per cent and 45 per cent, respectively (Connor and Dewson 2001). More recent data (House of Commons 2002) provide a social-class breakdown of the age participation index; this reveals that 76 per cent of those from professional backgrounds participated in higher education in 2000, compared with only 14 per cent of those from unskilled backgrounds. A clear gap still exists in terms of participation in higher education between those from the highest and lowest socio-economic groups (see also Egerton and Halsey 1993).

We can see from our discussion so far that social class is an important factor in predicting young people's achievement in a UK context. We now turn to international data to examine whether the UK findings are replicated elsewhere.

## International tests, achievement and socio-economic status

The Programme for International Student Assessment (PISA), first administered in 2000, covered three domains: reading literacy, mathematical literacy and scientific literacy. An international socio-economic index of occupational status was used, which grouped pupils according to their parents' occupations.

The findings from PISA 2000 revealed that differences in the socio-economic index of occupational status were associated with substantial differences in student performance within countries, with students in the top quarters of the index obtaining higher scores on the reading literacy, mathematical and scientific literacy scales than those in the bottom quarters. Interestingly, the countries with the highest differences between students in the top and bottom quarters of the index were Belgium, Germany and Switzerland, followed by the Czech Republic, Hungary, the United Kingdom and the United States.

### Difficulties with the concept of social class

Whilst the concepts of social class and socio-economic status have been used interchangeably and unproblematically, there are a number of difficulties with both as they are determined, in general, on the basis of the occupation of the father.

This is important as an increasing number of children live in lone-parent families. In 2001 (National Statistics 2002) the number of such children was 22 per cent compared with 8 per cent in 1971, and of these, 20 per cent lived with their mother. The occupation of the mother is thus likely to be used more frequently when establishing social class, but importantly the distribution of women in different socio-economic groups varies from that of men.

Another problem arises in relation to parents who are unemployed and are then classified in terms of *employment* status as opposed to *socio-economic* status. An added complication relates to the socio-economic status of parents from minority ethnic backgrounds, particularly those who are newly arrived immigrants or refugees. As a result of problems gaining employment, because of racism or other barriers, such parents may not be able to obtain employment that is of a level that their educational status would merit. Thus the concept of social class, although of value, is problematic, particularly given the changing social context. An added difficulty is that within British society the proportion of individuals now working in manual occupations has declined in recent years (Glennerster 1998), making comparisons over time difficult. It is for these reasons that other measures may be used by researchers. The next section looks at poverty and its association with achievement and this is followed by an examination of the relationship between parents' educational level and achievement.

## Poverty and achievement

Research has shown that there is an impact of low income in addition to that of social class (see Sammons 1999). Much recent research has focused on the relationship between poverty and attainment particularly because of the ready availability of such data.

West *et al.* (2001) examined the relationship in England between the proportion of children dependent on an individual claiming a state benefit, income support, and academic attainment at the level of the LEA. They found a very high correlation between the proportion of children dependent on income-support claimants and low attainment. The inclusion of other markers of disadvantage – such as the proportion of children in lone-parent families, the proportion of children from minority ethnic groups, the proportion of children with English as a second language and the proportion of children with and without statements of special educational needs – added little to this prediction. Thus, a single measure of poverty (proportion of children dependent on recipients of income support) can act as a good marker of educational need.

Research at school and individual pupil level has focused on the relationship between levels of achievement and an indicator of poverty, namely known eligibility for free school meals. Children are eligible for free school meals if they are from a family in receipt of the state benefit known as income support or a related benefit known as the job-seeker's allowance. In England as a whole the proportion of children known to be eligible for free school meals was 18 per cent for primary schools and 16 per cent for secondary schools in January 2001 (DfES 2001b). These data are collected annually by the DfES from schools and they provide a readily available measure of deprivation.

At a school level, DfES (2001c) data demonstrate a clear relationship between the concentration of poverty levels in schools and examination results. On average, the greater the level of poverty the lower the aggregate GCSE results. The median percentage of pupils achieving five or more GCSEs (or GNVQ equivalent) at grades A$^*$ to C was 67 per cent in non-selective schools (i.e. schools that are not grammar schools), with up to and including 5 per cent of pupils known to be eligible for free school meals. The equivalent figures in schools with more than 50 per cent of pupils who were known to be eligible for free school meals was 21 per cent. With other indicators of achievement similar trends are apparent (e.g. the percentage of pupils obtaining GCSE English, mathematics or science at grades A$^*$ to C and the average GCSE point score). Across England as a whole there are thus clear links between poverty and low attainment levels in schools.

## Studies on attainment, progress and poverty

Many research studies confirm these strong links between poverty and attainment. For example, Sammons et al. (1997) found that young children from low-income families (who were known to be eligible for free school meals) performed at a lower level than others at Key Stage 1, and Mujtaba and Sammons (1999) also obtained similar results at both Key Stages 1 and 2.

Other research studies have examined progress as well as attainment. Mortimore et al. (1988) in their inner London research examined not only the relationship between social class and attainment but also the relationship between eligibility for free school meals and attainment and progress. They found that known eligibility for free school meals had an impact on both reading and mathematics progress. Children who were eligible for free school meals made poorer progress than predicted, given their initial attainment, in both reading and mathematics. They also found that children from low-income families were more likely to have poor attendance than others, with pupils eligible for free school meals being absent for around 10 per cent of the time, and those not eligible being absent for only 8 per cent of the time. These findings, the researchers hypothesised, may reflect a link between ill-health and unemployment or low family income.

More recently, Strand (1999) examined pupils' progress between the ages of 4 and 7 years. His study of over 5,000 pupils in an inner London LEA analysed educational progress made between 'baseline' assessment at age 4 and national end of Key Stage 1 tasks/tests at age 7. He found that, after controlling for other factors, pupils known to be entitled to free school meals made less progress in all subjects than pupils not entitled to free school meals.

## Parents' education level

The earlier discussion has highlighted the links between social class and attainment and poverty and attainment. Related to social class is the level of education obtained by parents. As we have seen, children with parents in higher socio-economic groups are more likely to enter higher education than those in lower socio-economic groups. Research has demonstrated a strong association between social class and educational level for both fathers and mothers (e.g. West *et al.* 1998). Thus it should come as no surprise to find that parents' educational level is also strongly related to children's attainment.

The National Assessment of Educational Progress research carried out in the United States is an ongoing representative sample survey of core subjects (Braswell *et al.* 2001). This shows that parents' educational level is an important indicator of achievement. For example, in mathematics in 2000 it was found that, in general, students in grades 8 and 12 (typical ages 13 and 17 years) with higher scores on the test reported higher levels of parental education.

The PISA examined the relationship between mothers' level of education and student performance. The analysis undertaken used the International Standard Classification of Education (ISCED) to group the educational attainment of students' mothers (completion of primary or lower secondary education, completion of upper secondary education and completion of tertiary education). The education of the mother was chosen as the literature often identifies this as a stronger predictor of student achievement than the education of the father (OECD 2001).

Students whose mothers had completed upper secondary education were found to achieve higher levels of performance in reading than other students. This was the case in all countries. In most countries the completion of tertiary education by the mother was found to be associated with a further advantage in terms of performance. On the other hand, students whose mothers had not completed upper secondary education were seen as being 'particularly vulnerable' (OECD 2001: 149).

## What accounts for these differences?

Whilst research has consistently demonstrated links between the home environment and attainment, we know less about the processes that might explain this association. However, the Effective Provision of Pre-school Education project (Sammons *et al.* 1999) has examined the associations between a range of personal, family and home environment characteristics and cognitive attainment of children aged around 3 years at entry to pre-school. Sammons *et al.* (1999) found that a number of measures of home environment had an independent association with cognitive attainment. The frequency with which parents reported reading to their child was significant, with those who read twice a day showing the most impact, though reading daily or several times a week also showed a positive relationship compared with reading less than once a week. The frequency with which children were taken to the library also showed a significant positive association, with weekly visits showing the strongest relationship. In addition, children whose parents reported that their child frequently played with letters or numbers also showed higher scores, as did those who reported that they taught their child the alphabet, and those who taught a variety of songs to their children. However, what is particularly interesting is that these aspects of the home environment remained significant after having taken account of parents' educational level and occupational status.

It is also possible that the ways in which parents are involved in their children's education are important at a later stage too. West *et al.* (1998) examined parents' involvement in their children's education and found that differences in terms of educational level emerged even when social class differences did not. Children with more highly qualified mothers were significantly more likely to have used workbooks at home than the children of mothers with lower levels of educational qualifications.

And research by Greenhough and Hughes (1998) suggests different types of interaction with children's reading according to parents' educational level.

## Conclusions

The research and data that we have examined in this chapter are clear. On average, students from lower socio-economic groups (particularly those from unskilled manual backgrounds) and who are from low-income families achieve less well in a range of tests, examinations and assessments than those who are from higher socio-economic groups and who are not from low-income families. The data also indicate that students from families where the parents have higher levels of education tend to gain better results. It is important, however, that policy makers and practitioners do not take a negative stance and assume that improvements cannot be made in disadvantaged schools.

Neither should it be assumed that children's families are necessarily the reason for the lower performance of children from lower socio-economic groups or from families where the parents are less highly qualified. As we have seen, research indicates that teacher expectations appear to be lower for children from working-class backgrounds and teachers may be more likely to label children from certain social backgrounds as disruptive. In some cases school policies and practices may also be part of the problem. Of course, some schools do have challenging pupils and in these cases behaviour-management schemes can be put in place to help create an ethos where pupils and staff feel secure.

In terms of progress made by students from lower socio-economic groups and from low-income families, the evidence suggests that schools have *less* impact in terms of progress in subjects where parental involvement is likely to be greater – such as reading and writing. This implies that parental involvement is an important factor. Whilst we are not able to say that the relationship is indeed causal, it is certainly worth investigating in future research studies. Given that parental involvement is considered by policy makers and practitioners to have a range of benefits, it is important for further policy initiatives in this area to be explored.

However, what is less clear, at this stage, is what sort of involvement is important and what kinds of involvement should be further encouraged. Activities such as reading with children and visits to the library have been highlighted in research and it is clear that such findings have important implications for policy makers and schools as they reinforce the notion that parental involvement of a very clearly defined type may have an impact on attainment and progress.

Whilst there is evidence to suggest that young people from lower socio-economic groups have made larger proportionate increases in attainment over the past ten years, absolute achievement levels are still markedly poorer than for higher socio-economic groups. This suggests that further changes are needed to counter the pervasive impact of social class on achievement, which is apparent at the earliest of stages.

## Reflective questions

1   To what extent is the education system controlled by the middle class? If so, what positive effects and what negative effects might this have?
2   Socio-economic status still accounts for most of the variance in pupil achievement. Is this because of economic, cultural or political factors? Is it inevitable?
3   To what extent might this be a result of narrow or inappropriate expectations among largely middle-class teachers, and therefore a self-fulfilling prophecy?

# References

Blackburn, R. M. and Jarman, J. (1993) 'Changing inequalities in access to British universities', *Oxford Review of Education*, 19(2): 197–215.

Bramley, G. (1989) 'A model of educational outcomes at local authority level, with implications for local expenditure needs', *Environment and Planning C: Government and Policy*, 7: 39–58.

Braswell, J. S., Lutkus, A. D., Grigg, A. D., Santapau, S. L., Tay-Lim, B. and Johnson, M. (2001) *The Nation's Report Card: Mathematics 2000*, Washington DC: US Department of Education. http://www.nces.ed.gov/nationsreportcard/pubs/main2000/2001517.asp (2 September 2002).

Connor, H. and Dewson, S. with Tyers, C., Eccles, J., Regan, J. and Aston, J. (2001) *Social Class and Higher Education: Issues Affecting Decisions on Participation by Lower Social Class Groups*, Research Report No. 267, London: Department for Education and Employment.

Department for Education and Skills (2001a) *Youth Cohort Study: The Activities and Experiences of 16 year olds: England and Wales 2000*, National Statistics First Release, SFR 02/2001, London: DfES. http://www.dfes.gov.uk/statistics/DB/SFR/s0230/sfr02-2001.pdf (2 September 2002).

Department for Education and Skills (2001b) *Statistics of Education: Schools in England 2001*, London: The Stationery Office. http://www.dfes.gov.uk/statistics/DB/VOL/v0288/vol04-2001.pdf (2 September 2002).

Department for Education and Skills (2001c) *Autumn Package of Pupil Performance Information, 2001*, London: DfES. http://www.standards.dfes.gov.uk/performance/pdf/GCSE-GNVQ_2001.pdf (2 September 2002).

Department for Education and Skills and Office for Standards in Education (2002) *Departmental Annual Report*, London: DfES. http://www.dfes.gov.uk/deptreport2002/index.shtml

Egerton, M. and Halsey, A. H. (1993) 'Trends by social class and gender in access to higher education', *Oxford Review of Education*, 19(2): 183–96.

Glennerster, H. (1998) 'Education: Reaping the harvest?', in H. Glennerster and J. Hills (eds) *The State of Welfare: The economics of social spending*, Oxford: Oxford University Press.

Greenhough, P. and Hughes, M. (1998) 'Parents' and teachers' interventions in children's reading', *British Educational Research Journal*, 24(4): 383–98.

House of Commons (2002) *Hansard Written Answers for 8 July 2002 on Higher Education Statistics*. http://www.publications.parliament.uk/cgi-bin/dialogserverTSO

House of Common Education and Employment Committee Eighth Report (1999) *Access for All? A survey of post-16 participation*, London: House of Commons. http://www.publications.parliament.uk/pa/cm199899/cmselect/cmeduemp/57/5702.htm (4 November 2002).

Mortimore, P., Sammons, P., Stoll, L., Lewis, D. and Ecob, R. (1988) *School Matters: The Junior Years*, London: Paul Chapman.

Mujtaba, T. and Sammons, P. (1999) *Accounting for Variation in Pupil Attainment Across Key Stage 1 and Key Stage 2 in an Inner City LEA*. Paper presented at the British Educational Research Association Annual Conference, Brighton, September 1999.

National Statistics (2002) *Social Trends, Number 32*, London: The Stationery Office. http://www.nationalstatistics.gov.uk/downloads/theme_social/Social_Trends32/Social_Trends32.pdf (2 September 2002).

Organisation for Economic Co-operation and Development (OECD) (2001) *Knowledge and Skills for Life, First results from the OECD Programme for International Student Assessment (PISA) 2000*, Paris: OECD.

Payne, J. (2000) *Progress of Low achievers After Age 16: An analysis of data from the England and Wales youth cohort study*, Research Report No. 185, London, DfEE.

Sammons, P. (1995) 'Gender, ethnic and socio-economic differences in attainment and progress: A longitudinal analysis of student achievement over 9 years', *British Educational Research Journal*, 21(4): 465–85.

Sammons, P., West, A. and Hind, A. (1997) 'Accounting for variations in pupil attainment at the end of key stage 1', *British Educational Research Journal*, 23(4): 489–511.

Sammons, P. (1999) *School Effectiveness: Coming of Age in the Twenty-First Century*, Lisse: Swets and Zeitlinger.

Sammons, P. *et al.* (1999) *Technical Paper 2: Characteristics of the EPPE Project Sample at Entry to the Study*, London: Institute of Education, University of London.

Strand, S. (1999) 'Ethnic group, sex and economic disadvantage: associations with pupils' educational progress from baseline to the end of key stage 1', *British Educational Research Journal*, 25(2): 179–202.

West, A., Noden, P., Edge, A. and David, M. (1998) 'Parental involvement in education in and out of school', *British Educational Research Journal*, 24(4): 461–84.

West, A., West, R., Pennell, H. and Travers, T. (2001) 'Financing school-based education in England: Poverty, examination results and expenditure', *Environment and Planning C: Government and Policy*, 19(3): 461–71.

# CHAPTER 6

# THE CONTEXT
## A problem of gender

T. Maynard

*Boys and Literacy: Exploring the Issues* (2002), London and New York: RoutledgeFalmer, pp. 9–21

In 1996 Chris Woodhead, then Chief Inspector of Ofsted (Office for Standards in Education), was reported in *The Times Educational Supplement* (*TES*) as stating: 'the failure of boys and in particular white working-class boys is one of the most disturbing problems we face within the whole education system' (Pyke 1996). A year later Ted Wragg maintained that it is 'the under-achievement of boys that has become one of the biggest challenges facing society today (Wragg 1997). Such headlines, while in one sense shocking, were – and continue to be – fairly commonplace. Indeed, from the early 1990s the problem of the 'under-achieving boy' has rarely been out of the media. Boys are frequently portrayed as loutish, lazy, 'lads' caught up in an anti-school, anti-learning culture. This culture, according to the then government Education Secretary, David Blunkett, has grown out of 'deprivation and a lack of self-confidence and opportunity' (Woodward 2000).

Politicians – for example, Estelle Morris (1996) and Stephen Byers (cited in Lepkowska 1998) have emphasised the direct link that is believed to exist between under-achievement in school and truancy and crime. But it is not simply the cost of crime at a local level that is seen as a cause for concern but the damage that is being done to society as a whole. Thus concerns about the 'laddish' anti-learning culture have resulted in a 'moral panic' – that is, this culture is seen 'as a threat to societal values and interests' (Cohen 1987: 9). But how has this situation come about? Who is seen as to blame? And what are the suggested solutions? In order to explore these questions I refer not only to writers of academic texts but also to the voices of politicians and others as reported in the media – this has, after all, been a drama played out on a public stage. First, however, I will sketch in the historical and political context; it is necessary to understand this context if we are to make sense of the current concerns about under-achieving boys.

## The historical and political context

Measor and Sikes (1992) point to the long history of education and schooling being closely tied up with views of feminity and masculinity and the sexual division of labour. They maintain that even before the 1870 Education Act females were taught that males were superior to them in every way – physically, intellectually, morally and socially – and that as women their role in life was to serve and service men. What has come to be termed 'Victorian values' reinforced the view that men and women inhabited 'separate spheres': 'the public world of work and achievement was to be occupied by the independent and autonomous male and the private, enclosed domain of the "home, care, harmony and relationships" by the intuitive and dependent female' (Brabeck 1996, cited in Arnot *et al.* 1999: 34).

As Arnot *et al.* (1999) explain, this view is linked to what are seen as biologically derived 'natural' male and female characteristics. Thus, they argue, with the creation of a national system of education in the late nineteenth century, boys and girls were educated according to their gender as well as their class. Upper- and middle-class males were essentially prepared for leadership roles whereas working-class boys were schooled for the manual labour force. Similarly, upper- and middle-class girls were taught household management whereas working-class females learned housework and laundry skills. Girls' education (whatever their class) was linked to what was seen as girls' eventual destiny as wives and mothers (Arnot *et al.* 1999). This was supported by a proposed connection between female over-education – that is, mental strain – and infertility (Measor and Sikes 1992). As Measor and Sikes (1992) point out, middle-class girls who *were* educated usually had to make a choice between a career on the one hand or marriage and motherhood on the other.

## Post-war education

In the first half of the twentieth century, challenges to Victorian values were mounted from the women's movement, those advocating social democracy and the 1944 Education Act which, in theory at least, supported equality of opportunity (Arnot *et al.* 1999). Measor and Sikes (1992) note that, despite these challenges, various reports (e.g. the *Hadow Report* 1926; the *Crowther Report* 1959; the *Newsom Report* 1963) appeared to accept the 'common-sense' view that boys and girls should be prepared for the different roles they were to fulfil in adult life. As Arnot *et al.* (1999) explain, while there was now the expectation that boys and girls should have equal 'access' to education, there was not the expectation that this equality would follow on into the world of work.

## Outside the school walls

Outside the school walls, in the early years of the twentieth century, women's dependency on men was reinforced by their low rates of pay – this applied even to jobs taken up by middle-class women such as teaching, nursing and clerical work (Rowbotham 1999). With the outbreak of the First World War, however, the notion of a segregated jobs market was set aside as women were recruited to work in industry. Rowbotham (1999) notes that even protective legislation was waived so that women could work at night – thus enabling them to do their housework during the day!

As war ended, however, there was strong pressure on these women to relinquish their jobs in order to make way for the men and, during the 1920s and 1930s, the idea of woman as homemaker and full-time mother was promoted. However, as Rowbotham (1999) explains, the declaration of war in 1939 created a problem for the government: how could this ideal be safeguarded when women were needed yet again to make up the shortfall in the workforce? The solution,

Rowbotham notes, was the introduction of National Service for single, childless women aged 20–30. In addition, fears that some women might be deterred by the idea of working long hours led to the introduction of the possibility of part-time work.

Following the war, Beveridge's vision of the welfare state was intended – yet again – to promote the idea of the man as breadwinner and head of the household with the woman playing a supportive role as full-time wife and mother. However, as Arnot *et al.* (1999) point out, an unintended consequence of the welfare state was the expansion of employment opportunities for women within the welfare and service industries. But just as more married mothers began to go out to work in the 1950s, new ideas about child-rearing practices revived concerns about women's role. Prominent amongst these were the theories of John Bowlby who stressed the importance of the young child's need for a continuous relationship with the mother: indeed, any separation from the mother was viewed as 'deprivation' and as potentially damaging.

Even so, in the 1960s and first half of the 1970s the number of women in paid work increased, although the notion of separate labour markets for men and women persisted and women continued to earn a great deal less than men. However, attitudes had begun to change, influenced, in part, by the Civil Rights and Women's Liberation movements in the United States (Weiner 1985).

Women demanded equal educational opportunities for boys and girls and child-care for pre-school children. Arnot *et al.* (1999) note that the one official policy which attempted to accommodate some of these ideas was the Sex Discrimination Act of 1975.

The aim of the Sex Discrimination Act, according to Arnot *et al.* (1999), was to create a more gender-neutral educational framework. For example, it now became illegal to exclude pupils from taking particular school subjects on the grounds of their sex, although in practice boys and girls continued (and still continue) to make stereotypical subject choices. Most significantly, perhaps, the Act did open up spaces for feminists to campaign for equality of opportunity in schools, gather evidence on the unequal treatment of girls and to call for action (Gaine and George 1999). But despite the growing interest in equal opportunities by parents, teachers and the government alike, it appeared that while supporting this development in theory, in practice many teachers argued that their role was to prepare pupils for 'society as it was' (Figes 1994).

Weiner (1985) maintains that government interest in the development of anti-sexist practices in school at this time had its origins in the sustained economic and educational growth of the 1960s and 1970s. If the country needed more skilled labour then (as during both world wars) the government was prepared to ensure legislation did not prevent women from meeting this need. Weiner notes that, although driven by different motives, it seemed at this point as if the interests of the legislators on the one hand and activist teachers and parents on the other were beginning to converge. However, by the late 1970s the period of post-war boom had ended and, as the country slid into recession and unemployment began to grow, the Conservative government of the day grew less interested in equity issues and again began to promote the ideals of motherhood and domesticity (Weiner 1985). Gradually, the discourse of equality gave way to New Right notions of 'individualism', 'competition' and 'performance' (Arnot *et al.* 1999). By the late 1980s, government interest had shifted away from gender differences in policy and practice and towards issues such as patterns of gender difference in examination results (Gipps and Murphy 1994).

### 'Women are doing it for themselves'

All the while, the predominantly female workforce of teachers had been sowing the seeds of change, supported by research findings which, as David *et al.* (2000) note, pointed to the shortcomings of schooling for girls. By the early 1980s, some teachers and Local Education Authorities (LEAs) (school districts) began to develop strategies to address these inequalities (David *et al.* 2000). There was a particular concern to encourage girls to study what were seen as traditionally 'male' subjects such as science, mathematics and technology. Arnot *et al.* (1999) note that, in encouraging and supporting girls' involvement in the most consistently male-dominated subject areas, an emphasis was placed on the significance of female role models as well as addressing the learning styles favoured by girls and 'the masculine content and orientation of most textbooks, topics and tests' (Arnot *et al.* 1999: 78).

Weiner (1985) comments that two distinct approaches to challenging sex discrimination in school emerged at this time: the equal opportunities approach and the anti-sexist approach. The equal opportunities approach, associated with liberal feminism, concentrated on equality of access to existing educational benefits for both boys and girls. This included an improvement of teaching methods for the benefit of all pupils, devising non-sexist materials aimed at challenging gender stereotypes, de-sexing registers and school uniform and, as we have seen, persuading girls to take subjects such as science and technology (Weiner and Arnot 1987).

Anti-sexist approaches, on the other hand, took a more radical stance and aimed to make school more 'girl-centred'. This approach was more concerned with equality of outcome and recognised the need to 'redress past imbalances' (Riley 1994: 13). Weiner (1985) notes that central to this approach was a recognition of the relationship between patriarchy, power and women's subordination. Those advocating this approach wanted a fundamental restructuring of the whole school system and to overthrow the male domination of curricula, classrooms and schools (Weiner 1994).

Unsurprisingly, perhaps, it was the liberal feminist 'equal opportunities' approach that was (and still is) most favoured by the government and local education authorities. And, it could be argued, it was this approach that was also reflected in the introduction of the National Curriculum and Statutory Assessment requirements in July 1988. Based on the concept of entitlement, the National Curriculum set out a common set of subjects to be taken by girls and boys up to the age of 16 some of which were to be assessed through Standard Assessment Tasks (SATs). And it was with the introduction of the National Curriculum that the pattern of subject choices that had been shaped by Victorian values appeared to be finally broken (Arnot *et al.* 1999).

The National Curriculum has not been without its critics. Gaine and George (1999), for example, comment that the rigid and fixed nature of this curriculum only serves to reinforce traditional values upheld by white, male-dominated areas of knowledge. Nor, they argue, does it challenge boys' and girls' subject choices, teachers' expectations or the pervasive 'informal' curriculum.

## The 1990s

If during most of the twentieth century there had been concerns about girls' under-achievement in school, from the 1990s these concerns were reversed: it is boys who are now seen as having difficulties. Moreover, underlying these difficulties is a concern that boys' under-achievement is not only linked to truancy and crime but to a more fundamental crisis: that of masculinity itself. Morris (1996) has argued that this crisis has come about as, in the past, young men who did not achieve academically had the chance to take up apprenticeships and to be self-reliant within a framework of the traditional family unit. But, as we have seen, manual work – particularly in the manufacturing industries – is no longer a viable option for these boys. In addition, the 'traditional' family unit (with man as head of the household and main breadwinner) has become something of a rarity. As a result, Morris claims, many young men have become disaffected, marginalised from mainstream society and trapped within a culture of dependency.

But recent changes appear to have had a much more positive effect on young women. As we have seen, the growth of the service sector and information technology (IT) has resulted in more jobs for women – even if these tend to be temporary and low-paid. Moreover, changes in employment pattern have contributed towards what has been described as the feminisation of work (Stainton Rogers and Stainton Rogers 2001). Stainton Rogers and Stainton Rogers (2001) maintain that, in the new jobs market, men's traditional strengths, such as their physical prowess and competitiveness are seen as a less valuable asset than women's traditional strengths – flexibility, adaptability and cooperation. Consequently, not only have women become more employable but pressure has been put on men to adopt what are viewed as more feminine traits.

As a result of these changes it is suggested that, compared with men, young women generally have greater self-esteem, are happier, more ambitious and more positive about the future (Stainton Rogers and Stainton Rogers 2001). Having broken out of their traditional sphere of home and dependency, women are redefining feminity and, as a consequence, requiring masculinity to be redefined. But definitions of masculinity, it is argued, appear resistant to change – Arnot *et al.* (1999) indicate that this may be because, unlike generations of women and girls, men are not used to being challenged to make personal, social, educational and occupational changes. While some men have been successful in making the necessary adjustments in terms of their masculine identity, others have failed to do so and have adopted a position of hyper-masculinity: the stereotypical macho man (Stainton Rogers and Stainton Rogers 2001).

Boys often construct and display their knowledge of masculinity through adopting a position of hegemonic masculinity; through playing the fool, engaging in anti-social behaviour and adopting an anti-school, anti-learning stance. For some boys the lure of hegemonic masculinity may be limited in both time and intensity. For example, it may be offset by other factors, such as home circumstances which challenge such behaviour, convey high expectations, encourage self-belief and provide material and emotional support. Other boys may find its appeal overwhelming – positioning themselves as a 'macho man' offers them a means (possibly the only means) by which they can claim power and status in the world.

How, then, have these more fundamental difficulties with masculinity been reflected in the attainment of boys in school?

## The gender gap

In this era of standards and performance, it is unsurprising that boys' difficulties have become visible through the published results of national tests and examinations. And, since the early 1990s, concerns have been raised not simply about boys' attainment but about the relative attainment of boys and girls – what has become known as the 'gender gap'. By the end of the 1990s it was noted, for example, that more girls than boys achieved five A*–C grades in the General Certificate of Secondary Education (GCSE) examination. While results were similar in mathematics and science, girls did better than boys in subjects such as history, geography and IT, and in particular in English, modern languages, and art and design. More boys than girls were leaving school with no GCSE passes while the vast majority of pupils being permanently excluded from school (figures for 1997/8) were boys. In addition, two out of three pupils in special schools were boys (figures for 1998/9; from the DfEE Standards Site).

At Key Stages 1 (KS1), 2 (KS2) and 3 (KS3) a similar pattern emerged. For example, the 1999 results in mathematics and science were broadly comparable, although in the English SAT around 10 per cent more girls than boys achieved the 'expected' levels of attainment in KS1 and KS2. Moreover, at KS2, while boys had made considerable improvements in reading to narrow the 'gender gap' to six percentage points, the gap between boys' and girls' writing stood at fifteen percentage points. By KS3 the gap between boys' and girls' results in English increased to eighteen percentage points. In Wales the statistics for 1999 followed a similar pattern to those in England with the gender gap only being striking in the results for Welsh and English.

In England, a concern with standards of attainment in English, as well as the use of particular teaching methods in schools, led to the introduction of the National Literacy Strategy (NLS). This strategy includes a framework for a daily hour of the explicit teaching of reading and writing, focusing on aspects of language such as phonics, spelling, grammar and punctuation. Based on the introduction of the NLS, David Blunkett, the then Secretary of State for Education and Employment, set a target of 80 per cent of 11-year-olds achieving the standards of literacy expected for their age by 2002 – that is level 4. (In Wales, this target is set at between 70 per cent and 80 per cent of 11-year-olds attaining level 4 or above in English and Welsh.) In order to help children reach these targets, since 2000 schools in England have received additional funding to be spent on 'booster' classes for children on the borderline between level 3 and 4 (OFSTED 2001).

## Size matters?

It is, however, the size of the gender gap – the relative attainment of boys and girls in English – which appears to preoccupy researchers, the government and the media alike. In January 1999 it was reported that the gender gap had 'widened to a gulf' (Cassidy 1999). By October, following the analysis of another year's test results, it was announced that boys had 'turned the tide' in literacy (Thornton 1999), although a further report on the same day maintained that 'Boys Close Reading Gap but Still Trail in Writing' (Hackett 1999).

But these headlines only tell part of the story. A closer look at the 1999 (Key Stages 1 and 2) results for Wales, for example, indicate that in the English SAT at KS1 a higher percentage of boys than girls were working at below level 2 – the expected level of attainment – in both reading and writing. Moreover, when examining the 'fine-grading' of level 2 (i.e. levels 2a, 2b and 2c), it is apparent that boys were achieving at the lower end of 'average' – particularly in writing. Overall, the figures indicate that the number of boys and girls achieving level 2 were comparable in reading with girls taking the lead in writing: 76 per cent of girls compared with 71 per cent of boys achieved level 2. However, the number of boys attaining level 3 (above the expected level of attainment) in reading was 20 per cent compared with 31 per cent of girls. In writing, this figure was 5 per cent of boys compared with 11 per cent of girls. Similarly, at KS2 the number of boys and girls achieving the 'required' level 4 in the English test/task appears not to be too dissimilar: 46 per cent for boys and 48 per cent for girls. However, the number of boys achieving above level 4 was 17 per cent compared with 26 per cent of girls.

These results indicate that while the number of boys and girls achieving 'expected' levels of attainment in English were, in fact, broadly comparable (or at least the difference between them was less extreme) a higher percentage of boys than girls were represented in the lower levels of attainment. In addition, a higher percentage of girls than boys were represented in the higher levels of attainment. If there is or ever was a 'gulf' between boys' and girls' results, it appears to be related essentially to children performing at the extremes – for example, the larger percentage of girls achieving the higher grades at both Key Stages 1 and 2 in reading and writing (results from the National Assembly for Wales 1999a, b).

This reading of the statistics also resonates with a more sophisticated and wide-ranging analysis of the comparative performance of boys and girls at school in Wales which was undertaken by Gorard *et al.* (1999). Their study, which examined statutory assessment and examination results at KS1, 2 and 3, at GCSE and at A level, concluded that over the period studied (1992–7) the only changes in the achievement gap between boys and girls were confined to the highest levels of attainment at KS1–4 in English, Welsh and the humanities.

## Why boys? Why now?

But the knowledge that boys are not well represented at the highest levels of attainment in some subjects – particularly English – does not tell us exactly *which* boys are doing badly in school. Is boys' under-achievement, as Chris Woodhead suggests and Estelle Morris implies, a problem relating to white, working-class boys? Plummer (1998) agrees in part and suggests that it is social class rather than gender or race that continues to have the' single most important influence on educational attainment in Britain. She maintains that the correlation between social class and educational attainment can be seen in infant school and becomes even more marked by post-16.

Gillborn and Mirza (2000) also recognise the impact of social class on attainment but maintain that neither social class factors nor gender differences override the influence of ethnic inequality – particularly in relation to African-Caribbean, Pakistani and Bangladeshi pupils. What is particularly worrying, they note, is that (paralleling social class) inequalities of attainment for African-Caribbean pupils become progressively greater as they move through the school system.

It would appear, then, that the impact of social class and race might have been under-emphasised in recent analyses of educational attainment. But so, too, has an acknowledgement that there has been a long-standing recognition of boys' difficulties in relation to their attainment in some subjects – particularly the languages, the arts and the humanities. In fact, within these subject areas, the gender gap is nothing new. Cohen (1998) suggests that underlying the current media panic is a mistaken view that until recently there was a 'golden age of boys' when their achievements across the curriculum outstripped those of girls. But, she claims, in the period she has been researching (from the late seventeenth century) boys have *always* 'under-achieved' in relation to the learning of languages.

Cohen (1998) points out that in the eighteenth century, for example, the greater elegance, fluency and liveliness of women's conversation compared with that of men was recognised. By the end of the eighteenth century, however, girls' quick thinking was interpreted as a sign of their inferiority while boys' 'dullness' was seen as a sign of their deep and thoughtful minds. Similarly, in the first systematic and public assessment of girls' and boys' performance (the Schools' Inquiry Commission of 1868, see Cohen 1998), not only were girls found to outperform boys but their more positive attitude towards learning was also noted. But, Cohen maintains, at this time the problem was defined not as one of boys' under-achievement but as the danger of 'overstrain' for girls. Girls' excessive conscientiousness and their almost morbid obsession with learning were castigated as unhealthy and con-trasted with boys' 'breezy attitude' towards life. Cohen comments that boys' poor academic performance and their negative attitudes towards school and school-work were tolerated – even admired – as natural expressions of their rebellious, boyish ways, and seen as evidence of their real understanding and superior intellect (see also Walkerdine 1989). Even in the 1950s and 1960s, the relatively poor per-formance of boys in the 11+ examinations was recognised and justified in terms of boys' later development. Girls were therefore required to achieve better results than boys in this examination in order to achieve a place at selective grammar schools – 'to do otherwise would have meant that grammar schools would have been overwhelmingly populated by girls' (Epstein *et al.* 1998: 5).

So, it could be asked, why across the Western world (e.g. the United Kingdom, Australia, New Zealand, Canada, the United States as well as in other European countries) is there now such a concern with the attainment of boys, particularly in relation to literacy? Does it reflect a shared realisation that, in order to compete in the global economy, literacy matters? Is it that boys' difficulties with literacy (seen as a feminine subject) were tolerated so long as boys were believed to excel in 'harder-edged' subjects such as mathematics and science? Or is it because, as Yates (1997) suggests – referring to the Australian context – that there has been a reali-sation that not only working-class boys but also middle-class boys are beginning to lose out to girls: for many, the problem is getting 'too close for comfort'?

It may be, of course, as Cohen (1998) suggests, that despite (or even because of) their poor attainment in tests and examinations, boys are seen as having innate, if untapped, potential. While girls' successes are neatly explained away by their obsessive attitude towards work, boys' failures are attributed to something 'exter-nal' to them. Moreover, it seems that in current explanations of boys' under-achievement in school, these external factors are related back to the 'female': essentially it is women who are to blame. This argument is built around two interrelated elements: 'missing men' and 'the feminised school'.

## Who's to blame?

### The missing men

I noted earlier that in recent years concerns have been raised about the breakdown of the 'traditional' family. One consequence of this breakdown is that many chil-dren are brought up by lone parents – usually their mothers. Young boys who do not have a male presence in their lives may take their ideas about masculinity from the often stereotypically male characters they see in cartoons, comics, television, videos and computer games: there will be no-one to demonstrate a positive model of masculinity (see Beal 1994). The problem of missing men is exacerbated by the fact that the primary school is also a female-dominated environment. The result is that boys, particularly those who are brought up by their mothers, may not be exposed 'to the "masculine" dimension of some values' – such as a more overt competitive edge (Bleach 1998: 9). Certainly, in the media, the lack of male teachers and male role models in schools has been cited as a particular cause for concern (e.g. Woodhead, reported in Lightfoot 1996). This is considered particularly worrying in relation to boys' attainment in literacy.

At a deeper level, however, the domination of young males by female teachers and the impact that this has on boys' developing sense of masculinity has been a long-standing and widespread cause for concern (see Miller 1996). Mahoney (1998) notes that in Denmark, for example, concerns have been raised that 'school is a terrible place for boys. In school they are trapped by "The Matriarchy" and are dominated by women who cannot accept boys as they are. The women teachers mainly wish to control and suppress boys' (Kruse 1996, cited in Mahoney 1998: 44).

## The feminised school

The notion that boys' under-achievement is connected to the feminisation of the curriculum, pedagogy and assessment methods has been a further recurring theme in the media. Writing in *The Times Educational Supplement*, for example, Budge (1994) suggests that women teachers may have unknowingly been moulding education and assessment to suit their gender. Concerns about teaching methods have been particularly apparent in relation to the teaching of literacy, which, it is claimed, has been dominated by (feminine) child-centred approaches that girls can tolerate but which do not suit the learning styles of boys. Stephen Byers, then schools standards minister, maintained that since the late 1970s there has been an emphasis on these unstructured teaching methods and a move away from phonics. It is this, he claims, that caused boys to fall behind in English (Lightfoot 1998), while the more formal methods of the NLS account for the recent rise in standards of attainment, particularly in relation to boys' reading scores (Blunkett 2000).

Moreover, it is suggested, boys' relatively poor performance in GCSE examinations is associated with the move away from the old system of O level examinations where knowledge and abstract facts – seen to favour males' cognitive styles – were prioritised. The GCSE, it is argued, has placed greater emphasis on course work, open-ended tasks, context-dependent knowledge, analytical skills and verbal reasoning skills – all said to favour girls' cognitive styles (see, e.g. Warrington and Younger 1997; Arnot *et al.* 1998).

## Solutions?

If females and 'girl-friendly' teaching and assessment methods are to blame for boys' under-achievement, then it is unsurprising that strategies suggested to improve boys' attainment have included: the introduction of single-sex teaching; an increase in the number of male teachers and male role-models in schools; the adoption of boy-friendly teaching strategies and assessment methods; the motivation of boys through the establishment of links between (predominantly male) sports, learning and literacy; and the inclusion on school reading lists of the kinds of books boys prefer. This has been reflected in headlines such as 'Single-sex Lessons Plan to Counter Laddish Culture' (Woodward 2000); 'Labour Seeks More Male Teachers to Inspire Boys' (Petre 1998); and Girls' 1, Boys 0: Can Football Help Boys Draw Level in the Classroom? (Crace 2001).

The effectiveness of some of these strategies has been questioned. For example, Bleach (1998) and Phillips (2000) both recognise that male teachers may actually exacerbate the problem of 'laddish' behaviour amongst under-achieving boys. It could be argued, for example, that the influence of female teachers might lead to the adoption of a *less* aggressive and more flexible masculine identity (see Beal 1994). Similarly, other writers have suggested that tackling male under-achievement through emphasising boy-friendly books may also be counterproductive (Ghouri 1999) in that they may only serve to entrench the macho attitudes which caused boys to fail in the first place. As we shall see, there are no easy solutions to this problem.

## Conclusions

In this chapter we have seen that through most of the last century men and women inhabited 'separate spheres' – men dominating the world of work and women the world of home. Women were encouraged to venture into the male sphere when they were needed and to assume their position as full-time mother and homemaker when they were not. But agitation by feminists for equality of opportunity, changes in women's expectations and in the traditional family structure, as well as funda-mental shifts in employment patterns, have challenged males to make adjustments and to redefine masculinity. It is their difficulty with making the necessary adjust-ments that seems to be the problem for some men who have subsequently embraced a position of 'hyper-masculinity'. It is a commitment to the ideal of hyper-masculinity which appears to have a negative impact on boys' attitudes towards school and towards learning.

It is interesting to consider why so much emphasis has been placed on gender when it is argued that factors such as race, poverty and class may have a greater impact on educational attainment than whether one is male or female. Is it that by framing this issue as a problem of 'gender' it then leaves open the possibility of ratio-nalising boys' under-achievement in terms of 'gender-related' issues: for example, the 'feminisation' of the curriculum, of teaching strategies and of methods of assessment, as well as the domination of schools by female teachers? Moreover, is it that it then becomes the responsibility of teachers to find a solution to this problem through, for example, changing their expectations, teaching methods and curriculum content? And if there is a genuine concern with gender equity, why is it that school and soci-ety has so easily been 'un-hitched'? Why, for example, is there no comparable 'panic' about the position of young women in the post-school years, even though, as Treneman (1998) reminds us, 'the statistical under-achievement of boys in school is nothing compared with the statistical over-achievement of men in life'?

If we are to understand what teachers might do to raise standards – particularly standards of boys' attainment in literacy – then we need to examine how we acquire a sense of who we are as a 'gendered being' and how this might impact on children's attitudes towards and attainment in reading and writing.

## Reflective questions

1   Is the 'moral panic' about male under-achievement the result of the preponderance of male politicians – or the preponderance of female teachers?
2   Is male performance declining, or are males merely on a plateau but being overtaken by females? How specific and limited is any relative decline in male performance?
3   To what extent is male disaffection in the education system a result of economic and political forces operating outside the education system?
4   What interactions are there between gender and class in relation to pupil performance? What might be the implications for action?

# References

Arnot, M., Gray, J., James, M. and Rudduck, J. (1998) *A Review of Recent Research on Gender and Educational Performance*, OFSTED Research Series, London: The Stationery Office.

Arnot, M., David, M. and Weiner, G. (1999) *Closing the Gender Gap: Postwar Education and Social Change*, London: Polity Press.

Beal, C. (1994) *Boys and Girls: The Development of Gender Roles*, New York: McGraw-Hill.

Bleach, K. (ed.) (1998) *Raising Boys' Achievement in Schools*, Stoke-on-Trent: Trentham Books.

Blunkett, D. (2000) cited in 'Test Results Show Lag in Boys' Literacy', *The Guardian*, 20 September.

Budge, D. (1994) 'A World Made for Women', *The Times Educational Supplement*, 24 June.

Cassidy, S. (1999) 'Gender Gap Widens to a Gulf', *The Times Educational Supplement*, 29 January.

Cohen, M. (1998) 'A Habit of Healthy Idleness: Boys' Underachievement in Historical Perspective', in D. Epstein, J. Elwood, V. Hey and J. Maw (eds) *Failing Boys? Issues in Gender and Achievement*, Buckingham: Open University Press.

Cohen, S. (1987) *Folk Devils and Moral Panics: The Creation of the Mods and Rockers*, 2nd edn, Oxford: Blackwell.

Crace, J. (2001) 'Girls 1, Boys 0', *The Guardian*, 30 January.

David, M., Weiner, G. and Arnot, M. (2000) 'Gender Equality and Schooling, Education Policy-making and Feminist Research in England and Wales in the 1990s' in J. Salisbury and S. Riddell (eds) *Gender, Policy and Educational Change: Shifting Agendas in the UK and Europe*, London: Routledge.

Davies, N. (2000) *The School Report: Why Britain's Schools are Failing*, London: Vintage.

Epstein, D., Elwood, J., Hey, V. and Maw, J. (eds) (1998) *Failing Boys? Issues in Gender and Achievement*, Buckingham: Open University Press.

Figes, K. (1994) *Because of Her Sex: The Myth of Equality for Women in Britain*, London: Pan Books (Macmillan).

Gaine, C. and George, R. (1999) *Gender, 'Race' and Class in Schooling. A New Introduction*, London: Falmer Press.

Ghouri, N. (1999) 'Football Approach Risks an Own Goal', *The Times Educational Supplement*, 4 June.

Gillborn, D. and Mirza, H.S. (2000) *Educational Inequality: Mapping Race, Class and Gender*, (Ofsted), London: HMSO.

Gipps, C. and Murphy, P. (1994) *A Fair Test? Assessment, Achievement and Equity*, Buckingham: Open University Press.

Gorard, S., Salisbury, J., Rees, G. and Fitz, J. (1999) *The Comparative Performance of Boys and Girls at School in Wales*, Cardiff: ACCAC.

Hackett, G. (1999) 'Boys Close Reading Gap but Still Trail in Writing', *The Times Educational Supplement*, 8 October.

Lepkowska, D. (1998) 'Minister Promises to Act on Boys' Failure', *The Times Educational Supplement*, 9 January.

Lightfoot, L. (1996) 'Lack of Role Models Holds Back Boys at School', *The Telegraph*, 18 November.

Lightfoot, L. (1998) 'Boys Are Left Behind by Modern Teaching', *The Telegraph*, 5 January.

Mahoney, P. (1998) 'Girls Will Be Girls and Boys Will Be First', in D. Epstein, J. Elwood, V. Hey and J. Maw, J. (eds) *Failing Boys? Issues in Gender and Achievement*, Buckingham: Open University Press.

Measor, L. and Sikes, P. (1992) *Gender and Schools*, London: Cassell.

Miller, J. (1996) *School for Women*, London: Virago.

Morris, E. (1996) *Boys Will Be Boys? Closing the Gender Gap*, London: The Labour Party.

National Assembly for Wales (1999a) *National Curriculum Assessment Results in Wales: Key Stage 1*, Cardiff: National Assembly for Wales.

National Assembly for Wales (1999b) *National Curriculum Assessment Results in Wales: Key Stage 2*, Cardiff: National Assembly for Wales.

OFSTED (2001) *The Annual Report of Her Majesty's Chief Inspector of Schools (1999–2000)*, London: HMSO.

Petre, J. (1998) 'Labour Seeks More Male Teachers to Inspire Boys', *The Telegraph*, 4 January.

Phillips, A. (2000) 'Clever Lad!' *The Guardian*, 29 August.

Plummer, G. (1998) 'Forget Gender, Class Is Still the Real Divide', *The Times Educational Supplement*, 23 January.

Pyke, N. (1996) 'Boys Read Less than Girls', *The Times Educational Supplement*, 15 March.

Riley, K. (1994) *Quality and Equality: Promoting Opportunities in School*, London: Cassell.

Rowbotham, S. (1999) *A Century of Women*, London: Penguin Books.

Stainton Rogers, W. and Stainton Rogers, R. (2001) *The Psychology of Gender and Sexuality*, Buckingham: Open University Press.

Thornton, K. (1999) 'Boys Turn the Tide in Literacy', *The Times Educational Supplement*, 8 October.

Treneman, A. (1998) 'Will the Boys Who Can't Read Still End Up as the Men on Top?' *The Independent*, 5 January.

Walkerdine, V. (1989) *Schoolgirl Fictions*, London: Verso.

Warrington, M. and Younger, M. (1997) 'Gender and Achievement: the Debate at GCSE', *Education Review*, 10(1): 21–7.

Weiner, G. (1985) 'Equal Opportunities, Feminism and Girls' Education', in G. Weiner (ed.) *Just a Bunch of Girls?* Buckingham: Open University Press.

Weiner, G. (1994) *Feminisms in Education*, Buckingham: Open University Press.

Weiner, G. and Arnot, M. (1987) 'Teachers and Gender Politics', in M. Arnot and G. Weiner (eds) *Gender and the Politics of Schooling*, London: Hutchinson.

Woodward, W. (2000) 'Single-sex Lessons Plan to Counter Laddish Culture, Leader: The Trouble with Boys', *The Guardian*, 21 August.

Wragg, T. (1997) 'Oh Boy!', *The Times Educational Supplement*, 16 May.

Yates, L. (1997) 'Gender Equity and the Boys Debate: What Sort of Challenge Is It?' *Journal of Sociology of Education*, 18(3): 337–47.

# CHAPTER 7

# CONNECTING THE DISCONNECTED

Exploring issues of gender, 'race' and SEN within an inclusive context

L. Gerschel

In C. Tilstone and R. Rose (eds) *Strategies to Promote Inclusive Practice* (2003), London and New York: RoutledgeFalmer, pp. 48–66

## What are the current issues in ethnicity, gender and special educational needs/disability?

Despite the focus on social and educational inclusion and on 'joined-up thinking' (DfEE, 1999), the discourses of SEN and of equal opportunities, in terms of race and gender, have remained distinctly discrete. Although the literature on learning difficulties and disability sometimes makes reference to 'social class', the gender or ethnicity ('race') of pupils is rarely mentioned. Similarly, research on ethnicity and gender issues rarely acknowledges Special Educational Needs (SEN) and disabilities. In a useful overview of race and SEN in the 1990s, Diniz (1999) identifies only four publications which report studies involving Asian children with SEN and three involving Black-Caribbean children. In most research, however, it is as if children with SEN or disabilities are white and genderless or 'degendered', to borrow a term from Arnot (Arnot *et al.*, 1999), and minority ethnic groups do not include children with SEN or disabilities. For the parents and children for whom ethnicity, gender, social class and SEN or disability interact, these factors cannot be separated.

Some examples of the current issues that link the fields of ethnicity and race, gender, SEN and disability are listed later. Although the list is not comprehensive and presents hypotheses without detailed exploration, areas where experience suggests that more research is needed are identified. An author's name is included where the published work could make a helpful starting point for reading.

### The issues of ethnicity and SEN

* Little acknowledgement of the impact of ethnic and cultural diversity on learning in some schools and in some professional services (Cline, 1998);
* little research on ethnicity ('race') and SEN (Diniz, 1999);
* institutionalised racism and the impact of the Macpherson report on the inclusion of minority ethnic group pupils (Ofsted, 2000a; Gillborn, 2001);
* the significant over-representation of African-Caribbean pupils in the provision for emotional and behavioural difficulties (Cooper *et al.*, 1991); changing populations in MLD schools (Male, 2000);

- the over-representation of Chinese and Asian pupils in the provision for Severe Learning Difficulties (SLD) and Profound and Multiple Learning Difficulties (PMLD); their under-representation in Moderate Learning Difficulties (MLD) and specific learning difficulties and when assessed as dyslexic (Diniz, 1999);
- the over-representation of Pakistani and Bangladeshi children in hearing loss and deafness (Ahmad *et al.*, 1997);
- African-Caribbean pupils identified as having 'general learning difficulties' rather than specific literacy difficulties and the consequent poorer provision (Daniels *et al.*, 1996);
- early high attainment followed by increasing underachievement among African-Caribbean boys (Gillborn and Mirza, 2000);
- the gap between attainment at GCSE of African-Caribbean and Pakistani pupils and that of white pupils is bigger than a decade ago (Gillborn and Mirza, 2000);
- a wider attainment gap as a consequence of ethnic origin, social class and gender (Gilborn and Mirza, 2000);
- the lack of research into the experiences of the parents of pupils with SEN from minority ethnic groups (Shah, 1995; Gross, 1996; Diniz, 1999; Warner, 1999);
- evidence that poverty and lower social class may impact more on minority ethnic groups and are related to increased SEN (Mittler, 1999, 2000);
- effects of teacher expectations based on ethnicity and class stereotypes on the identification, assessment and provision for pupils with SEN from minority ethnic groups (Epstein *et al.*, 1998; Wright *et al.*, 2000; Newham, 2001);
- confusions between language difficulties and learning difficulties for pupils with English as an Additional Language (EAL) (Troyna and Siraj-Blatchford, 1993).

## The issues of gender and SEN

- Gender imbalance: more boys than girls with SEN (2 boys, 1 girl in SEN generally; up to 12:1 in EBD) (Hill, 1994; Vardill, 1996);
- boys receive more teacher attention for inappropriate behaviour, and their emotional needs are recognised less than their behavioural needs (McNamara and Moreton, 1995);
- boys and girls are not treated with equity in identification, assessment and provision for SEN (Daniels *et al.*, 1999; Daniels *et al.*, 2001);
- boys get more and better provision for their identified needs (Daniels *et al.*, 1999);
- girls' emotional needs are often ignored or seen as health problems (McNamara and Moreton, 1995; Klein, 1999; Tierney and Dowd, 2000; Newham, 2001);
- the effects of the national emphasis on literacy on boys (Barrs and Pidgeon, 1998; Epstein *et al.*, 1998; QCA, 1998; Noble and Bradford, 2000);
- growing disaffection and underachievement amongst boys (Mac an Ghaill, 1994; Bleach, 1998; Holland, 1998; Klein, 1999);
- the increasing exclusion of boys; particularly the impact on Black-Caribbean, white working class, and those with SEN (DfEE, 2000; Wright *et al.*, 2000; Osler *et al.*, 2001);
- fewer opportunities for less able boys to find employment in unskilled or manual jobs (Holland, 1998);
- failure to acknowledge the needs of a minority of girls in some special schools (especially EBD);

- the need to address the sexuality of pupils with learning difficulties and disabilities; homosexuality is rarely addressed in special schools (Stewart and Ray, 2001);
- the issue of choice of, or consent to, sterilisation and contraception for girls with learning difficulties;
- the effects of teacher expectations (based on gender stereotypes) on the identification, assessment or provision for girls and boys with SEN (Green, 1993; Hill, 1994; Mac an Ghaill, 1994; Vardill, 1996; Wilson, 2000; Newham, 2001).

## The issues of SEN, equality and equity

- Increasing inclusion of pupils with learning difficulties and disabilities in mainstream education but inconsistencies in the quality of education received;
- a lack of data on the ethnicity and gender of pupils with statements, and inadequate ethnic and gender monitoring of pupils with SEN at school, local and national level for placement, identification, assessment, provision and attainment (Male, 2000);
- a lack of data on children 'looked after' by local authorities in relation to ethnicity, gender and SEN (Brodie, 2000) and exclusion (Osler *et al.*, 2001);
- little awareness in some schools of the minority ethnic group cultures of pupils with SEN, or the different needs of girls and boys with SEN (Daniels *et al.*, 2001);
- a lack of clarity about what is 'underachievement' and what is SEN (Bleach, 1998);
- although the National Curriculum 2000 supports parallel inclusions, there is a need to develop connective pedagogy (Corbett, 2001a); the effects of league tables on pupils with SEN (Gillborn, 2001);
- although Ofsted reviews of National Literacy Strategy (NLS) and National Numeracy Strategy (NNS) in special schools do not mention ethnicity or gender, they acknowledge that NLS has been successful for many pupils with SEN but that those with PMLD are still not fully included (OFSTED, 2000b, 2001; Byers, 1999);
- the effects of policies and programmes for pupils which are 'gender and colour blind' (Mittler, 2000; Gillborn, 2001);
- QCA programmes offer access for pupils with learning difficulty but are 'gender and colour blind' (QCA, 2001);
- too little recognition of the rights of young people with SEN as sexual beings (Scott, 2001);
- a need for better sex education for pupils in special schools (Scott, 2001);
- little recognition of the links between pupils 'looked after' by local authorities, and SEN;
- 'summer-born' children have more identified SEN (Wilson, 2000); race, gender, SEN and setting (Ollerton, 2001);
- the links between poverty, health and social class and SEN (Dyson, 1997; Mittler, 2000);
- inconsistencies in SEN resource allocation associated with parental power and class (Gross, 1996);
- too little known about bullying within the field of SEN (Torrance, 2000);

- the increasing number of exclusions of pupils with statements of SEN (DfEE, 2000; Osler, 1997); the use of exclusion to access support for SEN (Osler *et al.*, 2001);
- the higher rates of permanent exclusion from special schools (DfEE, 2000);
- the effects of the Disability Discrimination Act (1995) and the SEN and Disability Act (2001) on the education and the rights of pupils;
- the effect of the Human Rights Act on the rights of pupils with SEN;
- inequitable and sometimes ineffective distribution of resources to support pupils with SEN (Corbett, 2001b; Dyson, 2001; Gillborn, 2001);
- the effects of teacher expectations, based on gender, ethnicity or class stereotypes, on group organisation and settings (Wilson, 2000; Gillborn, 2001; Ollerton, 2001).

Some of these issues are long standing: Coard (1971) showed that disproportionately large numbers of pupils of African-Caribbean origin were labelled ESN (educationally sub-normal) and sent to special schools. Two decades later, the labelling (now EBD) continues (DfEE, 2000; Wright *et al.*, 2000). Sewell (1997) and Mac an Ghaill (1994) see this as the result of a mismatch between pupil and school cultures. Exploring the reasons for exclusion, Osler *et al.* (2001) suggest practical school and LEA action. The traditional remedy (pupils to 'adapt' to school culture) has failed and the increasing exclusion of some pupils is an indicator of the failure of the school to plan for the inclusion of all pupils and to adapt its teaching and learning culture accordingly (Mittler, 2000; Osler *et al.*, 2001). The implementation of DfEE Circular 10/99 on social inclusion has created considerable concern in some schools but offers specific advice on reducing the number of exclusions by recognising the impact of social and cultural disadvantage on learning. Nevertheless, the majority of pupils excluded from school are boys (many from ethnic minority groups or lower social classes) and over one-third are registered as having SEN.

There has long been a concern about the relationship between pupils who are learning EAL and who also have SEN. There has often been a lack of clarity in whether pupils are experiencing language or learning difficulties and how their needs are identified and met (Troyna and Siraj-Blatchford, 1993; Gerschel, 1998). There was a tendency in the 1970s and 1980s to identify pupils with language difficulties as having learning difficulties. A more recent problem, however, has been caused by the unwillingness of some schools to recognise that some pupils who speak EAL also have SEN, which are consequently not being met.

On the other hand, there has been considerably less attention to some issues linking SEN and gender. For example, a DfEE-funded study by the London Borough of Newham (2001) of girls' experiences of schooling draws attention to the lack of recognition given to girls' emotional difficulties; a neglected area compared to the attention given to the behavioural difficulties of boys. Although the sexuality and sexual orientation of pupils with learning difficulties and disabilities has been largely ignored in the literature, current approaches to sex education for pupils with SEN are being explored at Shepherd School in Nottingham, through the Standards Fund and innovative work in drama undertaken by 'Image in Action' (Scott, 2001; Stewart and Ray, 2001).

## Underachievement or SEN?

Of particular significance to the media, is the underachievement of boys (see e.g. Henry, 2001a,b). Although girls have outperformed boys for many years in many areas of the curriculum, the publication of national test results (SATs, GCSEs and A-levels) highlights the differences and a body of literature is emerging which explores cause and effect (Ofsted, 1993; Mac an Ghaill, 1994; Pickering, 1997; Epstein *et al.*, 1998; QCA, 1998; Arnot *et al.*, 1999; Frater, 2000). Lively debate has focused on the extent to which the recent introduction of the NLS has exacerbated the difficulties boys experience with literacy and the solutions (Millard, 1997; Barrs and Pidgeon, 1998; Fisher, 2001; Rundell, 2001).

Gillborn and Mirza (2000) make it clear that the comparative attainment of boys and girls from different ethnic groups and social classes reflects a complex pattern, but that 'the gender gap is considerably smaller than the inequalities of attainment associated with ethnic origin and social class background' (p. 23). They stress that neither social class nor gender differences:

> ...can account for persistent underlying ethnic inequalities: comparing like with like, African Caribbean, Pakistani and Bangladeshi pupils do not enjoy equal opportunities.
>
> (p. 27)

To what extent are these ethnic and social factors considered in relation to planning and the teaching of pupils with SEN?

The current pattern of underachievement among boys applies across all abilities, most ethnic groups and all social classes, although it is difficult to say where 'underachievement' ends and 'special educational needs' begins. In some cases the demarcation is simply resource-driven and, as an example of the relationship between underachievement and SEN, Bleach (1998) cites the fact that the 'cut-off point' for providing support for SEN in a secondary school was placed at a maximum reading age of 8.5. Therefore, a reading age of 8.3 at age 11 recognises that a pupil has SEN; a reading age of 8.7, in these terms, means that the pupil is 'underachieving'!

This complex relationship is further blurred by the increasing recognition of disaffection and its impact on learning (Klein, 1999). At what point does the disaffection and underachievement of a Black-Caribbean boy at a secondary school, who is increasingly resisting schooling (possibly as a result of what he sees as a racist experience), become an emotional or cognitive need, recognised as a SEN meriting necessary additional resources organised by the SENCo? The greater probability is that he will be seen as a behavioural problem which may be 'dealt with' (or disciplined) through the pastoral system (head of year, head of house) rather than as a pupil whose experience of barriers to learning has left him behind in the great race to literacy and to A*–C grades at GCSE. He might, however, be helped through a more inclusive approach, possibly suggested by the SENCo. The following questions need to be addressed:

- What would be the difference in the school's response had our resistant pupil been a white working-class girl?
- How often is underachievement among pupils with statements for learning difficulties discussed in special or mainstream schools?

The current media discussion on underachievement risks focusing attention on the attainments of a small minority of able students (measured in A*–C grades at GCSE or A/AS-level) rather than reflecting on the wider wastage of potential skills and abilities among a greater number of pupils (Gillborn, 2001). Klein (1999) explores the difficult relationships between disaffection and SEN and, like Daniels *et al.* (1999), stresses the importance of recognising that not all disaffection or 'naughtiness' is an emotional or behavioural difficulty.

It is clear that, despite accusations of 'excuses', there is a strong direct association between social class and success in education (Gillborn and Mirza, 2000). Children without safe living conditions, food, warmth and clothing, let alone access to books, computers and other stimuli, and whose parents are stressed by poverty, are less likely to succeed at school. Mittler (2000) is explicit about class and economic links to underachievement, suggesting that:

> ...boys are more susceptible to social disadvantage in early childhood, girls more vulnerable at adolescence.
>
> (p. 58)

He further points out that:

> ...at the age of seven, five times as many children from social class five had reading difficulties, as compared with those from social class one.
>
> (p. 52)

Acknowledging gross inequalities in health and their social consequences, Mittler makes the link between children who experience social and economic deprivation, and those with special needs and illness or disability, and also shows that the poorer health suffered by ethnic minorities is a reflection of poverty. Put simply, with poorer health and poorer living conditions, pupils are more likely to have SEN. Corbett (2001b) recognises this and emphasises the need to see pupils holistically, within the wider community of their housing and leisure activities.

## Culture clashes: inclusion or competition?

The statement of aims of most schools usually stresses that each pupil is valued as an individual and it is the intention of staff to help to fulfil her or his potential. Although an inclusive approach clearly supports this aim, there are major tensions between inclusive and competitive philosophies both in the government and in schools. Government advocates inclusion but simultaneously expects schools to achieve increasingly high academic targets. The prevailing culture in schools is influenced by government pressures to raise standards and to achieve targets set in literacy and numeracy, in order to appear in a favourable position in published league tables. In some schools, considerable resources have been provided for pupils whose performance falls just short of achieving the desired targets. Additional literacy support is sometimes given at KS2 to pupils who can be encouraged to move from level 3 to level 4 in time for Standard Assessment Tasks. Pupils whose attainment is well below national expectations have sometimes suffered comparative neglect, as their results do not impact on the league tables in the same way (Gillborn, 2001). The pressure on schools to set targets and to raise standards may well directly militate against the admission and inclusion of pupils whose academic performance will not prove sufficiently competitive. Gillborn (2001) effectively critiques the inherent conflict between the Government's expectation of inclusion and its recent Green Paper (DfEE, 2001) which encourages increased specialisation and the use of selection.

## Connecting the disconnected: moving towards inclusive education

The Government has sought to increase the inclusion of pupils with SEN and disabilities in mainstream schools (DfEE, 1997, 1998; DfEE/QCA, 1999; DfES, 2001) and to improve the provision for such pupils in mainstream and special contexts. Mittler (2000) argues that the inclusion debate has been reinvigorated by disability rights groups who have presented inclusion as a fundamental issue. For many, the word 'inclusion' suggests a necessary shift in the culture of mainstream schools to expect and welcome pupils with disabilities and learning difficulties. However, the publication of *Social Inclusion: Pupil Support* (Circular 10/99, DfEE, 1999) increased the 'catchment group' for discussions on inclusion to embrace pupils 'at risk of disaffection and exclusion' and recognised the impact of social and cultural disadvantage on learning. As O'Brien (1998) states:

> Inclusion is not only about eliminating discrimination for those who are cognitively or physically disadvantaged; it is also about improving provision for vulnerable children who suffer relentless economic and emotional deprivation.
>
> (p. 151)

Mittler is even more specific; for him:

> ...the inclusion agenda...challenges all forms of exclusion and discrimination, whether arising from society's response to disability, gender, race, sexual orientation or poverty and social disadvantage.
>
> (Mittler, 2000, p. 93)

For the first time, and some years after its introduction, the National Curriculum (DfEE and QCA, 1999), implemented in September 2000, sets out a 'statutory inclusion statement on providing effective learning opportunities for all pupils' (p. 32), and acknowledges that pupils from certain identified groups may be at a disadvantage unless curriculum planning is specifically designed to meet their needs. These groups are:

- boys and girls;
- pupils with SEN;
- pupils with disabilities;
- pupils from all social and cultural backgrounds;
- pupils of different ethnic groups, including travellers, refugees and asylum seekers;
- pupils from diverse linguistic backgrounds.

A clear expectation is spelt out for staff to be aware of the requirements of the equal opportunities legislation covering race, gender and disability, in order to meet the full range of pupils' needs. It appears that the move towards inclusion is simultaneously bringing about a consistency of approach to differing groups and a recognition of the diverse needs of distinct groups of pupils. At the same time, the new Code of Practice has come into place (DfES, 2001). We have yet to see whether these changes will simply result in more rearranging of the ways in which special education is delivered or whether they will:

> ...construct a form of education which is more equitable in itself and which will promote wider social equity.
>
> (Dyson, 1997, p. 153)

## Stephen Lawrence's legacy: the impact of the Macpherson report

As the disability rights movement has had a galvanising effect on national inclusion policy, so special education may be said to have benefited from the Stephen Lawrence Inquiry. Recommendations of the Stephen Lawrence Inquiry (Macpherson, 1999) state that:

> ...consideration is given to amendment of the National Curriculum aimed at valuing cultural diversity and preventing racism, in order better to reflect the needs of a diverse society.
>
> (Recommendation 67)

The Labour Government has ensured that 'institutional racism' is addressed through policy and action at all levels, from Ofsted and local education authorities to individual classrooms, through the Race Relations (Amendment) Act (2000). It has ensured that every school has been sent a copy of two publications which support self-evaluation through audit and a checklist; one specifically addresses racism in education (*Learning for All*, CRE, 2000) and includes audit statements relevant to pupils with SEN.

Diniz (1999) and Gillborn (2001) argue convincingly that the identification and assessment of the SEN of pupils from minority ethnic groups are affected by institutionalised racism. This is demonstrated, for example, by a willingness to attribute pupils' difficulties and disabilities to 'within-culture' factors rather than, for example, linking inadequate health-care provision for Pakistani and Bangladeshi children to the high numbers identified as having hearing loss and deafness (Ahmad *et al.*, 1997), or a lack of awareness of heritage languages and cultures in schools and services, for example, the use of standardised SEN assessment tests with Asian children (Desforges, 1995; Cline, 1998). An increasing body of literature refutes the within-child explanations of the disaffection and exclusion of Black children, especially boys, and recognises the responsibility of schools to re-examine their cultures. Macpherson has brought the issues into the open: those in special education must recognise their own roles in bringing about greater equity for pupils from minority ethnic groups. Using the audits provided in *Learning for All* may help schools and LEAs to identify areas for change within their control.

The second publication, sent to all schools, the *Index for Inclusion* (Booth *et al.*, 2000) addresses issues of equality and inclusion more broadly. At the same time, Ofsted (2000a) has published valuable guidance on evaluating educational inclusion and introduced compulsory training for all its inspectors, as a direct result of Macpherson's recommendation (Macpherson, 1999) that Ofsted be required to inspect the implementation of strategies by local education authorities and governors to 'prevent and address racism' (Macpherson, 1999, Recommendations 68 and 69). However, Ofsted's guidance wisely focuses on evaluating the inclusion of a wide spectrum of pupils, adding to those groups identified earlier (Macpherson, 1999, p. 56):

- pupils from minority ethnic and faith groups;
- pupils who need support to learn EAL;
- gifted and talented pupils;
- children 'looked after' by the local authority;
- others such as sick children; young carers; those children from families under stress; pregnant schoolgirls and teenage mothers;
- any pupils who are at risk of disaffection and exclusion.

(p. 1)

Notably omitted from all lists are gay and lesbian pupils, who remain a hidden and vulnerable minority in all schools and whose learning may consequently be disadvantaged (Rivers, 2000).

The emotional behaviour of children who belong to one of these groups may be affected both by the factor that makes them different (e.g. their giftedness or the stress that they experience in their home situations), but also by their responses to school as a place that either recognises or ignores their 'differences', and enables them to learn.

Many children will 'belong' to more than one of the groups listed earlier, and in all there are likely to be children with SEN or disabilities. This point can be illustrated by asking you to define yourself – perhaps by sex, 'race', class, (dis)ability or impairment, age, marital status, role in the family, profession, skills, talents, size...the list could go on!

- Which of these attributes defines you most distinctly in your own eyes?
- Which are most important in how other people define you?
- How have any of these attributes affected your learning as a child, as an adult and, subsequently, in your current job?

Each person's learning is affected by multiple factors, and there are implications for schools in turning inclusion policies into practice for pupils who have SEN and/or disabilities, and for whom barriers to learning are compounded by their gender, culture, class or ethnicity.

It may be that the term 'special educational needs' is no longer helpful, reflecting a 'within-child' or medical model to guide planning. O'Brien (1998), Mittler (2000) and Dyson (2001) all offer systemic approaches to planning which are far broader and more inclusive. Dyson (2001) emphasises the rights of children to a guarantee of concern for their individual progress, within an inclusive context where systemic planning is embedded in classroom practice. O'Brien (1998) focuses on the needs that are common to all, those that are relevant to a discrete group and finally to those features of planning which will be necessary for a few specific individuals. This way of thinking about a class or school which is mixed in terms of gender, ethnicity, social class and ability or disability, emphasises commonality while recognising difference, and includes all those within it. Teachers may then ask:

- What is it that all children need in order to participate and to learn? (common needs)
- What is it that this group of pupils needs – because they are (for example) boys and/or with Down's syndrome and/or with hearing impairments and/or from the Bangladeshi community and/or Muslims – that is distinctive or different? (distinct needs)
- What else is it that this individual needs which is specific to her or him? (specific/individual needs)

O'Brien (1998) points out that:

> ...the membership of groups highlights distinct needs...an individual's membership of such groups has to be reflected positively in the curriculum and in classroom interaction.

(p. 148)

An excellent example of this practice is given by Corbett (2001b), describing how work with young trainees with learning difficulties addressed their needs specifically and holistically. But it is essential that we do not create divisions or hierarchies of disadvantage: inclusion policy and practice must recognise the complexities of individual experiences and address their impact on learning: what Corbett (2001a) calls 'connective pedagogy', that is, taking a holistic view of the pupil.

The experiences and outcomes of differing discriminations often have commonalities. If a teacher has low expectations of a child because of her or his sex, sexuality, ethnic or social background, cognitive or physical ability or disability, those expectations will potentially have a negative impact on the child's learning. If inclusion is a process of change that will enhance the learning experiences and achievements of all pupils, it must address areas of potential disadvantage coherently, and develop what Daniels *et al.* (2001) call 'pedagogies for equity' in education.

## 'Regardless of' or 'focused on' disadvantaged groups?

The needs of distinct groups can be met through what I shall call 'regardless of' and 'focused on' approaches. The introduction to the documents from QCA, *Planning, Teaching and Assessing the Curriculum for Pupils with Learning Difficulties*, illustrates the first approach. It declares that:

> ...the guidelines relate to all pupils aged between five and sixteen who have learning difficulties, regardless of factors such as their ethnicity, culture, religion, home language, family background or gender, or the extent of their difficulties.
>
> (p. 4)

The curriculum opportunities and activities it advocates are applicable to all pupils but it does not recognise the distinct needs resulting from being part of a distinct group. For example, the suggestions for pupils at Key Stage 3 on learning about 'My body' refer to sanitary products and menstruation and masturbation but do not focus on gender and ethnicity issues in planning and teaching. The examples could have drawn attention to the importance of same-sex groups for discussions, or acknowledged the needs of male and female pupils who have been circumcised. Nor does the PSHE and Citizenship programme acknowledge the right of all pupils with learning difficulties to be seen as sexual beings; heterosexuality is assumed.

Although there is an advantage in policies and programmes which are intended to apply to all, there is a danger that if they do not identify the needs of particular groups or focus on specific examples, they will simply make no difference. As Gillborn (2001), says: 'Color-blind policies tend to have racialised effects' (p. 107). This lesson can be applied more widely: what is not specifically addressed will continue to damage pupils' opportunities. To be specific about the needs of distinct groups is not to undermine inclusion, as Mittler (2000) points out. Referring to the failure of what he calls 'colour blind' policies to meet the needs of children from ethnic minorities, he argues that:

> A conscious, focused attention on their needs is necessary to avoid marginalisation and unwitting discrimination.
>
> (p. 77)

This statement applies equally to all disadvantaged groups and we need to be able to translate policy and programmes from the general inclusive principle to the specific relevant practice: to be cognisant of, and 'focus on', the learning of distinct groups within an inclusive context.

## The principles and the questions: reviewing policy and practice

Schools that wish to address inclusivity and equity need to audit their current practice in order to identify where change is needed and where they can build on success. As long ago as 1988, Mortimore *et al.* (1988) held that:

> ...schools which are effective in promoting progress for one group of pupils (whether those of a particular social class, sex or ethnic group) will usually also be effective for children of other groups.
>
> (p. 217)

We could say that planning effectively for inclusivity promotes effectiveness; in the National Curriculum guidance (DfEE/QCA, 1999) three principles are explored that are described as 'essential to developing a more inclusive curriculum' and which all teachers are expected to address in their planning and teaching:

- The need to set suitable learning challenges for all pupils;
- The need to respond to pupils' diverse learning needs;
- The need to overcome potential barriers to learning and assessment for individuals and groups of pupils.

(p. 32)

For each principle, specific indicators and examples are given to help teachers to identify good practice.

These principles for inclusion knit well with the questions identified and addressed by Booth *et al.* (2000) in the *Index for Inclusion*:

- Who experiences barriers to learning and participation in the school?
- What are the barriers to learning and participation in the school?
- How can barriers to learning and participation be minimised?
- What resources are available to support learning and participation?
- How can additional resources be mobilised to support learning and participation?

(p. 14)

Teachers, governors, pupils and parents are invited to identify or address inclusive practice through questionnaires and indices for evaluating inclusion.

Ofsted (2000a) requires inspectors to consider three questions in order to evaluate inclusion which are pertinent and practical for staff to consider when devising policies:

- Do all pupils get a fair deal at school?

This relates to

- – what benefits pupils get out of school, particularly their achievements;
- – the opportunity to learn effectively, without interference and disruption;
- – the respect and individual help they have from their teachers;
- – pupils' access to all aspects of the curriculum;

  - the attention the school gives to pupils' well-being;
  - whether they and their parents are happy with the school.

- How well does the school recognise and overcome barriers to learning?

This is about

  - the school's understanding of how well different groups do in school;
  - the steps taken to make sure that particular groups are not disadvantaged in school and to promote their participation and success in learning;
  - the school's strategies for promoting good relationships and managing behaviour;
  - what the school does specifically to prevent and address racism, sexism and other forms of discrimination, and what it does about those cases of discrimination that do occur.

- Do the school's values embrace and inclusion and does its practice promote it?

The clues are

  - how the values of the school are reflected in its curriculum, resources, communications, procedures and conduct;
  - how people talk about and treat one another in the school;
  - the leadership provided by senior staff and the consistency of staff behaviour;
  - what the school intends and tries to do for 'people like me'.

(Ofsted, 2000a, p. 3)

There is a coherence in these three documents which is both refreshing and challenging. The expectations made of teachers and schools are explicit and the process of change can be supported by using these self-audit opportunities to review, amend and monitor inclusive practice, and to ensure that all pupils 'get a fair deal'. Nevertheless, it is also true that the practice of equality needs adequate resourcing and we have yet to see whether and how this will be available by government.

The issues of equity, equality and SEN are inextricably bound together. It is clear that if schools are to become truly inclusive they must recognise both commonalities and distinctions between groups of learners who have hitherto been understood as belonging to separate spheres of SEN, 'race', gender and class. There is a need for a clear philosophy of education that embraces issues of both entitlement and equity (Corbett, 2001b) and sees the parts in relation to the whole and the whole as the sum of its parts: a holistic and 'connective pedagogy' (Corbett, 2001a). The approach to meeting the diverse needs of pupils and to overcoming obstacles to learning and achievement can no longer be sustained at an individual within-child level and must be systemic (O'Brien, 1998; Mittler, 2000; Dyson, 2001).

The key question for schools must be that posed by Ofsted: do all pupils get a fair deal at school? If the answer for some groups is 'No', what must be done to ensure that they do? Children deserve a guarantee of entitlement and equity in their education (Dyson, 2001) which will come about only when schools consider their definition of inclusive education, and work towards its reflection in the reality of daily life by honest and ongoing evaluation. The tools are available; audits and checklists (Booth *et al.*, 2000; CRE, 2000; Ofsted, 2000a) are supplied to schools by the Government. However, unless there is willingness amongst staff, pupils, parents, governors, friends and neighbours of the school to carry out these audits, and a commitment by the whole school community to act on the findings and to bring about change, such audits will not impact on the daily experiences of children and young people. Macpherson said of institutional racism:

> It persists because of the failure of the organisation openly and adequately to recognise and address its existence and causes by policy, example and leadership.
> (Macpherson, 1999, p. 28)

The same can be said of the exclusivity in education systems which leads to disaffection, failure and the waste of young lives and potential. 'Being equitable requires conscious consideration and effort' (Corbett, 2001b, p. 118); schools must examine their leadership, policy and practice, whether at the micro level of the classroom where teachers' work reflects the inclusion statement of the National Curriculum (DfEE, 1999), or at the macro level of the impact of national and local government initiatives. Those involved with education must agree the changes necessary in what they actually do: for example, in curriculum content, teaching styles, organisation of teaching groups, deployment of resources, setting specific targets to recognise distinct needs and review policies for coherence and consistency. Effective monitoring and evaluation systems, including Ofsted, must ensure that all children do get 'a fair deal'. Inclusion will entail a shift in power, a review and redistribution of resources and a culture change that reconnects the disconnected, embracing distinct groups within a holistic educational philosophy for equity and achievement.

## Reflective questions

1 If children can have 'Special Educational Needs', can they also have 'Special Gender Needs' or 'Special Class Needs'? How might such needs be identified and met?
2 Should pupils with Special Educational Needs be excluded from attainment targets and school league tables?
3 What is the worst case scenario for a pupil – to be disabled, black, working class and male? Or not?

## References

Ahmad, P., Oxley McCann, A. and Plackett, C. (1997) 'Home-school liaison in multicultural schools in Cleveland', in J. Bastiani (ed.) *Home-school Work in Multicultural Settings*. London: David Fulton.
Arnot, M., David, M. and Weiner, G. (1999) *Closing the Gender Gap: Post-war Education and Social Change*. Cambridge: Policy Press.
Barrs, M. and Pidgeon, S. (1998) *Boys and Reading*. London: CLPE.
Bleach, K. (1998) *Raising Boys' Achievement in Schools*. Stoke-on-Trent: Trentham Books.
Booth, T., Ainscow, M., Black-Hawkins, K., Vaughan, M. and Shaw, L. (2000) *Index for Inclusion: Developing Learning and Participation in Schools*. Bristol: Centre for Studies on Inclusive Education (CSIE).
Brodie, I. (2000) 'Children's homes and school exclusion: Redefining the problem', *Support for Learning*, 15 (1) 25–9.
Byers, R. (1999) 'The National Literacy Strategy and pupils with special educational needs', *British Journal of Special Education*, 26 (1) 8–11.
Cline, T. (1998) 'The assessment of special educational needs for bilingual children', *British Journal of Special Education*, 25 (4) 159–61.
Coard, B. (1971) *How the West Indian Child is Made Educationally Subnormal in the British School System*. London: Beacon Books (reprinted 1991, London: Karia Press).

Commission for Racial Equality (2000) *Learning for All: Standards for Racial Equality in Schools*. London: CRE.

Cooper, P., Upton, G. and Smith, C. (1991) 'Ethnic minority and gender distribution among staff and pupils in facilities for pupils with emotional and behavioural difficulties in England and Wales', *British Journal of Sociology of Education*, 12 (1) 77–94.

Corbett, J. (2001a) 'Teaching approaches which support inclusive education: a connective pedagogy', *British Journal of Special Education*, 28 (2) 55–9.

Corbett, J. (2001b) 'Is equity compatible with entitlement? Balancing inclusive values and deserving needs', *Support for Learning*, 16 (3) 117–21.

Daniels, H., Creese, A., Hey, V., Leonard, D. and Smith, M. (2001) 'Gender and learning; equity, equality and pedagogy', *Support for Learning*, 16 (3) 112–16.

Daniels, H., Hey, V., Leonard, D. and Smith, M. (1996) Equal to the challenge?, *Special Children*, Autumn, 15–16.

Daniels, H., Hey, V., Leonard, D. and Smith, M. (1999) 'Issues of equity in special needs education from a gender perspective', *British Journal of Special Education*, 26 (4) 189–95.

Daniels, H., Visser, J., Cole, T. and Reybekill, N. (1999) *Emotional and Behavioural Difficulties in Mainstream Schools*. Research Report No. 90. London: DfEE.

Department for Education and Employment (DfEE) (1997) *Excellence for all Children: Meeting Special Educational Needs*. London: The Stationery Office.

Department for Education and Employment (DfEE) (1998) *Meeting Special Educational Needs: A Programme of Action*. London: The Stationery Office.

Department for Education and Employment (DfEE) (1999) *Social Inclusion: Pupil Support (Circular 10/99)*. London: DfEE.

Department for Education and Employment (DfEE) and Qualifications and Curriculum Authority (QCA) (1999) *The National Curriculum Handbooks for Primary/Secondary Teachers in England*. London: DfEE/QCA.

Department for Education and Employment (DfEE) (2000) *Statistics in Education: Permanent Exclusions from Maintained Schools in England* (Issue 10/00). London: The Stationery Office.

Department for Education and Employment (DfEE) (2001) *Schools: Building on Success: Raising Standards, Promoting Diversity, Achieving Results* (Cm 5050). London: DfEE.

Department for Education and Skills (DfES) (2001) *Special Educational Needs: Code of Practice*. London: DfES.

Desforges, M. (1995) 'Assessment of special educational needs in bilingual pupils: changing practice?', *School Psychology International*, 16, 15–17.

Diniz, F. A. (1999) 'Race and special educational needs in the 1990s', *British Journal of Special Education*, 26 (4) 213–17.

Dyson, A. (1997) 'Social and educational disadvantage', *British Journal of Special Education*, 24 (4) 152–7.

Dyson, A. (2001) 'Special needs education as the way to equity: an alternative approach', *Support for Learning*, 16 (3) 105–11.

Epstein, D., Elwood, J., Hey, V. and Maw, J. (1998) *Failing Boys? Issues in Gender and Achievement*. Buckingham: Open University Press.

Fisher, H. (2001) 'Achieving the best: gender and the Literacy Hour', *British Journal of Special Education*, 28 (1) 30–4.

Frater, G. (2000) *Securing Boys' Literacy*. London: The Basic Skills Agency.

Gerschel, L. (1998) 'Equal opportunities and special educational needs: equity and inclusion', in C. Tilstone, L. Florian and R. Rose (eds) *Promoting Inclusive Practice*. London: Routledge.

Gillborn, D. (2001) 'Raising standards or rationalising education? Racism and social justice in policy and practice', *Support for Learning*, 16 (3) 105–11.

Gillborn, D. and Mirza, H. S. (2000) *Educational Inequality: Mapping Race, Class and Gender (a Synthesis of Research Evidence*. HMI 232). London: Ofsted.

Green, L. (1993) 'Possible gender bias within teachers' perceptions of pupils with special needs', *Support for Learning*, 8 (2) 78–80.

Gross, J. (1996) 'The weight of the evidence: Parental advocacy and resource allocation to children with statements of special educational need', *Support for Learning*, 11 (1) 3–8.

Henry, J. (2001a) 'Boy-friendly tests unfair say heads', *Times Educational Supplement*, 25/5/2001, p. 3.

Henry, J. (2001b) 'Help for the boys helps the girls', *Times Educational Supplement*, 1/6/2001, p. 5.

Hill, J. (1994) 'The paradox of gender: Sex stereotyping within statementing procedures', *British Educational Research Journal*, 20 (3) 345–55.

Holland, V. (1998) 'Underachieving boys; problems and solutions', *Support for Learning*, 13(4) 174–8.

Klein, R. (1999) *Defying Disaffection: How Schools are Winning the Hearts and Minds of Reluctant Students*. Stoke-on-Trent: Trentham Books.

Mac an Ghaill, M. (1994) *The Making of Men: Masculinities, Sexualities and Schooling*. Buckingham: Open University Press.

Macpherson of Cluny, Sir William (1999) *The Stephen Lawrence Inquiry (The Macpherson Report, CM 4262-1)*. London: The Stationery Office.

Male, D. (2000) 'Who goes to MLD schools?', *British Journal of Special Education*, 23 (1) 35–41.

McNamara, S. and Moreton, G. (1995) *Changing Behaviour: Teaching Children with Emotional and Behavioural Difficulties in Primary and Secondary Classrooms*. London: David Fulton.

Millard, E. (1997) *Differently Literate: Boys, Girls and the Schooling of Literacy*. London: Falmer Press.

Mittler, P. (1999) 'Equal Opportunities – for whom?', *British Journal of Special Education*, 26 (1) 3–7.

Mittler, P. (2000) *Working Towards Inclusive Education: Social Contexts*. London: David Fulton Publishers.

Mortimore, P., Sammons, P., Stoll, L., Lewis, D. and Ecob, R. (1988) *School Matters: The Junior School Years*. London: Open Books.

Newham LEA (2001) *Girls' Voices: Are they on the Agenda?* London: London Borough of Newham (The Girls' Project, Tunmarsh Centre, Tunmarsh Lane, E13 9NB).

Noble C. and Bradford, W. (2000) *Getting it Right for Boys...and Girls*. London: Roudedge.

O'Brien, T. (1998) 'The Millenium Curriculum: Confronting the Issues and Proposing Solutions', *Support for Learning*, 13 (4) 147–52.

Office for Standards in Education (Ofsted) (1993) *Boys and English*. London: Ofsted.

Office for Standards in Education (Ofsted) (2000a) *Evaluating Educational Inclusion: Guidance for Inspectors and Schools* (HMI 235). London: Ofsted.

Office for Standards in Education (Ofsted) (2000b) *The National Literacy Strategy in Special Schools 1998–2000* (HMI 238). London: Ofsted.

Office for Standards in Education (Ofsted) (2001) *The National Numeracy Strategy in Special Schools. An Evaluation of the First Year* (HMI 267). London: Ofsted.

Ollerton, M. (2001) 'Inclusion and entitlement, equality of opportunity and quality of curriculum provision', *Support for Learning*, 16 (1) 35–40.

Osler, A. (1997) *Exclusion from School and Racial Equality: Research Report*. London: Commission for Racial Equality.

Osler, A., Walting, R., Busher, H., Cole, T. and White, A. (2001) *Reasons for Exclusion (Research Report 244)*. London: DfEE.

Pickering, J. (1997) *Raising Boys' Achievement*. Stafford: Network Educational Press.

Qualifications and Curriculum Authority (QCA) (1998) *Can Do Better: Raising Boys' Attainment in English*. London: QCA.

Qualifications and Curriculum Authority (QCA) and DfEE (2001) *Planning Teaching and Assessing the Curriculum for Pupils with Learning Difficulties*. London: QCA.

Rivers, I. (2000) 'Social exclusion, absenteeism and sexual minority youth', *Support for Learning*, 15 (1) 13–18.

Rundell, S. (2001) 'How to improve his stories', *Times Educational Supplement*, 1/6/2001, p. 28.

Scott, L. (2001) 'Adding drama! Sex and relationships for children with learning difficulties', *Sex Education Matters*, 24, Spring 2001, pp. 4–5.

Sewell, T. (1997) *Black Masculinities and Schooling: How Black Boys Survive Modern Schooling*. Stoke-on-Trent: Trentham Books.

Shah, R. (1995) *The Silent Minority: Children with Disability in Asian Families* (Revised edition). London: National Children's Bureau.

Stewart, D. and Ray, C. (2001) Ensuring entitlement: sex and relationships education for disabled children. Forum fact sheet from Sex Education Forum and Council for Disabled Children. London: National Children's Bureau.

Tierney, T. and Dowd, R. (2000) 'The use of social skills groups to support girls with emotional difficulties in secondary schools', *Support for Learning*, 15 (2) 82–5.

Torrance, D. A. (2000) 'Qualitative studies into bullying within special schools', *British Journal of Special Education*, 27 (1) 16–21.

Troyna, B. and Siraj-Blatchford, I. (1993) 'Providing support or denying access? The experience of students designated as ESL or SN in a multi-cultural school', *Educational Review*, 45 (1) 3–11.

Vardill, R. (1996) 'Imbalance in the numbers of boys and girls identified for referral to educational psychologists: Some issues', *Support for Learning*, 11 (3) 123–9.

Warner, R. (1999) 'The views of Bangladeshi parents on the special school attended by their young children with severe learning difficulties', *British Journal of Special Education*, 26 (4) 218–23.

Wilson, G. (2000) 'The effects of season of birth, sex, cognitive abilities on the assessment of special educational needs', *Educational Psychology*, 20 (2) 153–66.

Wright, C., Weekes, D. and McGlaughlin, A. (2000) *'Race', Gender and Exclusion from School*. London: Falmer Press.

# PART III

# EXCLUSION FROM SCHOOL
Problems and challenges

# CHAPTER 8

# THE CHALLENGE OF TRUANCY AND SCHOOL ABSENTEEISM

## K. Reid

*Truancy: Short and Long-term Solutions* (2002), London and New York: RoutledgeFalmer, pp. 1–19

## The extent of effort

More is happening to combat truancy and absenteeism in schools throughout the United Kingdom than ever before. The real question is: how much difference are all these initiatives making? And the simple truth is that no one really knows or can be certain.

Certainly, no one can be blamed for making a lack of effort. Not the DfES, Scottish Parliament or Welsh or Northern Ireland Assemblies. In fact, after reading this chapter, you may feel it is a question of initiative-itis. Moreover, no one can be really certain of which preventative initiatives are working better than others. Perhaps there is a feeling amongst high office holders that all new innovations to improve school attendance are helpful even if only from a raising awareness perspective.

Equally, teachers and headteachers in schools are playing their part. Many of them and their staff are spending long hours in the detection, prevention and investigation of their pupils' non-attendance. Most schools now have policy documents on attendance and promote a range of school-based solutions. Re-integration strategies to enable pupils to return and re-settle in schools generally remain weak and are often non-existent. This is generally true irrespective of whether the cause for the absence is a long-term illness, visit abroad or a period of truancy. In fact, many schools do not currently even have appropriate short-term re-integration or return to school strategies in place if evidence from truancy patrols is to be believed. In Swansea, for example, truancy patrols are regularly picking up the same pupils in the afternoon as those they returned to their schools in the morning, even though the process involves the school signing a form to acknowledge their pupils have been returned safely to them. Certainly, therefore, some schools are not retaining their disaffected pupils for very long.

Education welfare officers, too, are working their socks off despite national restructuring issues. Unfortunately, this service is notoriously blighted by having no national and uniform conditions of service. In some parts of the United Kingdom the service is seriously under strength. One Education Welfare Officer (EWO) in north-west England told a conference in Manchester in March 2001 that she was responsible for attendance issues at fourteen comprehensive schools and all their feeder primaries. Imagine trying to do that job! Following an internal review, one authority in South Wales will have only two full-time EWOs after September 2001. The same area once had thirty-five employees. So, on the one hand, whilst more initiatives than ever are taking place, and whilst schools are playing their part, the service with overall responsibility for attendance issues locally is struggling hugely. Moreover, the range and responsibilities given to the education welfare service are ever increasing partly because of new initiatives and partly because of legislative requirements. Thus, as from April 2001, the education welfare service has taken on a key role as part of the Connexions Service in England.

## The extent of truancy

Against this background of sheer gritty professional effort, illegal work for under-age schoolchildren continues to thrive. The TUC/MORI (2001) poll reported that nearly half a million school-age children are engaged in illegal work. Of these, approximately 100,000 truant from school on a daily basis in order to be able to do so.

And herein lies another serious deterrent to successful professional practice. No-one can be really sure precisely how many pupils are missing school daily. The government would have us believe that there are only 50,000 truants from schools in England on a regular basis. This is 0.7 per cent of the English school-age population. But, how do they reach this conclusion and are they certain of their data? If the real figure for truancy from schools in England is only 50,000, do we really have such a major problem? In fact, one might ask why is so much time being spent on one new initiative after another if this is the real extent of the phenomenon? Why, indeed, are the Department for Education and Skills (DfES) and other departments spending millions of pounds annually to combat it?

The issue is, of course, one of definition. Where does the 50,000 truancy figure come from? There are no universally agreed and uniform national statistics and those which have been collected in earlier decades suggest the national truancy rate *per se* is around 2.2 per cent of pupils daily (Reid, 1985). The suspicion is that the current truancy rate being used by the DfES excludes certain categories of pupils such as parental-condoned absentees because these are often marked as authorised absences within schools. Yet, parental-condoned absentees are really parental-condoned truants. And, in a whole array of surveys conducted over the past forty years, parental-condoned absentees tend to make up the single largest category of truants. Equally the returns to the DfES exclude post-registration truants and specific lesson absentees. In some schools these can also make up the largest single category of truants (O'Keefe *et al.*, 1993).

And, there is a much greater and more serious contributory problem – the recording of absence within schools. At present, the system is much too complicated and open to abuse, sometimes for the best of reasons. The major issue revolves around detecting and recording authorised from non-authorised absence. In some schools staff are instructed not to record unauthorised absence unless it is for exceptional circumstances. For example, pupils who turn up to school after a period of absence without good reason are asked to return the following day with a note providing a reason for the absence. The pupil's absence is then recorded as authorised in whichever category is subsequently chosen. By contrast, the same pupil under a different school's internal practices is marked as unauthorised absence. Surprisingly, some schools now go as far as giving returning pupils a list from which they are asked to tick a box selecting the reason for their absence. Thus, some schools are deliberately colluding with their pupils in order to maintain high attendance figures. In these cases, no unauthorised absences are ever recorded. Therefore, practical and policy differences between internal procedures for recording absence is one of the main reasons for the large variations in rates between schools' attendance. These differences are exacerbated by league tables although there are several other reasons for this phenomenon as well.

Take another example. Regulations regarding the taking of family holidays during school time are frequently misunderstood or misinterpreted. Officially, pupils are entitled up to ten days' holiday time during the school year with the prior consent of the headteacher. The parental application should be made in writing to the school. However, in practice in many schools, pupils who are taken on family holidays during term-time are marked as authorised absence even though they do not have the prior consent of the headteacher. In other schools, they are marked as unauthorised. At one conference held in the north of England, on a show of hands around half the teacher delegates reported that pupils on family holidays were marked as authorised absence; provided the school had been sent an official note or letter from a parent. In the other half of schools, taking family holidays is marked as unauthorised absence. Hence, it is clear that all the guiding regulations are simply not understood by schools. Given the constant changes of staffing in some schools and Local Education Authorities (LEAs) (school districts), perhaps this is hardly surprising. In one LEA in northwest England more pupil absences are attributable to family holidays than for all other categories put together. This is by no means unusual. In fact, there are several LEAs which currently report that absences due to family holidays are the single largest category of non-attendance and their greatest cause for concern.

Another grey area is parental-condoned absence. Again, a high proportion of schools mark parental-condoned absence as authorised absence. This practice can occur irrespective of whether parents retrospectively provide a note or whether a pupil is found to be with a parent in say, a shopping centre during a truancy sweep. This is one of the reasons why so many non-attenders currently being picked up by truancy sweeps are carrying 'excuse notes' in their pockets. Some, of these notes have been found to be written by a parent, others by the truants themselves or by a friend. This practice shows that even some truants are getting the message. As long as you have a note of some kind, the school is less likely to be as concerned about your absence.

All the variations between schools in practice mean that it is difficult to establish an accurate daily figure either for truancy or for other forms of non-attendance. Surveys suggest that between 600,000 and 1.2 million pupils miss school daily. Of these, a high proportion are young pupils who are away from primary or infants schools for reasons of illness. Official studies undertaken of attendance during a day, a week, a term and a school year continue to confirm findings emanating in the 1970s that the national daily average for attendance is between 85 and 92 per cent of secondary-aged pupils (Reid, 1985, 1999). The one-day national study on attendance of all secondary and middle schools in England and Wales (DES, 1975) reported that 9.9 per cent of all pupils were absent on the day. Of these, 22.7 per cent (2.2 per cent of all pupils) had no legitimate reason for their absence. The NACEWO Survey (1975) of secondary pupils in sixteen LEAs found 24 per cent of pupils to be absent on the day. The Pack Report (Scottish Education Department, 1977) found 15 per cent of pupils to have been unaccountably absent on at least one occasion during a six-week period.

Variations in attendance rates continue to abound. There are huge local variations by school, by time of year, by day of the week and by geographical location, with some large urban inner cities amongst the highest for non-attendance rates. Some rural areas are also disproportionately high. South Wales and Glasgow continue to have some of the highest rates for truancy and non-attendance in the United Kingdom.

But, whereas collecting accurate attendance statistics used to be a fairly routine matter, nowadays, with so many different categories being used to classify authorised absence, it is almost impossible to classify like with like. Not only do internal school policies and practice vary but so do those within LEAs. After all, no headteacher wishes her school to be at the bottom of a league table on attendance. Neither do LEAs wish to appear bottom of their regional league tables on attendance.

Classifying attendance would in some ways be very much simpler if the registration process reverted to the old system of merely recording those 'present' or 'absent'. Or, using today's terms, the absence column could be simply divided into two categories: either authorised (e.g. a visit to the dentist) or unauthorised absence (e.g. truancy, parental-condoned absenteeism). At least we might then have more accurate daily totals for pupils in school as well as for those who were not. Currently, too many headteachers have a vested interest in ensuring that their unauthorised non-attendance returns are kept as low as possible by obfuscating the reasons between authorised and unauthorised absence.

As the author has travelled around the United Kingdom on visits to schools, LEAs and to attend conferences on attendance-related issues, it has become increasingly obvious that the officially published statistics do not add up. You only have to consider the large number of secondary schools recently put into special measures partly because of their low attendance. Or, the number in which attendance is the first issue on Ofsted or Estyn action plans. Or, the large number of secondary schools whose overall attendance rates are below 80 per cent. Or, the large number of schools who have reported a decrease in attendance particularly in years 10 and 11 since the introduction of the National Curriculum. Or, the large number of headteachers, LEA officers and EWOs who will tell you in private with professional dismay about the differences between their official attendance returns and the reality on the ground. In an age when blame culture thrives, headteachers and directors of education can lose their jobs (and have done so) for appearing bottom of performance-related and attendance league tables, is it hardly surprising that the issue is fudged? After all, within this process, everyone benefits and no one is really sure quite who to blame.

So, despite all the good work of government departments, schools, LEAs, caring professionals and EWOs, truancy and other forms of non-attendance continue to flourish in British schools almost unchanged over previous decades and generations (Hoyle, 1998). And, whatever the true daily figure for truancy and other forms of non-attendance, the evidence from schools and professionals is that the problem is at least as great today as it was thirty, fifty, seventy or a hundred years ago. Moreover, we still need to find better ways of detecting and recording specific lesson absence, post-registration truancy and parental-condoned absence/truancy.

## Professional issues

There remain several outstanding professional issues which continue to cause concern. One of these is the work of the magistrate's court in attendance cases.

Here, also, there is very little consistency in practice. Variations in outcomes by magistrate, locality and region abound. Some magistrates are keen on parenting orders. Others are not. The DfFS believes parenting orders are used too infrequently. Some impose high fines. Others do not. Some clerks plan for attendance cases to be heard on the same day one after another. Most do not. In fact, in some areas clerks tend to fit attendance cases in and around other perceived more significant matters, thereby giving attendance cases too low a priority. Unfortunately, too few magistrates or magistrates' clerks have been trained in the subtleties or implications of attendance-related issues.

Similarly, some local authority social service departments have increasingly given attendance-related issues a lower priority than they should, often leaving attendance cases to the social-work skills of education welfare officers. Again, differences in local practices vary enormously. In many parts of the United Kingdom, it is becoming accepted as the norm that the social services are only seriously concerned in attendance cases when the child (or a parent) is perceived to be at risk perhaps because it is a child abuse matter or the subject of a care order. This is unfortunate and often seriously hampers joined-up interdisciplinary good practice.

The reverse is true in the case of the police. The police have become much more interested in attendance cases since the 1998 Criminal Justice Act and the introduction of truancy patrols. Following the publication of the first report on truancy and social exclusion (Cabinet Office, 1998) which highlighted the clear link between the genesis of truancy and day-time crime conducted by truants, as well as the link between juvenile and adult criminality, New Labour has been making a concerted effort to combat the links between truancy and crime. During March 2001, the DfES and Home Office launched a series of major seminars throughout England on the theme of Truancy and Crime: Together We'll Tackle It. Two hundred and fifty invited professionals from across the caring professions attended each of these events. From these people, new regional committees have been established to practise and share joined-up interdisciplinary and multidisciplinary good practice on truancy and school attendance issues. Partners in the venture include headteachers, teachers, the police, education welfare officers, magistrates, social workers, youth workers, community team workers, pupil referral unit staff and social inclusion officers as well as civil servants from the DfES. These regional committees provide a unique opportunity to establish agreed ways forward to combat truancy and crime and to further improve the boundaries between the professions. Emergent local information technology web-sites on good practice are to provide a key form of linkage between the groups alongside a national DfES database. This regional initiative is, of course, also supporting some of the DfESs other policy initiatives relating to truancy and attendance.

## Truancy and crime

Why is truancy so important in the fight against crime? Apart from the fact that many thousands of pupils are missing school daily, some of whom could be at risk, there are other reasons: 23 per cent of young people sentenced in court have engaged in truancy. A high proportion of young offenders are truants and often commit serious crimes while truanting (Reid, 1986). Moreover, truants are more likely to end up unemployed and have poor life chances – socially, professionally and economically (Reid, 1999).

In England, there have recently been a whole host of central government initiatives aimed at reducing the link between truancy and youth crime. These include:

(a)  a co-ordinated nationwide programme of truancy sweeps;
(b)  new legislation which ensures that parents of persistent truants have to go to court and face tougher fines;
(c)  new funding of £11 million for electronic registration schemes in 500 schools in 2002/3; Sheffield LEA, for example, is one authority at the forefront of these developments;
(d)  truancy buster awards;
(e)  the formation of a cross-Whitehall Group including DfES, Home Office, Children and Young People's Unit (CYPU), Department of Health and Social Exclusion Unit which meets regularly to discuss issues affecting the truancy and crime agenda.

Further government-led schemes are included in the next section on initiatives in England.

We will now consider how police and schools working together can tackle truancy, crime and disorder. First, this is what schools can do. Headteachers can give a public commitment to local initiatives to reduce crime and anti-social behaviour. Schools can help to identify pupils who are at a high risk of being involved in anti-social or criminal behaviour and work with local agencies to help combat this behaviour. They can help to establish a youth action group focusing on crime prevention. They can involve police in classroom activities, where appropriate, to help pupils form positive relationships with the police. They can advise the police of any actual criminal activity or suspicious behaviour. Finally, they can have effective first-day absence schemes: in particular, have in place competent electronic registration schemes which will enable them to contact parent(s) or guardian(s) on the first day of a child's absence.

Second, the police can do the following:

(a)  participate in truancy sweeps;
(b)  work closely with schools to help challenge young people's attitudes to criminal behaviour;
(c)  develop youth participation in community projects;
(d)  work with schools to develop joint truancy protocol.

Other local issues for schools and the police to consider together are: protocols with other caring agencies; information sharing; the vexed problem of confidentiality; the relationship between drugs-related activity and truancy; multiracial dimensions; mobile phone policies and the use or otherwise of restorative justice in schools.

Working in partnership means that schools should be readily involved with other partners to support anti-truancy initiatives. Schools should appoint a dedicated teacher as police liaison officer. Schools need to work with other local key players in the area such as community agencies, child guidance and, at a practical level, bus companies. Schools should also be represented on community safety partnerships. Evidence suggests that the best and most successful results tend to happen when police and schools target their efforts on high-risk individuals and help to identify 'hot spot' locations. Some of these 'hot spot' locations can often be frequented by truants.

## Initiatives in England

The DfES is spending large sums of money on a variety of initiatives to combat truancy and, in some cases, related crime. The main schemes implemented by New Labour and organised by the DfES include:

(a) *Social Inclusion: Pupil Support (SIPS) grant* The government has set schools a target to reduce truancy and exclusion by a third and provide a full-time education to all pupils who are excluded by 2002 To help schools and LEAs meet these targets, the DfES provided £174 million to schools and LEAs in 2001/2; 33 per cent more than available in 2000/1 and a tenfold increase since 1996/7. The majority of the grant is devolved to schools so that they can decide how best to meet the needs of disaffected pupils before the need to exclude. The £174 million includes £127 million for schools and £36 million for authorities under the SIPS grant. In addition, a further £10 million is available from the Capital and Infrastructure grant to fund new onsite learning support units in schools. Finally, the department provides a further £1 million to flexibly support the national drive against truancy.

(b) *Connexions Service* Connexions is the name of the multi-agency support service that is available for all 13–19-year-olds and which commenced on 1 April 2001 and was phased in over the next 2–3 years. Connexions brings together a range of partners currently working with young people, such as schools, colleges, career services, the youth service, EWS, health agencies, and youth offending teams in order to provide a coherent, holistic package of support that enables every young person to remain engaged in learning and make a successful transition to adulthood. Connexions is designed to ensure that every teenager receives individual and appropriate learning and career advice.

(c) *Childrens Fund* The Children's Fund has been established as a key part of the government's strategy to tackle child poverty and social exclusion. It attempts to ensure that vulnerable children get the best start in life, remain on track in their early years, flourish in secondary school and choose to stay on in education and training at 16.

The Children's Fund supports two major programmes. £380 million of the Fund is distributed to local partnerships to develop preventive services to identify children and young people aged between 5 and 13 who are showing early signs of difficulty and provide them and their families with the support they need to overcome barriers and disadvantage. £70 million is distributed directly to local community groups through a network of local funds.

(d) *National Strategy for Neighbourhood Renewal (NSNR)* The NSNR is about turning round the most deprived neighbourhoods by tackling the underlying causes of urban and rural poverty. It is a key priority for No. 10 and has cross-Whitehall ownership. The document 'A New Commitment to Neighbourhood Renewal: National Strategy Action Plan' was launched by the Prime Minister on 15 January 2001 in East London. It marks a radical change in the way government is tackling social exclusion. The idea is to gradually rid the country of a sub-culture of dependence, deprivation and violence that is the breeding ground for disaffection, truancy and crime.

(e) *Sure Start* Sure Start promotes the physical, intellectual, social and emotional development of young children by ensuring that children are ready to flourish when they start school. By 2004, the DfES was investing almost £500 million each year in Sure Start, reaching a third of children under the age of 4 born to poor families. In addition, New Labour is planning bursaries for all new children at birth which will be invested for their later use in education or to provide them with a start in adult life.

(f) *Learning Mentors in Excellence in Cities*   There are some 1,500 learning mentors in post in Excellence in Cities secondary schools and by the end of 2001 also 900 in primary schools in the areas. By 2004, there was an estimated total of 3,200 learning mentors in primary and secondary schools in Excellence in Cities and the new Excellence Clusters.

As part of the Excellence in Cities programme, learning mentors are school-based employees who, together with teaching and pastoral staff, assess, identify and work with those pupils who need extra help to overcome barriers to learning inside and outside school. In this way, they take some of the burden off teachers, who often feel as though they should be helping pupils to overcome problems inside and outside school. Having a learning mentor to help pupils tackle these problems frees teachers to teach. Some headteachers who are not in Excellence in Cities areas are using their school improvement funding to recruit their own learning mentors.

(g) *Education Action Zones*   Education Action Zones (EAZs) were proposed in the White Paper 'Excellence in Schools' and have their legislative basis in the School Standards and Framework Act, 1998. EAZs were intended to create urgent focus on raising standards through local partnerships between parents, schools, businesses, LEAs, TECs and others. Zone initiatives generally focus on four main themes: improving the quality of teaching and improving the quality of learning; social inclusion including attendance; providing support to families and providing support to pupils; and working with business and other organisations. EAZs have now been merged into other initiatives.

(h) *On Track*   On Track is a long-term crime reduction programme aimed at preventing children at risk of getting involved in crime. It is a key element of the government's agenda on tackling the causes of crime. The programme was launched at the end of 1999. Twenty-four areas were initially selected to develop On Track projects. Partnerships in each area consisting of the key agencies that work with families and children have put together detailed delivery plans and are implementing them. Each area initially receives funding of around £400,000. The programmes are expected to be funded for seven years. The projects are based in high crime, high deprivation communities.

The On Track programme is currently being led by a team made up of staff from the Family Policy Unit and the Research, Development and Statistics Directorate of the Home Office. It is overseen by a project board involving a range of government departments. Since April 2001, On Track has been incorporated into the new Children's Fund and the projects are monitored and supported by the government's Children and Young People's Unit.

## The National Curriculum

There is considerable anecdotal evidence amongst teachers that the originally prescribed and rigid nature of the National Curriculum was hampering their efforts within schools to combat disaffection and attendance-related issues. Yet, no one can be certain of the real extent of pupils' non-attendance which is related to the National Curriculum. We do know that a lot of pupils are taking subjects in schools, including GCSEs, in which they have little interest or aptitude. As some pupils begin to recognise that they are unlikely to achieve good passes at

GCSE-level, and have little interest in some of their subjects, so their attendance starts to become more erratic.

It is for this reason that the DfES empowered schools to introduce more flexibility into the National Curriculum. First, schools were permitted to allow disaffected pupils the chance to spend up to half their allocated time on vocationally-orientated subjects often outside schools in, for example, a further education college. Second, schools are in the process of introducing vocational GCSEs which it is hoped will cater better for disillusioned pupils. Third, the DfES is considering extending vocational partnerships for pupils aged 14 or over. These partnerships might involve longer work placements with local business partners or other special partners which could mean that certain categories of pupils might remain at school after 14 in a part-time capacity.

Headteachers and teachers' professional organisations are welcoming the advent of much greater flexibility in the management and implementation of the National Curriculum within schools. Only time will tell whether these new initiatives will make a real impact upon truancy and other forms of non-attendance.

## Familial breakdown

Despite all the considerable efforts being made by a whole host of caring professionals and by government, truancy and other forms of non-attendance from school are constantly being refuelled by another parallel factor. Most persistent school absentees emanate from deprived home backgrounds often suffering from multiple deprivation, low social class and with a whole host of social, psychological and institutional aspects providing the root cause for their non-attendance in school (Reid, 1985, 1999). Yet, just as standards in school are being driven up, so the number of children attending schools from broken or turbulent homes is ever increasing.

Truancy, in one very real sense, mirrors the spiralling decline in society's standards. Far too many children are being caught up as the innocent victims of marital break-up, familial disharmony and familial dysfunction. Given their lack of stability at home, many pupils' self-concepts are being lowered often to the point where the natural parental support they need for their schooling is non-existent. As their personal confusion at home is compounded by a lack of success at school, some pupils decide to play truant or start missing occasional days or lessons. Whereas before the 1950s and early 1960s, divorce or parental separation was unusual, today it is becoming the norm for up to half of all pupils as they go through their school lives. And this figure keeps on rising. Moreover, there is often a communication gap between the parents of the needy child and the school.

Therefore, the origins of truancy are thriving. The increasing number of pupils who require regular emotional help and support means that however hard teachers and caring professionals work to support their pupils, they are losing out against the sheer weight of numbers. And it is this key factor that is at the heart of the need for vigilance in the continual fight against truancy and other forms of non-attendance. As professional practice improves, so people are having to work harder all the time in order to maintain the status quo by containing the ever growing numbers of potentially serious child-related problems. Just imagine what would happen if all the professional and state help and support currently being given to these children and their families stopped overnight. In what condition would British society be left?

Whilst familial breakdown appears to be on the continual increase, so professionals are having to learn to cope with the consequences of working and living in a multicultural society which also brings with it new pressures for schools. Early studies suggest that underachievement, truancy and related criminal activity appear to be higher in inner city and cosmopolitan regions (Social Exclusion Report, 1988). Yet, there remains very little specific information on the reasons for this trend or on whether the causes of truancy amongst minority multiracial groups are the same as those for the indigenous population.

## The pressure of truancy

The pressure upon schools caused by the local consequences of truancy tends to vary dependent upon its nature, extent and the efforts of the local media. There are three major forms of truancy. The first is low-level truancy which can be equated with harmless fun, growing up and natural child rebellion. This is manifest by usually regular attending and able pupils taking the occasional day off school as an alternative to their strict daily routines. Such truancy is regarded as less than serious and almost as a healthy part of growing up.

The second type is of persistent low levels of truancy which is manifest by significant parental-condoned absenteeism, specific lesson absence and post-registration truancy. To the majority of the public, persistent low levels of truancy are not seen as a major symptom of social dysfunction but of the extent to which schools are in or out of control of their pupils and are educating or not educating them properly.

The third type is high-level truancy. This equates with pupils whose schooling is seriously damaged by non-attendance, disruptive behaviour and links with crime. It is normally this latter form of truancy which grabs the national and local headlines and receives most attention.

Yet, at present, there is no way of differentiating between the extent of these forms of truancy. Indeed, most schools probably include pupils from all three categories to a greater or lesser extent. Clearly, high truancy schools will contain a greater proportion of high-level truancy cases than those with lower levels of absenteeism.

Equally, apart from the author's own work (Reid, 1985, 1999), there is no way of distinguishing between the extent of traditional, psychological and institutional absence on a school-by-school basis. There is also no current way of distinguishing between the five different types of parent(s) who are perceived by the authorities to 'condone' absence. That there are in reality four different types of parent(s) who condone their children's absence while the fifth category actually endeavours to do everything possible to ensure their children attend school but are unable to do so. Hence, the study of truancy *per se* is by no means quite as simple as some people seem to believe.

## Truancy and the United Kingdom

One of the questions repeatedly asked is why high truancy and absenteeism rates are such a hallmark of schools in Britain when, for example, in many other countries in Europe equivalent rates are minimal. So far, no one can answer this question with certainty. We know that rates of truancy and absenteeism have been high in the United Kingdom since the introduction of compulsory schooling. We know the rates increased significantly in some parts of Britain after the introduction of comprehensives. We also know that absences have always been much higher in years 10 and 11 than in earlier years. Recent evidence however, indicates that the onset of absenteeism is becoming younger and younger. Whereas thirty years ago, truancy from primary schools was almost unknown, today up to 35 per cent of pupils begin their histories of non-attendance whilst at primary school (Reid, 1999).

It is also well known that the causes of non-attendance amongst persistent school absentees are unique and diverse (Reid, 1985). Schools are notoriously poor at detecting the causes of initial absentees and taking early steps to rectify the situation (Reid, 1985). Moreover, the more pupils absent themselves, the more confident and brazen they tend to become over a period of time.

Ofsted have shared the concern of the DfES about attendance rates within some primary and secondary schools. This is why school attendance targets were raised in late 2001 from 90 to 92 per cent for secondary schools and to 95 per cent for primary schools. Ofsted and the DfES are also worried about the increasing numbers of 'missing children' from school rolls, the numbers of pupils who are not on any official school register, and the number of pupils for whom the 'specific trigger' for their absence appears to be the primary secondary transfer stage or the selection of public examinations between years 9 and 10.

## Pupils' traits

Evidence from research so far suggests that there are certain psychological traits within some pupils which make them more prone to absenteeism than their peers. These include lower general levels of self-esteem, lower academic self-concepts, a tendency (especially amongst institutional absentees) towards neurotic and anti-social conduct, a susceptibility towards being vulnerable to peer group pressure (especially amongst traditional and psychological absentees) and bullying, reacting badly to poor academic progress and social failure within schools, having vulnerable personalities, being prone to illness or psychosomatic conditions (allergies, asthma, and so on), having unusual appearances (e.g. obesity) or being picked upon by staff within schools (Reid, 1999). It is quite probable that further personality aspects will be linked to persistent absentees over time although, to date, research has not proved any other clear-cut traits.

What we do know is that the age of maturation amongst pupils – both boys and girls – is becoming younger all the time. Whereas the age of puberty amongst girls a hundred years ago was around $15\frac{1}{2}$ to 16, today it is between 12 and 13. Many girls now start to menstruate at primary school. Even some boys have broken voices by the age of 12. Therefore, the tendency towards even earlier maturation begs the question as to whether schools have changed sufficiently over time in recognition of their pupils' needs.

The answer is almost certainly no. Average secondary schools only allow 'special' privileges in school for 'sixth formers'. Even the application of these rights varies from school to school. Within most comprehensives, there are few, if any, facilities for younger age pupils. Explicitly, year 9, 10 and 11 pupils tend not to have their own separate common rooms, tuck shops, counsels or quiet rooms. In many schools, they do not even have their own independent access to information technology or their own lockers. Typically, in most schools, space is limited, pupils are cramped and the design and state of repair of some buildings woefully inadequate. Is it any wonder therefore, that some underachieving pupils who already feel inadequate because of their adverse social and home backgrounds and perceived limited aptitude react in the way they do by missing school? These psychological feelings of inadequacy are exacerbated by the fact that today there is much more peer and social pressure exerted upon pupils than in previous generations.

The effects of advertising aimed at teenagers means that they are all wanting to grow up as soon as possible. In real terms, the childhood phase is shortening. Secondary schools are catering for young adults who wish their near-adult status to be recognised.

Ask many parents and you will find that one of the chief complaints of their children is that teachers should have more respect for them. The typical daily school regime for most pupils is rule-orientated, monotonous and geared towards the masses rather than focused upon individual needs. In fact, the increased pressures upon teachers since the introduction of the National Curriculum, attainment targets, records of achievement and policies of devolution to schools, had meant that many pupils feel even more vulnerable than before. It is becoming more and more difficult to find individual time for pupils. Against this argument, of course, is the increased emphasis upon literacy and numeracy, on mentoring, or providing classroom assistants as well as more proactive special needs policies. There is little doubt that schools are becoming busier and busier. And, the demands of paperwork are equally ever increasing.

Nevertheless, it is clear that regular non-attenders are found among those pupils whose literacy and numeracy scores are two or more years (often three or four) behind their peers by the ages of 7, 9 and 11. Unless these pupils receive sufficient and appropriate individual and group support to assist them with their numeric and literacy skills, they will remain at risk of long-term school failure and of dropping out of a system in which they receive constant negative reinforcement in the form of low grades, being placed in the bottom sets and being unable to choose subject for public examination from the same list as their higher achieving peers (e.g. second languages).

The challenge to teachers and to teaching as a profession is to find ways of being able to get to know and work with all pupils on a needs-orientated and individual basis which not only protects pupils' levels of self-esteem but also enables them to feel that they are being successful and making progress. Sadly, despite some laudable recent initiatives, the opposite fate continues to be the norm for far too many pupils. And it is precisely these pupils who become truants and persistent non-attenders.

There is good evidence for making this assertion. Reid (2000, Unit 9) has presented evidence on factors which cause pupils to miss school; a checklist of pupil-related factors which cause truants to miss school; a checklist of teacher-related factors which cause pupils to miss school; reasons given by persistent absentees for missing school; how regular attenders in years 9, 10 and 11 think school can be improved; how truants think schools can be improved and the qualities which truants and regular attendees in years 9, 10 and 11 look for in good teachers.

Reid's work has also shown that once pupils have begun to absent themselves from school, and the initial 'cause' lies undetected, it is likely that the pattern of absence will continue and escalate throughout the pupils' subsequent school careers. This reinforces the need for (a) early identification; (b) early preventative strategies operating in schools; and (c) for schools to implement appropriate re-integration strategies for short- and long-term absentees once they return to school. Future research may be able to show that absentees will return to school and start to attend regularly when they see it as being relevant to their individual needs.

Through my research, teaching and consultancy activities over more than thirty years with truants and persistent absentees, certain points stand out clearly. First, playing truant imposes significant psychological consequences upon the individuals concerned. Second, the first act of truancy requires a certain amount of courage. Third, the vast majority of truants and persistent absentees are bored when absent from school. Fourth, the majority would never become persistent absentees or truants if they had their time over again. Fifth, the effects of playing truant include further reducing already fragile self-concepts, often to the point that it encourages a dependency culture to develop which, in some cases, continues throughout adult life. It is this very vulnerability which leads some absentees and truants into a shadowy and unhappy life ahead which can be punctuated by crime, failed relationships, poverty and frequent job changes. Very few school-aged truants become successful employees, businessmen or upstanding citizens within society. Many become totally dependent upon the state throughout their adult lives at a major cost to the taxpayer.

## Teachers' attitudes

Research also shows that the causes of truancy are unique, multidimensional and interdisciplinary (Reid, 1985). Sometimes teachers and schools are to blame in individual cases. Sometimes it is a pupil's own fault. Sometimes, it is the parent(s) and the pupil colluding together. Sometimes, it is the fault of schools, parent(s) and pupils. Too often however, pupils' own problems are exacerbated by the attitudes and/or culture within some schools. Examples of these unfavourable attitudes towards non-attenders are now presented. These views have been recorded verbatim from statements made by delegates at conferences on attendance and/or truancy over a two-year period starting in February 1999. Whereas most teachers are empathetic towards pupils with attendance problems, this is not universally the case; indeed, some teachers are notoriously unsympathetic towards truants and absentees as well as the whole notion of social inclusion.

> My school asked me to attend this course today. To be frank, I'd rather have been sent on anything else. It makes me feel that my head doesn't value my contribution to the school.
> (Male teacher, Conference in north of England, June 2000)

> When my head asked me to take charge of attendance I nearly flipped. Why me? I had no idea where or how to start.
> (Male teacher, Conference in Birmingham, May 2000)

> Quite frankly, when I find the class has only got twenty pupils instead of thirty I jump for joy and get on with it.
> (Female teacher, Manchester, November 1999)

> As a form tutor I can tell you that I have had no problems with any of my truants – apart from not seeing any of them.
> (Female teacher, Leeds, October 2000)

> I came into teaching to help people. Why should we be interested in helping people who do not want to help themselves?
> (Cardiff, October 2000)

## Headteachers' attitudes towards truancy

This unsympathetic attitude held amongst some teachers is also shared by some head-teachers as the examples below show:

> I object to the Government telling me that I have to spend my time on down-and-out pupils like truants and exclusion cases. I have enough paperwork already for three people without worrying any further about those who have either rejected the system or have caused my school serious problems.
>
> (Male headteacher, London, July 2000)

> In our school we have a simple philosophy. If they don't want to attend and learn, we are not going to force them. The school has enough problems without chasing any new ones.
>
> (Male headteacher, Liverpool, June 2000)

> I think schools should only have to teach and support those pupils who want to be there.
>
> (Female deputy headteacher, Bristol, October 2000)

> I care for all my pupils. However, I have to admit that the most frustrating are those who never attend and whose parents can't be bothered either.
>
> (Male primary head, Weston-Super-Mare, May 2000)

There now follow some interesting statements made by good attenders about persistent school absentees. Finally, some verbatim statements made by pupils in Scotland for missing school (Scottish Office Focus No. 5, 2000) concludes this short section.

## Good attenders' attitudes towards persistent school absentees

Many regular school attenders also tend to hold pupils like persistent absentees and truants in contempt as the following verbatim examples illustrate:

> If I had my way, I'd give them the cane, stop their pocket money and make them catch up with all their work on Saturdays and Sundays.
>
> (Year 9 boy, Cardiff, October 2000)

> I couldn't care whether they come to school or not as long as they don't interfere with me. My parents have told me that all truants come from broken homes and are jealous of people like me.
>
> (Year 6 boy, Ormskirk, July 2000)

> I feel sorry for truants. It must be awful being so dull that you can't read or write and are afraid of coming to school in case a teacher sees you.
>
> (Year 7 girl, Rhondda Cynon Taff, February 1999)

> I don't blame Shaun for not coming to school. Most of the class picks on him and so does Mr J. If I was him, I'd stay away as well.
>
> (Year 10 boy, South Midlands, December 2000)

Kevin used to come to school until he got blamed for something which wasn't his fault. He was made to stay behind and got put in detention when everyone in the class knew it was Harrison who flicked the pellet. I liked Kevin. Now, I never see him and he hates Mr C.

(Year 9 girl, Leeds, November 2000)

## Some reasons for not going to school in Scotland

Finally, it is worth noting the range of excuses given by pupils in Scotland for not attending their schools on a regular basis (see Scottish Office, 2000).

'I just felt sick every time I thought about turning the conrer and seeing that school in front of me.'

'I was always in the top class. I just couldn't stand everyone saying I was a swot. After second year I never went back.'

'There's nothing I'm good at. What's the point going every day just to learn what you already know – nothing.'

'I don't mind school but most of my pals just say let's go down the town, so you go.'

'The teachers all look down on you because you're from the scheme. It's like you're contaminating their lovely school.'

'Mr X makes me stand in the middle of the floor and say I am a pratt. It is humiliating. I'd rather have the hassle for dogging it than put up with that.'

'You can't go to the toilets or you get beaten up. Half the time you can't go into the playground because someone will do you over, and if they don't get you in school they get you on the way home.'

'I stay off sometimes when I'm at my dad's. My mum is really strict and makes me go in even if I've got a headache.'

'The only time I don't go in is when I have nae done ma homework. That can be quite often mind.'

'The white boys all slag me and my family. Sometimes they wait behind a hedge and throw stones at me.'

'If I'm late I think, well, maybe it's better to stay off sick than get a big row an that.'

'I often get a sore stomach or a sore throat and my mum just lets me stay in my bed.'

'I can be a lot mair use staying in the hoose looking after the weans for my ma.'

'I had a puni and it got doubled and I couldn't do it so I just thought I'd no go in.'

'I start my milk round at four. If I've been up late the night before I'm too knackered to go to school, I should maybe give it up but it's 45 quid a week and that's a lot of dough.'

'The only day I dog it is PE days. I just can't stand it.'

In another detailed study, Reid (1985) in *Truancy and School Absenteeism*, produced a breakdown of the detailed initial and later causes of the reasons given by 128 persistent absentees for missing school for at least 65 per cent of school time based on a three-year project undertaken with pupils in years 9, 10 and 11 from schools in South Wales supported by appropriate case studies. He found that school-based reasons were named most frequently by the persistent absentees for missing school with aspects relating to the curriculum, school transfers (all types), bullying, rules and punishment, boredom and poor teacher–pupil relationships to the forefront.

Why then should Britain top the European league tables on truancy and absenteeism? The answers seem to be in the resolution of the following points. First, by making sure that all pupils have their learning needs met on an individual as well as a group basis. Second, by preventing and overcoming the direct causes of truancy. These include poverty, the anti-educational attitudes of some parents, low literacy and numeracy skills, boredom amongst certain pupils whilst in school, poor undemanding teaching and adverse peer pressure allied to unattractive school buildings and adverse school climates. Is it purely coincidence, for example, that until now Britain has been one of the few parts of Europe not to have a complementary vocational curriculum for appropriate pupils alongside an academic one? And even now, there is a very long way to go before British schools have a proper alternative vocational curriculum which is valued by all parties in the education enterprise.

## Pupils' perspectives

It is clear that the government has begun its fight back against these festering negative ills. It will take a great deal of resources, time, effort and capital funding before the United Kingdom will cease to continue to top league tables for absenteeism in Europe. If the government is eventually to be successful, it has to take account of the needs of pupils like Sara, Kelly, Ryan and Jake and to ensure that all pupils are treated with respect; after all, this is everybody's fundamental human right.

### Sara

Sara is 14. She truants from school regularly usually condoned by her mother. She says she misses school because the 'teachers pick on me. I have all the dull teachers. Some of my friends have got really good teachers. The school needs more younger teachers like Mr P who really understands kids and knows how to talk to us. Some of the teachers should be put out to graze. They don't like teaching and they don't like kids. If I had good teachers, I'd go to school every day.'

### Kelly

Kelly is 12. She started to miss school at the age of nine. She is now a persistent absentee missing on average two to three days a week.

'I started to miss school because I did badly in my tests. Miss R read out my results in front of the whole class and said I could do better. The other kids started to call me names like "stupid". Then, when I came here, they told me I had to go into the bottom set for maths so I thought "Why should I bother?". Since then, things have got worse. I wish they would help me to read and write properly 'cause I know I've got to learn and one day get a job. At the moment, going to school is a waste of time. But, I'd like to go and start again if I could.'

## Ryan

Ryan is 14 and misses a lot of school to go surfing about which he is a fanatic. He accepts the problem is entirely of his own making and his truancy will do him no good in the long run.

'One day my parents will find out and they'll kill me. I get up and wait for the school bus. Then I hang around until my parents have gone to work. Every morning I wait for the mail to come in case there's a letter for my parents from the school. So far, I've ripped two up. When they come, I go back to school for a few days before bunking off again. I'd like to go to school part-time but I know no one will let me.'

## Jake

Jake is 15. Up until the age of 13, he was achieving well at school. After entering year 10 and starting his GCSE programme things started going badly wrong. 'I used to like all my subjects. Then, I was told what I could and could not take. I thought that I would leave school with a lot of good exam passes. Then, my year tutor told me that I was likely eventually to do GNVQs rather than A levels so I thought "Why bother?" I've decided to join the army and so will probably go to college and take subjects I like after leaving school. I tried to explain my point of view to the teachers at school but they would not listen. They said they knew what was best for me. So, I lost interest and now you're talking to me. It's all a shame because I thought I was doing well. But why should I have to take what I'm told when everyone else could choose their subjects?'

## The costs of non-attendance

No one can be sure of, probably not even estimate, the long-term costs of truancy and non-attendance from school. All we know is that there are a multiplicity of reasons why some pupils do not attend school regularly (Reid, 1999) and that subsequently these pupils cost the taxpayer enormous sums of money; not least in terms of the social security, unemployment, housing, crime prevention and adult psychiatric budgets. Moreover, a lot of truants become young offenders; some committing their first offences whilst away from school. If we could find ways to successfully prevent and/or stop truancy and other forms of non-attendance, we would save the Exchequer millions and millions of pounds annually. And, we would help these types of youngsters become more useful citizens in adult life and, probably, better parents as well.

There is, however, another cost of non-attendance. This is the cost to the caring professions – especially teachers – of dealing with the consequences of non-attendance, including often the resulting abusive behaviour.

Finally, there is the cost to the professions. In Scotland in 2001, five headteachers and two deputy heads were suspended for falsifying attendance data. The Scottish Parliament launched an investigation into the causes of this phenomenon. In South Wales, a director of education, his deputy and a headteacher were dismissed for claiming too much public funding for 'shadow' pupils. A similar incident has occurred at a small primary school in Mid Wales. In England, a director of education was asked to resign because her authority came bottom of the league tables on attendance when it was hardly her fault as she had only been in post for eighteen months and, to the author's certain knowledge, this authority had been experiencing similar problems for over twenty years. A headteacher in the north-east was forced to resign when she 'suspended' twenty truants and disruptive pupils prior to an inspection and their parents subsequently complained. And the number of these kinds of cases seems to be growing.

This is one reason why Jane Davidson, the Minister for Education and Lifelong Learning in Wales decided to abolish publishing league tables in the Principality after September 2001. It seems the adverse publicity and extra pressure exerted on professionals has become counterproductive.

## Summary

This chapter briefly describes key issues relating to the challenge of tackling truancy and other forms of school absenteeism. Included is a consideration of the extent of truancy, current registration difficulties, professional issues, new initiatives in England, the growing problem caused by escalating familial breakdown, the 'pressure' of truancy, truancy and the United Kingdom, pupils' traits, teachers' attitudes, pupils' perspectives and attitudes, some reasons for not going to school in Scotland, and, finally, the cost of non-attendance.

Truancy and persistent school absenteeism are difficult issues which in some ways divide the teaching profession. Most teachers work exceptionally hard and often inwardly feel contempt for non-conformist pupils like truants. At the same time, schools, teachers and other caring professionals are doing more work and trying harder to reduce absence in schools than ever before. Notwithstanding, putting teachers in charge of attendance within a school when they do not want the role can be counterproductive. Handling truancy and attendance issues within schools is a skilled and delicate issue. Staff given this responsibility need help and support including appropriate professional development.

## Reflective questions

1   Is truancy a cause of or an effect of underachievement?
2   Is truancy a rational response to ineffective provision? If so, what might effective provision look like?
3   Why are there such large local variations in school attendance rates? What might be done about this?
4   Truancy is a gamble. That is part of the excitement. You never know if you will get away with it. But there is a reasonable chance you will. What might be done about this?

## References

Cabinet Office (1998) *Truancy and School Exclusion Report*, Social Exclusion Unit, London: Cabinet Office.
Department of Education and Science (1975) *Survey of Absence from Secondary and Middle Schools in England and Wales on Thursday, 17 January 1974*, London: HMSO.
Hoyle, D. (1998) 'Constructions of pupil absence in the British Education Service', *Child and Family Social Work*, 3, 1–13.
O'Keefe, D. *et al.* (1993) *Truancy in English Secondary Schools*, London: DfES.
Pack (1977) *Truancy and Indiscipline in Schools in Scotland (The Pack Report)*, Scottish Education Department, London: HMSO.
Reid, K. (1985) *Truancy and School Absenteeism*, London: Hodder & Stoughton.
Reid, K. (1986) *Disaffection from School*, London: Methuen.
Reid, K. (1999) *Truancy and Schools*, London: Routledge.
Reid, K. (2000) *Tackling Truancy in Schools*, London: Routledge.
Scottish Office (2000) *Focus No. 5 on Truancy*, Edinburgh: Scottish Office.
Social Exclusion Report (1998) *Truancy and School Exclusion Report*, London: Cabinet Office.
TUC/MORI Poll (2001) *Half a Million Kids Working Illegally*, TUC, 21 March 2001.

# CHAPTER 9

# SCHOOL EXCLUSIONS IN THE UK

## Numbers, trends and variations

C. Parsons

*Education, Exclusion and Citizenship* (1999), London and New York: RoutledgeFalmer, pp. 22–34

## The dimensions of the exclusions problem

The data presented in this chapter come from three sources: first, from surveys of Local Education Authorities (LEAs) (school districts) carried out over four years with funding from DfE, Christ Church College and the Association of Teachers and Lecturers; second, from the Office for Standards in Education (OFSTED) school inspection reports; and third, from DES/DfE/DfEE reports. The earliest figures on exclusions available are acknowledged to be inaccurate by the DES. Indeed, that monitoring covered years from April to April rather than school years.

Though first sanctioned by the Education (No. 2) Act 1986 (sections 23–27), exclusion was a rare occurrence at the beginning of the 1990s. School exclusions have risen to become educationally and socially significant and costly. Figure 9.1 shows the steady year on year rise to 1996/97, where a slight fall occurred with the downward trend continuing into 1997/98.

## The excluded population

The percentage annual increases, as set out in Table 9.1, can be reliably used only from 1993 onwards. Before this time LEAs were not required to keep accurate data, no reliable surveys were conducted across the country and the government's National Exclusions Recording System was known to have collected incomplete data and not compensated for non-response (hence the hatched line above the first two figures). The lower, bold italicised figures for 1994/95, 1995/96 and 1996/97 on Figure 9.1 are derived by the DfEE from the addition to the Form 7 which is completed by all schools in January each year (DfEE, 1997b, 1998). The fact that the figures from school level data differ from those based on LEA level data raises questions about what the 'real' figures for permanent exclusions are. There are motivations for schools to under-record. Exclusions are held to be a performance indicator and schools want to show themselves in the best light they can. There is also the problem that exclusion names and numbers are historical data; schools are recording events that happened some six and eighteen months before, while simultaneously completing a form about numbers on roll at the present time which

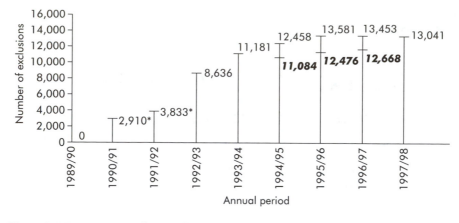

*Figure 9.1* Permanent exclusions from schools in England, 1990–98
*Note*:
* Known to be under-recording by National Exclusions Registration System.

*Table 9.1* Numbers of permanent exclusions from schools in England and annual rates of increase/decrease, 1990–98

| Year | Primary | | Secondary | | Special | | Total |
|---|---|---|---|---|---|---|---|
| | Number | Increase/ decrease % | Number | Increase/ decrease % | Number | Increase/ decrease % | |
| 1990/91[a] | 378 | | 2,532 | | ** | | 2,910 |
| 1991/92[a] | 537 | 42 | 3,296 | 30 | ** | | 3,833 |
| 1992/93[b] | 1,215 | 126 | 7,421 | 125 | ** | | 8,636 |
| 1993/94[c] | 1,291 | 6 | 9,433 | 27 | 457 | | 11,181 |
| 1994/95[d] | 1,438 | 11 | 10,519 | 12 | 501 | 10 | 12,458 |
| 1995/96[e] | 1,872 | 30 | 11,159 | 6 | 550 | 10 | 13,581 |
| 1996/97[f] | 1,856 | −1 | 10,890 | −2 | 707 | 29 | 13,453 |
| 1997/98[g] | 1,796 | −3 | 10,639 | −2 | 605 | −14 | 13,041 |

*Notes*:
** no data available.
a The National Exclusions Reporting System figures are an under-recording, based on incomplete responses from schools. The yearly figures were also April to April rather than for a school year.
b From Hayden (1994).
c The figures for permanent exclusions for 1993/94 for all 109 LEAs in England were estimated from responses from 101 LEAs (DfE, 1995).
d The figures for 1994/95 for all 109 LEAs were estimated from responses from 41 LEAs.
e The figures for 1995/96 were estimated from returns from 91 of the, then, 117 LEAs.
f The figures for 1996/97 were estimated from returns from 102 LEAs.
g The figures for 1997/98 were estimated from returns from 119 LEAs.

affect income in the coming year. There are similar motivations for LEAs to over-record but this is likely to be variable. Over-recording for the LEA would usefully exaggerate the problem they face. The fact that LEAs receive the Form 7 from all LEA schools, and the DfEE expects the forms to be checked by the LEA, offers little in the way of safeguards, especially when it is numbers on roll that are regarded as most important for that exercise.

Primary school exclusions are a small proportion of the total, a remarkably constant 13.8 per cent in 1995/96 and 1996/97 (13.9 per cent in 1997/98), but the rate of exclusion for this group had been accelerating while the rate of increase at secondary level was slowing. The time period is too short to make much of trends but the problems in terms of individual children and the nature of primary schools as institutions marks them out as different from secondary schools. Primary schools, with class teachers working most of the week with their own classes, have an intrinsic pastoral quality. The problems facing the primary school child who is disruptive are manifold – poor prior learning, disruptive and disorganised home circumstances and psychological disturbance. The child is not in control of its behaviour. This contrasts with some seemingly truculent 14 and 15-year-olds who are often making rational choices about their behaviour in the light of competing forces and attractions. Carol Hayden's (1997) research vividly conveys the problems which many excluded primary school pupils and their families already face in terms of poverty, family breakdown and other misfortunes serious enough to involve Social Services. These problems may not be peculiar to the primary phase but they certainly characterise the exclusion-related problems there.

At primary level permanent exclusion is almost exclusively a problem associated with boys; that is largely the case in special schools also, as set out in Figure 9.2. An examination of Figures 9.3 and 9.4 suggests that not until Year 9 (Y9) do girls significantly approach the boys' rates of exclusion.

Exclusions from special schools are small in number but a worryingly high percentage of the special school population. It is not rare to hear of statemented children with emotional and behavioural difficulties (EBD) being excluded from residential EBD schools. They may then be placed part-time in Pupil Referral Units (PRUs) which are less well resourced and staffed to deal with them. In the 1996/97 school year, permanent exclusions fell very slightly in primary and secondary schools but they rose by 29 per cent in special schools. In 1997/98 special school exclusions fell by 14 per cent.

The distribution of exclusions across secondary school years shows few surprises. Fixed term exclusions are about eight times more numerous than permanent exclusions and excluded boys at secondary level outnumber girls by approximately four to one. This pattern mirrors truancy rates and fits with a frequently held view of young people who increasingly 'buck the system', particularly a compulsory system, as they get older.

Figures 9.3 and 9.4 show that for both fixed term and permanent exclusions the rates increase with age to peak at Y10 and drop back in Y11. This is possibly due to the effective shortness of the school year for Y11s who (until September 1998) had been able to leave at Easter (the end of the spring term) if they had reached the age of 16. The same pattern applies for boys and for girls, though the fall off in permanent exclusions for girls in Y11 is more marked. Boys have much higher rates of exclusion in every year. The difference between boys' and girls' rates is least in Y9. DfEE (1997b) figures confirm this overall trend and distribution. Either their explicit oppositional behaviour arises later and/or schools' tolerance of it diminishes for 13–14-year-old girls.

The difference between different types of LEAs is marked. Figure 9.5 shows that, while metropolitan and county authorities differ little in their rates of exclusion, London authorities exclude at much higher rates, with Inner London boroughs

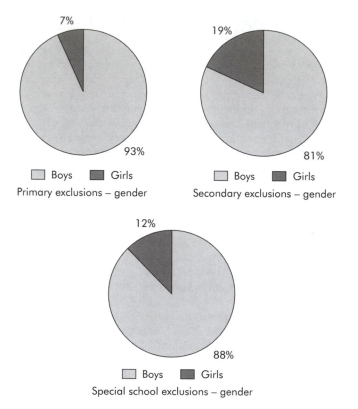

Figure 9.2  Gender and permanent exclusions by school type, 1995/96

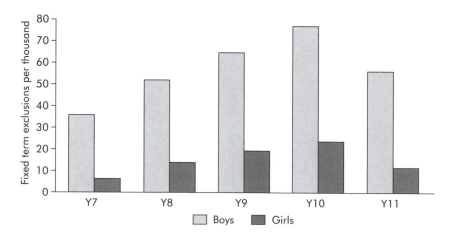

Figure 9.3  Fixed term exclusion rates by National Curriculum year, 1995/96

having double the rates for metropolitan authorities and counties. The permanent exclusion rate for Inner London authorities at secondary level is equivalent to 1 in every 130 pupils. This amounts to almost one pupil for every four classes for 11 to 16-year-olds. There is considerable variation within LEA types. Variation among

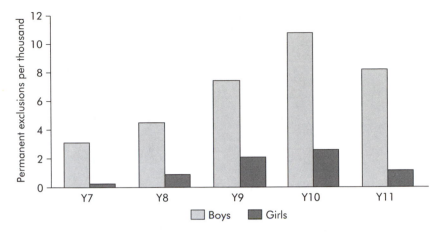

*Figure 9.4* Permanent exclusion rates by National Curriculum year, 1995/96

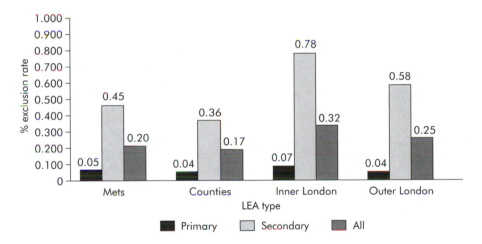

*Figure 9.5* Permanent exclusion rates by school type and LEA type, 1995/96

LEAs in rates of exclusion is such that they are ten times higher in some LEAs than in others. This variation is greater than can be explained by the socio-economic characteristics of the area alone.

Interestingly, rates of permanent exclusion change from one year to another in LEAs. In 1995/96 exclusions overall rose by nearly 10 per cent, yet for six out of the thirty LEAs for which there were also figures for the year before, there was a fall of more than 10 per cent. In 1996/97, out of the seventy-seven LEAs for which there were also figures for the previous year, five LEAs experienced a rise of more than 25 per cent and four a decrease of more than 25 per cent. In 1997/98 in ten LEAs, increases of more than 25 per cent were recorded, and in seven, decreases of more than 25 per cent, suggesting considerable volatility in permanent exclusion figures. Overall the fall was less than 1 per cent in 1996/97 and a bare 3 per cent in 1997/98. It would be most instructive to examine policies and practices in low excluding LEAs, which manage to reduce exclusions still

*Table 9.2* Permanent exclusions by ethnicity in 1994/95 and 1995/96

|  | Number excluded | | Percentage of excluded pupils | | Percentage of school population | |
|---|---|---|---|---|---|---|
|  | 1994/95 | 1995/96 | 1994/95 | 1995/96 | 1994/95 | 1995/96 |
| White | 8,785 | 10,096 | 83.8 | 82.6 | 89.8 | 88.9 |
| Black Caribbean | 769 | 867 | 7.3 | 7.1 | 1.1 | 1.5 |
| Black African | 148 | 216 | 1.4 | 1.8 | 0.6 | 1.0 |
| Black Other | 182 | 241 | 1.7 | 2.0 | 0.8 | 0.7 |
| Indian | 98 | 109 | 0.9 | 0.9 | 2.7 | 2.5 |
| Pakistani | 208 | 255 | 2.0 | 2.1 | 2.1 | 2.5 |
| Chinese | 46 | 14 | 2.4 | 0.1 | 0.8 | 0.4 |
| Bangladeshi | 11 | 58 | 0.1 | 0.5 | 0.4 | 0.9 |
| Other ethnic group | 241 | 366 | 2.3 | 3.0 | 1.5 | 1.7 |
| Total with ethnicity data provided | 10,508 | 12,232 | | | | |

further. The inner cities, most particularly London, suffer from the greatest deprivation and have the greatest concentrations of ethnic minority pupils. Table 9.2 shows the great over-representation of Black Caribbean pupils, over five times as likely to be excluded compared with white pupils. Other ethnic minority groups are also excluded at higher rates than their presence in the population would lead one to expect. Indian, Bangladeshi and Chinese pupils are exceptions to this pattern.

The interrelation of socio-economic status and ethnicity has never been well examined. The contributors to *Outcast England* (Bourne *et al.*, 1994) write emotively about the exclusion of black children but do not explore the link with class. Blyth and Milner (1996) and Sewell (1997) point to cultural and other interactional factors of importance. The OFSTED (1996b) report on exclusions from secondary school presented evidence that excluded black pupils did not have such severe home and social problems and were not under-achievers as frequently as white pupils who were excluded. This evidence alone supports the case that there is a racist response to black children's 'difficult' behaviour which lies behind the exclusions. It needs to be recognised, however, that if there were *no* ethnic minority permanent exclusions in 1995/96 the remaining total (white) permanent exclusions would still have been over 10,000 and this is on the DfEE's lower number of exclusions on the 12,232 where ethnicity is known.

## Provision for excluded pupils

Figures 9.6 and 9.7 show the pattern of provision made for permanently excluded primary and secondary school pupils. The survey (DfE, 1994) indicated that the 238 PRU in the 101 LEAs responding to the questionnaire accommodated 8,685 pupils, 90 per cent of them secondary. One-quarter of excluded primary pupils for whom there were records and 39 per cent of pupils excluded from secondary school attended PRUs during the autumn term 1994. Home tuition catered for 27 per cent of secondary pupils and 38 per cent of primary pupils. The earlier DfE recording of exclusions (DfE, 1993) reported that 45 per cent of those permanently

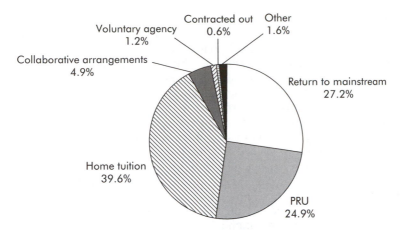

*Figure* 9.6 Proportions of permanently excluded primary school pupils in different types of provision, autumn term 1994

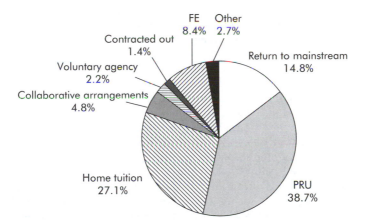

*Figure* 9.7 Proportions of permanently excluded secondary school pupils in different types of provision, autumn term 1994

excluded received home tuition. Return to mainstream schooling appeared more common with primary pupils than with secondary. This is understandable in view of the challenges presented by Year 10 and 11 pupils who have set themselves resolutely against the school regime as the point of leaving approaches.

The proportion of excluded secondary school pupils returning to mainstream school was recorded as low as 14.8 per cent during that period (autumn term 1994), while 27 per cent of primary school pupils managed the return to full-time mainstream education. This is set out in Figures 9.6 and 9.7. The questionnaire asked how many pupils, who were registered as excluded in the autumn term of 1994, returned to mainstream during that period. A larger proportion of pupils would have returned after a longer period out of school. Our judgement is that the figures underestimated by 25 per cent the proportion who eventually returned to mainstream education (reproduced as a note in OFSTED, 1996a: 60) and this figure may still be low. If less than 50 per cent return and complete their schooling, there are serious implications for the young people themselves, for the community and for society, the adult membership of which they are to join. There are questions to be posed about the extent to which these young people are equipped with skills, during the exclusion period, to manage themselves on return to school, whether schools are disposed as institutions to face the challenges and responsibilities of receiving an excludee, and whether individual teachers have the skills and attitudes to do what is necessary to support reintegration.

The more recent study, carried out for the Commission for Racial Equality (CRE), identified only seven out of twenty-six pupils (27 per cent) returning to mainstream school (CRE, 1996, Table 3: 22). Of the remaining nineteen, five were leavers who did not return to school. It was calculated that 46 per cent of excluded pupils continued as excluded into the following school year (CRE, 1996: 26). It is unlikely that the situation in autumn 1998 was better. This same research illustrated the variety of experiences following exclusion with a small number (three out of thirty) finding a place within fifteen days in a new school but most remaining out of school for a long period.

The existence of PRUs may encourage exclusions. Some LEAs or areas within LEAs have closed PRUs down with a view to reintegration after an interim period of home tuition. The effects of this measure are, as yet, unrecorded. PRUs in some areas have filled their places quickly, even with part-time provision, with the result that they have waiting lists.

Collaborative provision, usually with Social Services, was a feature in thirty-eight LEAs, but in only fourteen cases did this involve more than ten pupils in any one project. Voluntary agency and contracted out provision, often difficult to separate (e.g. Cities in Schools/INCLUDE), accounted for 297 pupils altogether, 3 per cent of all those for whom provision was being made. Further education (FE) provision for Year 11 pupils, sometimes associated with a PRU placement, was made for 658 pupils, 8 per cent of the secondary pupils.

Figures 9.8 and 9.9 show that, while a proportion of LEA PRUs provided full-time and half-time education, for the large number of pupils receiving home tuition it was mostly for under ten hours per week; indeed over half those receiving home tuition received less than five hours per week This was the case with over 60 per cent of the 338 primary pupils in receipt of home tuition and over 50 per cent of the 2,122 secondary pupils in the same position. These figures have two direct implications. First, the withdrawal of opportunities for learning takes the form of a punishment for the family, and for the child whose examination chances are diminished; second, many of these excluded pupils need more, not less, time with professionals, usually to address problems of low educational attainment and basic skills but also to resolve social and emotional problems. A subsidiary implication is that, if the finance is not allocated to meet these needs, the decision which could be interpreted as a legitimised withholding of funds from the undeserving.

Judgement of the value and success of PRUs must await further experience, evidence and evaluation. They were a new initiative for excluded pupils, established from September 1994, often catering for other categories of pupils as well those permanently excluded from school. Evidence at the time of the survey (spring 1995) indicated that provision for excluded pupils was patchy and stretched. While inspectors may have been looking for the wrong things, the report of the first twelve inspections (OFSTED, 1995) began very negatively.

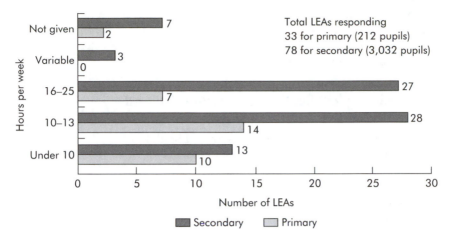

Figure 9.8 Time allocation for permanently excluded pupils 'normally' made by LEAs in PRUs, autumn term 1994

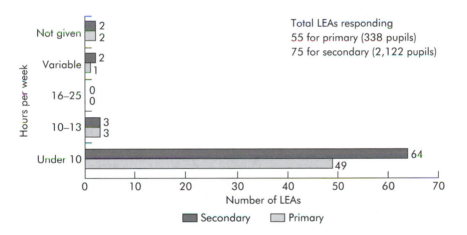

Figure 9.9 Total time allocation for permanently excluded pupils on home tuition, autumn term 1994

> Standards of attainment in the pupil referral units (PRUs) inspected thus far are variable, but generally too low, even when the educational history of pupils is taken into account.
>
> (OFSTED, 1995: 5)

The Education White Paper (DfEE, 1997a) suggested a continuing dissatisfaction, 'The quality and cost-effectiveness of many Pupil Referral Units need to be substantially improved' (p. 57). However, later reviews suggest that only five out of a hundred PRUs inspected had been found to be failing, and generally, 'PRUs are becoming more successful, in improving attendance and stimulating positive attitudes to learning and behaviour' (Social Exclusion Unit, 1998: 12).

OFSTED inspections of PRUs (as 'schools') have been in place only since 1996. In a number of cases a negative judgement was reached because of the part-time nature of the educational provision and the admission that suitable progress cannot be made with this limited input.

## Exclusions in Wales, Scotland, Northern Ireland and countries of the European Union

Exclusions in Wales are covered by the same legislation as applies in England. Figures supplied by the Welsh Office put the numbers of permanent exclusions at a fairly low level:

1994/95    476 permanent exclusions
1995/96    543 permanent exclusions
1996/97    473 permanent exclusions

The Scottish system has always been different. The power to exclude a pupil from school and the circumstances under which this power may be exercised were originally set out in the School's General (Scotland) Regulations 1975, and have been amended subsequently. A key difference, compared with England, is that the responsibility for exclusion rests with the education authority, not with the headteacher or principal. It is possible for an authority to devolve the ability to exclude to school level. Some Scottish education authorities do not allow permanent exclusions. Even when estimates are added in for authorities where small but undisclosed numbers of pupils (recorded as 'fewer than five') were excluded, the picture for Scotland is of falling numbers of permanent exclusions:

1994/95    343 permanent exclusions
1995/96    185 permanent exclusions
1996/97    117 permanent exclusions

It is with some interest that one views the list of Scottish education authorities for 1996/97 which reveals that the numbers of permanent exclusions registered for the City of Edinburgh and for Glasgow City are nought.

In Northern Ireland the situation is again different. Article 49 of the Education and Libraries (Northern Ireland) Order 1986, amended by article 39 of the Education and Libraries (Northern Ireland) Order 1993, regulate the procedures to be followed in relation to the 'suspension' and 'expulsion' of pupils from schools. As in England and Wales, a pupil may be suspended by the headteacher or principal. As in Scotland, where the local authority has powers to put a brake on exclusions, so in Northern Ireland regulations built into the 1995 statutory rules make expulsion more difficult and have a somewhat different orientation to the regulations prevailing in England. It is the requirement that expulsion meetings 'shall include consultations about the future provision of suitable education for the pupil concerned' that marks the Northern Ireland approach as less punitive and more balanced. The number of pupils excluded in 1995/96 was 62 out of a population of 343,000 pupils; 76 were permanently excluded in 1996/97.

Comparing the four countries of the United Kingdom is not straightforward. Suspensions may be applied in Scotland and Northern Ireland like indefinite exclusions were used in England and Wales until September 1994, but this is unlikely to explain the differences. Table 9.3 shows that for 1994/95, permanent exclusions in Wales occurred at only two-thirds of the rate current in England. Scotland's rate

*Table 9.3* Permanent exclusions from schools in the countries of the United Kingdom, 1994/95

|  | Wales | Scotland | Northern Ireland | England |
| --- | --- | --- | --- | --- |
| Total school population | 492,600 | 820,800 | 349,500 | 7,824,600 |
| Number of permanent exclusions | 476 | 343 | 62 | 21,458 |
| Percentage rate of permanent exclusions | 0.097 | 0.042 | 0.018 | 0.159 |

was one-quarter of England's. For Northern Ireland it was close to one-tenth of the exclusion rate in England.

The countries of western Europe from which information was obtained about the management of behaviourally difficult children showed some contrasts with the law and practice in England and Wales. These other countries have young people with similar characteristics and in similar proportions found in schools in England and Wales. The management of such pupils has not been characterised by easy solutions but a *fundamental principle* in all these countries is that all children who are nationals of that country or resident in that country should be receiving a full-time education. There are not the provisions for regulating the exclusion of a child that exist in English law. It remains commonly the case that, if a child is to be expelled from school, it is the headteacher's responsibility to find another placement for the child before the exclusion occurs. This is the situation in Denmark, the Netherlands, Belgium, France, Germany, Austria, Luxembourg, Spain and the Republic of Ireland. In the last case, the Irish Department of Education and Science Circular 20/90 makes plain the limitations on fixed term exclusion, and Rule 130 forbids permanent exclusion 'without the prior consent of the Patron and unless alternative arrangements are made for the enrolment of the pupil at another suitable school'.

## Conclusion: the social function of school exclusion

In the management of exclusions we witness an example of the atomisation of the services for these young people when it is well known that there are multiple causes for the many social problems which lead to their difficulties. There is a punitive response which accords with an attribution of blame which is highlighted by significant media responses to stories of school exclusion. In the provision of public services, exclusion from school serves as an exemplar of the way the attribution of blame has changed in British society since the late 1970s: public issues are rendered personal choices, and intervention and support are withheld or reduced in favour of punitive responses.

Careful consideration needs to be given to what is seen as an 'effective school' and *effective for whom* (Slee and Weiner, 1998). Currently the effective school is seen in government and research terms as one with good academic results – learning is proven to have taken place. The 'good' school may be different, placing an emphasis on its caring role (without detriment to its academic functions). The 'very good' school, very much a moral project, may be the inclusive school which keeps its clients and retains the responsibility to cater for their needs – however demanding these may be.

There are forces which increase the likelihood of exclusion from school and these operate at the macro level of socio-economic and cultural factors, at the institutional level and at the personal/individual level. Our argument is that, while 'inclusion' has much rhetorical and moral backing, inclusion is not for these challenging children. Indeed, exclusion is designed into the system at macro level, shaping the institutional response, and limiting options at the individual level.

## Reflective questions

1    Whose problem does exclusion from school solve?
2    What good might exclusion do to which stakeholders?
3    What damage might exclusion do to which stakeholders?
4    Might a school have to exclude some children to provide a more inclusive environment for the others?

## References

Blyth, E. and Milner, J. (1996) 'Black boys excluded from school: race or masculinity issues?' in Blyth, E. and Milner, J. (eds) *Exclusion from School: Inter-Professional Issues for Policy and Practice*, London: Routledge.

Bourne, J., Bridges, L. and Searle, C. (1994) *Outcast England: How Schools Exclude Black Children*, London: Institute of Race Relations.

Commission for Racial Equality (CRE) (1996) *Exclusion from School: The Public Cost*, London: CRE.

DfE (1993) *Press Release on National Exclusions Reporting System*, London: Department for Education.

DfE (1994) *Code of Practice on the Identification and Assessment of Special Educational Needs*, London: Department for Education.

DfE (1995) *National Survey of Local Education Authorities' Policies and Procedures for the Identification of, and Provision for, Children who are out of School by Reason of Exclusion or Otherwise*, London: Department for Education.

DfEE (1997a) *Excellence in Schools*, London: HMSO.

DfEE (1997b) 'Permanent exclusions from schools in England 1995/96', DfEE Press Release 342/97, 30 October, London: DfEE.

DfEE (1998) 'Morris reveals ambitious new plan to cut truancy and exclusion from school', DfEE Press Release 386/98, 29 July.

Hayden, C. (1994) 'Primary age children excluded from school: a multi-agency focus of concern', *Children and Society*, 8(3), 257–73.

Hayden, C. (1997) *Children Excluded from Primary School*, Buckingham: Open University Press.

OFSTED (1995) *Pupil Referral Units: The First Twelve Inspections*, London: OFSTED.

OFSTED (1996a) *Recent Research on the Achievements of Ethnic Minority Pupils*, London: OFSTED.

OFSTED (1996b) *Exclusions from Secondary Schools 1995/96*, London: OFSTED.

Sewell, T. (1997) *Black Masculinities and Schooling*, Stoke-on-Trent: Trentham.

Slee, R. and Weiner, G. (1998) 'Introduction: school effectiveness for whom?', in Slee, R., Tomlinson, S. and Weiner, G. (eds), *Effective for Whom?*, London: Falmer.

Social Exclusion Unit (1998) *Truancy and School Exclusion*, London: The Stationery Office.

# PART IV

# ACTION IN SCHOOLS

# CHAPTER 10

# ADAPTING CURRICULUM AND INSTRUCTION

## P. Westwood

*Commonsense Methods for Children with Special Educational Needs: Strategies for the Regular Classroom* (4th ed.) (2003), London and New York: RoutledgeFalmer, pp. 202–17

> Adaptive teaching is an educational approach that clearly recognizes differences between learners – especially cognitive differences or other specific characteristics. Teachers accept that their students differ in capabilities and take these differences as the starting point for teaching and learning.
>
> (Van den Berg *et al.* 2001: 246)

Attention has been given to the teaching and learning of what are known as the 'basic academic skills' – reading, writing, spelling and using numbers. Strategies have been presented for adapting methods and curriculum content in these areas to meet the special requirements of some students. The basic academic skills are obviously not the only areas of the curriculum where adaptation may be necessary when teaching students with special needs. In this chapter some generic principles for developing inclusive practice through differentiation across the curriculum will be discussed, together with specific suggestions for adapting curriculum content and resources, or modifying teaching approaches.

## Differentiation

In the simplest of terms, differentiation can be defined as '... teaching things differently according to observed differences among learners' (Westwood 2001: 5). Differentiation strategies can be applied to:

- teaching approach;
- content of the curriculum;
- assessment methods;
- classroom organisation;
- student grouping;
- teachers' interactions with individual students.

Differentiation is attempted mainly as a response to diversity among students, but it is also a strategy for accommodating students with disabilities by removing some of the barriers to learning (Byrnes 2000). It should be noted that differentiation within the classroom addresses not only the needs of students with disabilities or learning problems but also the needs of the most able or gifted students (Kerry and Kerry 1997).

It must be acknowledged from the start that differentiation is never a simple matter in practice. Teachers may believe that their teaching should address students' individual needs and differences in principle, but in reality they have great difficulty in translating this belief into action. Effective differentiation invariably places very heavy demands on teachers' time, knowledge and organising skills (Babbage *et al.* 1999; Peetsma *et al.* 2001; Pettig 2000). Webster (1995: 47) has observed:

> ...whilst most teachers see the value in planning their teaching to enable all pupils to participate effectively at one level or another, classroom realities sometimes constrain good intentions. Differentiation is probably best viewed as an aspiration, and whatever steps teachers make towards achieving the kind of flexibility described here, will certainly benefit all pupils, not just those with special needs.

Differentiation first involves recognising that children differ one from another in many ways, and then planning and teaching lessons so that any educationally significant differences are taken into account. It is argued that when differentiation occurs all students can make optimum progress. The main advocate for differentiated instruction in the United States, Carol Tomlinson (1996, 1999, 2001), refers to *personalising* instruction to take account of students' current levels of ability, prior knowledge, strengths, weaknesses, learning preferences and interests in order to maximise their opportunities to learn.

To achieve a personalised approach it is necessary to respond to individual differences among students by (for example):

- setting individualised objectives for learning;
- modifying curriculum content to match more closely the cognitive level of the students;
- providing different paths to learning to suit differing learning styles and preferences;
- varying time allocation for classroom tasks to take account of students' differing rates of learning;
- adapting instructional resource materials;
- encouraging students to produce their work in different forms or through different media;
- using flexible groupings of students;
- varying the amount of guidance and assistance given to individual students.

Most advocates of an adaptive approach to teaching consider the above eight areas to be the major focus for differentiated practice (e.g. Dettmer *et al.* 2002). Each area will be discussed more fully, but first it is important to stress the *simplicity principle*.

## Keep it simple

The whole process of applying differentiation in the classroom can sound very daunting for teachers because so many different ways of adapting instruction and modifying curricula have been described in the literature. Although in theory there are many potential strategies for meeting students' different needs in practice, it is not always feasible or desirable to apply more than one or two such strategies at any one time, particularly in large classes. The following advice from Deschenes *et al.* (1999: 13) is well worth noting:

> Adaptations are most effective when they are simple, easy to develop and implement, and based on typical assignments and activities. Adapting in this way is feasible for the classroom teacher because it is relatively unobtrusive, requiring little extra time for special planning, materials development, and/or instruction.

Applying the simplicity principle, Falvey *et al.* (1996) have recommended that adaptations and modifications should not be used unless absolutely necessary, and should be faded as soon as possible in order to liberate, not limit, a student's possibilities. It is important to ensure that a differentiated curriculum does not become an *impoverished* curriculum, with the lower-ability students always receiving less demanding work than the more able students.

## Specific examples of differentiation

The mnemonic CARPET PATCH can be used to summarise the main ways in which teachers might adapt their approach in order to establish more inclusive classroom practice and meet their students' individual needs.

C = *Curriculum content:*   The curriculum to be studied may be increased or decreased in terms of depth and complexity. Aspects of the curriculum may be sequenced into smaller units and presented in smaller steps. Lesson content may draw more on students' own interests.

A = *Activities:*   Teachers can vary the difficulty level of the tasks and activities the students are required to undertake in the lesson.

R = *Resource materials:*   Teachers could select or create a variety of different texts and instructional materials for students to use (e.g. some requiring less reading or writing).

P = *Products from the lessons:*   Teachers might plan for students to produce different outputs from a lesson, according to their abilities, interests and aptitudes.

E = *Environment:*   The classroom might be set up to support more individualised or group work. Use may be made of learning centres, computer assisted learning, or resource-based learning.

T = *Teaching strategies:*   Teachers might adopt particular ways of teaching designed to stimulate the poorly motivated students; or they may use more explicit and direct forms of instruction for certain groups in the classroom. Teachers may use tactics such as differentiated questioning, more frequent revising, practising, prompting, cueing, according to individual needs and responses from students. They may also set individual learning contracts for students.

P = *Pace:*   Teachers may vary the rate at which teaching takes place, or the rate at which students are required to work and produce outputs.

A = *Amount of assistance:*   Teachers could vary the amount of help given to individuals during a lesson. They may encourage peer assistance and collaboration among students.

T = *Testing and grading:*  Teachers may vary the ways of assessing students' learning and may modify grading to reflect effort and originality as well as the standard achieved.

C = *Classroom grouping:*  Teachers can use various ways of grouping students within the class to allow for different activities to take place, under differing amounts of teacher direction.

H = *Homework assignments:*  Teachers may give some students homework that involves additional practice at the same level of difficulty, while others have more demanding homework involving application and extension exercises.

Much longer lists of specific differentiation strategies exist – for example, Falvey *et al.* (1996) identify over 120 different ways of organising and delivering what they term 'multi-level instruction' in inclusive mixed-ability classrooms. Other practical ideas are contained in James and Brown (1998), Janney and Snell (2000) and Udvari-Solner (1998).

### Starting points

Kameenui and Simmons (1999) recommend that teachers begin to plan for differentiated instruction by focusing on essential core content they would hope *all* students will learn from the lesson or series of lessons (information, concepts, rules, skills, strategies). They refer to this as identifying the 'big ideas'. Planning and differentiating the topic then becomes a process of creating many different ways the students can encounter these big ideas through a variety of coherent experiences matched to their abilities. For example, some students may encounter new ideas through reading about them in books; some may understand them only if they encounter them visually through direct experience or via video; others may gain most from talking with peers about the issues or problems; some will understand new ideas best by creating their own pictures or models; and some will acquire the concepts most easily through direct teaching. As a general rule, all students in the group will learn best if provided with a variety of activities and paths to learning. To avoid fragmentation of the total learning experience the teacher must not lose sight of the big ideas for the topic, regardless of the many and varied activities and tasks set for students.

Several writers have described appropriate procedures for adapting curriculum and instruction (e.g. Deschenes *et al.* 1999; Dettmer *et al.* 2002; Hoover and Patton 1997). The steps they identify can be summarised as:

- selecting the subject or topic to be taught;
- identifying the specific content to be included;
- prescribing the learning goals and objectives for the majority of students in the class;
- deciding on the way the lesson will be organised and conducted for most students;
- identifying any students who will need modifications to the general lesson format;
- modifying the objectives for these students, if necessary;
- preparing any necessary adaptations (e.g. shorter assignments, easier textbook, extra use of concrete materials);
- teaching the lesson, and making any necessary additional changes while teaching;

- providing extra assistance to certain students while the lesson is in progress;
- planning appropriate methods for assessing students' learning, based on the goals and objectives.

When planning the differentiated objectives for the lesson it is usually helpful to have in mind the three sentence starters:

- All students will...
- Some students will...
- A few students might...

These subheadings help teachers to identify the essential core of knowledge and skills that *all* students will be expected to master, possibly through different activities and varied pathways. Some students will achieve more than this core; and a few may achieve one or two higher-order objectives through the medium of extension activities (Kenward 1997).

In terms of organisation for the lesson, it is important to consider how students will be grouped and how the available time will be used most effectively. Planning needs to include consideration of strategies for facilitating the delivery of additional help to certain students during the lesson (e.g. via peer assistance, a learning support assistant, or from the teacher).

The following questions may need to be answered concerning any student requiring adaptations:

- Does the student have the prerequisite skills for this work (e.g. adequate reading ability)?
- Can the student work without constant supervision?
- Can the student work cooperatively with others?
- What is the attention span of the student?
- Does the student have any behaviour problems?
- What will represent appropriate work output from this student?
- What feasible modifications to the activities or resources will need to be made?
- Will the assessment procedure have to be modified for this student?

## Modifying curriculum content

Modifying curriculum content usually implies that:
- students with learning difficulties are required to cover less material in the lesson;
- the tasks or activities they attempt are usually easier to accomplish;
- in the case of gifted or more able students, the reverse would be true; they might cover more content and in greater depth;
- for certain students in the class the objectives set for the lesson might involve mastery of fewer concepts and the application of easier skills;
- the nature of the learning tasks set for the students will be matched to their learning rate and abilities; some tasks may take longer time to complete than others;
- differentiated content for homework assignments could be used as one way of meeting the needs of gifted and able students, as well as those of students with difficulties.

Some definitions of differentiation refer specifically to 'matching' the level of curriculum content to the differing capabilities of the students in the class (e.g. Carpenter and Ashdown 1996). Other writers argue that differentiation should be less about changing the level or type of work set by the teacher but much more about providing alternative paths and giving as much assistance as is necessary to enable all students to study the same curriculum content and achieve satisfactory outcomes (e.g. Dettmer *et al.* 2002; McNamara and Moreton 1997).

### Potential problems with modified curriculum

Reducing the complexity and demands of the curriculum and setting easier objectives may sound like very good advice; but watering down the curriculum in this way can have the long-term effect of increasing the achievement gap between the students with learning difficulties and other students. By lowering the demands placed on students of lower ability we may be exaggerating the effect of individual differences and perpetuating inequalities among students. It can be argued, particularly in countries with national curricula, that rather than reducing our expectations for what students can achieve we should be finding ways of providing students with sufficient assistance to ensure that they can achieve the same core objectives applicable to the majority of the school population. The problem is one of giving additional support (scaffolding) rather than the provision of alternative curricula. Obviously this argument cannot easily be extended to cover students with moderate to severe disabilities integrated in inclusive classrooms. In such cases it will be necessary to modify significantly the demands of the mainstream curriculum to match more closely the students' cognitive level. In many countries this is achieved through the medium of an individual education plan (IEP) and the provision of additional services.

## Adapting resources

One of the main areas where modifications are recommended to improve access to the curriculum is that of instructional resources. The resource materials used within a lesson (texts, worksheets, exercises, blackboard notes, computer software) may need to be modified, and apparatus or equipment may need to be provided for some students (e.g. blocks for counting or grouping in mathematics; pages taped to the desktop for a student with gross motor difficulties; a 'talking' calculator for a student with impaired vision; a pencil with a thick grip for a student with poor hand coordination).

When preparing print materials for students with learning difficulties the following strategies may be helpful (adapted from James and Brown 1998; Squires 2001):

- simplify the language (use short sentences, substitute simple words for difficult terms);
- pre-teach any new vocabulary (if a difficult word cannot be simplified, ensure that it is looked at and discussed before students are expected to read it unaided);
- provide clear illustrations or diagrams;
- improve legibility of print and layout;
- remove unnecessary detail;
- present information in small blocks of text, rather than dense paragraphs;
- use bullet points and lists, rather than paragraphs where possible;
- make printed instructions or questions clear and simple;

- use cues or prompts where responses are required from the students (e.g. provide the initial letter of the answer, or use dashes to show the number of words required in the answer);
- highlight important terms or information (e.g. use underlining, or print the words in bold type or colour);
- consider sentence construction to facilitate comprehension. (Active voice is easier to process than passive voice: e.g. 'The teacher draws a line' rather than 'A line is drawn by the teacher'.)

Applying some of the strategies listed earlier will often be sufficient to allow a student with a mild disability or with a literacy problem to access text elements of the curriculum without the need for further adaptation. Evidence indicates, however, that in general teachers do not engage in much modification of resource materials, possibly through lack of time or lack of knowledge and skills (Chan *et al.* 2001).

### Potential, problems with modified resource materials

Bearne (1996) warns against the tendency to provide differentiation merely by using graded worksheets. While there may be occasions where the use of graded worksheets is appropriate and helpful, their frequent use can label the students as belonging to particular ability groups. It is also relevant to heed the warning from Robbins (1996: 33) that differentiation should not lead to 'death by a thousand worksheets'!

Use of too many worksheet assignments in class can produce poorer outcomes than the use of direct teaching. Based on classroom evidence from research into mathematics teaching in British primary schools, Reynolds and Muijs (1999: 21) report that:

> ...there was often an over-reliance on worksheets and published [texts]. While these were not necessarily poor in themselves, they simply isolated pupils in ways that made it difficult for them to receive any sustained, direct teaching at all. In other words, more often than not complex arrangements for individual work were self-defeating; they dissipated rather than intensified the quality of the teaching and reduced the opportunities for children to learn.

On the issue of using simplified resources with some students there has been an interesting finding – in general, students *don't like* to use modified materials or to be given easier tasks (Hall 1997; Klinger and Vaughn 1999). Students with special needs, particularly those in the secondary and upper primary age range, want to have the same activities, books, homework, grading criteria, and grouping practices as their classmates – but they appreciate any extra help the teacher may give them while attempting that work. Students do not like to be given simplified tasks, materials or tests because these practices mark them out as 'different' and undermine their status in the peer group. Adolescents in particular are acutely sensitive to peer-group reactions, and they may deeply resent being treated as if they are lacking in ability. There is also some evidence that parents don't like their children to be given what they perceive to be easier work in the class.

## Adapting instruction

Adapting instruction covers all the major and minor changes that may be made to the way teaching occurs in the classroom. It includes the method of instruction, how students are grouped, the nature of their participation in the lesson, and the interactions between teacher and students, and among the students themselves.

When teaching and learning processes are modified some of the following strategies may be used:

- The teacher may give more assistance or less assistance to individual students according to their needs.
- The teacher may reteach some concepts or information to some students, using simpler language and more examples.
- Questions asked during the lesson may be pitched at different levels of difficulty for different individuals.
- Closer monitoring of the work of some students may take place throughout the lesson.
- The teacher may use particular tactics to gain and maintain the interest of poorly motivated students.
- Feedback may be given in more detail or less detail, according to the students' needs.
- The rate at which the students are expected to work may be varied, with extra time allowed for some students to complete tasks.
- Extra practice may be provided for students who need it, often via differentiated homework assignments.
- Extension work may be set for the most able students, requiring mainly independent study, investigation and application.
- The ways in which students are grouped for specific purposes (e.g. by ability, interest, friendships) may also be part of differentiation within the teaching process. The aim may be to encourage cooperation and peer assistance; or grouping may facilitate the matching of learning tasks to students' ability levels; or grouping may help the teacher to give more assistance to certain students.
- Classroom learning centres may be set up, individual contract systems established, and computer-assisted-instruction (CAI) may be used.

### Difficulties in adapting teaching process

There is evidence to suggest that teachers are much better at using the modifications to teaching process described earlier than they are at modifying the curriculum – there are fewer difficulties (Chan *et al.* 2001; Leyser and BenYehuda 1999). They appear to find teaching process modifications more natural and much easier to accomplish within their personal teaching style. For example, skilled teachers do tend to provide additional help to students when necessary, they do use differentiated questioning, and they do make greater use of descriptive praise, encouragement and rewards during lessons. These are all strategies that can be applied while the teacher is still following a common curriculum with the whole class – and for this reason they are regarded as the most feasible adaptations for teachers to make. They certainly provide a very sound starting point for any teacher moving from a formal, whole-class method of instruction to a more personalised approach. What we know about the dynamics of change processes in education suggests that change is most likely to occur when teachers are required to take small steps in a new direction rather than giant leaps, and when they can build on their current practices.

# Differentiating student output

The term 'student output' refers here to the products from the learning process. Often these will be tangible products such as written work, graphics, or models; but sometimes the 'product' refers to other forms of evidence of learning such as an oral report, a performance, a presentation to the group, participation in discussion, or the answering of oral questions.

Differentiating the products of learning may mean that:

- Each student is not expected to produce exactly the same amount or quality of work as every other student.
- A student may be asked to produce work in a different format; for example, an audio recording, a drawing or poster, rather than an essay.
- The student may complete a multiple-choice exercise rather than prepare a project involving extensive writing.
- Individual students might negotiate what they will produce, and how they will produce it, in order to provide evidence of their learning in a particular topic.

## *Potential problems with differentiating output*

Whether or not teachers expect students to produce different amounts and varying qualities of work, they will of course do so – and have always done so. The potential danger in setting out from the start to accept less work from some students or a poorer quality of work, is that this strategy represents a lowering of expectations that can result in a self-fulfilling prophecy. The students produce less and less, and we in turn expect less and less of them. A different perspective suggests that teachers need to help students achieve more, not less in terms of work output, than they would have achieved without support.

The second suggestion of encouraging quite different products can be applied more easily in some subject areas rather than in others. For example, in social studies, language arts, expressive arts, and environmental education it is quite feasible and desirable to differentiate the product and encourage diversity in what the students produce. On the other hand, in mathematics for example, it is more difficult to find acceptable variations in the way that students can demonstrate their mastery of key understandings and skills.

Differentiation of product should never be seen as offering a 'soft option'. It should never lead to a student consistently managing to avoid tasks he or she does not like to complete.

# Differentiation of assessment and grading

'Assessment' refers to any process used to determine how much learning, and what quality of learning, has occurred for each student in the class. Assessment provides an indication of how effective a particular episode of teaching and learning has been. The process of assessment also highlights anything that may need to be taught again, revised, or practised further by some students.

'Grading' refers to the fairly common practice of indicating the quality of the work a student has produced for assessment purposes. Often a letter grade (e.g. A, B, C, D) is used, or the work may be given a mark out of 10 or 100. In some countries there has been a trend away from this form of grading in favour of more descriptive comments and written feedback.

Modifications to assessment processes include such options as:

- simplifying the assessment task for some students;
- shortening the task;
- allowing longer time for some students to complete the task or test;
- allowing a student with special needs to have some assistance in performing the task (e.g. dictating answers to a scribe);
- enabling the student to present the work in a different format (e.g. scrapbook rather than essay).

Classroom tests are one of the ways in which some teachers assess the progress of their students. Students with special needs may require modification to the test format, or additional time allowed to complete the test. Some may need a variation in the mode of responding.

Standard adaptations for test formats include:

- enlarging the print;
- leaving more space for the student to write the answer;
- using more variety in question type (e.g. short answer, multiple-choice, sentence completion, gapped paragraphs, matching formats);
- rewriting the instructions in simple language, and highlighting key points;
- keeping directions brief and simple;
- providing prompts such as: *Begin the problem here* ⇒.

Modifications to test administration procedures include:

- using oral questioning and answering;
- using a scribe (someone else to write down what the student says);
- allowing the student to dictate the answers on to audiotape;
- giving short rest breaks during the test without penalty;
- allowing extra time to complete the test;
- avoiding any penalty for poor spelling or handwriting;
- allowing the student to use a laptop computer to complete the test;
- giving credit for drawings or diagrams if these help to indicate that the student knows the concept or information;
- spending adequate time making sure that *all* students understand the requirements before the test begins;
- reducing the anxiety that some students have in test situations;
- for some students, testing in an environment other than the classroom (e.g. social worker's office, withdrawal room) may help the student to relax and do his or her best.

Some ways of modifying grading to take account of learning difficulties, adapted from Wood (1998), include:

- using 'Satisfactory/Unsatisfactory' as the yardstick for grading a subject;
- reporting achievement not as a grade but as the number of specific objectives achieved in the course. This becomes a more *descriptive* report and can include indications of areas still needing to be improved as well as what was achieved;
- providing two grades for every subject. One grade represents 'effort' while the other grade represents 'achievement' (e.g. D for achievement; A for effort);

- recording results in numerical form (e.g. achievement: 66 per cent; effort: 90 per cent). Achievement is calculated from test scores or marks obtained for assignments. Effort is estimated rather more subjectively, but might also have specific criteria made known to the students before the course begins (e.g. 'You will receive 25 per cent if all classroom assignments are completed; 20 per cent for neatness and presentation; 30 per cent for participation during lessons; 25 per cent for all homework completed').

## Potential problems in differentiating assessment and grading

Differentiation of grading procedures for students' work in inclusive classrooms is particularly problematic. The main debate concerning modifications to grading systems for students with special needs tends to focus on 'fairness'. For example:

- Is it fair to judge the standard of work produced by a student with mild intellectual disability, or a student who is deaf, against the standard applying to students of average or good ability in the class?
- Is it fair to give a student of very limited ability a report card showing Ds and Fails when he or she has worked extremely hard: doesn't this lower motivation and self-esteem?
- Is it fair to students who do not have learning difficulties or disabilities if we give 'good' grades to lower achievers simply based on the fact that they 'tried hard' and to encourage them?
- Is it fair to parents and employers to misrepresent a student's actual abilities and achievements on school reports by giving grades to encourage the student rather than to represent actual attainment? Shouldn't a grading system be the same for all students if it is to be fair and accurate?

For these and other similar questions there are no easy answers. Those who provide simplistic advice on adapting assessment procedures and grading criteria seem, at times, to be unaware of the complexity of some of the underlying dilemmas.

## Accommodations for students with disabilities

The term 'accommodation' usually conveys the notion of making sure that students with disabilities can participate fully or partially in a particular lesson by varying the type of activities or the method of instruction, providing additional human and technical resources, giving extra support, modifying the ways in which the student will respond, or changing the classroom environment. Janney and Snell (2000: 16) suggest: 'Accommodations are changes that others make to assist the student. They are provided to enable the student to gain access to the classroom or the curriculum.'

Many of the modifications and adaptations already described earlier are equally appropriate for students with disabilities. For example, simplifying objectives and tasks, frequently reteaching important concepts and skills, allowing more time for students to complete work, encouraging different outputs from students, and facilitating peer assistance are all strategies that reduce or remove barriers to learning. Some students will also need additional support and modified equipment.

Technological accommodations often involve the use of assistive devices to help a student to communicate or to produce work output (e.g. modified keyboard, a computer with a visual display and touch screen or with voice synthesiser, braillers for blind students, greatly enlarged text on a computer screen for a student with partial sight, radio-frequency hearing aids for students with impaired hearing). Less sophisticated aids might include school-made communication boards for students without speech, or using symbol or picture-card systems for communicating. Technology has also increased the mobility and independence of many students with severe physical disabilities. It is beyond the scope of this chapter to discuss assistive technology in detail. Appropriate texts have been listed under Further Reading.

The specific needs of students with disabilities are usually identified in their Individual Educational Programmes (IEPs). The IEP should be seen as the main source of advice of the types of differentiation needed by the students.

## Differentiation is not easy

It is important to state again that many teachers experience significant difficulty in implementing and *sustaining* a differentiated approach (Babbage *et al.* 1999; Pettig 2000; Scott *et al.* 1998). When advising teachers to become more responsive to individual differences among their students it is important not to overlook the real difficulties in practical implementation. As Rose (2001: 147) has remarked, 'The teaching methods and practices required for the provision of effective inclusion are easier to identify than they are to implement.' The problems, as well as the practices, have been addressed in this chapter.

Davies (2000) suggests that differentiation might prove to be impracticable for three main reasons:

- Teachers' inability to judge accurately the different ability and performance levels in their students.
- Teachers' inability to change their teaching to match observed differences among students.
- Unintended effects of differentiation that negate any benefits (e.g. students' negative reactions to being treated differently; failure to cover the work required within a prescribed curriculum or for public examinations).

The following five barriers have been identified as preventing teachers from engaging in adaptive teaching (Schumm and Vaughn 1995):

- Planning for differentiated lessons is extremely time consuming.
- It is difficult to implement different procedures and tasks while managing the whole class.
- To simplify the curriculum or slow the pace of instruction may compromise the progress of the higher-achieving students.
- Using different tasks and resources may draw more attention to the students with difficulties.
- Simplifying everything (and making success easy) does not reflect the real world in which the students will need to function.

### Prerequisites for using a differentiated approach

Based on information from international literature, it seems that the following five conditions need to be satisfied if teachers are to introduce differentiation in their classrooms and sustain the practice over time:

- Teachers have to *believe* that the investment in time and effort will produce significantly better results in terms of students' learning and motivation (Weston *et al.* 1998).
- Teachers have to have adequate *time to plan lessons* much more carefully if tasks are to be set for different levels of ability and if different resources are to be designed (Dettmer *et al.* 2002).
- Teachers need to *know the individuals in their classes extremely well* in order to match class work to students' differing abilities (Pettig 2000; Udvari-Solner 1998). It should be noted that teaching large classes militates against getting to know students well; and being a subject specialist who teaches many different classes also militates against knowledge of individual students.
- Teachers need to have access to a *varied range of resource materials* in their subject area, rather than being confined to a single standard textbook (James and Brown 1998).
- There needs to be *general support* for a differentiated approach to teaching within the school (Weston *et al.* 1998). It is even suggested that there must be an explicit commitment in the school's written policy to indicate that students' individual needs will be met through differentiated practices.

Given that differentiation as a strategy within classroom teaching has the potential to increase success rates for all students and remove some of the barriers to learning for students with disabilities it is hoped that teachers will continue to become more adaptive in their approach. Despite the difficulties mentioned in this chapter, many teachers already do a great deal to respond to their students' unique needs; given appropriate motivation, they will continue to increase their expertise. Advisers, inspectors and support teachers need to be aware of the ways in which classroom instruction can be adapted so that the advice they give to teachers is of practical value. They also need to be fully aware that teachers will not necessarily find it easy to implement such advice and will require much support in moving in that direction.

## Reflective questions

1  Is individualisation of learning possible given constraints on resources?
2  Does differentiation work?
3  If so, is it cost-effective?
4  Would time spent writing Individual Educational Plans (IEPs) be better spent teaching?
5  How many IEPs are put into practice in a way that would not happen if the IEP did not exist?

## Further reading

Deschenes, C., Ebeling, D. and Sprague, J. (1999) *Adapting the Curriculum in Inclusive Classrooms*, New York: National Professional Resources.
Fisher, D. and Frey, N. (2001) *Responsive Curriculum Design in Secondary Schools: Meeting the Diverse Needs of Students*, Lanham, MD: Scarecrow Press.
Flippo, K.F. (1995) *Assistive Technology: A Resource for School, Work and Community*, Baltimore, MD: Brookes.

Gregory, G.H. and Chapman, C. (2002) *Differentiated Instructional Strategies: One Size Doesn't Fit All*, Thousand Oaks, CA: Corwin Press.

Hart, S. (1996) *Differentiation and the Secondary Curriculum*, London: Routledge.

James, F. and Brown, K. (1998) *Effective Differentiation*, London: Collins.

Janney, R. and Snell, M.E. (2000) *Modifying Schoolwork*, Baltimore, MD: Brookes.

McNamara, S. and Moreton, G. (1997) *Understanding Differentiation: A Teacher's Guide*, London: Fulton.

Schumm, J. (1999) *Adapting Reading and Math Materials for Inclusive Classrooms*, Reston, VA: Council for Exceptional Children.

Stakes, R. and Hornby, G. (2000) *Meeting Special Needs in Mainstream Schools* (2nd edn) London: Fulton.

Tomlinson, C.A. (1999) *The Differentiated Classroom: Responding to the Needs of All Learners*, Alexandria, VA: Association for Supervision and Curriculum Development.

# References

Babbage, R., Byers, R. and Redding, H. (1999) *Approaches to Teaching and Learning: Including Pupils with Learning Difficulties*, London: Fulton.

Bearne, E. (1996) *Differentiation and Diversity in the Primary School*, London: Routledge.

Byrnes, M. (2000) 'Accommodations for students with disabilities: removing the barriers to learning', *NASSP Bulletin*, 84, 613: 21–7.

Carpenter, B. and Ashdown, R. (1996) 'Enabling access', in B. Carpenter, R. Ashdown and K. Bovair (eds) *Enabling Access: Effective Teaching and Learning for Pupils with Learning Difficulties*, London: Fulton.

Chan, C., Chang, M.L., Westwood, P.S. and Yuen, M.T. (2001) 'Teaching adaptively: How easy is "differentiation" in practice? A perspective from Hong Kong', *Asia-Pacific Educational Researcher* 11, 1: 27–58.

Davies, P. (2000) 'Differentiation: processing and understanding in teachers' thinking and practice', *Educational Studies*, 26, 2: 191–203.

Dettmer, P., Thurston, L. and Dyck, N. (2002) *Consultation, Collaboration and Teamwork for Students with Special Needs* (4th edn), Boston, MA: Allyn and Bacon.

Falvey, M.A., Givner, C.C. and Kimm, C. (1996) 'What do I do Monday morning?', in S. Stainback and W. Stainback (eds) *Inclusion: A Guide for Educators*, Baltimore, MD: Brookes.

Hall, S. (1997) 'The problem with differentiation', *School Science Review*, 78, 284: 95–8.

Hoover, J. and Patton, J. (1997) *Curriculum Adaptations for Students with Learning and Behaviour Problems* (2nd edn), Austin, TX: ProEd.

Kameenui, E. and Simmons, D. (1999) *Towards Successful Inclusion of Students with Disabilities: The Architecture of Instruction*, Reston, VA: Council for Exceptional Children.

Kenward, H. (1997) *Integrating Pupils with Disabilities in Mainstream Schools*, London: Fulton.

Kerry, T. and Kerry, C.A. (1997) 'Differentiation: teachers' views of the usefulness of recommended strategies in helping the more able pupils in primary and secondary classrooms', *Educational Studies*, 23, 3: 439–57.

Klinger, J. and Vaughn, S. (1999) 'Students' perceptions of instruction in inclusive classrooms: implications for students with learning disabilities', *Exceptional Children*, 66, 1: 23–37.

Leyser, Y. and Ben-Yehuda, S. (1999) 'Teacher use of instructional practices to accommodate student diversity: views of Israeli general and special educators', *International Journal of Special Education*, 14, 1: 81–95.

Peetsma, T., Vergeer, M., Roeleveld, J. and Karsten, S. (2001) 'Inclusion in education: comparing pupils' development in special and regular education', *Educational Review*, 53: 125–35.

Pettig, K.L. (2000) 'On the road to differentiated practice', *Educational Leadership* 58, 1: 14–18.

Reynolds, D. and Muijs, D. (1999) 'Contemporary policy issues in the teaching of mathematics'. In I. Thompson (ed.) *Issues in Teaching Numeracy in Primary Schools*, Buckingham: Open University Press.

Robbins, B. (1996) 'Mathematics', in B. Carptenter, R. Ashdown and K. Bovair (eds) *Enabling Access: Effective Teaching and Learning for Pupils with Learning Difficulties*, London: Fulton.

Rose, R. (2001) 'Primary school teacher perceptions of the conditions required for including pupils with special educational needs', *Educational Review*, 53, 2: 147–56.

Schumm, J.S. and Vaughn, S. (1995) 'Getting ready for inclusion: Is the stage set?' *Learning Disabilities Research and Practice*, 10, 3: 169–79.

Scott, B.J., Vitale, M.R. and Masten, W.G. (1998) 'Implementing instructional adaptations for students with disabilities in inclusive classrooms', *Remedial and Special Education* 19, 2: 106–19.

Squires, G. (2001) 'Dyslexia: strategies for support', *Special Children*, 149: 23–6.

Tomlinson, C.A. (1996) *Differentiating Instruction for Mixed-ability Classrooms*, Alexandria, VA: Association for Supervision and Curriculum Development.

Tomlinson, C.A. (1999) *The Differentiated Classroom: Responding to the Needs of All Learners*, Alexandria, VA: Association for Supervision and Curriculum Development.

Tomlinson, C.A. (2001) 'Grading for success', *Educational Leadership*, 58, 6: 12–15.

Udvari-Solner, A. (1998) 'Adapting the curriculum', in M.F. Giangreco (ed.) *Quick Guides to Inclusion: Ideas for Educating Students with Disabilities*, Baltimore, MD: Brookes.

Van den Berg, R., Sleegers, P. and Geijsel, F. (2001) 'Teachers' concerns about adaptive teaching: evaluation of a support program', *Journal of Curriculum and Supervision*, 16, 3: 245–58.

Webster, A. (1995) 'Differentiation', in G. Moss (ed.) *The Basics of Special Needs*, London: Routledge.

Weston, P., Taylor, M., Lewis, G. and MacDonald, A. (1998) *Learning from Differentiation*, Slough: NFER.

Westwood, P.S. (2001) 'Differentiation as a strategy for inclusive classroom practice: some difficulties identified', *Australian Journal of Learning Disabilities*, 6, 1: 5–11.

Wood, J.W. (1998) *Adapting Instruction to Accommodate Students in Inclusive Settings* (3rd edn), Upper Saddle River, NJ: Merrill.

# CHAPTER 11

# POLICIES FOR POSITIVE BEHAVIOUR MANAGEMENT

## T. Cole

In C. Tilstone and R. Rose (eds) *Strategies to Promote Inclusive Practice* (2003), London and New York: RoutledgeFalmer, pp. 67–83

Does the advance of inclusion (Thomas *et al.*, 1998; Tilstone *et al.*, 1998) hold good for pupils labelled as being disruptive or having emotional and behavioural difficulties (EBD)? Clark *et al.* (1999) noted intractable problems of behaviour even in the most inclusive of settings. Research has underlined the severity of the management problems posed by some pupils with learning and behavioural difficulties, the stress caused to peers and staff, and the extensive demands on senior management time. Difficulties continue despite differentiated and appropriate teaching and proficient behaviour management, but Ofsted reports indicate that some schools in disadvantaged areas are more successful in managing difficult behaviour than some in more affluent areas. What are the characteristics of successful schools and what policies do they operate to minimise the segregation of pupils with learning and behavioural difficulties?

## Definitions and parameters

The government definition of EBD is given in Circular 9/94 (DfE, 1994b):

> Children with EBD are on a continuum. Their problems are clearer and greater than sporadic naughtiness or moodiness and yet not so great as to be classed as mental illness.
>
> (p. 4)

Their differences range from 'social maladaptation to abnormal emotional stresses' (p. 7); 'are persistent and constitute learning difficulties' (p. 7), and children with EBD are seen as having problems in relationships. Cole (1998) noted that behaviour difficulties are usually accompanied by underachievement in class and sometimes by pronounced learning difficulties.

These pupils' difficulties can stem from both within-child factors (sometimes including the biological or genetic) and without-child factors, usually in interaction with each other and with a complicated ecosystem involving peers, family and neighbourhood influences (Cooper *et al.*, 1994). In this chapter, 'pupils with EBD' is used not only for students with statements for EBD (and those on the Code of Practice Stages for learning difficulties associated with behaviour) but also for the far greater number of pupils termed 'disruptive' or 'having attention deficit disorder'

(ADHD) or said to 'have mental health difficulties'. The epidemiology depends not only on local interpretations of national guidance but also on different professions' contrasting perspectives and traditions. The writers of one local education authority's behaviour support plan noted: 'The lively youngster in one setting can be deemed a major problem in another' (Cole *et al.*, 1999, p. 22). Government statistics and LEA behaviour support plans appear to indicate that the number of pupils with significant EBD or those deemed 'seriously disruptive' amounts to 5 per cent of the national school population (Cole *et al.*, 1999).

## Creating and maintaining an inclusive school ethos

A prerequisite for effective mainstream policies for pupils with EBD and learning difficulties is the creation and maintenance of an appropriate inclusive school ethos. Daniels *et al.* (1998) noted that some schools are fortunate in having a history of 'looking after' at risk pupils, of forging close community links and working towards successful inclusion. In contrast, in schools where a suitable balance between stressing the academic and the pastoral has never been achieved (Galloway, 1990; Power, 1996), initiatives are necessary to bring about fundamental changes in attitudes and policies. In other schools, the quasi-market reforms of the 1980s and 1990s may have weakened their capacity for coping with pupils who challenge the 'standards' and published league table agendas (Parsons, 1999; McLaughlin and Rouse, 2000; Hallam and Castle, 2001).

In all schools, the quality, style and attitudes of leadership (in particular those of the head teacher) are crucial to creating and maintaining an inclusive ethos. One head stated, 'We are a comprehensive school', before stressing his duty to all - children in his community, including those with learning and behavioural difficulties. In schools coping well with behavioural issues, statements such as this were an articulation of deeply held beliefs, and senior staff, imbued with inclusive values, possessed the skill and motivation to influence the attitudes and actions of their sometimes more-doubting colleagues. Many teachers and Learning Support Assistants (LSAs) have become receptive to senior staff initiatives to engender positive behaviour management. Conversely, head teachers and senior staff are receptive to, and supportive of, teacher ideas and initiatives. These is evidence of a desire to experiment with reward systems and a common reluctance to reject pupils, for example, through the frequent use of fixed-term and permanent exclusions. Daniels *et al.* (1998) noted that the direction, coherence and cohesiveness in these schools was generated by the leadership, but made possible by staff who were committed and caring towards their less gifted and more challenging pupils.

Research indicates that, when not in direct contact with children, staff spend time talking to colleagues about work-related topics or student needs to support each other; to provoke reflection and self-analysis; to explore new ideas and to help colleagues to learn new skills (Hopkins, 1997). As well as being 'talking' schools, they are 'learning' schools using the 'do-review-learn-apply' planning and practice cycle in most aspects of school life (Dennison and Kirk, 1990) including behaviour management. Practitioners were engaged in an on-going re-evaluation of their work through formal development days, training and advice from LEA support services or through staff working groups. Lessons learnt led to adjusted practice (Daniels *et al.*, 1998) and Cole *et al.* (2000) provide further evidence of 'learning' schools. Teachers and LSAs are then willing to use their school's Behaviour Co-ordinators (BCos), details of whose roles are given later, to observe and discuss their classroom performance and to review school systems.

Behavioural difficulties are usually linked to underachievement and to learning difficulties (Daniels *et al.*, 1998; Hallam and Castle, 1999; Cole and Visser, 2000). Missed schooling or social and emotional upsets are likely to be combined to make young people acutely aware of their recurrent failure in front of their peers. Their reaction is commonly 'fight' or 'flight', and help needs to be channelled diplomatically to address their learning difficulties. Close working between pastoral, subject and learning support departments is required although, too often, it seems that Special Educational Needs Co-ordinators (SENCos), heads of department and heads of year act separately, to the detriment of individuals and groups and ultimately to the ethos and effectiveness of the school. It is a feature of the 'good practice' schools in Daniels *et al.* (1998) that such divisions did not exist or at least that senior management was actively trying to bring the activities of pastoral and SEN staff closer together. An example was the placing of an assistant SENCo in each subject department in order to provide early specialist intervention for 'at risk' pupils and 'front-line' advice to subject specialists in differentiation techniques or behaviour management. In another school, in a staff meeting, the deputy head confessed to having just experienced a particularly difficult lesson with a new Year 9 pupil. The SENCo offered to see the young person immediately to establish what, if any, learning difficulties he had. This was their standard practice (Daniels *et al.*, 1998).

The research underlines a predictable but crucial factor identified in the literature on behavioural difficulties (Redl, 1966; Cooper, 1993): schools coping well with 'difficult' children are characterised by having many talented and effective staff who are able to form helpful relationships with challenging young people. Cole *et al.* (1998) listed the characteristics, as perceived by teacher respondents to a national survey, of successful teachers with pupils with EBD. They did not need to be masters of psychoanalysis or of therapies or different from good, committed mainstream staff. They should be well organised, consistent, humorous, calm, enthusiastic; skillful in delivering their specialist subjects; set clear boundaries; be flexible; understand 'behaviour' causation (Cole, 1998) and be empathetic to the young people. Talking to children with EBD elicited a similar view: they respect teachers who set firm boundaries, are skillful classroom managers and deliverers of their subject. More, however, is needed: a Year 10 girl with a statement for EBD described good staff as:

> ...teachers who understand you and take an interest in you. After you have finished your work they ask you how you are. They socialize. You get to like them.
>
> (Daniels *et al.*, 1998, p. 83)

A Year 10 boy who had recently 'come off' a statement for EBD compared good and bad teachers:

> They [the good] are polite and treat you with respect. If a teacher...is in a foul mood or shouting at you, you do the same back.
>
> (Daniels *et al.*, 1998, p. 83)

A group of young people at a small rural secondary school commented:

> Staff are seen as friends and helpers to children and each other. The caring ethos has been absorbed by generations of children and teachers. Children

show concern for other pupils and will say if another child is having a bad day and needs special attention or help.

(Daniels *et al.*, 1998, p. 20)

For a school to minimise feelings of disaffection and resulting challenging behaviour, form tutors have to *embrace* and not *resist* their pastoral role as mentors and supporters (Cole and Visser, 2000; Munn *et al.*, 2000). In primary schools, there is more likely to be a tradition of caring and talking and of creating inclusive cultures in which all pupils and their families feel welcome. The challenge is clearly greater in large secondary schools, particularly those having catchment areas with a history of resistance to schooling and less local faith in teachers. Cultures can, however, be changed: pastoral staff and subject specialists can alter practice until they are perceived by pupils more as *pastors* than agents of punishment.

## Whole-school behaviour policy

Relevant and 'lived' comprehensive whole-school behaviour policies help to minimise EBD (DES, 1989; Daniels *et al.*, 1998). Such policies should:

- be succinct but detailed and in written form;
- used as a vehicle for promoting desired staff practice;
- contain school pro formas;
- give explanatory notes as well as flow-charts for referrals;
- make the links explicit between pastoral, subject and special needs departments;
- be seen as a resource to be consulted by teachers in times of need;
- be open, consultative and ongoing if reflection and self-evaluation amongst staff is to be promoted and the stakeholders are to feel 'ownership' of the process.

There can be teacher resistance to the regular use of such policies (Daniels *et al.*, 1998) and, where this happens, policy documents need to be used as the basis for ongoing staff development, referred to by senior staff periodically as particular issues arise throughout each school year and not allowed to gather dust at the back of teachers' cupboards. All school staff (including administration and caretaking staff) should be involved (see Box 11.1). In the long term, *imposed* policies tend to be subverted, circumvented or ignored.

Useful advice on the content of behaviour policies has been given by DES (1989), Ofsted (1993), DfE (1994a) and Clarke and Murray (1996). Box 11.2 shows the contents of an exemplary policy observed in a large secondary school (Daniels *et al.*, 1998).

The consistent application of agreed policies is crucial as emotional and behavioural difficulties are exacerbated by uncertain and unpredictable policy application. In Daniels *et al.* (1998), senior staff worked hard to ensure that all staff applied agreed policies thoroughly in, for example, the use of:

- 'positive behaviour' credit and certificate systems;
- systems for reporting worrying or unacceptable behaviour;
- records of the interventions used;
- behaviour report and monitoring forms;
- supervision rosters for break times;
- rules for movement of pupils through buildings;
- attendance registers, their maintenance and the follow up of absentees.

---

*Box 11.1 Creating and maintaining a whole-school behaviour policy in a six-teacher primary school*

Despite a positive Ofsted report that praised the behaviour of pupils and might have prompted the school to rest on its laurels, it was felt beneficial to review the behaviour policy. Pupils, full-time teachers, part-time teachers, LSAs, midday supervisors, governors and parents were all actively involved in a review of existing policy over a period of months. This happened in discussions in class, in formal meetings and in informal discussions in breaks and after school. A revised draft policy was widely circulated before final approval by the school governors. The result was a policy owned by all stakeholders. Research in the school suggested that the consistency and cohesion of the staff in the operation of this policy contributed to the inclusion of children on the SEN register for behavioural reasons.

(Daniels *et al.*, 1998)

---

*Box 11.2 The content of a whole-school behaviour policy*

A whole-school behaviour policy should describe:

(a)  the mission statement and the general aims of the school;
(b)  the rights and responsibilities of staff, pupils and parents;
(c)  the school's Code of Conduct/rules;
(d)  approaches to the encouragment of good behaviour;
(e)  routines and staff responsibilities;
(f)  'Cause for Concern', 'Incident Forms' and other pro-forma devised with the help of the school psychologist;
(g)  sanction and reward systems;
(h)  pastoral support systems;
(i)  links to other school policies;
(j)  advice on working with parents.

---

The need for some sanctions was seen in all schools, the emphasis of which was on the reinforcement of desired behaviours and it was evident that staff should ensure that they model the values and attitudes they wish to see permeating their own communities.

## Proficient classroom management

Positive behaviour policies should encourage teachers to review their own practice and to identify their sometimes unwitting part in creating challenging behaviour. In addition, senior managers should be proactive in creating school climates in which reviews of practice are embedded and in which skilled help can easily be sought, without feelings of failure or blame, to tackle identified weaknesses.

Classrooms in EBD schools which bring together groups of pupils that have been highly disruptive in mainstream settings are not infrequently quiet, purposeful environments with little outward sign of disturbance (Laslett, 1977; Cole *et al.*, 1998). Similarly, in mainstream settings, some pupils with EBD (including some said to have ADHD and who are not taking psychostimulants such as 'Ritalin') behave well for some teachers, but are severely disruptive for others. Clearly, disruptive behaviour is often situation-specific, relating in part to how the adults in school settings act. Jordan (1974) (cited in Smith and Laslett, 1993) identified 'deviance-provocative' and 'deviance-insulative' teachers. Identifying and 'where possible' rectifying teacher shortcomings is an aspect of school life to which more time and resources should be devoted as pupils with EBD tend to be the first to respond with disruptive behaviour to inappropriate or unskilled teaching. These children often lack patience, become easily frustrated, have short attention spans and low anger thresholds, give up on tasks and are frightened of new work. Unless they are taught skillfully, these factors will readily come into play, particularly if the style of teaching exacerbates the low self-esteem of many pupils with EBD and 'shows them up' in front of their peers.

Conversely, they can respond well to proficient teaching (Ofsted, 1999) and in Daniels *et al.* (1998) teachers were observed successfully controlling and motivating pupils with EBD. These teachers were confident presenters of their subject and masters of basic classroom craft, clearly possessing Kounin's (1970) 'withitness'! They were skilled in the use of eye-contact for engaging interest or of 'the look' to express disapproval; they used varying tone of voice and an appropriate choice of language, sometimes blended with humour to defuse situations or to stop minor disruptions. They anticipated and avoided trouble through diversionary tactics or low-level interventions that did not provoke pupil resentment. They tended not to be desk-bound but moved around the room as appropriate, thereby exercising 'proximity control' (Redl and Wineman, 1952). Their craft contrasted with the limited repertoires of less effective teachers who were clearly in need of training and development as DfEE (1997) stressed.

One structured approach to practical on-site teacher development is Birmingham LEAs 'Framework for Intervention' (FFI) scheme (City of Birmingham Education Department, 1998; Daniels and Williams, 2000; Cole *et al.*, 2000). At the heart of FFI are LEA advisory teachers and on-site BCos, who urge class teachers first to look at their own basic practice before searching for an 'explanation' of a child's perceived misbehaviour 'within the child'. Disruptive behaviour can too readily be seen as the outward manifestation of inner disturbance or of a medical condition, such as wrongly diagnosed ADHD (Elliott and Place, 1998; Baldwin, 2000). Making such a diagnosis should be resisted, at least until after the teacher, supported by the BCo, has checked the key elements of the total *behavioural environment* including the teacher's own contribution (see Box 11.3).

Where FFI is well established, both newly qualified and experienced teachers have found it useful to ask themselves the questions posed in Box 11.3 while completing a detailed Behavioural Environmental Checklist (BEC) about the impact of wider school life upon this class, as well as the teacher's own practice. Often the BCos are asked to observe the lessons. A Behavioural Environment Plan (BEP) is then constructed, not to target the individual child but rather the teacher's management of the whole problematic class, and events outside the classroom that may be influencing difficulties within it. Completing BECs and BEPs, supported by the BCo, are described as Level One interventions. Some evidence shows that these can obviate the need to develop interventions targeted at individual pupils which initially cause concern to the teacher (Cole *et al.*, 2000). If the Level One intervention proves unsuccessful, the focus can then turn to the individual child and Level Two approaches. For example, the construction of individual behaviour plans, peer or mentor support schemes, interventions from specialist staff or anger management

---

*Box 11.3  Checking the behavioural environment*

(1) How is the 'difficult' child influenced?

  - by the school's rules/expectations?
  - by what happened in a previous lesson or break time?
  - by the rest of the class?

(2) How does the class enter the classroom before the start of the lesson?
(3) Are the seating arrangements suitable for what I am teaching?
(4) Are the children grouped in the most appropriate way?
(5) Are the necessary materials and equipment readily accessible to the pupils?
(6) Is heating, lighting and ventilation suitable?
(7) Am I giving clear instructions in an audible and 'non-grating' voice?
(8) Am I teaching at an appropriate level: not too hard, not too easy?
(9) Am I modelling the suitable use of polite language?
(10) Am I providing variety and pace in my lessons?

---

training. The provision of time and the creation of structures for BCos (and in large schools, assistant BCos) to operate effectively requires resources and at least medium-term LEA support. The Birmingham system has relied on time-limited government grants, but the indications are that this is a fruitful approach worthy of imitation and perhaps meriting the employment of some of the funding made available to tackle social exclusion under, for example, Pupil Retention Grants (DfEE, 1999).

Other research work (Hallam and Castle, 1999; Cole and Visser, 2000) suggests the potential of advisory teachers in developing classroom practice. Staff self-support and development groups run along the lines of Teacher Support Teams (Creese *et al.*, 1997) can also be invaluable.

## Curricular factors

An effective teacher can make almost any subject interesting to pupils with EBD. Certainly Shakespeare (tales of lust, excitement and violence?) does not have to be an obstacle and can be brought alive by imaginative teachers. Likewise, religious education, music and modern foreign languages, viewed by senior staff of the nation's EBD schools as the most difficult subjects to deliver, ceased to be a problem when skilled specialist practitioners sympathetic to the problems of pupils with emotional and learning difficulties were employed in some schools (Cole *et al.*, 1998). However, teachers who perhaps are not 'born to the profession' or are required to teach outside their subject specialism predictably find behaviour management and student motivation easier when they are allowed flexibility of approach, sometimes outside a statutory framework. Where possible that which is taught and the manner of teaching should play to their students' areas of relative strength, as well as their interests outside the classroom (particularly for Years 9 through to 11). Schools should explore and develop policies that take these factors into account without sacrificing rigour or challenge or becoming patronising to their students.

Somewhat surprisingly, the notion of a general National Curriculum was not seen as an obstacle to effective practice with pupils with emotional and learning difficulties. Instead, senior staff tended to recognise that it had increased the range and quality of education offered in special and mainstream schools (Cole *et al.*, 1998). Aspects of different subjects (e.g. creative writing in English or algebra in Mathematics), however, did evoke criticism from some mainstream teachers. In Cole *et al.* (1998) and Daniels *et al.* (1998) there was support for recent reductions in the number of subjects that had to be taught and for the Green Paper's (DfEE, 1997) and Programme of Action's (DfEE, 1988) encouragement of more vocational and practical subjects and links with colleges of further education for pupils in Key Stage 4 (KS4). Such a policy is sensible, subject to the important proviso that is not used as an excuse for offering an undemanding, alternative curriculum not linked to national accreditation. Our data suggest many successful placements of KS4 pupils in well-organised Further Education (FE) colleges, sometimes leading to General National Vocational Qualifications (GNVQs) and directly paving the way to lasting employment. A Year 10 girl with EBD described her enjoyment of a GNVQ beauty 'taster course' at the local FE college (Daniels *et al.*, 1998).

The head teacher of a school that had retained a grammar school image and was noted for good examination results, argued for curricula that played to many pupils' 'natural propensities' for the practical and the verbal rather than the abstract and the written (Daniels *et al.*, 1998). There is not unanimity on this argument, however, and the head teacher of a large inner-city comprehensive thought he had 'turned round' his school by ridding it of its vocational, 'boys' secondary modern approach. At this school the emphasis on academic entitlement for all students had increased, and teacher expectations of the capabilities of their pupils risen. Clearly an appropriate balance has to be struck between the academic and the vocational and the written and the verbal, but with an emphasis on flexibility and responsiveness to individual pupil capabilities and, perhaps, local circumstances. Where a balance is managed in relation to curriculum delivery, there can be a marked reduction in behavioural difficulties.

## Managing the behaviour of individual pupils

Strategies adopted in 'good practice' schools to target the specific challenges presented by individual pupils were refinements of 'normal' behaviour systems and approaches used across their schools (Daniels *et al.*, 1998) for pupils without notable EBD. Whenever possible, strategies were instigated against a backdrop of a policy of early identification and intervention and an additional key factor is the ability of back-up staff to offer a swift 'catcher' and support system when a class teacher needs to ask a pupil to leave the class. Behaviour management is unlikely to be successful if it is not part of a wider set of supportive relationships between pupils and key staff.

Behaviourist-learning approaches are useful. Commonly they involve careful observation and tallying of behaviours on frequency charts, and specific target setting linked to clearly defined reinforcements. Reward systems can range from points or merit certificates through lunchtime use of computers to small sums of money or vouchers for shops, the choice being made in negotiation with the pupil (Daniels *et al.*, 1998). Schools can also offer a mixture of extrinsic rewards and verbal reinforcement (adult approval and praise) sometimes given at weekly award assemblies. School policies should stress the dictum 'Catch Them Being Good' (Madsen *et al.* cited in Cole *et al.*, 1998) and outline the rewards on offer, as well as stressing the principles sketched in Box 11.4.

Pupils with emotional and learning difficulties can usually accept sanctions perceived by them as fair, unless they have become substantially alienated from

---

*Box 11.4  Reward principles*

- *Rewards have to be earned.* Pupils will not respect rewards perceived as unearned, nor respect staff who give them too freely. Rewards can become appeasement.
- *Rewards must relate to clear, agreed targets.* Targets should be specific, limited in scope to maintain a child's focus, realistic, negotiated and agreed as worthwhile by the child. Global injunctions on a child's Behaviour Plan or Report Card 'to behave' or 'be good' are of very limited use.
- *Rewards must be given at appropriate time intervals.* Large rewards offered half-termly or weekly may not work as well as small rewards offered daily or twice daily or after the attainment of targets for a particularly problematic lesson with a particular teacher. Flexible time scales offer more chances for 'forgiveness' of the pupil.
- *Praise should be delivered appropriately.* Praise can take the form of lavish words. Some pupils, however, may be embarrassed by public praise (Hanko, 1994; Rogres, 1994), but will respond to non-verbal communication (e.g. a 'thumbs up' or nod of the head). Praise might best be offered away from a student's peer group (e.g. in a head of year's office).
- *Rewards should come from a 'significant other'.* Rewards or sanctions given by teachers perceived as hostile or indifferent are likely to be ineffective (Deniels *et al.*, 1998).

---

the school community and have very poor relationships with most staff. Sanction systems must avoid being mechanistic and punitive, thereby failing to achieve the necessary balance between overall fairness and allowing for individual capacity and difference. Rigidity of application can be a danger for simplistic interpretations of, for example, *assertive discipline* (Canter, 1990; Daniels *et al.*, 1998). Sanction systems must be accompanied by regular monitoring, which does not need to be punitive, by staff who are 'significant others'. A head teacher was observed in a secondary school sitting next to a child at school dinner to chat to him informally as well as to check with him the entries on his lesson report card (Daniels *et al.*, 1998), the 'message' being that it was the pupil's bad behaviour alone that had been criticised.

Beyond the application of as school's formal behaviour system, school policies must create opportunities for talking and listening to 'at risk' young people. Staff interviewed as part of Daniels *et al.* (1998) frequently referred to the difficult home circumstances and the emotional turmoil of most of the pupils considered to have EBD. They tended to be knowledgeable and sympathetic to these wider problems, had gained their understanding through contact with the child's family or careers or through ongoing contacts in school with the children themselves. Time had been found for these children, and time is essential for successful work with children with EBD whatever the setting. Positive relationships had been nurtured by regular communication between teachers, support and (sometimes) administrative staff and the vulnerable and disruptive and staff made a point of stopping for a brief chat with pupils with EBD in the corridors, or before or after 'problem' lessons. These frequent 'naturalistic' interactions, part of sharing the same 'life-space' (Cole *et al.*, 1998), are used to reassure and to remain pupils with EBD that they are valued and that they remain part of the school community despite the challenging behaviour they often present.

When difficult problems do occur, it is essential that assistance for the class teacher is on hand immediately from experienced staff, as it is vital that class teachers do not feel alone, without recourse to help, in extreme situations and that other pupils do not experience excessive disruption and inappropriate behaviour. Cole *et al.* (1998) and Daniels *et al.* (1998) found such 'catcher system's to be widely valued. Their role was to remove and counsel seriously disruptive pupils, to calm down others in the aftermath of tantrums or fights, and it was found that 'the calm after the storm' of serious classroom or break time incidents could be used to provide 'emotional first aid' (Redl, 1966) to an upset pupil with serious emotional difficulties. Children can be most open to sharing confidences and listening to the opinions of valued staff when the immediate storm of an emotional outburst has subsided (Redl and Wineman, 1952).

Given the central part played by LSAs in enabling inclusion, a sensitive approach to offering learning support is necessary and some pupils, usually those with moderate learning and behavioural difficulties, seem to be at ease with the presence of an LSA beside them. These pupils in secondary schools may well have grown used to such an arrangement in their primary schools and were reported to be heavily reliant upon, and to expect and to enjoy the presence of, their LSA (Daniels *et al.*, 1998). In contrast other pupils disliked LSA support as they interpreted it as a highly visible sign of their difficulties, which 'showed them up' in front of their peers. Schools need policies that are understood and followed in relation to learning support (Lorenz, 1998; Thomas *et al.*, 1998; Lacey, 2001).

Valuable support can also be offered by staff or volunteers not directly employed by the school (Box 11.5). Girls sometimes found it useful to talk to the school nurse and both boys and girls to peripatetic EBD teachers or to youth workers (Daniels *et al.*, 1998; Cole and Visser, 2000). At one school, Bengali children received counselling from a Bengali Education Welfare Officer (EWO). 'At risk' black pupils are disproportionately included in the exclusion figures (Osler, 1997; Osler *et al.*, 2001) and often appreciate support from black staff. The value of adult mentors is increasingly being recognised, particularly where the mentor shares the same ethnic heritage (DfEE, 1999; Cole and Visser, 2000).

Flexible curricular organisation and timetabling is also important. Full inclusion with their regular class for every lesson was judged to be against some children's medium- and long-term interests. Given the degree of their underachievement and/or disruption in some lessons, or unsatisfactory relationship with particular

---

*Box 11.5 Offering classroom support sensitively*

An underachieving Year 10 pupil, formerly on an EBD statement, appreciated:

- a teacher who managed to brief the pupil about lesson content ahead of class;
- other staff who would wait until the other pupils were engaged in quiet writing before discreetly moving to his table to offer support.

An LSA described her strategy; she made a point of sitting close to a girl who liked her in close proximity. For another child, the LSA would bide her time and wait until the teacher was moving round a room offering support to other children so that it was not unusual or stigmatising for her to go over and offer to be a scribe for the child who was uneasy about her presence (Daniels *et al.*, 1998).

teachers, some withdrawal was judged wise (Daniels *et al.*, 1998). Ideally, children's timetables should reflect their individual needs and capabilities. In practice, a compromise is sometimes needed to give overwrought staff and the pupils' peers respite from some children's extreme behaviours.

Finally, it is advisable to consider the physical environment as a prop to the management of a few pupils' more extreme behaviour. A comfortable *physical and private space* (a room or an area) can be a haven or sanctuary for a few pupils when in throes of a damaging behavioural outburst. It can be part of children's individual behaviour plans, understood by the subject teachers, as an escape from the classroom or playground when:

• they are having difficulty in controlling their anger or emotions;
• they feel the need for 'time out' from peers who are goading them;
• they need to talk with specialist staff;
• a subject teacher decides that the child's behaviour has become too disruptive.

Pupils can return from this sanctuary to rejoin their usual groups when in a calmer mood.

## Conclusion

The policies and practices described earlier will help children and staff, but it is recognised that no easy prescriptions can be offered for schools serving neighbourhoods where there are acute social problems and an entrenched culture of disaffection and dissatisfaction with education. Schools can, and often do, make a difference (Mortimore *et al.*, 1988) but it was discouraging to hear a teacher say of a school serving a disadvantaged community, 'You have to like the children, like the work and like being here' (Daniels *et al.*, 1998, p. 53), clearly implying that some staff in this school, probably through tiredness and chronic disappointments, did not. Similarly worrying was the comment, 'You can talk to staff here' by a Year 10 pupil (Daniels *et al.*, 1998, p. 84). Sadly, this was a novel experience for him and contrasted with his previous schools from which he had been excluded. Inclusion can only advance when sufficient skilled and committed staff win the respect and liking of pupils and create school communities of which they want to be a part. Data repeatedly indicate that once pupils and their families reach the firm conclusion that a school has little to offer and sometimes has rejected them, there will remain intractable problems, perhaps only solvable by a move to another mainstream school or to a contrasting 'segregated' setting (Cole *et al.*, 1998; Cole and Visser, 2000).

This is only partly a criticism of some teachers as staff can be forced by school traditions and government diktat to move away from fulfilling a pastoral role adequately and to work in an anti-inclusionary way. A generation ago, Balbernie (Foreword to Millham *et al.*, 1975) portrayed successful work with difficult young people as 'the art of making oneself available in relationships for others'. Such strategies can be achieved only if staff are enabled to create time and space for talking and listening to pupils as a central part of their professional role, without detracting from skilled and rigorous teaching. In secondary schools in particular this has been a difficult challenge since long before the introduction of the National Curriculum and the 'marketisation' of education (Leavold, 1984; Cole, 1989), but the reforms of the 1980s and early 1990s probably exacerbated the situation (Booth *et al.*, 1998; Cole, 1999; McLaughlin and Rouse, 2000). Nevertheless, some schools meet the challenge better than others and their policy and practice must be shared.

# Reflective questions

1   Physical disability is relatively easily defined and objectively and consistently observed in a variety of contexts, and evokes sympathy. Social, emotional and behavioural disability tends to be perceived subjectively in a particular context and evokes strong antagonistic reactions. What are the implications for practice and policy stemming from this?

2   It has been argued that pupils with special educational needs do not need special teaching, they need good teaching. Does this apply equally (or perhaps especially) to pupils with social, emotional and behavioural difficulties?

# References

Baldwin, S. (2000) 'How should ADHD be treated: a discussion with Paul Cooper', *The Psychologist,* 13(12) 598–602.

Booth, T., Ainscow, M. and Dyson, A. (1998) 'England: inclusion and exclusion in a competitive system', in T. Booth and M. Ainscow (eds) *From Them to Us.* London: Routledge.

Canter, L. (1990) 'Assertive discipline', in M. Scherer, I. Gersch and L. Fry (eds) *Meeting Disruptive Behaviour.* London: Macmillan.

City of Birmingham Education Department (1998) *The Framework for Intervention.* Birmingham: City of Birmingham Education Department.

Clark, C., Dyson, A., Millward, A. and Robson, S. (1999) 'Theories of inclusion, theories of schools: deconstructing and reconstructing the inclusive school', *British Educational Research Journal,* 25(2) 157–77.

Clarke, D. and Murray, A. (1996) *Developing a Whole School Behaviour Policy: a Practical Approach.* London: David Fulton.

Cole, T. (1989) *Apart or A Part? Integration and the Growth of British Special Education.* Milton Keynes: Open University Press.

Cole, T. (1998) 'Understanding challenging behaviour: prerequisites to inclusion', in C. Tilstone, L. Florian and R. Rose (eds) *promoting Inclusive Practice.* London: Routledge.

Cole, T. (1999) 'Defining and developing proficient education for pupils with emotional and behavioural difficulties in special and mainstream schools'. Unpublished PhD dissertation. University of Birmingham.

Cole, T., Daniels, H. and Visser, J. (1999) *Patterns of Educational Provision Maintained by Local Education Authorities for Pupils with Behaviour Problems* (A report sponsored by the Nuffield Foundation). Birmingham: University of Birmingham.

Cole, T. and Visser, J. (2000) *EBD Policy, Practice and Provision in Shropshire LEA and Telford and Wrekin LEA.* Birmingham: University of Birmingham.

Cole, T., Visser, J. and Daniels, H. (2000) *The Framework for Intervention: Identifying and Promoting Effective Practice* (Second Evaluation Report). Report commissioned by the City of Birmingham Education Department. Birmingham: The University of Birmingham.

Cole, T., Visser, J. and Upton, G. (1998) *Effective Schooling for Pupils with Emotional and Behavioural Difficulties.* London: David Fulton Publishers.

Cooper, P. (1993) *Effective Schooling for Disaffected Students.* London: Routledge.

Cooper, P., Smith, C. and Upton, G. (1994) *Emotional and Behavioural Difficulties.* London: Routledge.

Creese, A., Daniels, H. and Norwich, B. (1997) *Teacher Support Teams.* London: David Fulton.

Daniels, A. and Williams, H. (2000) 'Reducing the need for exclusions and statements for behaviour', *Educational Psychology in Practice,* 15 (4) 221–7.

Daniels, H., Visser, J., Cole, T. and de Reybekill, N. (1998) *Emotional and Behavioural Difficulties in the Mainstream* (Research Report RR90). London: DfEE.

Dennison, B. and Kirk, R. (1990) *Do, Review, Learn, Apply: a Simple Guide to Experiential Learning.* Oxford: Blackwell.

Department for Education (1994a) *Pupil Behaviour and Discipline* (Circular 8/94). London: DfE.

Department for Education (1994b) *The Education of Children with Emotional and Behavioural Difficulties* (Circular 9/94). London: DfE.

Department for Education and Employment (1997) *Excellence for All Children: Meeting Special Educational Needs* (Green Paper Cm 3785). London: The Stationery Office.

Department for Education and Employment (1998) *Meeting Special Educational Needs: a Programme of Action*. London: DfEE.

Department for Education and Employment (1999) *School Inclusion: Pupils' Support* (Circular 10/99). London: DfEE.

Department of Education and Science (1989) *Discipline in Schools: Report of the Committee of Enquiry* (The Elton Report). London: HMSO.

Elliott, J. and Place, M. (1998) *Children in Difficulty: a Guide to Understanding and Helping*. London: Routledge.

Galloway, D. (1990) *Pupil Welfare and Counselling*. London: Longman.

Hallam, S. and Castle, F. (1999) *Evaluation of the Behaviour and Discipline Pilot Projects (1996–99)* (Supported under the Standards Fund Programme: Research Report, RR163). London: DfEE.

Hallam, S. and Castle, F. (2001) 'Exclusion from school: What can help prevent it?', *Educational Review* (Special Issue: Inclusion in Practice), 53 (2) 169–79.

Hanko, G. (1994) 'Discouraged children: when praise does not help', *British Journal of Special Education*, 21 (4) 166–8.

Hopkins, D. (1997) 'Improving the quality of teaching and learning', *Support for Learning*, 12 (4) 162–5.

Kounin, J.S. (1970) *Discipline and Group Management in Classrooms*. New York: Krieger.

Lacey, P. (2001) 'The role of learning support assistants in the inclusive learning of pupils with severe and profound learning difficulties', *Educational Review* (Special Issue: Inclusion in Practice), 53 (2) 157–67.

Laslett, R. (1977) *Educating Maladjusted Children*. London: Granada.

Leavold, J. (1984) 'A sanctuary for disruptive pupils', in M. Lloyd-Smith (ed.) *Disrupted Schooling: the Growth of the Special Unit*. London: Murray.

Lorenz, S. (1998) *Effective In-Class Support*. London: David Fulton Publishers.

McLaughlin, M. and Rouse, M. (2000) (eds) *Special Education and School Reform in the United States and Britain*. London: Routledge.

Millham, S., Bullock, R. and Cherrett, P. (1975) *After Grace – Teeth*. London: Chaucer.

Mortimore, P., Sammons, L., Stoll, L. and Ecob, R. (1988) *School Matters*. Wells: Open Books.

Munn, P., Lloyd, G. and Cullen, M. (2000) *Alternatives to School Exclusion*. London: Paul Chapman.

Ofsted (1993) *Achieving Good Behaviour in Schools*. London: HMSO.

Ofsted (1999) *Principles into Practice: Effective Education for Pupils with EBD*. London: Ofsted.

Osler, A. (1997) 'Drama turns into a crisis for blacks', *Times Educational Supplement*, 10 October 1997.

Osler, A., Watling, R., Busher, H., Cole, T. and White, A. (2001) *Reasons for Exclusion from School* (Research Brief 244). London: DfEE.

Parsons, C. (1999) *Education, Exclusion and Citizenship*. London: Routledge.

Power, S. (1996) *The Pastoral and the Academic: Conflict and contradictions in the Curriculum*. London: Cassell.

Redl, F. (1966) *When We Deal with Children*. New York: Free Press.

Redl, F. and Wineman, D. (1952) *Controls from Within*. New York: Free press.

Rogers, B. (1994) *Behaviour Recovery: a Whole-school Program for Mainstream Schools*. London: Longman.

Smith, C. and Laslett, R. (1993) *Effective Classroom Management: a Teacher's Guide*. London: Routledge.

Thomas, G., Walker, D. and Webb, J. (1998) *The Making of the Inclusive School*. London: Routledge.

Tilstone, C., Florian, L. and Rose, R. (eds) (1998) *Promoting Inclusive Practice*. London: Routledge.

# CHAPTER 12

# PEER AND CROSS-AGE TUTORING AND MENTORING SCHEMES

F. Mallon

In H. Daniels (ed.), *Special Education Re-formed: Beyond Rhetoric?* (2000), London and New York: Falmer Press, pp. 204–21

## Introduction

Worldwide there is evidently massive interest in the use of peer tutoring within education systems. Searches uncover a host of research programmes testifying to the efficacy of peer tutoring and to a wide variety of applications in primary, secondary and higher education, in business and commerce and in all the professions.

Yet, this author continues to cause surprise when advocating to teachers approaches which include peer tutoring as potential solutions to problems they refer. Reactions span from apparent surprise at the 'novelty' of the idea; through concerns about the practicalities, particularly with certain pupil populations; ethical considerations about 'education on the cheap'; to fears that while tutees might gain, tutors may be held back or miss out on aspects of the curriculum. Clearly not all are convinced. Yet the literature and research contain powerful evidence not only for the potency of peer tutoring as an approach but for the positive benefits to both tutors and tutees. In reviewing the literature and considering in detail one radical approach which specifically targets disaffected adolescents as tutors, the Valued Youth Program (Cardenas *et al.*, 1992), it is hoped that more teacher colleagues will be stimulated to consider possible applications of peer or cross-age tutoring.

## An historical perspective

The process of transferring skills or knowledge from peers who possess such to those who do not must date from the earliest days of humankind (see, e.g. Jenkins and Jenkins, 1987). It is our immense capacity to learn from one another, together with the power of language, that has made *Homo sapiens* the most successful and best adapted species on the planet. Descriptions of educational practice in ancient Rome and in early Judaism have features we might recognize as peer tutoring (Topping, 1988) and we know that monitors were used in Elizabethan classrooms (Seaborne, 1966).

Most authors, however, accept that the earliest systematic use of a system whereby peers were used in formal teaching was by Andrew Bell, a school superintendent, who saw the potential power of children teaching children (Bell, 1797). Bell established elaborate hierarchies whereby in each class there were pairings of tutors and pupils, typically 12 more able pupils paired with 12 less able, with an assistant teacher who instructed and supervised tutors. In turn, the assistants were overseen by teachers who has overall responsibility for pupil progress and class-room discipline. However, the assistants and teachers themselves were aged between 7 and 14 years of age! The hierarchies were completed by subushers and ushers, who were ultimately responsible to schoolmasters. Thus we have in Bell's system both peer and cross-age tutoring. Bell was a truly remarkable educator who recognized the many advantages of peer tutoring, not only in terms of educational progress but in the improved self-esteem of all involved and the accruing improved discipline in classroom and school as a whole. Over two hundred years ago, he realized that, far from being held back in his studies, 'the tutor far more efficiently learns his lesson than if he had not to teach it to another. By teaching he is well taught' (Bell, 1799). As will be apparent from the research quoted later, this obser-vation has since been confirmed empirically, time and time again.

Joseph Lancaster opened a school in Southwark in 1798, eventually catering for 350 boys. He adopted and developed Bell's system, establishing classes each of which had a monitor, an able pupil with superior knowledge of the subject matter (Lancaster, 1803). Large classes also had assistant monitors. Interestingly, Lancaster saw the monitor role as not being to teach so much as to ensure the pupils taught each other. Thus a monitor would not correct a mistake but would ensure another pupil offered a correction (Goodlad and Hirst, 1989). Lancaster grouped pupils by ability in individual subjects, further subdividing these into smaller groups, each with a monitor. Lancaster also reported improvements in behaviour among monitors, concluding that 'the best way to form them is to make monitors of them'.

From these beginnings the monitorial system flourished throughout the nine-teenth century, but with the increasing professionalism of teaching and increased state aid to education, it waned in the early twentieth century. Topping (1988) com-ments that peer tutoring projects continued on a small scale but have made a great resurgence since the 1960s through concerns about underachievement and the per-ceived benefits of individualized instruction. The use of peers or older pupils as tutors represented an economical means of achieving more individualization of teaching.

## So what are peer tutoring, cross-age tutoring and mentoring?

Damon and Phelps (1989a) define peer tutoring as an 'an approach in which one child instructs another child'; but they go on to say 'in material on which the first is an expert and the second is a novice'. Clearly, there are numerous successful pro-jects where peer tutors demonstrably are not expert in the subject matter yet pro-duce positive outcomes for tutors and tutees (see, e.g. Scruggs and Osguthorpe, 1986, and Cook et al., 1986, where studies with learning disabled tutors are described). The earlier part of the Damon and Phelps definition will suffice for this chapter. While there is considerable literature describing the reciprocal benefits of students in further or higher education tutoring school-age pupils (e.g. Goodlad, 1995), the focus here will be on school-age tutors and mentors.

Many authors and researchers do not make a distinction between peer and cross-age tutoring. In this chapter the distinction will be applied in that peer tutoring will refer to tutors who are approximately the same age as their tutees, while cross-age tutors are older than their tutees. Topping (1987) makes reference to 'reciprocal tutoring', where peers are the same age and with similar abilities, an approach which is receiving increasing attention. A related area is that of 'peer collaboration', where children are approximately at the same competency level and collaborate on tasks to seek solutions (Damon and Phelps, 1989b). While research in this area is promising, Wood and O'Malley (1996) were concerned that observational studies showed that this approach did not produce the promised benefits in the classroom. In general, therefore, when referring to both peer and cross-age tutoring, there will be a focus on curriculum areas with the tutor helping one or more tutees to learn subject matter.

Mentoring involves providing a positive role model to another and acting as an informal guide (Donaldson and Topping, 1996) sometimes with a focus particularly on life skills (Goodlad, 1995). Sometimes this role may be extended and include informal or formal *peer counselling* (Cowie and Sharp, 1996). This invariably involves mentors being provided with initial training in counselling and on-going support.

## Peer and cross-age tutoring programmes/approaches

It is a virtual impossibility to synthesize the vast research literature concerning children teaching children, but in the following section an attempt has been made to give the reader a flavour of the many creative uses of peer tutors and the research outcomes.

### Academic skills

Topping's seminal book, *The Peer Tutoring Handbook* (Topping, 1988) remains an excellent introduction to and overview of research in peer tutoring. He describes many projects which involve children helping to develop literacy and numeracy skills, stressing the importance of providing tutors with some basic training but emphasizing that this need not be lengthy nor involve extensive monitoring. A preferred methodology is *paired reading* (Topping, 1986; Morgan, 1986) which is acquired rapidly and used relatively easily by tutors. Another approach frequently used in peer tutoring programmes is 'Pause, Prompt and Praise', which Wheldall and Mettem (1985) demonstrated could be used effectively by tutors after only 60 minutes of training.

Quoting the most extensive review of academic research available at that time by Sharpley and Sharpley (1981), Topping (1986) reported that reading was most frequently chose as the subject of peer tutoring approaches, 'with varying degrees of success'. This and other reviews (e.g. Feldman *et al.* (1976), Goodlad (1979), and Ehly and Larsen (1980)), while generally reporting positive outcomes from peer and cross-age tutoring programmes, nevertheless raised cautions that many (indeed most) studies were poorly controlled and methodologically unsound. There was also some caution that while no studies reported negative effects, there were some which did not produce significant gains. Sharpley and Sharpley (1981), for example, reported that 27 out of the 62 studies considered had non-significant effects. Topping was therefore judiciously cautious at that time to avoid raising unrealistic expectations.

Topping also refers to a *meta-analysis*, an attempt to quantify and assimilate the research findings from many different studies, carried out by Cohen *et al.* (1982). The overall conclusion drawn was similar to that mentioned earlier, in that when the results of 52 studies were combined, the overall effect size could only be described as modest (Topping, 1988). However, within this meta-analysis some studies produced highly significant effects, with cross-age tutors tending to produce larger effect sizes. In 38 of the studies, tutors themselves improved in achievements, and in 33 of these tutors performed significantly better than controls in the curriculum areas that they had tutored.

Another leading researcher into peer and cross-age tutoring in the United Kingdom is Sinclair Goodlad, who has consistently demonstrated positive cognitive and achievement effects of using students in higher education to tutor school-age pupils (Goodlad, 1995). Goodlad and Hirst (1990) cites another meta-analysis by Cook et al. (1986) which assimilated 19 research articles in which pupils with a range of special educational needs acted as tutors. This analysis demonstrated academic gains for both tutors and tutees compared to control subjects. Attitude to school improved for both tutors and tutees, and the behaviour ratings for tutors also improved.

Carol Fitzgibbon is the other foremost UK researcher into peer and cross-age tutoring. Comparing the outcomes of five controlled field experiments, she found that cross-age tutoring, mostly with a focus on improving maths skills, was more successful than two peer tutoring studies (Fitzgibbon, 1990a). Important to the Valued Youth Programme described later is her conclusion that:

> the cross-age tutoring role will evoke in tutors strong feelings of responsibility towards tutees, insights into the learning process, expressions of empathy with teachers, relief-from-boredom, a recognition that peer tutors may be able to assist learning and, very importantly, high levels of co-operation with their own teacher.
>
> (Fitzgibbon, 1990a: 57)

In another paper (Fitzgibbon, 1990b), she cites a meta-analysis of Levin et al. (1984) which compared cross-age tutoring with increased instructional time, reduced class sizes and computer-assisted learning and concluded that cross-age tutoring 'won hands down' (Fitzgibbon, 1990b: 262). Slavin et al. (1991) surveyed research on early intervention programmes aimed at preventing failure and came to a similar conclusion. Of nine types of intervention, which included reduced class sizes, provision of instructional aids and pre-school provision for 4-year-olds, they concluded that the most effective strategies were those which included one-to-one tutoring.

Another study with a focus on developing basic number skills (Beirne-Smith, 1991) concluded that the input from cross-aged tutors was the key factor for acquisition of basic facts, rather than the method of instruction. As with reading, the research evidence consistently shows gains for both tutors and tutees in maths skills from involvement in both peer and cross-age tutoring approaches (Damon and Phelps, 1989a; Britz et al., 1989).

While the focus here has been on studies relating to basic academic skills, it is evident that peer and cross-age tutoring is now being used in virtually every educational area, including personal and social education. Topping cites its usage in:

> contraception, sexually transmitted diseases, smoking, diet and nutrition, alcohol abuse, drug abuse, drinking and driving, oral English language proficiency, violence prevention, suicide prevention, gang membership, dealing

with divorce and loss, drop-out prevention, coping with chronic/terminal illness, rape awareness, sexual harassment and post-traumatic stress syndrome.

(Topping, 1996: 24)

He argues that not only are peers effective in these areas, but that professional teachers would find many of these areas difficult to address.

## Peer and cross-age mentoring programmes/ approaches

Mentoring schemes are established at almost all American universities, as evidenced by the number of such schemes which came up as 'hits' on an Internet search for 'peer mentoring'. There is even a phenomenon called 'cyber-mentoring', where students gain support on-line, via e-mail, and chat-rooms. There is growing interest in the United Kingdom in mentoring schemes to help and support students and pupils with various difficulties, particularly those seen to be disaffected. One such in Birmingham is the KWESI project, which aims to provide black adult male mentors for African-Caribbean boys at risk of exclusion. No formal evaluation is as yet available, but anecdotally KWESI mentors report successes in preventing exclusion. There is also interest in peer and cross-age mentoring and, as with tutoring, some of the research is promising.

The face validity of peer and cross-age mentoring as an approach with intrinsic merit is compelling, particularly with adolescents. Many of us can recall the powerful effect of having talked through a life problem with an adolescent peer or of receiving useful advice from such. For pupils who have difficulty forming relationships, such spontaneous counselling may not be available and may need to be engineered by teachers.

There is growing evidence that peer mentoring and counselling approaches are perceived by the pupils as highly beneficial in helping them to cope with and to counter bullying (e.g. Cowie and Sharp, 1996). Sharp (1996) concludes that indeed effective intervention must involve peers. These authors advocate strongly that young people can be readily trained in counselling skills such as active listening, reflection and paraphrasing, and can put these into practice to good effect (Sharp *et al.*, 1994).

Some studies have compared the effectiveness of girls to boys as tutors. Sharpley and Sharpley (1981), in their review, concluded that while girls produced significantly better results than boys, same sex pairings did not produce better results than opposite sex pairings. Topping and Whiteley (1993) combined the results from projects in 15 schools. They found that male pairings worked particularly well, female pairings tended to produce better scores for tutees though not for tutors, and mixed gender combinations produced good results for tutors but not for tutees, especially where a female tutor was paired with a male tutee. However, they point out that in these studies mostly same or similar aged peers were involved, whereas a third of reported studies of cross-aged tutoring showed good results for mixed gender pairings. Ainsborough (1994) found that boys and girls were equally effective as tutors using the 'Pause, Prompt and Praise' approach, but interestingly presents some evidence that if tutees are given the choice of gender of their tutor they gain more.

In the remainder of this chapter, a detailed description is given of a programme with a strong cross-age tutoring component which has deliberately recruited disaffected pupils as tutors.

## The Valued Youth Program

The Intercultural Development Research Association (IDRA) is a non-profit-making educational foundation based in San Antonio, Texas, USA. It gives as its mission statement: to improve schools for the benefit of all students. In southern Texas there is large student population from Hispanic (Spanish-speaking) backgrounds. Research carried out by IDRA in the 1980s revealed that a very high percentage of these students dropped out of school before reaching high school, and many more dropped out of high school itself (Cardenas et al., 1988). Recent studies have shown that while only 12 per cent of high school students are Hispanic, they account for 22 per cent of the drop-out population (US Census Bureau, 1997). Out of concern at these alarming statistics, IDRA has focused much of its energy and resources on reducing the drop-out rate, particularly among the Hispanic groups.

The reasons American students gave for dropping out of school varied considerably. Woods (1995) cites a comprehensive literature survey which concluded that there appeared to be four main categories of risk factors which add up to a profile of characteristics that can lead to a student dropping out of school. These were student-related, school-related, family-related and community-related factors. As the combination of risk factors becomes more complex, the greater is the probability of the student dropping out of school.

Among the school-related factors, the strongest predictor of dropping out was poor academic performance (Hess et al., 1987; Woods, 1995) with students who repeated a grade being twice as likely to drop out. Student-related factors include substance abuse, pregnancy and behaviour difficulties related to school such as truancy, lateness and exclusion for disciplinary offences. The degree to which parents could give support to a student was dependent upon factors such as the stability of the family unit, socio-economic status, membership of a minority group, single-parent household, parents' education, and English as an additional language (Horn, 1992). Crucially, of the community-related factors, poverty constituted the strongest predictor. Many students stopped attending school for largely economic reasons, in many cases to supplement the family income, with the likelihood of dropping out increasing with the number of hours worked per week (Winters et al., 1988).

IDRA was concerned that traditional responses to the problem of students dropping out failed to take account of many of these factors but equally did not build on the strengths of students at risk (Robledo et al., 1986). They surveyed existing intervention programmes that had been implemented and evaluated in the United States and attempted to distil from these what might be the vital ingredients to make up a successful package to keep students in school. Ten elements were identified and can be summarized as follows:

1 the provision of bilingual instruction for limited-English-proficient students, the development of higher-order thinking skills and provision of accelerated learning for disadvantaged students;
2 a cross-age tutoring component which gives the role of tutor to the at-risk student;
3 activities to enrich, expand, extend and apply the content and skills learned in the classroom;
4 school–business partnerships to provide financial resources, job opportunities and role models;
5 reinforcement of student accomplishments, talents, leadership and participation;

6 parent participation in meaningful activities which contribute to their empowerment;

7 formative evaluation of the programme to develop and improve the programme;

8 cooperative staff development with campus activities to take account of curriculum and student needs;

9 strong programme leadership to reinforce success and establish educational goals;

10 the development of a curriculum incorporating self-paced, individualized instruction using cooperative learning and whole language approaches.

(Cardenas *et al.*, 1992)

These elements were incorporated in the IDRA's 'Coca-Cola Valued Youth Program' (VYP), so named after the principal sponsor and funding agent. The programme is established in 91 separate school sites in a number of states in the United States. The programme is comprehensively evaluated in each school site with invariably highly positive outcomes for participating students (IDRA, 1996).

A comparative study between a group of Valued Youth (VY) Tutors ($N = 101$) and a control group ($N = 93$) matched for limited English proficiency and reading level was carried out between 1988 (baseline) and 1990 (Cardenas *et al.*, 1992). Both VY tutors and control group students were from the same pool of at-risk students. At baseline there were no differences between the groups on age, ethnicity, grade retention, average grade in reading, Quality of School Life (QSL) (Epstein and McPartland, 1978) and self-esteem (Piers and Harris, 1969) scores. There was, however, a statistically significant difference between the groups in terms of eligibility for free or assisted school lunches, indicating that the VY tutor group were significantly lower in socio-economic status. Since Winters *et al.* (1988) concluded that poverty was the strongest of the community-related predictors of dropping out, it is possible that the VY group may, if anything, have been more at risk than the controls.

The results of the two-year study showed that only one VY tutor (i.e. 1 per cent) dropped out of school, compared to 11 (12 per cent) of the control group. The VY tutors also had significantly higher gains in reading. After the first year of their involvement in the VYP, the tutor group had significantly higher self-concept scores, and this difference was sustained by the end of the second year. The same pattern emerged for the attitude to schools as measured by the QSL. As we have seen, these results are consistent with the findings of many other studies on the beneficial effects of peer and cross-age tutoring. What was unique at the time about this study was that the target group was seriously at risk of dropping out of school. Not only did the programme bring success for the tutors as outlined earlier, but the indications were that these effects were being maintained over time.

## The Valued Youth Programme in Birmingham, England

Impressed with these results, the unusual combination of programme features, the high-risk target group and the highly positive orientation of the approach, the present author became interested in the Coca-Cola VYP and established regular correspondence with IDRA. There was considerable concern in Birmingham at the increasing numbers of pupils being excluded from school, and in particular the over-representation of boys of African-Caribbean origin in the exclusion statistics, Shortly after his appointment in 1993 as Chief Education Officer, professor

Tim Brighouse commissioned Ted Wragg (professor of Education, Exeter University) to report on areas of concern within Birmingham and to recommend courses of action the City might consider to address such problems as the exclusion rates. Wragg challenged Birmingham to seek innovative approaches to the phenomena of underachievement and widespread disaffection of African-Caribbean students. The parallels with the Hispanic students in the United States were apparent to the author, who renewed his resolve to research the VYP further and in particular to seek funding to attend the annual VYP conference in San Antonio.

In early 1996, a new charity, Second City, Second Chance (SCSC), was established in Birmingham, dedicated to reducing exclusions by promoting and extending the use of adult mentors in helping to motivate disaffected pupils from different cultures. The VYP, with its emphasis on training at-risk middle school students to become tutors for younger elementary school pupils, seemed consistent with the basic aims of SCSC, which raised funds from local industry to enable a fact-finding group to visit San Antonio to participate in the VYP Annual conference, to see the VYP in action in Texan schools, and to discuss with IDRA the possibility of transplanting the programme to Birmingham, recognizing the very different educational contexts of the two cultures. Impressed with the organization of the programme and the high commitment of teachers, students and IDRA staff, the group set about devising a pilot programme to attempt to replicate the VYP as closely as possible within the British school context.

## So what is the VYP?

As the title of the programme suggests, the philosophy of VYP is that all students are regarded as valuable and no student is expendable. VYP sets about finding ways of conveying this sense of being valued to the selected students, virtually all of whom may well have developed negative self-perceptions, seeing themselves as trouble-makers or educational failures.

As stated earlier, there are a number of interesting features in the VYP, some of which have evolved since the early programmes, but at its core is a cross-age tutoring programme where students aged 12 and over, who have been identified as at-risk of dropping out or being excluded from school, are trained to act as tutors to younger pupils. Following two weeks' initial training, the VY tutors are allocated up to three pupils (tutees) in a class at a nearby elementary school, whose education they support under the direction of the class teacher. There is always a four-year gap in terms of attainment between tutor and tutee to ensure the former has a sufficient educational basis for the task of tutoring. Tutors who themselves are behind educationally may therefore be allocated pupils as young as kindergarten age to preserve the four-year gap.

Typically, tutors provide a session of up to an hour per day for four days each week during the programme. On the fifth day, they meet together as a group led by the 'teacher co-ordinator' of the programme for ongoing training, preparation, basic skills support work, peer support and debriefing. There are many reinforcers built into the programme but, most particularly, tutors earn a stipend for their work, often equivalent to the state minimum hourly wage, which they receive in a fortnightly pay packet. At its best, the VYP programme provides students with peer and adult support, engendering group solidarity and teamwork. Many American educators are convinced, and the research tends to support them (Cardenas et al., 1992), that the VYP provides young people with a positive alternative to street gang culture.

## The Birmingham VYP

Seven secondary schools opted to join a hastily constructed pilot programme commencing in October 1996 to run through until July 1997. The basic aim of this pilot was to examine the feasibility of operating the VYP, given the constraints of the British educational system. IDRA was contracted to provide training, materials and their standard evaluation, all of which was felt necessary to ensure the programme met IDRA's minimum standards. SCSC was already committed to the use of adult mentors, and it was intended from the outset to compare the outcomes for pupils who became VY tutors with those who had mentors only and with those who had both. Although initially pupils were assigned to one or other of these conditions, pragmatic decisions by teacher coordinators (TCs), often for ethical considerations, resulted in pupils being transferred to another condition, most usually from mentor only to VYP. Thus the intended comparison was not possible.

A separate strand of this programme relates to the Behaviour Support Service (BSS). From January 1997, three BSS Centres which provide education for permanently excluded pupils recruited a number of pupils to train as VY tutors. These were all either year 10 or year 11 pupils, and hence the aims of involving them in the VYP were to increase their self-esteem, to provide them with additional worthwhile experiences to three sessions they received per week in the Centres, and to enhance their Records of Achievement.

## Adaptations to the Coca-Cola VYP

### Criteria

Criteria were adapted for the British context from the American programme to identify target groups of pupils. An essential criterion was given as:

> Higher than average disciplinary referrals: for example, at least one fixed term exclusion in the last year; two or more referrals to senior staff in the past term; high 'at risk of permanent exclusion' rating from two or more senior staff.

In addition, at least two of the following were required:

- higher than average (for the school) absentee rate;
- non-participation in extra-curricular activities;
- two or more National Curriculum levels below year average;
- lack of career orientation;
- low socio-economic level (e.g. free school meals).

### Group size

Up to eight pupils meeting these criteria in each school were invited to take part in the programme. This group size is smaller than those in the American Programme, where typically whole tutor groups of up to 18 pupils would be usually involved on a single school site. The smaller numbers for this pilot programme were suggested (a) on the assumption that this would be more manageable for TCs, and (b) as potentially providing a modest sample for comparison. As will be seen later, both these assumptions proved to be false.

## Teacher Coordinators

Typically in the United States, TCs are released for significant periods of time from their curriculum duties to enable them to undertake the many tasks demanded in the pure programme. This was simply not possible in all our schools, particularly since timetables had already been fixed prior to the pilot being agreed. In virtually all cases, the TC – usually a year tutor or deputy head – fitted in as many of the tasks as possible on top of their regular commitments. This had significant consequences for the programme and particularly the evaluation, as will be seen later.

## Time for tutoring

As stated earlier, typically American VY tutors spend to an hour a day for four days per week tutoring their group. Our National Curriculum has much less flexibility, and as a compromise tutors worked for a minimum 30 minutes per day on three days of the week. This was deemed acceptable by IDRA. Also, American tutors have a weekly group preparation/debriefing session which was not usually possible in Birmingham due to timetabling difficulties. However, TCs did provide back-up support in almost all cases, in the form of individual or small group sessions to prepare VY tutors and offer them advice. However, this is seen by the author as a serious weakness in the pilot which will need to be addressed in future years.

## Rewards

The main rewards for American VY tutors take the form of stipends equivalent to the state minimum hourly wage (currently about $4.75, or approximately £3.00) which they receive in fortnightly wage packets. After much consultation and deliberation, it was decided to reward Birmingham VY tutors with tokens which had a nominal monetary value but which could be saved towards a back-up reward of the tutor's choice. The tutors agree these rewards with their mentors, who ensure the reward is appropriate and in the tutor's interest. Thus the mechanics of the system are that for each 30-minute session a tutor works, a teacher signs a record form. Each signature represents a token, worth (in the pilot year) £1.00, and a running total is kept. The tutor agrees with his/her mentor what the back-up reward will be, and at a minimum of a half-termly interval the tokens may be exchanged for the agreed reward. Some tutors opted to save for expensive back-ups which may take considerably longer than half a term to achieve. (One tutor opted for an electric guitar!) It is possible for tutors to opt for a cash reward with the agreement of their mentor. In this event, a bank account is opened for the tutor, into which earnings are paid half-termly.

## Mentors

The use of volunteer, external (to the school) adult mentors is a Birmingham addition to the VYP but one which has the full support of IDRA. Integral to the American model is the use of positive role models who typically pay one-off visits to schools adopting the VYP to talk about their background and experiences. Such visits have been encouraged by SCSC, which has met some of the expenses of visitors. Mentors provide much more by giving ongoing support on a fortnightly basis to VY tutors. These mentors receive basic training from SCSC: for example, on listening skills and important issues such as child protection.

## Reading Is Fundamental (RIF)

RIF is another American import and is that country's largest children's literacy organization. RIF seeks to establish community-based, volunteer-supported literacy projects which provide books for young people to choose and own at no cost to them. It is aimed at motivating children to read for pleasure, by engaging them in planned activities involving parents, families and the whole community. SCSC is the Birmingham agent for RIF, and this provided an opportunity to reward primary schools which were prepared to accept VY tutors. In the year of the study (1998), VY tutors consequently focused on literacy skills, although in the light of their and the primary teachers' feedback, in future VY tutors will engage in whatever support pupils require during their visit and in any curriculum area.

## Initial VY tutor training

As stated earlier, in American schools two weeks' preparation is given to VY tutors, which again was not possible in our context. The amount of training has varied between schools but in all cases appears to have been both brief and relatively superficial. The author considers this another weakness which will need to be addressed in the future.

## Schools

Of the seven secondary schools which originally opted to be involved in the VYP pilot programme, one school had an OFSTED inspection during the winter term and consequently delayed starting the programme. There was therefore insufficient time to judge whether or not the programme was having any effect here, as tutors were involved for less than two terms. Another school had serious difficulties conforming to the minimum requirements of the programme and ultimately abandoned it. One of the remaining schools was in the inner city, while all others were on the outer ring, predominantly in areas of economic deprivation. In addition, another secondary school approached SCSC with a request to include one girl pupil who was causing serious concern, and this was accepted as a goodwill gesture. Seven primary schools hosted VY tutors. Our experience of San Antonio was that elementary (primary) schools were on the same campus as the middle (secondary) schools, whereas all but one of our primaries were some distance away, requiring a bus ride for the tutors in most cases. In one instance, the primary school was several miles away, which proved ultimately unsatisfactory.

## Pupils

In all, 43 pupils – 31 boys and 12 girls – commenced the programme in one or other of the conditions. The ethnic distribution was as follows: 21 white European, 15 African Caribbean, 2 Asian and 5 mixed race. Tutors visited their nearest host primary schools and were allocated to classrooms in pairs, working with up to three tutees each.

The pilot programme had serious difficulties in data retrieval from schools in this pilot year, due to a number of factors which have been addressed for a full trial run which is nearing completion at the time of writing.

## General conclusions from the pilot

It has not been possible to compare outcomes for VY tutors with those who had mentor only and with those who had both, and this kind of comparison has for the moment been abandoned. Teachers invariably argued that the at-risk pupils identified should be given access to whatever support was available and that it would be unethical to limit them to one condition only.

In this pilot phase, five schools successfully implemented the programme for two terms, and 31 tutors were involved. As stated earlier, a further school requested one pupil to be involved, making a total of 32 tutors. Five tutors dropped out of the programme quite quickly for a variety of reasons, some finding tutoring too stressful, others simply finding it unrewarding. One other pupil was withdrawn from the programme for a positive reason, in that an alternative programme became available which more closely matched his needs. Three pupils were taken off the programme due to poor attendance and one for disciplinary reasons. It should be noted that the support for tutors in this pilot fell well short of the American model, and this is one of several limitations.

Thus, of the 32 tutors starting the programme, 22(68 per cent) completed it successfully, with reported gains from teachers in self-esteem, social skills, disciplinary record and attitude to school. Although this percentage is lower than one would have hoped, given the population and the programme limitations it represented a positive beginning for the VYP in the United Kingdom. Anecdotally, several successes were remarkable, in the several pupils deemed to be on the brink of exclusion not only completed the programme but were now expected to remain in school.

Following this crude pilot, seven secondary schools opted to implement the programme and adhere to the minimum programme requirements set by IDRA. Data collection and analysis are incomplete, so it is not possible here to report on the outcomes. However, what is apparent already is that the vast majority of pupils meeting the at-risk criteria and who were deemed by their schools as likely to be excluded have 'survived' their year on the programme. All schools remain enthusiastic about the programme and are committed to continuing with it – and, indeed, making it available to more pupils. All receiving primary schools also wish to continue with help from VY tutors and report anecdotally that tutees are benefiting from the input they receive. By word of mouth, several other secondary schools have heard of the programme and wish to adopt it on the strength of recommendation from their colleagues, and at the time of writing five other LEAs are negotiating with IDRA and SCSC to commence VY programmes in selected schools.

## Final thoughts

Nationally, there is major concern about the rising number of pupils being excluded from school. In addition, there are unacceptable numbers of pupils who are dropping out of school and are lost to the education system. Paradoxically, with this level of exclusion and self-exclusion, many teachers and educationalists have embraced the rhetoric of *inclusion*, but while there are demonstrable successes of schools including pupils with learning, communication, physical and sensory difficulties in mainstream, pupils who present challenging behaviour are an exception to the inclusive trend.

The VYP in the United States was recognized by the National Diffusion Network as a programme which works to counter dropping out. As such, it was recommended to schools throughout the country, and consequently was favourably regarded for funding at federal and state level. Apart from the genuine humanitarian concerns of IDRA, it is clear that the sponsorship of VYP by a company such as Coca-Cola brings with it economic considerations. Coca-Cola clearly wishes to be associated with a successful programme. However, the federal and state governments are aware of the huge economic and social costs of pupil failure in terms of crime and the penal system, and hence there is a mutual interest of the state and private enterprise in cooperating to support programmes of this kind. Investment in preventive programmes which work makes social *and* economic sense. In the United Kingdom, we cannot afford to ignore the success of such a programme if we wish to be truly inclusive and embrace a philosophy that 'All pupils are valuable, no pupil is expendable'.

The early, admittedly soft indicators are that the VYP can be transplanted to our system and can make an impact with suitable local modifications, prime among which is the additional component of mentoring with which our American colleagues are extremely impressed. This author is committed to rigorous evaluation of the VYP, and will be presenting future papers which it is hoped will add to the impressive volume of work on the benefits of children teaching and helping other children.

## Reflective questions

1   What is the difference between tutoring and mentoring?
2   How can peer tutoring be organised to ensure that tutors as well as tutees benefit?
3   How can peer tutoring be managed so that pupils with special educational needs or other barriers can serve as tutors?

## References

Ainsborough, S.E. (1994) 'The peer tutoring of reading using Pause, Prompt and Praise: a study examining the differential effects of gender pairings'. Unpublished MEd thesis, School of Education, University of Birmingham.

Beirne-Smith, M. (1991) 'Peer tutoring in arithmetic for children with learning difficulties', *Exceptional Children*, 57, 330–7.

Bell, A. (1797) *An Experiment in Education Made at the Male Asylum of Madras: Suggesting a system by which a school or Family may Teach Itself under the Superintendence of the Master or Parent.* London: Cadell and Davis.

Britz, M.W., Dixon, J. and McLauchlin, T.F. (1989) 'The effects of peer tutoring on mathematics performance: a recent review', *British Columbia Journal of special Education*, 13(1), 17–33.

Cardenas, J.A., Robeldo, M.R. and Waggoner, D. (1988) *The Under-Education of American Youth.* San Antonio, TX: Intercultural Development Research Association.

Cardenas, J.A., Montecel, M.R., Supik, J.D. and Harris, R.J. (1992) 'The Coca-Cola Valued Youth Program – dropout prevention strategies for at-risk students', *Texas Researcher*, 3, 111–30.

Cohen, P.A., Kulik, J.A. and Kulik, C-L.C. (1982) 'Educational outcomes of tutoring: a meta-analysis of findings', *American Educational Research Journal*, 19(2), 237–48.

Cook, S.B., Scruggs, T.E., Mastropieri, M.A. and Casto, G.C. (1986) 'Handicapped students as tutors', *Journal of special Education*, 19(4), 483–92.

Cowie, H. and sharp, S. (eds) (1996) *peer Counselling in Schools – A Time to Listen.* London: Fulton.

Damon, W. and Phelps, E. (1989a) 'Critical distinctions among three approaches', in N.M. Webb (ed.) *Peer Interaction, problem-solving and Cognition: Multidisciplinary perspectives.* New York: Pergamon Press.

Damon, W. and Phelps, E. (1989b) 'Strategic uses of peer learning in children's education', in T.J. Berndt and G.W. Ladd (eds) *Peer Relationships in Child Development*. New York: Wiley.

Donaldson, A.J.M. and Topping, K.J. (1996) *Promoting Peer Assisted Learning amongst Students in Higher and Further Education*. Birmingham: SEDA.

Ehly, S.W. and Larsen, S.C. (1980) *Peer tutoring for Individualised Instruction*. Boston: Allyn and Bacon.

Epstein, J. and McPartland, J.M. (1978) *The quality of school Life Scale*. Boston, MA: Houghton Mifflin Co.

Feldman, R.S., Devin-Sheehan, L. and Allen, V.L. (1976) 'Children tutoring children: a critical review of research', in V.L. Allen (ed.) *Children as Teachers: Theory and Research on Tutoring*. NY: Academic Press.

Fitzgibbon, C.T. (1990a) *Success and failure in peer tutoring experiments. Explorations in Peer Tutoring*, CEM Publication 52. Newcastle: Curriculum, Evaluation and Management Centre.

Fitzgibbon, C.T. (1990b) *Empower and Monitor: The EM Algorithm for the Creation of Effective Schools*, CEM publication 16. Newcastle: Curriculum, Evaluation and Management Centre.

Goodlad, S. (1979) *Learning by Teaching: An Introduction to Tutoring*. London: Community Service Volunteers.

Goodlad, S. (1995) 'Students as tutors and mentors', in S. Goodlad (ed.) *Students as Tutors and Mentors*. London: Kogan Page.

Goodlad, S. and Hirst, B. (1989) Peer Tutoring: A Guide to Learning by Teaching. London: Kogan Page.

Goodlad, S. and Hirst, B. (1990) *Explorations in Peer Tutoring*. Oxford: Blackwell.

Greenwood, C.R., Delquadri, J.C. and Hall, R.V. (1989) 'Longitudinal effects of classwide peer tutoring', *Journal of Educational Psychology*, 81(3), 371–83.

Hess, G.A., Well, E., Prindle, C., Liffman, P. and Kaplan, B. (1987) 'Where Room 187? How schools can reduce their dropout problem', *Education and Urban Society*, 19(3), 330–55.

Horn, L. (1992) *A profile of parents of Eighth Graders: National Education Longitudinal Study of 1988. Statistical Analysis Report*. Washington, DC: National Center for Educational Statistics, Office of Education Research and Improvement, US Department of Education.

IDRA (1996) *Coca-Cola Valued Youth Program – 1995–1996 Stewardship Report*. San Antonio, TX: IDRA.

Jenkins, J.R and Jenkins, L.M. (1987) 'Making peer tutoring work', *Educational Leadership*, 44(6), 64–8.

Lancaster, J. (1803) *Improvements in Education as it Respects the Industrious Classes of the Community, Containing, among Other Important Particulars, an Account of the Institution for the Education of One Thousand Poor Children, Borough Road, Southwark; and of the New System of Education on which it is Conducted*. London: Darton and Harvey.

Morgan, R.T.T. (1986) *Helping Children Read – The Paired Reading Handbook*. London: Methuen.

Piers, E.V. and Harris, D.B. (1969) *The Piers-Harris Children's Self Concept Scale*. Los Angles: Western Psychological Services.

Robeldo, M.R., Cardenas, J.A. and Supik, J.D. (1986) *The Texas School Dropout Survey Project: A survey of Findings*. San Antonio, TX: IDRA.

Scruggs, T.E. and Osguthorpe, R.T. (1986) 'Tutoring interventions within special educational settings: a comparison of cross-age and peer tutoring', *Psychology in the schools*, 23, 187–93.

Seaborne, M. (1966) *Education: The History of Modern Britain*. London: Studio Vista.

Sharp, S. (1996) 'The role of peers in tackling bullying in schools', *Educational Psychology in Practice*, 11(4), 17–22.

Sharp, S., Sellors, A. and Cowie, H. (1994) 'Time to listen: setting up a peer counsellng service to help tackle the problem of bullying in schools', *Pastoral Care in Education*, 12(2), 3–6.

Sharpley, A.M. and Sharpley, C.F. (1981) 'Peer tutoring: a comparison of cross-age and peer tutoring', *Collected Original Resources in Education (CORE)*, 5(3), 7-C11 (fiche 7 and 8).

Slavin, R.E., Karweit, N.L. and Wasik, B.A. (1991) *Preventing Early School Failure: What Works?* Reports no. 26. Baltimore, MD: Centre for Research on Effective schooling for Disadvantaged Students.

Topping, K. (1986) *The Kirkless Paired Reading Training pack* (second edition). Huddersfield: Kirklees Directorate of Educational Services.

Topping, K. (1987) 'Children as teachers', *Special Children*, 14, 6–8.

Topping, K. (1988) *The peer Tutoring Handbook*. Beckenham: Croom Helm.

Topping, K. (1996) 'Reaching where adults cannot', *Educational psychology in practice*, 11(4), 23–9.

Topping, K and Whiteley, M. (1993) 'Sex differences in the effectiveness of peer tutoring', *School Psychology International*, 14(57), 57–67.

US Census Bureau (1997) *School Enrolment – Social and Economic Characteristics of Students:* October 1995. Washington, DC: US Census Bureau.

Wheldall, K. and Mettem, P. (1985) 'Behavioural peer tutoring: training 16-year old tutors to employ the "Pause, Prompt and Praise Method" with 12-year-old remedial readers', *Educational Psychology*, 5(1), 27–44.

Winters, K.C., Rubinstein, M. and Winters, R.A. (1988) *An Investigation of Education Options for Youth at Risk, Ages 9–15: Demographics, Legislation and Model Programs. Research Report no.* 88–10. Washington, DC: National Commission for Employment Policy(DOL).

Wood, D. and O'Malley, C. (1996) 'Collaborative learning between peers', *Educational Psychology in Practice*, 11(4), 4–9.

Woods, E.G. (1995) *Reducing the Dropout Rate. School Improvement Research Series*. Washington, DC: Office of Education Research and Improvement (OERI), Northwest Regional Educational Laboratory.

# PART V

# PROMOTING AND MANAGING
# SYSTEMIC CHANGE IN SCHOOLS

# CHAPTER 13

# VIRGINIA WOOLF HIGH SCHOOL

P. Cooper, M.J. Drummond, S. Hart, J. Lovey and
C. McLaughlin

*Positive Alternatives to Exclusion* (2000), London and New York:
RoutledgeFalmer, pp. 53–73

## Introduction

Virginia Woolf High School is an 11–16 urban mixed comprehensive school. At
the time of the research, there were approximately 950 students aged 11–16 on
roll. Of these 31 per cent were eligible for free school meals, and there were
275 pupils on the special needs register, of whom 46 had statements. The great
majority of the intake is from local authority housing.

Unemployment in the area is higher than the national average. Over recent
years several of the traditional local light manufacturing industries, who used to
employ from our catchment area, have closed down. It is not unusual to look in
the local newspaper and read about ex-pupils appearing in the Magistrate and
Crown Courts. Incidents such as joy-riding, drug abuse and sales, vandalism and
violence are not uncommon; we also have significant numbers of children who live
with domestic violence or who are young carers.

This is not to say that we are what may be labelled as a 'rough inner city
school' with its stereotypical problems. We have a proportion of students who
have genuinely high aspirations – a proportion which is slowly increasing –
though the magic five General Certificate of Secondary Education (GCSE) examination passes at grades A to C are attained by only about 25–30 per cent of children, placing us near the bottom of the Local Education Authority (LEA) (school
district) league table. Nevertheless our catchment can be seen as suffering from
economic and social deprivation.

When I received the first flyer about the research, I was a temporary member of
the school's senior management team, running an externally funded project
intended to support vulnerable and disaffected students. Known as 'Personal
Tutoring', this was a scheme of individual support whereby volunteer members of
staff used a mix of counselling and mentoring skills to attempt to help students
remain integrated and successful within the school's structures, expectations and
demands. There were also a number of other initiatives underway in the school
that were relevant to the themes of the research. I was keen for the school to be
involved in order to give us an opportunity to review and evaluate what we were
currently doing. Networking with other schools would enable us to exchange
ideas, discuss strategies and learn from one another.

With the head's agreement, a small steering group was set up. In negotiation
with members of the research team from Cambridge, it was agreed that the

research would be principally concerned with exploring the perceptions of staff and students of the various initiatives that we were currently working on. Volunteers were invited to be actively involved in researching each initiative, and seven members of staff joined the research team. All staff were invited to express their views through a questionnaire. Members of the university team were asked to research the 'Personal Tutor' (PT) scheme and to carry out case studies of two selected pupils deemed to be at risk of exclusion.

The various initiatives that were selected for examination were of two kinds. On the one hand there were initiatives – like the Personal Tutoring scheme – which aimed to have an immediate impact, by offering additional support to individuals who were considered to be particularly vulnerable or at risk of exclusion. On the other hand, there were initiatives designed to develop and enhance features of existing practice in school for the benefit of *all* pupils (e.g. developing the Personal and Social Education (PSE) curriculum, introducing Circle Time in Year 7, provision for developing literacy). Their contribution to the task of reducing and preventing exclusion would be a more indirect and long-term one: attempting to create a stable, secure and positive environment which would in turn make it more likely that students would engage productively in school life.

Over the nine months of our involvement in the project, differences of perspective amongst staff became such an important feature of the process that it would not be true to reality to present the findings of the research as if these reflected a common, collective understanding. In this chapter, I offer a personal account of the new insights that emerged with respect to the various initiatives that were currently under way. The analysis focuses in more depth and detail on the strategies for individual support, because there were the areas of work that I was most directly involved in.

## The personal tutor scheme

At the time of the research, there were ten members of staff acting as 'Personal Tutors'. Each worked with about six students. The PTs were an extra layer of support, not replacements for those within the existing pastoral system. The funding made it possible for them to spend time with their tutees, either meeting frequently for one-to-one work or providing support in the classroom.

Initially staff were asked to volunteer to become PTs. The main criteria I used for approaching staff and sounding them out as potential PTs were that they had a high level of self-esteem and emotional literacy themselves. They also needed to be resilient and committed to giving of themselves. This included a commitment towards being trained, in their own time, and supporting others in the team. I also felt that while I may have been seen as manager of the scheme, it was vital that I had a number of students to whom I could act as PT myself.

I was fortunate that one PT was already trained as a counsellor. She was able to act as a guiding light and support to the rest of us, especially when we felt out of our depth. However, it soon became clear that we needed formal supervision from an active professional and I found a local medical General Practitioner's (GP's) counsellor who acted as supervisor and trainer for us all. I employed her to meet with us at least twice a term. She taught us how to support one another, keep things in proportion and to off-load within the team. She also helped PTs develop counselling skills. Because of the nature of the work we were doing it was essential that we became mutually supportive in a deep and totally non-judgmental way. It would have been easy for PTs to feel isolated and overwhelmed.

Students were, at first, identified by heads of year for possible inclusion on the scheme. There were no criteria set in tablets of stone; indeed there were many and various reasons why children were taken onto the project. Fundamental to whether or not they would be offered the chance of having a PT – and it was their choice – was whether or not they showed a commitment. If they failed to turn up to sessions they were warned; if those warnings had no effect then they were dropped from the project. We always had a 'waiting list' of children. One of my roles as manager was to protect PTs from themselves. As they were conscientious and very caring staff there were times when they wanted to take on more vulnerable children and I had to direct them not to.

As we became more expert in this work it seemed to become easier to identify those who would benefit from having a PT, even if their names were not put forward. This was especially true for pupils who were going through some sort of short-term crisis, either in school or at home.

The project was originally set up with the intention of helping reduce exclusions, so those at risk of exclusion were the first to be identified. However, as time went on and PT skills levels increased, we took on students who, for a number of reasons, were 'opting out' of working in school or showed signs of personal (but usually disguised) distress. We also had dozens of children who wanted to either self-refer or refer friends. Some had to be turned away. Not an easy thing to do, but it was an essential part of my management role.

Amongst those whom we worked with, there were children who were suicidal, who were bullied or were bullies, who had eating disorders, who took drugs and who exhibited self-destructive behaviours. There were some who had suffered bereavements, who had problems with sexuality, who lived with alcoholics in the family, who were habitually involved in petty crime and who were aggressive. I worked in liaison with social services, the police, local GPs, the school nurse and the Family Psychiatry unit. We knew our limitations and the professional boundaries; there were times when I had to reassure PTs that they had done all they could; just being there for the child was sometimes enough.

Personal Tutors saw their selected pupils once a week at least, for a lesson or longer. Records were kept of meetings and individuals were discussed, anonymously, at shared mini case conference meetings. This was a chance for tutors to discuss among ourselves possible ways forward with these children. And a chance to off-load. Sometimes, we asked our supervisor to attend these meetings. We tried to share strategies and be as creative as we could within the limits we had of working in a school. Sometimes children were supported in particular lessons by their Tutor who would sit alongside them in the classroom; sometimes parents were invited in to a joint meeting; sometimes a talk and/or advice session sufficed; sometimes we used art therapy. Whatever we tried, the children always knew we were there for them, and would actively listen to them. In spite of some initial concerns, the fact that this was a different relationship to the usual teacher – pupil one, was not as great a problem as feared we had. Children were able to understand when a particular adult was being a 'teacher' and when a PT.

In-depth individual interviews were carried out by a Cambridge researcher with three staff and six pupils who were involved in the scheme. The aim was to find out from staff what they saw as the aims of the work, how they felt it contributed to reducing and preventing exclusion, what skills they needed, and what training and support they received. Students were asked what they understood the Personal Tutoring scheme to be for, how it helped them, and how it was different from other sorts of help they received. Interviews were tape recorded and later transcribed; direct quotes are verbatim extracts from the tape transcripts.

There were many issues on which all three students agreed. For example, they commented on the importance of having someone who would listen to them, and knowing that what they said was respected and treated in confidence. The regularity of meetings, and knowing that the PT was always there for them, were also crucial. The students wanted someone in whom they could confide, and who would trust them, and give them a chance.

Problems at home, feelings of frustration and anger, difficulties with friendships and the way teachers treated the students, were all brought to PT sessions. There were also concerns expressed about coping with the work in class and homework. The fact that there was an adult who cared about them and showed non-judgemental commitment towards them as individuals, freely giving time and energy and showing belief in them, was valued a great deal.

The students felt cared for, supported and attended to. It was different from the other sorts of help available in school. For one student, this seemed to be the only opportunity to speak with an adult who understood. The opportunity to express feelings and frustrations in a 'safe' way and a secure environment was also recognised as important. The students commented positively on some of the specific strategies introduced by PTs. Asked about the part that they felt the scheme had played in preventing exclusion, the students were convinced that, without access to, and work with, the PT, they would not still be in school. The students' perception of the vital part played by the scheme in helping to prevent exclusion was echoed in the interviews with the PTs.

The tutors described the aims of the work in terms of building students' self-esteem and helping the students deal with a variety of issues including curriculum difficulties, bereavement, sexuality, rejection by parents, emotional and physical neglect and promoting emotional literacy. Although there were some differences, in their comments, in the relative emphasis placed on coping with school and coping with personal issues, all saw themselves as trying to help students to become independent and to learn how to take responsibility for themselves, their behaviour and its consequences.

Tutors felt that their work was generally valued by other staff, but there were concerns. They found the sessions with individual students very demanding. Consequently, support from other PTs was important, as was the opportunity for outside supervision twice a term. The outside supervision 'really made a difference' in situations where tutors felt a lack of confidence about how best to tackle a situation. Having somebody say 'You're doing an OK job' was also important. At times they found themselves feeling blameworthy and responsible for the misbehaviour of their students but were developing the capacity to stand back.

## Support for excluded pupils on re-entry

A further form of support that was available for individuals was a monitoring system for students returning from fixed-term exclusion. For some time, I had been concerned that when excluded students returned, there was maybe an interview with a senior member of staff, and sometimes with parent(s), and then they would be plunged straight back in to sink or swim. I felt that they were more likely to reintegrate successfully, and avoid problems escalating into further exclusions, if some sort of system of support was in place to assist their re-entry.

Since I was still officially managing the externally funded project, I had a few extra free periods; also, I did not have a tutor group and this meant that I was more often available to monitor individual children at key times of the day. I decided, in liaison with a head of year, to redesign our existing behaviour report cards in order to use them as a tool for my own monitoring. Like many secondary schools, we had a system where identified individuals carried a card with them from lesson to lesson for teachers to sign and write comments on, in order to keep a track of behaviour over a given period of time. My aim was to make them target-specific – thus allowing staff to recognise and reinforce the positive in their comments and interactions with individual students. I also wanted to remove the space for teacher comments as some staff used this space to sound off about a child or incident involving the child. This could aggravate a situation.

The students were invited to decide, with my guidance, what their behaviour targets would be. These were made clear on the card. Staff were asked to put a 'one' in the space for their lesson if the target was completely met, a 'two' if partially met, and 'three' if not met at all. It was important to allow students to set only a few (maybe three or four) targets and at least one of them to be a target which I believed would allow the teachers to assign a 'one'. There was no point in reinforcing failure.

The intention behind what I was doing was to help the students survive and be successful. I met the students, individually, at the start of the day, before registration. I could then carry out basic checks with them, such as whether they had a pen, books, their completed homework. If necessary I would lend them a pen or provide them with paper. If they did not have text books then we discussed how they could avoid confrontation with a member of staff who would be understandably displeased.

I also met the students at break-time, lunchtime and after school. In this way I was able to monitor, through the report card, what had happened in a relatively short time and try to nip potential problems in the bud. I knew from experience that, without some sort of intervention, problems were often carried from one lesson to another and gradually each small incident could escalate into something serious.

If it looked as if a student was hooked into a downward spiral of this kind, I could offer the chance of flexibility. It was sometimes appropriate to suggest that individuals came to me, rather than went to their usual lesson, and worked in my teaching room, or alone. I would then see the relevant member of staff, gather in some work, explain the situation and take responsibility for that student. At other times the student and I could discuss possible tactics for a potentially difficult lesson: I would try to give them choices about effective strategies and set up a win-win situation between them and their teacher.

As I became more familiar with the students' perceptions of how they experienced their week I became more able to anticipate where the tensions might arise. Parallel with this, the students were becoming aware of my understanding. This made it easier for all of us. I knew I could say to a student, 'If it gets too difficult in XXX you can come to me'. The very fact that they had a bolt-hole was often enough, though there were a few times when there were as many as two or three seated at the back of the classroom while I taught another class.

One of the university researchers examined the impact and effectiveness of the monitoring strategy described earlier as part of a case study of two Year 10 pupils who, at the start of the year, were considered to be at risk of exclusion. The report card had been highlighted by staff, students and parents as one strategy that did seem to make a positive difference to students' behaviour in lessons. As part of this enquiry, I was asked to keep an audio diary of what happened each day in my work with individuals over a period of several weeks. Three students who had experience of individual monitoring were also interviewed, in order to explore their perceptions of what was helpful in enabling them to get on better in school and avoid further trouble.

What emerged from this part of the study was that it was not just the report card that was important for the students, but also the sustained personal support being offered via a range of strategies. The report card itself was considered to be helpful, but there were reservations. The fact that there were targets brought its own pressures. For one student, it was very important to have written proof that targets had been met.

There were many parallels here with what students said was important about the Personal Tutoring scheme. Students valued the contact with someone who they knew cared about how they were getting on, whom they knew was there if needed, and who could be trusted to take action on their behalf if it seemed likely to help. Just having a brief contact and conversation could make all the difference.

The anger-management strategies I had taught them included breathing exercises, self-awareness of their physical state, 'cognitive restructuring' or self-talk (whereby they tried to interpret what was going in a way which would be less personally offensive to them) and visualisation. While finding these helpful, the students' accounts of their experience suggested that there were times when they just could not stop themselves doing things which would get them into trouble. They felt reassured that they had the option to get up and leave, with the teacher's permission, in order to cool off elsewhere.

One student felt that the legitimacy of the strategy was not accepted by all staff. Requests to leave the room were sometimes refused. This could then provoke a situation where the student would get sent out anyway.

I was certainly aware, in my day-to-day contacts with staff, that there were considerable differences in terms of their perception of the value, overall, of this form of support for students. Some were pleased to know that the students were getting support; others were concerned that it was rewarding students for misbehaviour; others felt that it was an intrusion into their own discipline and practices. I always tried to negotiate with staff and keep them informed but sometimes I would only hear of incidents involving the students I was monitoring by accident. I often only got the students' perceptions of what had happened and had to spend time seeking out staff to hear their version. By the time I had gathered what I considered to be enough of the 'facts' it sometimes meant that the moment to respond effectively had passed. I shall summarise five other areas of development work currently going on in the school. Brief details of the research carried out in each area and key findings are given in Table 13.1.

## Other initiatives

First, there was a new Personal Social and Health Education (PSHE) programme devised to meet what staff perceived as the specific needs of students at Virginia Woolf. The previous programme had leaned heavily on commercially produced resources and had little cohesion. It was intended that the new work would emphasise a skills-based approach, and that all staff should be involved in planning the identified modules. This would give the sense of ownership and commitment which had seemed to be missing. Furthermore, it would also allow not only content to be discussed among staff, but teaching methods.

*Table 13.1* Virginia Woolf High School

| Initiative | Data sources | Key findings |
|---|---|---|
| PSHE | Interviews with 15 students (by teachers) | • importance of tutor group and tutor as teaching unit<br>• valued lesson content<br>• made links with other curriculum learning<br>• actively used outside classroom |
| | Questionnaire for whole staff (24 returns, $n = 61$) | • valued teaching own tutor group<br>• content meaningful to students personally<br>• can enhance social skills/self-esteem |
| Circle time | Interviews with 18 students (by teachers) | • valued chance to talk about problems<br>• helped with relationships and with learning<br>• sometimes uncomfortable |
| | Whole staff questionnaire | • positively viewed by staff, particularly those with direct experience of approach |
| Role of Form Tutor (FT) | Form tutor logs and interviews (8 staff, by teachers) | • highlighted different perceptions of role<br>• administration could hinder other aspects of role<br>• tension between disciplinary role and building positive relationships<br>• desire to do more to support learning |
| | Parent questionnaires (40 Year 9) 100% returns | • majority saw FT as first point of contact for information or concerns |
| | Pupil interviews (by teachers) (2 per year group) | • valued stability and security provided by FT<br>• valued extra efforts made by FT (e.g. attending matches)<br>• key concept 'trust' |
| Literacy Working Group | Readability survey of texts | • texts age appropriate but many children have reading age below chronological age |
| | Survey of key language/ literacy skills | • interesting common patterns emerged which could provide basis for discussion/development work (e.g. discrepancy between value placed on pupils listening to teacher and to one another) |
| | Survey of reading levels of excluded pupils | • association confirmed between low reading levels and pupils excluded, but some exceptions |
| GNVQ project-based course | Interviews with 12 students | • liked active learning, working at own pace |
| | Interviews with 6 parents | • felt children enjoyed subject, keen for younger ones to take course |

*(Table 13.1 continued)*

*Table 13.1* Continued

| Initiative | Data sources | Key findings |
|---|---|---|
| | Interviews with 6 staff | • differing views about impact of course on motivation/behaviour<br>• highlighted demands on students as well as importance of short-term goals, opportunity for visits, for different type of relationship with teachers |
| Personal tutoring | Interviews with (3) PT (by university researcher) | • being a PT was frustrating and demanding, but highly rewarding |
| | Interview with project manager (by university researcher) | • importance for students of feeling genuinely listened to by an adult in school |
| | Interviews with 6 students in the scheme (by university researcher) | • importance of ongoing range of support strategies for students<br>• belief among students that being part of the project helped them avoid exclusion<br>• newly acquired anger-management strategies deemed effective |
| Re-entry from* fixed term exclusion | Audio diary<br>Interview with project manager<br>Interview with (3) students<br>Staff questionnaire<br><br>Parents interview? | • importance of frequent and regular monitoring to pre-empt possible problems<br>• creative solutions possible but skilful negotiation required<br>• concerns from some staff about resources devoted to 'the undeserving'<br>• the importance of reducing pressures on students, balanced with building students' inner resources. |

*Note*:
* The bullet points in this section summarise findings for all the data sources.

Because previous PSHE work had been worksheet heavy, it had tended to alienate students, specially those with poor literacy levels. It was also seen by staff as being rather dull. The new programme meant that more creative ways of delivering PSHE could be considered. Time was set aside for a variety of types of oral work, such as discussion and role play, and outside speakers were booked. Worksheets were revamped where necessary. A timetable for delivery of modules was formalised, allowing staff with particular interests and skills to deliver particular units of work, although most Form Tutors taught most modules. The whole course was, and continues to be, regularly evaluated at pastoral team meetings and each year team makes recommendations for fine-tuning so that succeeding teams, who will teach the modules later, benefit from their experience.

Much emphasis was placed on the need to develop student self-esteem. As Form Tutors teach their groups for two lessons a week – for both tutorial time and

PSHE – and as National Records of Achievement are firmly established and seen as having real value and currency among our students, there is scope for development and progression through work on self-esteem right through from Year 7 to 11.

## Circle Time

Closely linked to the new PSHE programme was an initiative to introduce Circle Time in Year 7 classes. It has since progressed up the school. Circle Time is a way to encourage self-responsibility, self-control and emotional literacy. Although Circle Time is often practised more in the primary sector I saw no reason why it should not be useful at secondary level in our repertoire of strategies for enhancing self-esteem and emotional literacy. I introduced Circle Time in Year 7 in September 1996 where it was run by Form Tutors once or twice a week during tutorial time.

At their first session of Circle Time the students make up their own rules: the process empowers the group and its members are more likely to conform to them. Rules are based on truth, trust, responsibility, active listening, no 'put-downs', kindliness and support. They are negotiated, agreed, written down, and then displayed in the Form Room. The role of the teacher is that of guide, being non-judgemental throughout, and setting the tone for future work.

Circle Time tends to last between fifteen and thirty-five minutes. Sometimes the teacher can set the agenda, sometimes the students, sometimes an agenda arises naturally from circumstances or an incident involving one of the class. To help the process of Circle Time, an object, such as a scarf, shell or paperweight (my Year 10 Tutor Group chose a teddy bear belonging to one of their peers who left the school), is passed around the circle. Rather like the assembly in William Golding's novel *Lord of the Files* (1954), where holding the conch signifies permission to talk and be listened to, the routine, imposed by the teacher, is that only the student (or teacher) holding the object may speak.

Because Circle Time gives a sense of security, identity, belonging, purpose and competence, sensitive issues can, eventually, be brought into the open. These issues might include bullying, dealing with bereavement – or endings in general – relationships, the hopes and fears of the children, what makes them sad or happy or angry and how to deal with peer pressure. All these issues help encourage discussion about feelings and how to work with them: for many of our students emotional literacy is a new idea. The culture of the catchment area mitigates against talking about feelings. It is often described as a 'macho' culture. Consequently, some boys find this aspect of the work especially difficult. Giving validity to the expression of feelings through a forum such as Circle Time can enhance self-esteem, provide security, and demonstrate publicly that feelings are a natural part of being human.

## The role of the Form Tutor

We were also in the early stages of reviewing and developing the role of the Form Tutor, due to be given priority in the School Development Plan the following academic year. Members of the research team felt that this was an important area to include in our work because Form Tutors can make a crucial contribution to reducing and preventing exclusion. In order to investigate how Form Tutors saw their role, eight of them were asked to keep a log of their activities, using a suggested proforma. They were then interviewed by colleagues on the research team to explore how they felt about how they were spending their time, and what seemed to help or hinder them from doing what they felt they ought to be doing in practice. By analysing these data, together with the views of parents and a small number of students selected randomly across year groups, it was hoped that ideas and questions would emerge that could become a focus for future development.

## Work on literacy

A Literacy Working Group had recently been set up to explore ways of enhancing pupils' literacy development. This group carried out a survey of the readability of texts used in different subject areas, in order to see whether texts currently in use were accessible, given our data on pupils' reading levels. The reading test scores of pupils who had been the subject of temporary exclusions were also examined. The views of subject departments were sought regarding the essential and desirable language and literacy skills for successful engagement with the content of particular subject areas, and the most common difficulties that students were found to experience. It was hoped that a synthesis of these various sources of information would help to define some areas for further development work.

## GNVQ

Another area that became a focus of interest during the course of the research was a project-based GNVQ course. Staff involved were keen to emphasise that it was not an alternative, low-level course for struggling or disaffected learners. What it offered, in theory, was an alternative (yet also demanding) style of learning, which might have more appeal for some students because there was considerable scope for developing projects in line with their own interests. While looking at attendance patterns in Year 10, one of the university team suggested that there might be a link between improved attendance and participation in the GNVQ course. She carried out interviews with selected staff, students and parents in order to see if their perceptions supported this hypothesis.

Accumulating evidence of the perceptions of staff, students and (in some cases) parents in relation to these various initiatives and developments provided encouraging confirmation that they were, in general, being well received (Table 13.1). Staff questionnaires also confirmed that their contribution – potential and actual – to the task of reducing and preventing exclusion was recognised by the wider staff group. The kinds of links made by staff are illustrated in the following comments taken from the questionnaire responses:

- (PSHE) Highlights issues related to personal value and well-being, two issues which drastically affect behaviour.
- (Circle Time) Gives students the opportunity to express their concerns and fears in a safe environment. Hopefully over time this may allow pupils to voice their difficulties before it is too late.
- (Role of Form Tutor) Very often hidden; but first route for many students and parents. Invaluable resource.
- (Literacy Working Group) Greater involvement across the curriculum. Less children 'switched off' by areas of difficulty, which can lead to disruptive behaviour.
- (GNVQ course) This should be an ideal way of contributing. The smaller groups and personal and individual nature of the work, and how it should be monitored, would help in providing motivation, regular feedback and a more mutual understanding of acceptable behaviour and attitude, and because of close monitoring, a better staff–student relationship.

## Tension between intermediate and long-term goals

While many staff clearly recognised the potential of these various initiatives, it was also evident from the questionnaires, and from interviews with staff relating to the individual case studies, that many teachers were looking for more direct and immediate support than was represented by the sum of the various initiatives. The pressures and stresses which they faced on a day-to-day basis were very consider-able. An approach which emphasised the long-term view left many people feeling unsupported in the immediate and short-term.

There were teachers who questioned whether it was in fact in anyone's interests, once things had reached a certain point, to pull out all the stops in order to prevent exclusion. Was all the human resource and effort, for instance, that was being expended in the individual monitoring scheme simply 'delaying the inevitable' (as one member of staff put it)? My own view was that unless something was done to support excluded pupils on re-entry, the kinds of problems that they would experience would be all too likely to provoke reactions that would lead to further exclusion. But did it depend upon maintaining indefinitely such intensive input, or was it (as I intended) a genuinely developmental strategy, in the sense of building up students' ability to manage independently and so become progressively re-engaged in school life?

Since one of the principles underpinning the research was commitment to give serious and equal consideration to the views of all those consulted, it was decided to take a closer look at the workings of the individual monitoring scheme in the light of these questions. Did the individual monitoring strategy indeed add up to more than an exercise in containment and damage limitation? On what grounds could it be claimed to be genuinely preventative? One interpretation of the nature of the support provided by the strategy – and grounded in the evidence – was proposed by the university researcher who had taken responsibility for this part of the project.

## Scaffolding to support positive change

Re-examining the detailed audio diaries, and students' accounts of the strategies that they found most helpful, what came across most strongly was the enormous complexity of the demands made upon students during the course of a school day. These tended to become visible only when students failed to negotiate them successfully.

All students have to learn to manage the emotionally charged task of building relationships with their peers in their immediate class group and in the whole school. They have to negotiate their relationships with a dozen or more teachers, each of whom has different idiosyncracies, expectations, rules and routines. They have to cope with the demands of the formal curriculum, and, at the same time, negotiate their place and status as learners in terms of the accepted norms of suc-cess and failure both in and outside school. They have to cope with the insecurities of their developing adolescent identities: working out who they are and who they want to become, in school and outside. And they have to manage all of this and more in relation to other pressures, responsibilities and competing interests from their lives outside school which vie for attention: factors which, for youngsters, have a higher priority than the expectations of their teachers.

Students' accounts of their experiences helped to illustrate why these tasks can be harder for some students than for others. It may be because the pressures on them are greater; or it may be that, for a variety of reasons, they have fewer inner resources to draw on to help them cope. One such pressure can be created by unsatisfying peer relationships, when students see themselves as disliked or rejected by their classmates. One student claimed that he was continually picked on by members of his peer group who saw him as 'weak'. He welcomed being sent to isolation (a disciplinary sanction which required students to work on their own away from their normal lessons) because 'you can get away from your class friends that really really bug you'.

Both staff and students, in interview, acknowledged the added pressures that come from having a reputation for trouble. This tends to make the student more visible to teachers, with the result that minor misdemeanours get picked up on when they may tend to go unnoticed when committed by others.

> The teachers are on the look out all the time, and so they see me do things that other people do but they don't get into trouble.

Tensions arise because it can feel to the student that teachers are 'going on and on' at them 'for every little thing', even though teachers are not intentionally being inconsistent in their responses to students. According to one student, having a reputation could also mean that, when he was in dispute with other students who were not usually in trouble, teachers were not so ready to believe his side of the story.

Teachers' perceptions of students' ability can also create pressures, since teachers may make more allowances for students whom they perceive struggling. As one student noted:

> Every time something goes wrong or I mess about or something, they go 'Come on, you're an intelligent person, you can do the work' and everything. But most of the time the reason I'm messing about is because I can't.

When a student is perceived as 'less able', teachers may be more ready to see difficult behaviour as a symptom of difficulty with learning. But if a student is perceived as 'bright', teachers are more likely to interpret difficulties as a failure of attention or effort on the part of the student. When students so perceived seek help with work which they genuinely do not understand, their requests may be denied and there may be a breakdown in the teacher–student relationship.

Once these pressures are recognised, it is easier to appreciate why the task of simply getting through the day without trouble can seem to be so enormously daunting for some students at risk of exclusion; and why so many attempts at a fresh start – so poignantly recorded in their school files – soon broke down. No matter how much students may genuinely desire to change their ways, they will be unable to sustain the effort as long as the pressures they encounter in school outweigh the resources that they can call on in coping with them. Something has to change in the current balance of pressures and resources in order to make it possible for students to cope with the pressures more successfully. Action needs to be taken either to bring about a significant reduction in the pressures experienced by the student such that he or she can cope with their existing resources; or provide students with opportunities to develop and strengthen their inner resources so that they are better able to cope successfully with the pressures they encounter.

This analysis provided a new way of thinking about the function of the various different strategies that were being used as part of the individual monitoring scheme. On closer inspection, some could be seen to be more concerned with reducing pressures on a short- or longer-term basis; others with building students' inner resources so that they become able to cope more effectively on their own. Some, in different ways, fulfilled both functions.

It could be argued, then, that these strategies, far from merely 'delaying the inevitable', are genuinely preventative, because they help to create the conditions that make it more likely that students who desire change and improvement can be successful in achieving them. The strategies provide a scaffolding for students' own efforts: not doing it all for them, but creating conditions in which those who cannot as yet manage it alone can – with help – gain the confidence and skill to manage independently in the long term.

## Building positive alternatives to exclusion

This analysis of the functions of the individual monitoring scheme can also be applied to the other initiatives that the school was developing in an effort to prevent and reduce exclusion. Each can be seen as contributing in different ways to either or both of these enabling functions. For example, the Personal Tutoring Scheme was clearly concerned with helping to develop students' inner resources so that they were better able to cope with the various pressures encountered in school (Table 13.2). The introduction of Circle Time in Year 7 was helping both to reduce pressures on students by enhancing peer group relationships and to build students' inner resources, by creating time for addressing personal needs and problems, and building confidence and self-esteem through the valuing of each individual's contribution.

Revisiting the various initiatives in this way raised the possibility that there might be other enabling functions reflected in current development work or in the ideas proposed by staff, students or parents as possible areas for future development. A third function was indeed identified, which was concerned with extending the range of opportunities provided within the regular curriculum for students to experience satisfaction and a sense of personal stake, or belonging. It was a source of considerable concern to some teachers, for example, and particularly some of those who were also PTs, that school seemed to have so little to offer some students by way of intrinsic, personal reward. In the words of one teacher, there was a need to 'give them a buzz about actually being here'.

Making the curriculum more personally meaningful and directly relevant to students was an important part of what the new PSHE curriculum sought to do. Circle Time, it was hoped, would give students a sense of having a genuine voice,

*Table 13.2* Reducing pressuress and building inner resources

| Reducing pressures | Building inner resources |
| --- | --- |
| Providing bolt hole | Anger-management strategies |
| Checking equipment | Reminder of strategies they have and can use |
| Removing from lessons strategically | Encouragement |
| Talking through problems arising | Talking problems through to reach new understanding of self and others |
| Moving to another group | Attention to personal needs |
| Teacher-monitor negotiating with staff on behalf of student | Conveying a sense that what happens to the student really matters to someone |

of being accepted, known, valued and integrated within the school community. Comments of both staff and students suggested a need to review and extend the opportunities more generally available for personal acknowledgement and satisfaction within the curriculum as a whole.

Thus, one way of understanding the work going on in the school to prevent and reduce exclusion is in terms of three kinds of supportive change that together might be able to make a genuine difference to students' ability and willingness to engage productively in school life. To summarise, they are strategies or initiatives designed to:

• reduce pressures, so that success in coping becomes more likely
• build inner resources so that students have a larger repertoire upon which to draw enabling them to manage the pressures on them more successfully
• extend opportunities for feeling a sense of personal satisfaction and belonging.

This three-dimensional view of what might be involved in building positive alternatives to exclusion constitutes a new perspective on the various different initiatives examined in this chapter, showing what they have in common and how each might be seen as contributing to a coherent and positive strategy.

It also provides grounds for optimism in a way that teachers may find helpful when situations may appear to have reached deadlock. It shows that there is always scope for positive change, if we can alter the current balance between pressures, resources and opportunities in ways that are enabling for students. It also identifies the kinds of changes that it may be most fruitful to pursue, in finding positive ways forward: in work with individuals, within the curriculum and within the school as a whole. These developments benefit not only those at risk of exclusion. A supportive, healthy, caring ethos put into action, combined with a relevant curriculum taught in ways which truly engage the students, will surely be of benefit to all.

In this chapter, I have described how the project helped to generate a new perspective on the different kinds of innovative work going on in the school, and how these were collectively contributing to the task of reducing and preventing exclusion. However, this was by no means the whole story. What also emerged through the research was a heightened awareness of the need to give equally careful thought to the needs of teachers, and to the part that addressing their needs might play in the task of building positive alternatives to exclusion.

## Reflective questions

1   To what extent can and should problems of a high proportion of disaffected pupils within a school be 'dealt with' by some form of supportive or therapeutic intervention targeted upon such pupils? What about targeting the system?
2   Does inclusion involve changing the pupil to fit the school, or changing the school to fit the pupil?

## Reference

Golding, W. (1954) *Lord of the Flies*, London: Faber and Faber.

# CHAPTER 14

# 'THE TIDE HAS TURNED'

## A case study of one inner city LEA moving towards inclusion

J. Wolger

In C. Tilstone and R. Rose (eds) *Strategies to Promote Inclusive Practice* (2003), London and New York: RoutledgeFalmer, pp. 187–202

During the past decade, the roles and responsibilities of local education authorities have become reduced and have changed direction in many areas although they still retain a significant responsibilities for pupils with Special Educational Needs (SEN). The extent of their responsibilities is surprising as SEN has, according to 100 Ofsted inspections between 1996 and 2000 consistently been one of its less successful areas of work (Ofsted and Audit Commission, 2001). Nevertheless, despite the moves towards the self-management and self-evaluation of individual schools (Caldwell and Spinks, 1988; MacGilchrist *et al.*, 1995, 1997) it would be unfortunate if the local knowledge and expertise that LEAs have built up in supporting children with SEN was lost (Ainscow *et al.*, 1999; Johnstone and Warwick, 1999; Mittler, 2000).

This chapter discusses the proposals for a practical inclusion policy of one inner city Local Education Authority (LEA) which, alongside a number of other similar authorities, was originally considered by Ofsted to have some major problems in its management and organisation, but which solved a difficult problem and produced positive policies for pupils with SEN.

## Case study

In May 1999 Islington Local Education Authority, in north London, received a critical Ofsted report (Ofsted, 1999) and, in April 2000, most of the LEA's statutory functions were transferred to Cambridge Education Associates (known as CEA@Islington). In the report, Islington's Special Education Department, although given a 'satisfactory' rating, was described as having:

> ... shortcomings in almost every aspect of provision, notwithstanding pockets of good practice,

a criticism which was overwhelmingly due to the absence of a

> ... clear and comprehensive strategy for special needs and the lack of translation of such a strategy into operational plans implemented to good effect...
>
> (Ofsted, 1999, para. 141)

In general, the LEA's work was described as having 'few strengths but many weaknesses' (Ofsted, 1999, para. 6) and, consequently, it was concluded that it was failing in its primary duty of supporting school improvement in order to secure a suitable and effective education for the pupils in its care. The development of a more inclusive approach to the education of pupils with SEN and the provision of higher-quality facilities for those pupils were identified as priority areas for action (Ofsted, 1999, paras A (iii), 22 and 52).

Some years from those damning comments the picture is very different, and a second Ofsted report, in March 2001, stated that:

> The tide has turned in Islington. Strong foundations have been laid...There is a forward momentum which is engendering the confidence needed to raise expectations on all fronts...
>
> (Ofsted, 2001a, para. 10)

This report describes the work of the Special Education Department as 'impressive' (para. 142) and specifically praises its work on inclusion. The comments are quoted in full as they provide a succinct critique of collaboration between special and mainstream schools:

> Islington's inclusion policy contains a clear and realistic vision, and set of principles that are well conceived. These principles have guided the development of strategy that over time should bring measurable improvements in provision and in pupil-related outcomes. This strategy, which is at an early stage, is based on the notion that all schools have a role to play in developing inclusive education, but some, supported by their local special school, are better placed to introduce specialist provision to meet particular types of need. Every school is linked to one of four service areas and thus to Islington's special schools. Each area is supported in the development of a particular range of expertise that will be available to the whole borough and, in time, resources will be devolved to area level. The provision developed at area level will include within its range, the needs of a significant proportion of children currently educated outside the borough. This should help vulnerable pupils to secure closer links with their families and at the same time reduce expenditure. The strategy is backed up by the 'SEN Framework for Action' the activities within which are clear, well matched to strategic aims and linked well with other activities, although more emphasis on success criteria and measurable outcomes would strengthen the monitoring impact, an essential ingredient of future success.
>
> (Ofsted, 2001a, para. 143)

According to the Ofsted grading system, such an endorsement places Islington in the top 5 per cent of LEAs in supporting pupils with SEN (Ofsted, 2001b), a situation which has inevitably been influenced by the progress on inclusive practice in the United Kingdom in general.

## The progress of inclusion in the United Kingdom

Mittler (2000) contends that the move towards inclusion is a 'journey without end', and if this is true then the speed by which the traveller has journeyed has certainly increased over the past five years in the United Kingdom. Books and journals dealing with the many aspects of inclusion have reflected the tensions and challenges to be found of the 'journey': some couched in terms of 'the ideal versus the pragmatic' (Croll and Moses, 2000); some carrying heated exchanges reflecting the strong feeling for and against the practicalities of inclusion (Barrow, 2000; Thomas, 2000; Vislie, 2000; Wilson, 2000); others providing an overview of current practice (Ainscow *et al.*, 1999; Mittler, 2000). There have been frequent discussions on 'definitions' and ideology' (see, e.g. Norwich, 1996; Wilson, 1999); and descriptions of specific practices in the United Kingdom (Jacklin and Lacey, 1993; Florian, 1998; Bannister *et al.*, 1999; Johnstone and Warwick, 1999; Knight, 1999; Richards, 1999) and abroad (LeRoy and Simpson, 1996; Meijer and Stevens, 1997; Zigmond and Baker, 1997).

The debates about *how* and *why* inclusion might be achieved have mainly focused upon the moral principles of 'human' and 'equal' rights and 'equality of opportunity' (Wilson, 1999, 2000; Mittler, 2000) and, less commonly, upon the financial arguments on the 'efficient' and 'effective' use of resources (Rubain, 2001). Interestingly, both arguments have been used 'for' and 'against' the inclusion of pupils with SEN into mainstream provision. The trend in the United Kingdom has been towards the *gradual* inclusion of pupils with SEN into mainstream schools, unlike in some other countries where special schools have closed almost overnight, and mainstream schools have been expected to cope with an influx of pupils with complex needs (Abbring and Meijer, 1994). Such a 'gentle' approach has meant that special and mainstream schools are still functioning alongside each other, although there have been some exceptions such as the developments in the London Borough of Newham (Burke, 1999), but even in such a vanguard authority, a special school is still in existence to meet particular complex needs, and other pupils with such needs are placed in specialist provision outside the borough.

Although gradual, the move towards inclusion in the United Kingdom has had some notable landmarks over the years. In the 1970s, for example, children with severe mental handicaps who were previously considered to be 'ineducable' were brought into the educational framework for the first time and, from the 1990s onwards, a whole raft of government documents and legislation has set out an educational vision in which the inclusion of children with SEN is seen as a major part of the future development of educational provision in this country, and the rights of children to that provision have been legally established (DfEE, 1997, 1998; DfES, 2001). Such initiatives have had at least three important effects:

1   Attention has been drawn to the wide continuum of need within the term 'SEN' which has fuelled a continuing debate on the categorisation of children with such needs. At one end of the continuum are those pupils who have profound and multiple disabilities and who are likely to need specialised education throughout their lives; at the other are those whose disabilities are transitory and can be met by prompt and effective action in the form of particular educational strategies and management.

2   The debate about assessment and the curriculum has moved from a deficit ('can't do') model, which describes the problem as being mainly 'within the child', to a positive ('can do') model, which focuses attention upon what the child is capable of achieving, and uses it as a starting point to make appropriate provision to meet his or her needs. Consequently, schools have been encouraged to consider what they are able to offer pupils with SEN in terms of appropriate teaching

strategies and environmental changes, rather than rejecting them because they do not *fit* the needs of the institution.
3   The rights of all children to equality of educational opportunity has been highlighted and, importantly, attention has focused on the basic right of any child to an education that is best suited to meeting his or her individual needs. Flexible patterns of inclusion have emerged which offer a variety of mainstream and special school experiences.

David Blunkett, formerly Secretary of State for Education, summed up the importance of focusing upon those with SEN:

> The education of children with SEN is a key challenge for the nation ... It is vital to the creation of a fully inclusive society in which all members see themselves as valued for the contribution they make. We owe all our children – whatever their particular needs and circumstances – the opportunity to develop to their full potential, to contribute economically, and to play a full part as active citizens.
>
> (DfEE, 1998, p. 2)

Despite such statements, Feiler and Gibson (1999) are critical of the lack of practical support from the Government and give a number of reasons why inclusive practice in the United Kingdom has not moved on the same pace as some other European countries. They include:

- the competitive atmosphere engendered in schools by the 1988 Education Act;
- the vested interests on the part of educationalist and researchers who are seen as coming either from the 'segregationist' or 'inclusionist' camps;
- confusion about terminology (e.g. what is meant by 'inclusion/integration' or 'SEN');
- the lack of empirical data on the benefits (or disadvantages) of inclusion either for pupils or for schools;
- 'internal exclusions' created by intentional streaming;
- highly structured and prescriptive organisational requirements stemming from curriculum initiatives such as the national literacy and numeracy strategies;
- the preference of some schools for using a deficit model, rather than the more positive 'can do' model, to protect their academic status;
- the use of 'popular' diagnoses such as dyslexia, ADHD and autism by both professionals and parents alike, to protect, or gain, scarce resources.

Lorenz (1995), in a similar list drawn up some years earlier, includes the introduction of Local Management of Schools; the National Curriculum; the use of standard assessment tasks (SATs); and the publication of league tables as being additional stumbling blocks to inclusion. She maintained that the reluctance or inability of schools to take on board some of these challenges was the reason why inclusion, in her own and similar LEAs, was driven by local 'political' imperatives rather than other motives such as a response to parental concerns.

## Index for inclusion

Recently, however, schools have had some practical help in overcoming the barriers to inclusion.

The *Index for Inclusion* published by the Centre for Studies on Inclusive Education (CSIE, 2000) was sent to all schools by the (then) DfEE and provides a set of materials to support institutions in the process of inclusive school development. The materials aim to help schools restructure their cultures, policies and practices and to enable *all* those pupils vulnerable to 'exclusionary pressures' (including those with SEN) to increase their participation in the life of the schools and in their local communities. Schools are encouraged to engage in challenging explorations of their practices through a consideration of indicators and questions. Within the *Index,* the concept of SEN is replaced by the term ' barriers to learning and participation', and the emphasis is on the capacity of the school to include students with diverse needs.

Although the DfEE was responsible for distributing the *Index* and therefore endorsed it, Mittler (2000) emphasises that the Government seems to be unclear on whether segregated provision should exist. The closing of all segregated provision is not a view to which all educators subscribe and Croll and Moses (2000) report the views of thirty-eight LEA officers and headteachers (of special and mainstream primary schools) across eleven LEAs who, although supporting the 'ideal' of full inclusion in principle, hold a more pragmatic view on its implementation. They saw it as an 'unrealistic' or 'Utopian' ideal'for some children with severe and complex needs and with emotional and behavioural difficulties, and suggested that these children would always require separate provision as their 'overriding right' to an educational environment that best served their needs. Norwich (1996), in discussing the 'dilemmas and tensions' of inclusion, sees the special school perspective as a useful reminder to mainstream colleagues of the diversity of values, assumptions and methods of education required for a minority.

The Government has certainly suggested ways in which special schools can take a more central role in the development of inclusive practices, including:

- building on their strengths to ensure that they become an integral part of an inclusive education system;
- allowing more flexibility on admitting pupils (e.g. taking them for shorter lengths of time to meet specific short-term needs);
- encouraging their staff to work with mainstream schools in order to plan support for pupils who may benefit from a mainstream setting;
- acting as a source of expertise, advice and professional development for mainstream colleagues;
- providing staff to work in resourced schools, and units in mainstream schools;
- amalgamating small special schools and encouraging them to work as a large part of a mainstream campus;
- giving their teachers an explicit remit to provide support and training for mainstream colleagues;
- sharing facilities and resources, including teaching and non-teaching expertise;
- providing support for pupils who move between special and mainstream schools;
- becoming part of 'cluster' arrangements with mainstream primary and secondary schools.

Many writers, whilst acknowledging that special schools can be barriers to the inclusion process, agree that such schools must have a positive role in the move towards inclusive practices (e.g. Ainscow *et al.*, 1999; Knight, 1999; Mittler, 2000). They consider that the principles of inclusion must be 'infused' rather than 'imposed', and Letch (2000), commenting particularly on the role that special school staff should play in preparing their mainstream colleagues for the task of including pupils with SEN, sees the work as extremely challenging for both:

> It will mean a reappraisal of the skills and competences of staff in specialist schools to see how far these can be applied in mainstream situations. It will also mean planning appropriate ways for these teachers to teach other adults since most teachers are used to teaching children but not their peers. Maybe most of all, it will entail mainstream teachers being ready to change time-honoured practices.
>
> (p. 117)

LEAs have a responsibility to support such tasks and, in a wide-ranging report on inclusive practice in Norway, Spain, Italy, Denmark and the United Kingdom, Johnstone and Warwick (1999) lay down some 'action points' for LEAs who are intending to support the process in a planned and proactive way. These include:

- regular staff discussions on the principles and values at the heart of inclusion policies;
- the encouragement of positive attitudes towards inclusion;
- the establishment of a realistic agenda towards inclusive practices; teachers and LEA officers must be empowered to use a clear set of guidelines; the regular revision of the policies;
- a strong commitment to a supportive framework for continuing professional development for teachers and support staff;
- a high-quality, broad-based, and responsive framework of support aimed at achieving inclusion must be in place within the LEA to ensure that all of the above can be carried through.

CEA@Islington has responded to these action points and has produced its own document for the future of its special needs provision, which takes into account many of the suggestions made by Johnstone and Warwick. A strong emphasis within this 'framework' document is the Government's vision of the creation of a new role for special schools.

## CEA@Islington's SEN framework for action

Islington LEA has been engaged in discussions on inclusive education, which has resulted in what could best be described as 'expressions of good intentions'. The launch of the first Annual SEN Conference in 1999 fuelled the debate, and as a consequence of the inception of CEA in April 2000, positive action has resulted. Widespread discussions have taken place at a variety of levels on CEA@Islington's new publication *Special Educational Needs Framework of Action 2000–2003* and included:

- officers of the Special Education Department and other senior officers from CEA@Islington;
- the heads and chairs of the governing bodies of the four special schools in the LEA (through a series of meetings and presentations);
- three annual SEN conferences involving borough officers and councillors, heads, deputies, governors and SENCos from all the mainstream and special schools in the borough;

- representatives from various professional teams including early years; learning support; educational psychology; social services and educational welfare; youth; play and community.

In addition to these discussions, a video was produced and widely circulated, and a series of public 'focus' meetings was held across the borough with governors, schools, pupil referral units and early years centres, parents, representatives from the trade unions and voluntary organisations. It was the biggest and most wide-ranging consultation ever to take place in the borough and written responses to the document highlighted the following key issues:

- the borough should be moving towards inclusive education (84 per cent);
- children have the right to attend a mainstream school (66 per cent);
- special schools should play a central role in developing inclusive practice (81 per cent).

## The document

It is understood and accepted by the LEA that there must be a clear policy framework backed by an achievable action plan and that the good practice of wide consultation should continue with the involvement of all key players at all stages in order to promote a shared vision and culture of inclusion. It was also recognised that proper support systems for mainstream schools would need to be in place, together with the development of ways of measuring progress in order that potential barriers to inclusive practice (such as test/examination results and league tables) could be monitored and nullified as far as possible. The framework document should build upon the strengths of practice identified by the Ofsted reports, mentioned earlier, which include: strong partnerships with the early years service; effective collaboration with Health and Social Services; good regional developments with other London boroughs in the areas of language and communications and dual sensory impairment; high-quality special schools, and a comprehensive network of advice and support for parents.

## Aims and principles of the new policy

The main principle, which governs the 'framework', is the improvement of the quality and co-ordination of services for children and families. It brings together placement and service planning and involves education, health and social service professionals. Consequently the overall needs of the child (during the school day, after school, at week-ends and during holidays) can be comprehensively provided for, whilst at the same time respite care and support for parents can be more readily available.

The aim of CEA@Islington's strategy for inclusion is that through supported teaching and learning, all children with SEN will have their needs met within local educational provision and that inclusive education will form an integral part of the vision for improving standards and raising achievement for all schools. A main task for the LEA is, therefore, how best to support schools to increase their ability to meet a wider range of SEN cost effectively and, at the same time, take into account the current profile of provision. Eight general principles have been identified which provide a useful checklist for the initial monitoring of the involvement of the LEA, to:

1  give greater flexibility and more power to the schools;
2  focus support in order to improve the schools' capabilities to meet the needs of a wide range of pupils;
3  create a transparent and equitable system of resourcing;
4  reallocate existing resources;
5  measure the impact of the additional support provided;
6  develop partnerships with parents and pupils;
7  ensure that *all* teachers are teachers of children with SEN;
8  enhance the skills and knowledge of the staff of schools and enable them to move confidently towards inclusion.

Headings from the research of Ainscow *et al.* (1999) into the role of twelve LEAs in developing inclusive policies and practices have been used to identify strategies needed to implement the 'framework'. These are: policy development; funding strategies; processes and structures; management of change; partnerships and external influences. The main tasks under each heading are discussed later.

## Policy development

All schools and service will have a SEN policy which reflects the principles and aims of the framework.

## Funding strategies

In the light of the consultation process it was decided that schools were best placed to assess the day-to-day needs of pupils with SEN and therefore funds for pupils, with and without Statements, will be delegated to schools on a 'whole-school basis' within one overall SEN budget. The duty of schools and governing bodies to ensure that provision is made for all pupils with SEN and additional educational needs (AEN) within their schools will be monitored by the LEA (which still has overall responsibility for children with Statements). By delegating funds in such a way it will be possible to:

* enable schools to identify and meet SEN at the possible stage;
* provide schools with more stability and flexibility;
* encourage the development of permanent specialist SEN teams;
* reduce bureaucracy;
* lessen the need for statements of need to be seen as the 'gateway' to SEN funding.

In addition, funding for pupils with low-incidence disabilities (visual impairment, hearing impairment, autism, physical disabilities, severe and profound and multiple learning difficulties) of such a severity that they would normally require a statement should continue to be devolved to schools following an individual assessment. Funding will also continue to be retained for pupils with severe and complex and emotional and behavioural difficulties whose needs cannot be met in mainstream settings.

A substantial number of Islington pupils with SEN attend mainstream schools (maintained and independent) outside the borough and at a considerable cost. It is intended that the quality of local provision will be developed to such an extent that parents will be more likely in future to choose local schools for their children rather than sending them out of the borough.

## Processes and structures

A new facilitative role for special schools will be developed, with less emphasis on the delivery of direct provision for individual pupils and more on a focused move towards inclusion. These schools will provide an education for their own pupils and also services for mainstream colleagues including:

- advice, support and information;
- help with the identification and assessment of need;
- the moderation of the levels of support required;
- curriculum and resource development;
- examples of evidence-based practice;
- shared professional development;
- time limited placements in special provision for some pupils.

Four service areas will be developed from the existing special schools, based upon the areas of disability identified in the *Draft Code of Practice* (DfEE, 2000): learning and cognition; emotional social and behavioural difficulties; communication and interaction; physical and/or sensory. These service areas will be responsible for developing a continuum of provision in order to facilitate the maximum level of inclusion for pupils with special needs in mainstream schools and will offer varied patterns of support which may include:

- total inclusion within a mainstream class;
- separate provision for a limited time;
- part-time or short-term placements;
- specific in-class support;
- learning support bases for withdrawal teaching.

It is envisaged that such a move will increase the ability of mainstream schools to provide for a range of pupils with SEN and to improve the links between special and mainstream schools (Figure 14.1). All four service areas will provide targeted support for high-incidence disability directly to mainstream schools. Mainstream schools will be encouraged to identify a low-incidence disability in which they are interested in developing further skills (e.g. hearing impairment, visual impairment, physical disability, autism, severe and profound and multiple learning difficulties). Working in clusters, they will be supported by the appropriate service area. It is likely that in future they will be become 'additionally resourced' schools, which will have developed expertise in a certain area of SEN and will consequently receive additional funding. Schools will determine the way in which their own provision develops and could vary from a discrete unit base to total inclusion. An example of such a model is provided later.

## Management of change

It is acknowledged that staff and parents will feel insecure as the SEN 'framework' is put into practice and strategies will need to be devised to ensure that current expertise is recognised and a full package of training is offered and developed for teachers, support staff, governors and parents. Islington's special education department will be responsible for developing work in a number of key areas:

- an agreed policy for placement in non-mainstream provision;
- developing links with the Connexions Service for children aged thirteen plus;

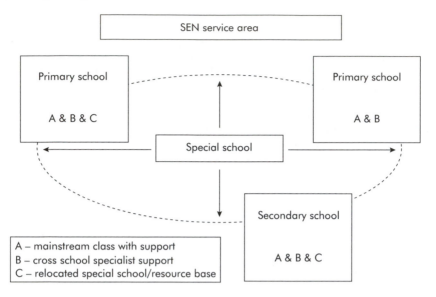

*Figure 14.1* School linkages to deliver services for children with SEN

- conciliation arrangements with an independent elements to help to resolve disputes;
- rigorous accountability for resources.

In addition improvements are planned in the arrangements for admission to schools and transfer between phases for children with statements of SEN. One of Islington's special schools already has established a training unit, which is offering training to teaching assistants in the LEA and a number of other London boroughs (Imray and Wolger, 1999). It is intended to develop this resource to form a training facility, capable of offering nationally accredited courses for teaching assistants and teachers and to support the work within Islington's service areas.

## Partnerships

Parents must feel confident that the needs of their children will be met in the move towards inclusive education. The following concerns were expressed by some parents during the consultation process:

- the practical realities of inclusive education;
- unsuccessful experiences in mainstream schools;
- health and safety issues and bullying in mainstream schools;
- funding and resources (some parents did not trust schools to spend money devolved to them for SEN for the intended purpose);
- transition from one phase of education to another (primary to secondary, example).

Parents did, however, have some suggestions on how to make the process more comfortable for them. In the main these centred on improved communications and information between parents and professionals. For example, proper support networks should be in place before the child's problems become critical, together with clearer guidance, in plain English. Parents also felt strongly that school staff needed to be better trained and more knowledgeable in SEN and that it was important for the whole child to be considered and not just his or her disability.

### External influences

It is important that the move towards inclusive education will be reflected in, and facilitated by, all educational initiatives in order to assist, rather than to obstruct, the process. Such initiatives will ensure that:

- inclusive education is the central theme of the LEA's Education Development Plan;
- the national literacy and numeracy strategies focus on raising the standards of *all* children including those with SEN;
- the LEA's School Organisation Plan provides opportunities for the development of resource bases and the relocation of current specialist provision;
- the needs of pupils with emotional, social and behavioural difficulties are a particular focus of the LEA's Social Inclusion Strategies and Behaviour Support Plan;
- early identification and preventative work will be the core of the Early Years Development Plan;
- the LEA's responsibilities for 'children in need' and 'looked after children' will be reflected in the Children's Services Plan and the Quality Protection Management Action Plan.

## Conclusion

In this chapter CEA@Islington's Framework for Action has been discussed with reference to the national initiatives on inclusive education and insights have been given into how parents and professionals within the borough view the proposals. Although it is impossible to discuss its effectiveness at this early stage, it can be reported that progress has been made on the planning, development and implementation of the four service areas and the heads of the special schools have been appointed as the heads of these services. Funding for mainstream schools in relation to the management of pupils with high-incidence disabilities is now in place, and further consultation with mainstream and special schools on the strategy for funding pupils with low-incidence disabilities has already started. The 'action points' identified in Johnstone and Warwick's research (1999) will ultimately be used to determine the success of the inclusion policy being promoted by CEA@Islington, but the recent Ofsted inspection reveals that the team consider the framework to provide:

> . . . a well-conceived, positive, clear and realistic vision that should bring benefits over the next three to five years.
>
> (Ofsted, 2001, para. 143)

The Inspection Team report that:

> . . . there is still a long way to go before all school staff are convinced about the merits of inclusion, but improved advice, training and support at all levels for teaching and non-teaching staff are beginning to improve confidence and expertise in schools.
>
> (Ofsted, 2001, para. 149)

It would seem that the tide has turned and that many of the correct strategies are in place for this policy on inclusion to become a reality.

## Reflective questions

1   As a local authority moves towards inclusion, what should be the balance between persuasion/infusion and a more managerial approach which offers rewards for inclusion and penalties for exclusion?
2   Might there be different time scales for these strategies to take effect?
3   In these developments, how important is the role of the local authority compared to that of national government and school inspection systems?

## References

Abbring, I. and Meijer, C.W.J. (1994) 'Italy', in C.W.J. Meijer *et al.* (eds) *New Perspectives in Special Education: A Six Country Study of Integration.* London: Routledge.

Ainscow, M., Farrell, P., Tweddle, D. and Malkie, G. (1999) 'The role of the LEA in developing inclusive policies and practices', *British Journal of Special Education*, 26 (3) 136–40.

Bannister, C., Sharland, V., Thomas G., Upton, V. and Walker, P. (1999) 'Changing from a special school to an inclusion service', *British Journal of Special Education*, 25 (2) 65–9.

Barrow, R. (2000) 'Include me out: a response to John Wilson', *European Journal of Special Needs Education*, 15 (3) 305–13.

Burke, B. (1999) 'LEA Support Services: a Newham Perspective', in B. Norwich (ed.) *Rethinking Support for More Inclusive Schooling.* Tamworth: NASEN.

Caldwell, B.J. and Spinks, J.M. (1988) *The Self-managing School.* London: The Falmer press.

Croll, P. and Moses D. (2000) 'Ideologies and Utopias: education professionals, views of inclusion', *European Journal of Special Needs Education*, 15 (1) 1–12.

CSIE (2000) *Index for Inclusion: Developing Learning and Participation in Schools.* Bristol: CSIE and London: DfEE.

DfEE (1997) *Excellence for All Children: Meeting Special Education Needs.* London: The Stationery Office.

DfEE (1998) *Meeting Special Education Needs: A Programme for Action.* London: DfEE.

DfEE (2000) *Draft code of Practice on the Identification and Assessment of Pupils with Special Educational needs and SEN Thresholds.* London: DfEE.

Department for Education and Skills (2001) *Inclusive Schooling: Children with Special Education Needs.* London: DfES.

Feiler, A. and Gibson, H. (1999) 'Threats to the inclusion movement', *British Journal of Special Education*, 26 (3) 147–51.

Florian, L. (1998) 'An examination of the practical problems associated with the implementation of inclusive education policies', *Supports for Learning*, 13 (13) 105–8.

Gerschel, L. (1998) 'Equal opportunities and special education needs: equity and inclusion', in C. Tilstone, L. Florian and R. Rose (eds) *Promoting Inclusive Practice.* London: Routledge.

Hegarty, S. (1993) 'Reviewing the literature on integration', *European Journal of Special Needs Education*, 8 (3) 194–200.

Imrary, P. and Wolger, J. (1999) 'A home-grown answer to the problem of support staff training'. *SLD Experience*, 25 (Autumn) 2–4.

Jacklin, A. and Lacey, J. (1993) 'The integration process: a development model', *Support for Learning*, 8 (2) 51–7.

Johnstone, D. and Warwick, C. (1999) 'Community solution to inclusion: some observations on practice in Europe and the United Kingdom', *Support for Learning*, 14 (1) 8–12.

Knight, B.A. (1999) 'Towards inclusion for students with special education needs in the regular classroom', *Support for Learning*, 14 (1) 3–7.

LeRoy, B. and Simpson, C. (1996) ' Improving student outcomes through inclusive education', *Support for Learning*, 11 (1) 32–6.

Letch, R. (2000) 'SEN and inclusion', in J. Docking (ed.) *New Labour's Policies for Schools: Raising the Standard?* London: David Fulton, in association with Roehampton Institute London.

Lorenz, S. (1995) 'The placement of pupils with Down's Syndrome: a survey of one northern LEA', *British Journal of Special Education*, 22 (1) 16–19.

MacGilchrist, B., Mortimore, P., Savage, J. and Beresford, C. (1995) *Planning Matters: The Impact of Development Planning in Primary Schools*. London: Paul Chapman Publishing.

MacGilchrist, B., Myers, K. and Reed, J. (1997) *The Intelligent School*. London: Paul Chapman Publishing Ltd.

Meijer, C.J.W. and Stevans, L.M. (1997) 'Restructuring special education provision', in S.J. Pijl, C.J.W. Meijer and S. Hegarty (eds) *Inclusive Education: a Global Agenda*. London: Routledge.

Mittler, P. (2000) *Working Towards Inclusive Education: Social Contexts*. London: David Fulton.

Norwich, B. (1996) 'Special needs in education for all: connective specialisation and ideological impurity', *British Journal of Special Education*, 23 (3) 100–4.

Ofsted (1999) *Inspection of Islington Local Education Authority*. London: Office of Her Majesty's Chief Inspector of Schools in conjunction with the Audit Commission.

Ofsted (2001) *Inspection of Islington Local Education Authority*. London: Office of Her Majesty's Chief Inspector of Schools in conjunction with the Audit Commission.

Ofsted and Audit Commission (2001) *Local Education Authority Support for School Improvement*. London: The Stationery Office.

Richards, I. (1999) 'Inclusive schools for pupils with emotional and behavioural difficulties', *Support for Learning*, 14 (3) 99–103.

Rubain D. (2001) 'Transforming legislation', in *The Times Educational Supplement* (Curriculum Special, 6 April), 4.

Thomas, G. (2000) 'Doing injustice to inclusion: A response to John Wilson', *European Journal of Special Needs Education*, 15 (3) 307–10.

Vislie, L. (2000) 'Doing justice to inclusion: A response to John Wilson', *European journal of Special Needs Education*, 15 (3) 311–13.

Wilson, J. (1999) 'Some conceptual difficulties about inclusion', *Support for Learning*, 14 (3) 110–12.

Wilson, J. (2000) 'Doing justice to inclusion', *European journal of Special Needs Education*, 15 (3) 297–304.

Zigmond, N. and Baker, J.M. (1997) 'Inclusion of pupils with learning disabilities in general education settings', in S.J. Pijl, C.J.W. Meijer and S. Hegarty (eds) *Inclusive Education: a Global Agenda*. London: Routledge.

**PART VI**

# POST-SCHOOL

# CHAPTER 15

# TRANSITION FROM SCHOOL
## How can it be improved?

### L. Dee

In H. Daniels (ed.) *Special Education Re-formed: Beyond Rhetoric?* (2000), London and New York: Falmer Press, pp.138–54

## Introduction

Tucked away at the end of the 1994 *Code of Practice on the Identification and Assessment of Special Educational Needs* (DfE, 1994a) are 20 paragraphs on the management of the transition of young people with special educational needs from school to their post-school destination. Yet, as several commentators have remarked, the Code's guidance on transition has been largely neglected by policy-makers, researchers, the Schools' Inspectorate and sometimes by schools themselves (Derrington *et al.*, 1996; Wilenius, 1996). Behind this helpful, though neglected, advice and guidance are complex issues and dilemmas which challenge its interpretation as well as the nature of some of the guidance itself. The purpose of this chapter is to attempt to unravel some of these complexities to inform both policy and practice and to suggest how the management of transition during the final years of schooling might begin to reflect the true complexity of the process.

In this chapter, I intend to argue that transition planning at the school-leaving stage needs to be seen much more broadly than currently is generally the case. The decisions that are made during this phase of a young person's life need to be understood in the context of an individual's total life span, as just one step in a much longer and gradually evolving process of deciding who they are and who they want to become. These processes in turn need to be placed within the context of their families, cultures and communities. If planning is driven by such considerations, then we may genuinely begin to support the process of the transition to adulthood by reducing the danger of the official procedures – for example, 14+ annual reviews and the completion of transition plans – becoming merely bureaucratic exercises.

## Transition and its meaning

The final years of secondary schooling are seen by the Centre for Educational Research and Innovation (CERI, 1986) as the first part of the transition of young people towards adulthood. More broadly, according to McGinty and Fish, transition is:

> ...a *phase* or period of time between the teens and twenties which is broken up educationally and administratively. During the phase there are changes of

responsibility from child to adult services, from school to further and higher education and from childhood dependence to adult responsibility.

...a *process* by which the individual grows through adolescence to adulthood and achieves the balanced state of dependence and independence which a particular community expects of its adult members.

(McGinty and Fish, 1992: 6)

Using McGinty and Fish's definition of transition, the focus of this chapter is on the interface between the final years of schooling and post-school options. During this period, there are shifts of responsibility for young people's education from local education authorities to the further or higher education sectors. Some young people may, by design or default, fall outside the remit of any of these services (Armstrong and Davies, 1995; Wilkinson, 1995). The procedural management of this phase for young people with identified special educational needs is governed by the guidance set out in the 1994 Code of Practice as well as various pieces of associated legislation including the 1986 Disabled Person Act, 1989 Children Act, 1990 NHS and Community Care Act, 1992 Further and Higher Education Act and the 1995 Disability Discrimination Act.

The Code proposed that planning for transition should begin at the young person's 14+ annual review meeting and that an individual transition plan should be drawn up. The meeting should be convened by the local education authority and parents and the careers service must be invited. The plan should address the young person's aspirations likely support needs, the contribution that each service and parents will make and the nature of the school curriculum. The Code stressed the involvement of young people and their parents in the decision-making process, noting in particular the need for young people to be given information about their options so that they could make informed choices. Young people should be supported to participate in the process by programmes of self-advocacy. Other services, including further provides of education or training, should be informed of any relevant information that would be useful in planning to meet the students' further requirements. The Code also reiterated the existing relevant legislation on inter-agency planning, described earlier. Finally, the Code proposed that guidance could be extended to include pupils without statements but who might benefit from some more planned support as they prepared to leave school.

As the result of a survey of LEAs, schools, parents and careers officers, Bowers *et al.* (1998) reinforced the perception that the Code's guidance on transition is neglected, nothing that 60 per cent of respondents in their questionnaire survey of 55 secondary schools did not complete the section on transition. Among the problematic issues identified by respondents were the quality of participation and involvement by parents and young people in the transition planning process, the timing of the first transitional review, and the relationship between this and subsequent reviews.

Some of these issues relate to the gap between policy and practice, how professionals interpret the guidance and how young people and their families experience the process of transition from adolescence to adulthood described by McGinty and Fish (1992). According to Erikson (1968), during this period young people begin to formulate goals for themselves based on their beliefs about who they are and who they might become. At the same time families are having to adjust to and deal with impact of these changes on the dynamics of the family and family relationships. When the young person has a disability or learning difficulty these processes are likely to be even more complex and stressful. Yet little is known about these experiences. Beresford (1995) in a survey of 1,000 parents of severely disabled children found that their second most pressing need was help with planning their child's future, and there were consistently higher levels of unmet needs among the parents of older children. Gascoigne (1995: 138), herself a parent of three disabled children, eloquently describes the feelings of many parents as their child approaches the school-leaving stage:

> Parents are torn by conflicting wishes for and on behalf of their children as they approach the end of their formal school education and begin to consider the range of future options. On the one hand they want their child to become as independent as possible, and on the other hand they wish to extend their protection of them. This is true of all parents, whether or not their child has special needs. The feelings are exaggerated however where the pupil has special needs. The parents have probably fought many battles both within the home and with external agencies over the years to maximise their child's independence. The approach of adulthood in their child may be a time when early hopes are finally dashed, or where the hopes being realised cause an onset of panic.

To understand more about these processes, it is worth examining some of the mainstream thinking on career learning, which, unfortunately, has generally ignored the experiences of young disabled people and their families. According to Szymanski (1994), discussions on transition have been limited in their scope, concentrating mainly on the school-leaving stage and the transition into employment. She refers to the work of Super (1980, 1994), for example, who challenged his own earlier thinking which saw career paths as being set during adolescence and instead suggested that who we are and our roles are influenced by our life-space – that is, the contexts of home, community, education and work – and this in turn influences our changing roles – for example, child, student, spouse, carer, citizen, etc. Furthermore, our roles change throughout our life span. By adopting a life-span or life-history approach, Hodkinson *et al.* (1996) believe that we can begin to see the school-leaving stage as merely one step in the process of career development which continues throughout our lives. In addition, most commentators also now define career more broadly than just relating to work. Banks *et al.* (1992) define career as the 'progress through domains of education, employment, leisure and domestic life'.

These are helpful ideas. Not only do they address many of the dilemmas faced by professionals working in special education by proposing a much broader notion of career which is thus more inclusive, but these ideas also provide a much clearer rationale for careers education and guidance in the school environment. They also help us to see that the so-called unrealistic ideas of many young people with learning difficulties and/or disabilities are part of a natural process of exploration which may take longer for some than others, as young people come to terms with their own strengths, needs and interests. Here is an extract from an interview conducted as part of some research into young people's aspirations. Sam is 15 and a wheelchair user.

> I would like to be a police officer. I know that it's going to be too difficult but I mean that is something that I have always wanted to be since I was a little kid . . . I don't like being behind desks, I have to be active. I like to move about as much as possible. . . . Now I am coming to terms with that, I won't be able to

be do that sort of thing, I will have to think of something that I can do because as I have grown up, I have got more used to being in a wheelchair but I still feel that I would like to get out of this and start walking on my own, get out of this and run off, but that is not going to be possible either.

It is also important to recognize that the period of transition from school to adult life is a relative concept influenced by cultural and contextual variables. Indeed, this transitional phase is becoming both more extended and more complex for many young people (Jones, 1995) as their entry into the labour market is increasingly delayed and they remain dependent on their families for longer. Thus, although the problems and difficulties associated with the transition phase are likely to be more complex and last well into their twenties and thirties for some young people, particularly if they have severe or complex learning difficulties and/or disabilities, their needs during this period will not be fundamentally different from their peers. In long term they will require support, advice, economic independence, opportunities to develop social networks and friendships and, above all, recognition as an adult and citizen with equal rights and responsibilities.

Before exploring the practical implications of these ideas during the final years of schooling, I want to consider one further aspect of the transition process, that of the relationship between the key decision-makers and the effects of these relationships on the decisions that are made. Most career learning theorists emphasize the explicit or implicit influence on individuals of the family, culture, friends, schooling, community and the availability of local opportunities in determining post-school destinations and eventual lifestyles. Arguments exist about the relative importance of each of these factors although most agree on the significance of families. While Foskett and Hesketh (1977) found, in a study of non-disabled school leavers, that young people are more instrumental in making choices at 16 than some earlier studies would suggest, these decisions are framed or circumscribed for them by their family circumstances and attitudes. Thus parents and children are both 'decision-makers' but the final decision is 'the product of internal processes within that partnership. The balance between the two partners will clearly vary from case to case and from issue to issue' (p. 307).

Following on from this and given the nature of the relationship between parents and their disabled child which Gascoigne describes earlier, it is not surprising parents are likely to have a substantial influence on the decisions that are made. Very little is known about the effect of feelings and emotions on decisions-making (Mellers *et al.*, 1998), yet it is self-evident that parental love for their child is bound to engender powerful feelings. For example, when asked about their aspirations for their child in a study of parental experiences of the transition process (Dee, 1997), parents found it easier to describe their fears than their aspirations: for example, concern for their child's safety, being forced to leave school, unemployment. The emotions which these fears can generate may lead parents to resist thinking about the future or alternatively rushing to make a decision without weighing up the options. Either way, such emotions are likely to make the transition process a complex and difficult time for parents, their child and the professionals involved in supporting them.

The part played by professionals in making decisions about post-school destinations has been highlighted by Hodkinson *et al.* (1996). They suggested that professionals play an equally important and influential role through virtue of the power that they have over policy and resources and which may in the end become the defining factors in what and how decisions are made. For example, a local education authority may decide that special schools only accept pupils up to 16, or the Further Education Funding Learning and Skills Council may endeavour to shift resources from specialist to sector provision, thereby reducing the choices that are available to parents and young people. Within special education there are numerous examples of the unequal power relationships that exist, for example, between parents and professionals (Harry, 1992; Sandow, 1994), between professional and professional (Weatherley, 1979) and between disabled students and professionals (Corbett and Barton, 1992). We have already seen that many people are sceptical about the genuine involvement of young people and their parents in the decision-making processes. For instance, Derrington (1997) found considerable variation in the practice of pupils' attendance at 14+ annual reviews between the schools in three LEAs, and even where pupils do express an opinion they are not always heard. Why is this the case?

Corbett and Barton (1992) locate the barriers to the full involvement of disabled people in decision-making within structural inequalities in the economy and society. Real choice does not exist, because options are manipulated to accomodate changes in the labour market and funding levels, for example, access to training or further education may be increased or decreased according to government or local priorities.

This could lead to the conclusion that the ostensibly rational, participatory decision-making procedures described by the Code of Practice are therefore used to 'cloak' an essentially political process (Weatherley, 1979). Like Weatherley, Hudson (1989) uses Lipsky's idea of the 'street level bureaucrats' (Weatherley and Lipsky, 1977), and maintains that public sector workers are accorded considerable power and discretion in how they conduct their professional roles because they are required to make decisions about other people. Hudson notes, 'It is through street level bureaucrats that society organizes the control, restriction and maintenance of relatively powerless groups' (Hudson, 1989: 397). In examinations of the conduct of transitional review meetings, both Tisdall (1996) and Wood and Trickey (1996) concluded that annual review meetings are generally focused around the needs of professionals to meet their procedural obligations rather than a concern to involve young people and their parents in the process.

Whatever the underlying motives, failure to involve parents and young people in processes which affect their lives is at worst a denial of their human rights and at best thoughtless. The conduct of meetings and their length appear to be important factors in the degree of satisfaction with meetings felt by the students and their parents. Tisdall found that where professionals had met beforehand and meetings were longer, parents and students felt a greater degree of satisfaction, while Miner and Bates (1997) found levels of satisfaction were more related to organizational factors than whether or not students and parents had been prepared for meetings.

So far, then, I have argued that, by broadening our understanding of transition during the final years of secondary schooling, we can increase our capacity to manage the process more effectively and improve the support that is offered to young people and their parents or carers. I turn now to examining in more detail the practical implications of these ideas in an attempt to close the potential gap between process and procedures. A set of underlying principles are proposed and the practical implications of each are described. Four elements of practice are considered: the curriculum, parent partnerships, annual reviews and individual transition plans.

# Implications for practice

## Curriculum

### Inclusive education policies should take account of the transitional needs of all pupils, including those with special educational needs

The reduction in the amount of time that has to be spent on the National Curriculum at Key Stage 4 has enabled schools to pay more attention to careers education and guidance. That said, there is now considerable evidence to suggest that pupils with special educational needs in special schools are likely to receive more extensive careers education and guidance than their peers in mainstream schools (CERI, 1986; OFSTED, 1995; Derrington, 1997). Bowers *et al.* (1998) found that careers officers believed that special schools teachers had a better understanding of their role as careers educators than their mainstream colleagues, a possible indication of the contribution made by them to the special schools' leavers programmes.

The quality and access to information and guidance also differs markedly between schools (Taylor, 1992). The kind of opportunities that may be provided include work experience, mini-enterprise schemes, link courses, business visits, residentials and community work. While Taylor did not include special schools in her study, she did find that differences existed not only between schools but within schools, and that boys and higher-attaining pupils were more likely to participate in career-related activities. This supports the OECD's (CERI, 1986) finding that lower-attaining pupils are less likely to experience careers education programmes in mainstream secondary schools than in special schools. As more young people begin to be included in general provision, due regard must be paid to ensuring the access of all pupils to a comprehensive and supportive careers education programme.

### Inclusive education policies should acknowledge that all pupils, including those with learning difficulties and/or disabilities, are likely to experience an extended period of exploration and floundering

Some teachers complain that young people with special educational needs are often unrealistic in their aspirations, yet this is an essential part of career learning (Krumboltz, 1979; Gottfriedson, 1981). Individuals need to fantasize and try out ideas about who they are and who they might become as part of the natural process of growing up. Indeed, the OECD (CERI, 1988) argued that disabled people are limited in this process by being socialized into their role as a 'handicapped' member of society. Families and society at large may perpetuate the myth of the 'dependent child'. Young people with disabilities can therefore be inhibited from ever seeing themselves as adults, adopting adult roles and responsibilities, and will not be encouraged to speculate about the adult they 'might become'.

Part of this process of exploring possibilities may include having to come to terms with having a disability, as Sam had to, and the effect that this may have on individual aspirations. This has important implications for the role of guidance in the curriculum, which needs to enable young people with special educational needs to explore their feelings and concerns as well as to experiment and try out other ideas.

Through this exploration clues can be gleaned about how best to support a student's learning. For example, John, who attends a school for pupils with moderate learning difficulties, wanted to work as a driver's mate, delivering catering equipment with his cousin. When asked what he thought might prevent him from doing this, he said simply, 'Maps', meaning his inability to read anything, including maps. To build on his motivation, an individual programme was designed to help him overcome this problem and gradually he began to be able to read simple maps.

### Inclusive education policies should develop students' sense of achievement and self-efficacy through the curriculum

The Code of Practice emphasizes the importance of pupil involvement in the decisions that are made during the transition process. The Code goes on to list a number of ways that the curriculum can promote pupil involvement by encouraging students to review and reflect on their own experiences and express their own views. An important vehicle for this process is the Progress File (formerly Record of Achievement) which can link the pupil's individual education plan and the individual transition plan. Some schools ensure that pupils take their Progress Files to the annual review meetings, and use them as a means of involving the pupil by getting them to talk through their achievements. For pupils with severe or complex learning difficulties, videoed Progress Files provide an immediate and powerful reminder for them of their interests and strengths as well as evidence of progress to parents and other professionals.

The Code also stresses the need to develop students' self-esteem. However, what seems more at issue for young people with learning difficulties and/or disabilities is not simply their self-esteem, which is important, as much as their self-efficacy and the extent to which they feel that they have control over events. A number of studies have drawn this distinction, including Jahoda *et al.* (1988), Fox and Norwich (1992), Ridell *et al.* (1993) and Ward *et al.* (1994). Hirst and Baldwin (1994) compared feelings of self-esteem among disabled young people to those of a control group. They concluded that those attending regular schools had higher self-esteem than those who had attended special schools, but lower than others attending regular schools. While some pupils scored higher than the general population on self-esteem, fewer felt a sense of personal control which, according to Oyserman and Markus (1990), may be a more important factor in realizing aspirations. They argued that self-efficacy is just as important as having positive self-esteem in negotiating a way through choices and options.

Strategies for promoting self-advocacy and the skills to make choices are well documented elsewhere (see e.g. Crawley, 1983; Clare, 1990; Flynn and Ward, 1991; Derrington, 1997). What seems harder to achieve is really allowing young people to be heard in the process of making complex decisions as opposed to the more mundane everyday choices with which they are often presented.

Being aware of our own professional practice and how we can unwittingly manipulate decisions is an important part of critical reflection on practice and can assist service providers in becoming more alive to the needs of young people and their parents or carers. For example, beliefs about an individual can help to form the implicit 'rules' which can govern decision-making. Where a young person goes on leaving school may be influenced by the destinations of other leavers from the same school: for example, common patterns may be seen in progression routes from special schools for the deaf to specialist colleges for the deaf. These decisions may be based on unspoken rules exercised by the professionals involved in providing information to students or parents about the options available to them – information based on custom and practice.

Choices can also be influenced through tone of voice, through the choices that are presented, through the order of choices and through the nature of the dialogue (Jenkinson, 1993; Mellers *et al.*, 1998). Jenkinson's research is particularly relevant to the kind of decisions that have to be made during the school-leaving years. She found that individuals are more likely to be influenced by others in complex decision-making situations, particularly where they experience stress or where choices are so controlled that they feel helpless.

## Parent and carer involvement

### Ensure that parents are provided in good time with information about the procedures for deciding post-school destinations as well as about the options that are available

How soon should discussions about leaving school start? To some extent, it depends on the individual needs of parents as well as the purpose of the discussions. Parents are not a homogeneous group. Some parents want discussions to start as soon as their child enters secondary school. Others cannot bear to think about the future. Some professionals argue that to begin discussing post-school options three or four years before they predict the child will leave school is too soon and creates unnecessary distress and alarm, particularly to parents. Yet, in a study conducted by Bowers *et al.* (1998) for the DfEE, a parent noted:

> It [the transition plan] gives us a clear guide to the future and plenty of time for parents and children to plan, i.e. look at every option. At first I thought it was too early but not now, having been through the system.
>
> (Bowers *et al.*, 1998: 100)

Furthermore, if we accept that the decision-making processes are not logical and rational but messy, with the potential to cause stress and anxiety, then the kind of support that is required will not just be about what options are available. Wertheimer (1989: 40) cites a mother who said:

> Life outside the boundaries that we and the school system have created in the past terrifies us. All our earlier feelings are reactivated. We may once again experience grief and upset, guilt and sadness, fear and despair. These feelings need to be acknowledged by the people who work with us.

Families have been identified as one of the main influences on the post-school destinations of all young people. Yet more often than not they rely for their information on informal rather than formal sources (Dee, 1997). An analysis of data gathered from three sets of parents showed that their main sources of information were other family members, neighbours and friends, the media, other parents, and their own experiences.

This informally gleaned information was sometimes positive and helpful but it could also be negative, helping to build up negative perceptions about a particular type of provision. Such perceptions, then, influence the choices that parents and carers make. They are not irrational decisions, but are based on their own experience and knowledge. Here is the mother of James, a deaf student, talking about their local college.

> Going back to the local colleges, I know nothing about them. There is a bit of a blockage because there is one place in Barchester that's not bad. Then I began

to hear different stories about it and it is a normal college but there is a group of people my friend works with and a few of them are deaf and the rest aren't but they are all what you might call mature students, I think, not 16 to 18 ones. I think they all tend to be 20 up to 30 and they are all mentally retarded and some of them happen to be deaf as well...I don't agree with them all being in a class together. ...There's nothing wrong with James. We don't hold anything against mentally retarded people but I've met these people she works with and they are pretty severely retarded.

So what do parents want to know? Sometimes they may not know what they want to know, and only in retrospect are they able to describe what would have been helpful at the time. Requirements will clearly vary, and it is important for schools in particular not to assume knowledge on the part of parents such as, for example, that the school has a post-16 section, what the role of the careers service is or what link courses are. The following list is derived from what parents have said would be helpful to them:

- A checklist of what happens, and when, with respect to school-leaving procedures, including parental rights and responsibilities. While the Code emphasizes the need for parents to know where to get practical help, they also want to know how decisions are made and over what period of time. The parents' guide to the Code is helpful (DfE, 1994b) but information will need to be customized to account for local differences.
- A list of the range of options available, including local and residential options and who to contact. Parents or carers require objective information with the opportunity for visits so that they can find out for themselves what the provision is like.
- A list of service providers, their responsibilities, names, telephone numbers and addresses.
- A mentor, that is, someone who is objective and whom they feel is outside the formal agencies and systems. Some parents feel, rightly or wrongly, that different professionals have particular agendas and may be operating under constraints which prevent them from passing on or processing certain information. While the concept of the named person or independent parental supporter is now a well-accepted part of the statutory assessment procedures, it has yet to be adopted during the transition years, when it arguably becomes even more important as parents and their child attempt to navigate a path between child and adult services and school and post-school provision.

## Improving procedures

### Work with other professionals to arrive at an agreed understanding of the purpose of the 14+ annual review as well as subsequent annual review meetings

It is important that professionals spend time clarifying how they see the purpose of these meetings. Decisions about what to do after school involve making plans, the outcomes of which are often uncertain. Thus the purpose of the 14+ review will be to begin the process of exploration rather than making a definite decision. Plans are made over a period of time and may involve making a number of smaller decisions which may or may not lead towards the desired goal – for example, I want to become an electrician, but I want to be with other deaf students and the specialist college doesn't offer the right course for me. If we place the 14+ and subsequent annual reviews in the context of Hodkinson *et al.*'s (1996) argument, that the school-leaving stage is just one step in a lifelong process of career development, then this allows us to begin to see the reviews as part of an incremental process of decision-making through which young people and their parents can explore ideas about the future and pursue different options as they change their minds. For example, the student in the above example might explore what a different residential college has to offer, try out a link course at the local further education college or change his mind about what he wants to do. The Code, as it stands, rather neglects the later stages of the transition process and the conduct of subsequent annual reviews. If the purpose of transitional reviews is seen more broadly than making decisions about post-school destinations, then this may help to resolve some of the current debates about the timing of the first transitional review.

## Develop a planning cycle to ensure that as far as possible the different activities associated with transition follow in a logical sequence

Schools, often in conjunction with the careers service, undertake numerous activities which help student and their parents to explore their options – parents' evenings, careers conventions, work experience, visits to colleges or workplaces, providing written guides, inviting speakers into the school. As far as possible, annual reviews need to be planned to take account of these, so that students and parents, as well as other professionals, have some basis of knowledge and experience to draw on in the meetings.

In preparing for the meetings, it is also important to ensure that, where possible, careers service colleagues have had the opportunity to meet the student beforehand and have made at least telephone contact with parents, so that there has been some opportunity to begin to explore roles and make some initial contact. There will probably need to be some negotiation with careers colleagues to take account of the constraints under which they operate as well as the expectations of their role. Equally, medical or other reviews need to be borne in mind so that as far as possible the outcomes of one review or meeting can inform the other.

## Ensure that the conduct of meetings facilitates contributions from all

As Tisdall (1966) points out, the presence of young people and their parents at annual review meetings does not guarantee their active involvement in the procedures. Indeed, Tisdall questions whether such meetings are the best way of ensuring young people's involvement. My own research into the experiences of parents during the transition phase revealed the power of professional in controlling events at meetings. When asked beforehand about his expectations of his daughter's annual review, a father replied:

> When we go for the review we will be asking a lot more questions. What does happen, you know, when they leave school? What do you think Grace will be capable of? What sort of college will she be able to go to?

In the event, Grace's parents only made three interventions which related to post-school placements before the class teacher changed the course of the discussion. When asked about the meeting afterwards, both the deputy head-teacher and the occupational therapist felt that the meeting had failed to consider any plans for Grace's future.

That said, there are steps which can be taken to support the involvement of both young people and their parents. First, it is important to ensure that review reports and other relevant documentation are circulated beforehand, so that less time is taken up during the meeting on going through reports, enabling at least one-third or more of the total meeting time to be given to immediate and longer-term plans. Second, effective meetings tolerate silences, allowing participants to process information and formulate their ideas. Third, using open as well as closed questions is more likely to encourage contributions and exploration of options.

Most important of all is the willingness of professionals to attach credence to the views and wishes of young people and their parents. Despite her severe communication disorder, Kim had already made a number of contributions about her achievements, prompted by questions from the chair. However, towards the end of the meeting she raised her wish to attend a youth club, something her parents had forbidden.

*Chair:*   Is there anything else?
*Kim:*   Club, don't go to club on Thursday.
*Father:*   Not really, we're only getting [involved] with our fears.
*Mother:*   Not really.
*Kim:*   Club…don't go to club on Thursday.

While her request was originally ignored, Kim's persistence made sure she was eventually heard and her mother agreed to explore the possibilities. The decision was recorded on the action plan and this was then followed up at the subsequent meeting.

## Transition plans

### Use transition plans to keep track of the decision-making journey

Most LEAs provide a proforma for transition planning on which the school are expected to, in the words of the Code, 'build on the conclusions reached and targets set at previous annual reviews'. The Code provides helpful guidance on the kind of information that will need to be recorded. The design of such proformas needs to allow for the fact that they will need to be updated and changed over the course of the student's final years of schooling.

### Ensure that copies of plans are passed between year groups as well as into further education

It is all too easy to file transition plans away and ignore what they say about what the school or other professionals should be doing to enable young people and their parents to make up their minds about the future. The Code also stresses the importance of passing this information on to further education and social services, provided that permission has been obtained from the young person and their parents, again emphasizing the longitudinal nature of the transition process reaching well beyond the school gate.

Information contained in transition plans is important, not only for individual planning purposes but for strategic planning as well. Some local authorities have developed concordats between local providers, including child and adult services, colleges and training providers, so that gaps in local opportunities are identified collectively and agreements made about how best these should be met. This has been particularly useful in identifying the likely needs of young people returning from residential school to their home areas.

## Conclusion

I began this chapter by suggesting that the guidance on transition has been largely overlooked and yet it is, arguably, one of the most important and complex aspects of the Code's guidance. For parents, the transition of their child from adolescence to adulthood is certainly one of the most stressful and worrying periods. To close the gap characterized by McGinty and Fish (1992) between the educational and administrative procedures and the psycho-social processes that the young person experiences, the school-leaving stage should be seen as just one step in an individual's total life span and part of a much longer journey. The decisions that are made are often tentative and incremental, and the process itself is often difficult and messy. Furthermore, decisions cannot be separate from the influences of family, culture and community. The services and the official procedures need, as best they can, to support the twists and turns of young people's lives, working with and respecting the inherent informal support networks that exist within the family and community.

## Reflective questions

1   To what extent do transition issues faced by pupils with special educational needs mirror those faced by all pupils? To what extent are they quite different in nature?
2   If education is preparation for life, why is transition from education to life so difficult?

## References

Armstrong, D. and Davies, P. (1995) 'The transition from school to adulthood: aspiration and careers advice for young adults with learning and adjustment difficulties', *British Journal of Special Education*, 22(2), 70–5.
Banks, M., Bates, I., Breakwell, G., Bynner, J., Emler, N., Jamieson, L. and Roberts, K. (1992) *Careers and Identities*. Milton Keynes: Open University Press.
Beresford, B. (1995) *Expert Opinions*. Bristol: Policy Press.
Bowers, T., Dee, L., West, M. and Wilkinson, D. (1998) *Evaluation of the User- Friendliness of the Special Educational Needs Code of Practice*. London: DfEE.
Centre for Educational Research and Innovation (1986) *Young People with Handicaps: The Road to Adulthood*. Paris: OECD.
Centre for Educational Research and Innovation (1988) *Disabled Youth: the Right to Adult Status*. Paris: OECD.
Clare, M. (1990) *Developing Self-Advocacy Skills with People with Disabilities and Learning Difficulties*. London: FEU.
Corbett, J. and Baron, L. (1992) *A Struggle for Choice*. London: Routledge.
Crawley, B. (1983) 'Self-advocacy manual'. Paper no. 49, Habilitation Techonology Project. Manchester: Hester Adrian Rehabilitation Centre, University of Manchester.
Dee, L. (1997) 'Whose decision? Factors affecting the decision-making progress at 14+ for students with learning difficulties and/or disabilities'. Unpublished paper presented at the British Educational Research Association conference, September.

Department for Education (1992) *Further and Higher Education (FHE) Act*. London: HMSO.

Department for Education (1994a) *Code of Practice on the Identification and Assessment of Special Educational Needs*. London: Central Office of Information.

Department for Education (1994b) *Special Educational Needs: Guide For Parents*. London: HMSO.

Department of Health (1986) *Disabled persons (Services, Consultation and Representation) Act*. London: HMSO.

Department of Health (1989) *Children Act*. London: HMSO.

Department of Health (1990) *NHS and Community Care Act*. London: HMSO.

Disability Discrimination Act (1995) London: The Stationery Office.

Derrington, C. (1997) *In on the Planning? Professional's Approaches to Involving Young People with Special Educational Needs in Transition Planning*. Slough: NFER.

Derrington, C., Evans, C. and Lee, B. (1996) *The code in Practice: The Impact on Schools and LEAs*. Slough: NFER.

Erikson, E. (1968) *Identity: Youth and Crisis*. London: Faber and Faber.

Flynn, M. and Ward, L. (1991) 'We can change the future: citizen and self-advocacy', in S. Segal and V. Varma (eds) *Prospects for people with Learning Difficulties*. London: Fulton.

Foskett, N. and Hesketh, A. (1997) 'Constructing choice in contiguous and parallel markets: institutional and school leavers' responses to the new post-16 market place', *Oxford Review of Education*, 23(3), 299–319.

Fox, P. and Norwich, B. (1992) 'Assessing the self-perception of young adults', *European Journal of Special Needs Education*, 7(3), 193–203.

Gascoigne, E. (1995) *Working with Parents as Partners in Special Education*. London: Fulton.

Gottfriedson, L.S. (1981) 'Circumspection and compromise: a developmental theory of occupational aspirations', *Journal of Counselling Psychology*, 28(6), 545–79.

Harry, B. (1992) *Cultural Diversity, Families and the Special Education System: Communication and Empowerment*. New York: Teachers College Press.

Hirst, M. and Baldwin, S. (1994) *Unequal Opportunities: Growing Up Disabled*. London: HMSO.

Hodkinson, P., Sparkes, A. and Hodkinson, H. (1996) *Triumphs and Tears: Young People, Markets and the Transition from school to Work*. London: Fulton.

Hudson, B. (1989) 'Michael Lipsky and street level bureaucracy: a neglected perspective', in L. Barton (ed.) *Disability and Dependency*. London: Falmer Press.

Jahoda, A., Markova, I. and Cattermole, M. (1988) 'Stigma and the self-concept of people with a mild mental handicap', *Journal of Mental Deficiency Research*, 32, 103–15.

Jenkinson, J.C. (1993) 'Who shall decide? The relevance of theory and research to decision-making by people with an intellectual disability', *Disability, Handicap and Society*, 8(4), 361–75.

Jones, G. (1995) *Leaving Home*. Buckingham: Open University Press.

Krumboltz, J. (1979) 'A social learning theory of career decision-making', in A.M. Mitchell, G.B. Jones and J.D. Krumboltz (eds) *Social Learning and Career Decision-Making*. Cranston: Carroll.

McGinty, J. and Fish, J. (1992) *Learning Support for Young People in Transition: Leaving School for Further Education and Work*. Buckingham: Open University Press.

Mellers, B., Schwartz, A. and Cooke, A. (1998) 'Judgement and decision-making', *Annual Review of Psychology*, 49, 447–77.

Miner, C. and Bates, P. (1997) 'The effect of person centred planning activities on the IEP/transition planning process', *Education and Training in Mental Retardation and Developmental Disabilities*, June, 105–11.

OFSTED (Office for Standards in Education) (1995) *The Implementation of the Code of Practice for Pupils with Special Educational Needs: A Report from Her Majesty's Chief Inspector of Schools*. London: HMSO.

Oyserman, D. and Markus, H. (1990) 'Possible selves and delinquency', *Journal of Personality and Social Psychology*, 59(1), 112–25.

Riddell, S., Ward, K. and Thomson, G. (1993) 'Transition to adulthood for young people with SEN', in A. Closs (ed.) *Transition to Adulthood for Young People with Special Educational Needs*. Edinburgh: Moray House publications.

Sandow, S. (1994) 'They told me he would be a vegetable: parents' views', in S. Sandow (ed.) *Whose Special Need? Some Perceptions of Special Education Needs.* London: Paul Chapman Publishing.

Super, D. (1980) 'A life-span, life-spaace approach to career development', *Journal of Vocational Behaviour*, 16, 282–98.

Super, D. (1994) 'A life-span life-space perpective on convergence', in M.L. Savickas and R.W. Lent (eds) *Convergence in career Development Theories: Implications for Science and practice.* Palo Alto, CA: Consulting Psychologists Press.

Szymanski, E.M. (1994) 'Transition: life-span and life-space considerations for empowerment', *Exceptional Children*, 60(5), 402–10.

Taylor, M.J. (1992) 'Post-16 options: Young people's awareness, attitudes, intentions and influences on their choice', *Research Papers in Education*, 7(3), 301–34.

Tisdall, E. (1996) 'Are young disabled people being sufficiently involved in their post-school planning? Case studies of Scotland's future needs assessment and Ontario's educational–vocational meetings', *European Journal of Special Needs Education*, 9(2), 125–44.

Ward, K., Thomson, G. and Riddell, S. (1994) 'Transition, adulthood and special educational needs: an unresolved paradox', *European Journal of Special Needs Education*, 9(2), 125–44.

Weatherley, R. (1979) *Reforming Special: Policy Implementation from State Level to Street Level.* London: The MIT Press.

Weatherley, R. and Lipsky, M. (1977) 'Street-level bureaucrats and institutional empowerment: implementing special-education reform', *Harvard Educational Review*, 47 (2 May), 171–97.

Wertheimer, A. (1989) *Self-Advocacy and Parents: The impact of Self-Adovocacy on the Parents of Young People with Disabilities.* London: FEU.

Wilenius, F. (1996) *Experiencing Transition: The Impact of the Code of Practice*, Occasional Paper no. 13. London: University of London Institute of Education.

Wood, D. and Trickey, S. (1996) 'Transition planning: process or procedure?' *British Journal of Special Education*, 23(3), 120–5.

# CHAPTER 16

# EVERYBODY IN? THE EXPERIENCE OF DISABLED STUDENTS IN FURTHER EDUCATION

A. Ash, J. Bellew, M. Davies,
T. Newman and L. Richardson

*Disability and Society* (1997), 12 (4), 605–21

## Introduction

The last 20 years have seen growing support for the inclusion of disabled children and young people in mainstream education. During the 1980s, the numbers of students in colleges of further education (FE) with special educational needs doubled to reach around 100,000 nationally (Berliner, 1993). However, this increase has frequently been accompanied by the development of separate teaching units, separate staff and separate courses (Whittaker, 1991). Provision has been found to lack rigour and to challenge students insufficiently [Further Education Funding Council (FEFC), 1994].

The expansion of numbers of students with special educational needs in FE has been accompanied by a growing body of literature on inclusion. However, the importance of student views on this subject has not been fully investigated (Bradley *et al.*, 1994). Moreover, the social experience of education, from the viewpoint of the students themselves, has frequently been missing from the picture.

This chapter, based on research carried out by Barnardo's, explores the views of students in colleges of FE, both disabled and non-disabled, on the inclusion of disabled peers.

## Background

How we think about disability is of central importance to the debate about the inclusion of disabled people within the mainstream of society. Two concepts most frequently described are the medical and the social models of disability (Reiser and Mason, 1992).

The medical model typically views disability as the result of physiological impairment due to damage or disease. Alleviating the impairment or interrupting the disease process would, it is argued, eliminate disability or reduce its impact. According to this model, the degree of disability (often quantified by the use of terms such as 'mild', 'moderate' or 'severe') depends on the extent to which physiological or intellectual performance deviates from standardised norms. The greater the deviance, the greater the degree of disability and hence the greater the intensity of any remedial treatments. Thus, disabled people are 'objects' to be 'treated' and changed in accord with standards commonly accepted by society. Failure to change becomes primarily the problem of disabled people themselves.

The social model, on the other hand, views disability as fundamentally a social construct. Individuals who have an impairment become disabled by social and cultural norms which reflect a preoccupation with 'normality' [British Association for Community Child Health (BACCH)/Department of Health (DOH), 1994]. Their inability to conform to these norms may result in oppressive and discriminatory experiences. Instead of requiring people who have an impairment to change in order to conform to, and not violate, social norms, this model suggests that it is the social and cultural norms themselves which require change.

Advocates of a social model of disability argue that inclusive education encourages personal and social relationships and attitudes based on a view that disability is part of, not outside, the ordinary range of human diversity. Excluding people who have an impairment to 'special' and segregated provision is seen as diminishing disabled and non-disabled people alike. Whilst the views of young people themselves about the inclusion of disabled peers in mainstream education is, as yet, under-researched, the involvement in research of young people and of those who receive services is also underdeveloped. The difficulties that older researchers may have in interviewing adolescents have previously been documented (e.g. Roberts *et al.*, 1995). In addition, traditional research methods have, typically, excluded the subjects of research both from its design, execution and dissemination (Minkes *et al.*, 1995).

The original idea for the work described here came from three of the authors who are disabled and had recently completed their education at a residential special school. From their continuing friendships with others who had attended the same school, they were aware that some of their friends had mixed experiences of going to college after leaving school. Sometimes poor relationships with other students were given as a reason, in other cases poor resourcing, planning and preparation by colleges. What seemed clear, however, was the lack of information that existed about the attitudes and views about inclusion of the students themselves, disabled and non-disabled.

The research described here was, therefore, developed and carried out by the three ex-students in conjunction with two other researchers. Our desire to work collaboratively was driven from a number of sources. First, the redefinition of the concept of disability from the perspective of the disabled person rather than the practitioner or researcher (Oliver, 1992) has challenged the assumption that the research community is best placed to define the purpose, direction and utility of research programmes. More recently, Oliver (1996, p. 143) has accused disability research as being irrelevant to the needs of disabled people and of failing to improve their quality of life. He suggests that:

> what should be researched is not the disabled people of the positivist and interpretive paradigms but the disabilism ingrained in the individualistic consciousness of institutionalized practices . . .

In addition to our wish not to add to the plethora of studies that treat disabled people as passive objects of inquiry, we were influenced, in a broader sense, by Alderson's work (1995), in which she argues forcefully both for the active participation of young people in the research process and the pursuit of emancipatory rather than exploitive social research. Most importantly, however, while intending the collaborative experience to be an empowering one for all the research team, our primary concern was to design a study and utilise the skills of the research team in a way that would enhance the integrity of the results. While the *process* of this kind of collaborative working may have value in itself, its real worth can only be measured by the extent to which the questions to be explored are illuminated. Apart from our colleagues' distinctive knowledge of special education and their lived experience of disability, we also believed that the quality and texture of interview material obtained would be richer and more spontaneous if obtained through peer encounters rather than by the other (somewhat more mature) members of the research team. In short, a combination of formal research skills and personal knowledge of the context of the enquiry was required, in order to conduct the kind of enquiry we believed necessary. The preparatory work involved training sessions in interviewing skills and collaboration on the generation and testing of interview schedules. (An account of this process from the perspective of the disabled members of the research team was published in the *Times Educational Supplement*, 21.7.95).

After discussion between members of the research team, it was agreed to explore three main areas:

- What are the views and attitudes of disabled and non-disabled students in colleges of FE to the inclusion of disabled students?
- What is the nature and extent of relationships between disabled and non-disabled students in colleges?
- To what extent can it be said that inclusion facilitates social and interpersonal relationships between disabled and non-disabled students?

## Methodology

Six colleges in South West England were initially identified and approached for permission to undertake the work. Resource limits meant that research could be carried out with a maximum of three colleges. The three colleges which eventually took part were selected on the basis of size, type and geographical spread.

The study had two parts. In the first, questionnaires were distributed to 200 students in each college. Questionnaires asked, *inter alia*, about friendships and contacts between disabled and non-disabled students, and invited respondents to give their views on various aspects of inclusion. Students in classes nominated by teaching staff were invited to complete questionnaires. In the second part, interviews, following a semi-structured format, were carried out with groups of students.

Within each of the three colleges, group interviews were set up by the hosts. These involved, first, the whole research team meeting up to the three separate class groups (which included disabled students) at each college and, second, the disabled members of the team meeting up to two groups of disabled students drawn from various courses in each college. Separate interviews with disabled students were arranged to explore the distinct experiences of this group. All interviews were taped.

Background material from colleges on plans, proposals, reports on inclusion and statements about equal opportunity policies were obtained prior to the fieldwork being undertaken.

### The colleges

Alpha College, with some 6000 full- and part-time students, was the second largest of the three colleges taking part in the research. The college occupies two sites, with the majority of disabled students attending courses on one of these. A separate unit exists for students with learning difficulties.

As a result of a recently undertaken environmental audit of the college, a programme of improvements was underway to improve access on the main campus. Alpha College has a special needs adviser and specialist support staff to assist students with additional learning requirements. However, its college policy relating to students who have additional support needs emphasises that 'front line responsibility for providing learner and learning support rests with course tutors and all lecturers'.

Beta College was the smallest of the colleges. Of its 1,300 students, about half are full-time, and attend courses relevant to land-based industries, particularly agriculture and horticulture. Beta College had the smallest number of disabled students (under 30) and few with physical impairments. The majority of students are residential.

The college provides students with a guide to learning support, which informs students who need extra help how the college will identify, assess and work to meet those needs. The college charter draws attention to the national FE charter and its requirements, and makes clear, for example, where information for students with physical impairments or learning difficulties can be found.

Delta College has three sites. One of these is largely inaccessible to disabled people due to its location and design. Delta was the largest of the three colleges included in this study, with 17,000 full- and part-time students. The college has a learner support section. At the time of the study, over 200 students with significant support needs were included into mainstream courses.

As in Alpha College, a separate teaching unit exists for students with learning difficulties. This unit advertises its services, curriculum and entry requirements alongside other courses in the college prospectus. An access guide, which identifies accessible and inaccessible areas of the college, is made available to disabled students. The equal opportunities policy commits the college to:

> take full account of the needs of students with physical difficulties when accommodation is being designed and allocated to particular courses [and] to allow for full social integration for all students, including those with learning disabilities, in student common rooms, cafeterias and other social areas.

All three colleges were, therefore, seeking to address many issues around access – to main curricula, buildings and social activity – and inclusion.


## Findings

Four-hundred-and-thirty students returned questionnaires. This was a response rate of 78 per cent, representing just under 2 per cent of the student population of all three colleges.

Slightly more men (57 per cent) than women (43 per cent) completed a questionnaire, and respondents were overwhelmingly white. Similarly, the vast majority (96 per cent) of students who replied said they did not have an impairment. The ages of respondents ranged from 15 to 58 years, with almost 80 per cent aged between 16 and 19 years. Because of the small numbers, the responses of the 19 students who described themselves as having an impairment are excluded from the data which follow.

# Non-disabled students: questionnaire

## Friendships

Over one-third (36 per cent) of respondents said they studied alongside a disabled student. However, only 8 per cent said they were very friendly with a disabled student, and a quarter reported being fairly friendly. Almost two-thirds (60 per cent) said they did not have any disabled friends, and slightly more said they could not remember any disabled students at the last school they attended.

Over half (54 per cent) of those saying they were very or fairly friendly with disabled students at school were also very or fairly friendly with disabled students at college.

## Leisure

Little leisure time in college was spent with disabled students. Less than one in ten respondents said they had either weekly or monthly contact.

Shared leisure time outside the college was even more limited. Four per cent of respondents said they shared leisure activities on a weekly basis, with 8 per cent saying they did so on average once a month.

## Anti-discrimination legislation

Almost three-quarters (72 per cent) of respondents considered anti-discrimination legislation was needed to protect the rights of disabled people, whilst 6 per cent disagreed. In addition, over three-quarters of non-disabled respondents thought that the chances of disabled students obtaining work after completing their college course were slightly or much worse than for other students.

## Views about disabled students in FE

Students completing the questionnaire were asked to indicate whether they agreed or disagreed with, or were unsure about, the following statements about disability:

1   All young people, whatever their kind of 'disability', should have the opportunity to study, if they wish, in a college of further education.
2   Some kinds of 'disability' make attendance at a college of further education impossible.
3   Disabled students at our college get all the help they need.
4   Disabled students would rather be in the same group together.
5   Disabled students make friends easily with the rest of the students.
6   Disabled students can get to all parts of the college.
7   Non-disabled students can gain a great deal from studying with disabled students.

Between one-third and a half of respondents chose the 'don't know' or 'not sure' categories, suggesting that lack of knowledge and exposure to disability issues was common. This was particularly so in relation to questions 3–5 inclusive.

Whilst nearly all students (98 per cent) agreed that 'All young people, regardless of "disability", should have the opportunity to study in FE college', 43 per cent believed that, in practice, some kinds of 'disability' made such participation impossible. Two-thirds of respondents agreed that 'Non-disabled students can gain a great deal from studying with disabled students', and a half agreed that disabled students had problems with physical access to all parts of the college.

# Non-disabled students: interviews

## The meaning of 'disability'

Group interviews started with an exploration of students' contact with disabled people and their attitudes towards 'disability'. Awareness and knowledge often appeared to be scanty and discussion required considerable prompting from interviewers about, for example, what 'being disabled' might mean and how people become disabled. Many of the responses mentioned specific conditions, for example, 'cerebral palsy', 'dyslexia', 'Down's Syndrome', 'epilepsy', or 'being deaf and blind'. Other comments mentioned the social restrictions placed on disabled people:

> They're not able to do the thing they want. A friend of mine was knocked off her bike in the summer so she's not able to do a lot of things any more.

> Trouble in communicating. She's OK but you can tell she struggles to communicate.

> Having to have someone else to help you meet your daily needs.

Students were asked about what could be done to mitigate the effects of an impairment. Students often found it hard to respond, and most replies were concerned with remedial aids and practical supports, for example:

> Aids to help substitute for their losses . . . like a hearing aid.

> Their meals taken, their beds made, dressing and washing.

> Education, like at schools they have special teachers to help them.

> My friend's got a spine thing, in his bedroom he's got a really big bathroom because he's in a wheelchair and can't have a bath.

Only one comment referred to non-physical needs of disabled people:

> Their emotional needs, like someone they can confide in, express their feelings.

Probing by the interviewers led to some comments which suggested some awareness of a different locus of 'disability':

> I think it all depends on how receptive the group of people they are going to is like. If they are a very hostile group then it will be very difficult for that person to overcome a 'disability'.

> Our local cinema hasn't got a ramp or anything so wheelchairs can't get in, that's a problem.

The framework of understanding disability for most students interviewed appeared rooted in the medical model. The focus was, broadly, on the perceived deficits of the individual and what compensations might be needed to counteract their effects. Few comments alluded to the need to reorder broader special responses and attitudes towards disability.

## Friendships and relationships with disabled peers

A small number of the students taking part in group interviews said they had disabled friends. However, in one group of mature students (all male) two described their friendships:

> A guy I went to school with – he's paralysed from the waist down – we were always close when we were at school, he's quite a good drinking buddy.

> I've got a friend who's paralysed from the waist down too, he's in a wheelchair. We go drinking.

Other students described the difficulties they experienced in their contacts with disabled peers. Ignorance, embarrassment, guilt and confusion – not knowing what to 'do' – were mentioned frequently:

> I haven't had much experience of disabled people but you get angry with them about a lot of things and then you find it difficult to communicate with them. Then you feel you are being bad towards them, then you feel you're being patronising and you are worried all the time about what you are saying, what you are doing, whereas if you could forget about everything and carry on as normal it would solve all the problems.

> Like a disabled person going through a door. You don't know whether to hold it for them – it would seem like you're patronising them – or just let them get on with it while you're thinking you could make it so much easier. You just don't know how to help people.

Some students attributed the awkwardness they felt to a lack of contact with disabled children when they were growing up:

> I think we just need to get younger children used to seeing disabled people ... when you're little, you don't see disabled people very often so when you do kids always stop and stare and parents always slap them and say 'don't stare at them' and things like that. So you're not aware of what their problem is and you never learn until, like now, when you come to meet them. You just don't know what to do ...

> I think we just don't mix with disabled people enough. There weren't any disabled people at my school at all and there aren't any I know at college. ... I think it would get rid of the barriers if children are used to having disabled people around.

### Learning together

Many students identified positive benefits of studying alongside disabled students:

> I think people stereotype a lot, just because they have a 'disability' they think they have a mental problem as well.

> I think there is a major problem because disabled and non-disabled have been divided over the years and I think that they should now be integrated, like brought together.

One student extended the notion of inclusion:

> Life is about different sorts of people, different cultural backgrounds. I mean, keeping people separate because of race or all kinds of problems isn't helping the situation at all.

## Problems with inclusion

Whilst it appeared that students were positive about the benefits of inclusion in principle, this approval became more qualified as they distinguished between students with different impairments. The full and equal inclusion of all students, whatever their needs, was not always seen as practical or possible:

> I think we still need different schools for people with more 'learning disabilities', because a lot more time needs to be spent with them.

> It depends on the 'disability'. I don't think you can – across the board – say that everyone can come, I think it's got to be worked on.

> You can reverse the question and say do you think it's right that somebody in a class who is able-bodied, mentally able and everything, should be deprived of as much education as he needs because of teachers having to spend so much time with somebody who can't cope?

## Anti-discrimination legislation

As with responses to the questionnaire, students were supportive of anti-discrimination legislation. Generally however, they did not support affirmative action:

> It's not fair [*to shortlist a disabled person who meets minimum qualifying criteria*] because you're singling them out because of their 'disability', putting them straight on the shortlist because they've got a 'disability'.

## Responses from non-disabled students: conclusions

Both the questionnaire results and interviews indicated limited exposure both to disabled students and to issues about the inclusion of disabled students in mainstream college curricula and social life. Students mostly recognised that disabled students have problems with physical access to buildings and thought that further legislation was needed to counter discrimination.

Non-disabled students' overwhelming support for the principle of inclusion was tempered with qualification, particularly around the inclusion of students with learning difficulties. Their embarrassment and uncertainty about how to behave towards disabled students was attributed to their own separation from disabled peers, in school and in the community.

The perceptual framework most in evidence from responses was one of focus on the impairment of the individual and their perceived difference from non-disabled people. An analysis based on a social model of disability was not, generally, evident.

# Disabled students: interviews

Two small groups, of between five and eight disabled students, were interviewed in the three colleges. In two of the colleges additional interviews were carried out with small groups of students with learning difficulties. The interviews were carried out by disabled members of the research team.

## Access

Students had varied experiences of physical access to college facilities. Students recognised the work that colleges were undertaking to make the campuses fully accessible to all students.

. . . while I was here with the mobility officer, I was approached by a gentle-man . . . 'did I need any tactile markings, any help getting around?' and things like that, which I don't but the offer was there. I can't get on with the canteen so as a concession I use the staff room for lunch. Everyone's been so helpful it's not true.

The experience of students at one college (in the process of carrying out improvements to access) showed how frustrating poor access was to students. Asked about their first week there, some students replied:

It was really difficult in the first week, it has taken a month to get something going and they have just started putting ramps in there now. It was really hard getting about.

The doors are the main problem, trying to push them open like fire doors, trying to push them open shuts them back on you again.

## Staff

In general, staff were seen as helpful, although not always well informed about issues of disability:

They are all OK but they don't know much, they haven't got much experience of, say, my 'disability'.

Depends on who they are I suppose. Usually they're OK. Some are a bit, you know, if they haven't come across it before, a bit sort of 'Oh what do I do?' sort of thing . . .

Some students were pleased at the preparatory work colleges did before they started their course, and with the support given by staff. Nonetheless, students disliked having to ask peers for help where their needs had not been anticipated:

If I need help, my tutor and the people on the course will all help, take you to the toilet or push you to the library but at lunchtime and on breaks everyone is very busy. . . . I don't really like to be relying on other people on my course because if I want to do something I feel I'm a burden on them . . . if I had someone else to help me I wouldn't feel such a burden on my group.

Whilst students had suggestions about what colleges could do to prepare for a disabled student starting a course, some saw an equal responsibility falling on students to make their needs known.

People coming together [*prior to admission of a disabled student*], talking to each other, conferring before you start so they know what you need, when you need it and not when you are doing the course ask you and then, five or six months later you get the stuff and you've got six months to catch up on.

I think it's up to you to approach your tutor if you have a problem, let them know about it.

. . . it's up to us to make them aware and I don't always ask for help when I need it because I'm too independent.

## Relationships with other students

Relationships with other students on their own courses were generally good, and comments suggested that these developed as all students in a class got to know each other:

> To start with they weren't that good, but as they got used to us they got better.

> They are pretty good to me and have taken to me like I don't know what because some people stand back and don't bother . . . they think you can do it yourself so you have to ask them because they don't like to interfere, but these students that I'm with, they aren't like that.

Interactions with students on other courses were less positive. Some disabled students described some of the comments and behaviour they had experienced from others:

> Sometimes I have problems with students on other courses. They take the mickey out of my 'disability', my back and the way I walk which I can't help. They call me names and I don't take very kindly to that.

> The first two weeks there were a lot of comments, not very pleasant ones.

They recognised, however, that this was not confined to disabled students:

> Some people are just like that, able bodied people get picked on too.

Disabled students showed considerable understanding and awareness of the feelings of their non-disabled peers:

> I think one thing we've got to be careful of is that if people do offer us help, to be polite and not to tell them to go away because then they won't offer a disabled person help again.

> I think what we've got to bear in mind is that a lot of people are embarrassed about us, they don't know whether to help or not, or how to treat us.

Students with learning difficulties educated in discrete units said they had little contact with students outside these groups. Their leisure time inside the college was usually spent with others with 'special needs'. These students, however, were very positive about attending a mainstream college.

## Friendships outside college

Whilst students generally had friendships *within* the college, these did not, on the whole, develop into shared activities outside. Again, the perceived embarrassment of other students, as well as practical difficulties, were seen as limits on the extent to which relationships might develop beyond college:

> I don't know how some of the girls in my group would actually feel about coming into the home of someone with 'disabilities'. . . . I've wanted to ask them but I don't know how they would actually feel because some people don't like it.

Some students talked of the reciprocity in their relationships with others. One described how he has been able to offer help:

> On my course there have been a few people with problems writing essays and I was fortunate in reading a good book on how to write an academic essay and got a very good mark. Consequently, I've been asked for lots of help. People have come round to my house and I think we'll keep in touch when the course has finished.

## Inclusion

Disabled students readily and universally supported the principle of inclusion, for themselves and for other students:

> I just wanted to be with able-bodied students. That was my goal and I think it's done me a tremendous lot of good. I've achieved more in a term in this college than I have in my previous college which was for disabled students.
>
> . . . they [*non-disabled students*] can start to learn everyday things about a disabled person. It does them good. They are learning as well as us.
>
> It gives you a test for when you go out into the real world because you have to get on with normal people.

Some students with learning difficulties saw inclusion as giving them the opportunity for a more academically challenging education:

> We didn't learn much [*in special school*], we used to do little kiddies' stuff. We didn't do hard work but at college we do hard work and then we learn more.
>
> We didn't do any exams – that was a bit disappointing. If your friends went to different schools and they would talk about the exams and say we were lucky 'cause we didn't get homework and stuff. But I wish we had 'cause we might have got better at things.

Another student located the issue in the social world, and the impact inclusive education has in reshaping wider social attitudes to disability:

> When you go into the wider community people will be used to wheel-chairs . . . we won't be sort of coming out, people won't stare at us, because it will just be normal.

The complex reality of inclusion for disabled students posed other issues for the students. They identified positives and negatives for the individual student, with one student, asked if she would have preferred to have gone to a mainstream school, commenting:

> Well, yes and no. Yes, because I would have been treated better but no because I might have got picked on because of my 'disability'.

Students frequently mentioned choice in relation to the type of educational provision they receive, and often saw that choice as dependent on the particular needs and preferences of the students themselves:

> I feel that disabled people should have a choice really. I know that there's always fighting for and against integration but some people do have problems. It's like any special needs, if you're dyslexic, some children might cope and some might find it very difficult, so the choice should be up to the disabled person.

Overall, disabled students were positive about the benefits of inclusive education for all students. They were, however acutely aware of some of the drawbacks, particularly in the way disabled students may be treated by their peers and the feelings of isolation and exclusion which might, for example, result from their not being able to take part in sport or social activities. They also, however, recognised that school years for many children, disabled or not, can be an isolating and unhappy experience.

### Values

Self-reliance and being in control of their own lives were core values held by many disabled students who took part in the interviews. Taking personal responsibility for oneself was frequently mentioned:

> If you've got courage and determination then you will get very far in life with your 'disability' but if you give up it's up to you. It's what you make of your life, what you the individual wants.

> I find, generally speaking, it doesn't matter what authority it is, social services etc., if you fight back, they'll cooperate, but if you give up, they'll walk away.

## Interviews with disabled students: conclusions

Despite the difficulties, considerable in some cases, students were aware that colleges were tackling issues to do with access and learner support. Where problems remained unresolved, they had the potential to damage disabled students' academic careers and social relationships. Students recognised that much effective work was done by specialist staff, but were aware that other staff did not necessarily have the knowledge, experience or awareness of disability issues. These views appear to support the main criticism of separate support teams.

Relationships with other students were generally good, although some disabled students had had unpleasant experiences in their contacts with other students. Disabled students were very aware of the embarrassment and difficulties other students experienced in knowing how to behave towards them. Social contacts outside the college with other students were less developed than those within the college.

There was widespread support for inclusion in education. Students identified benefits to social relationships and to their academic development as there were greater expectations on them to perform well.

Disabled students, more than non-disabled students, saw themselves as 'students first'. The relevance of their impairment to their college life was largely related to restrictions caused by physical or social factors which hindered their inclusion. They emphasized personal responsibility and saw their attainments as due to their efforts and application. Nonetheless, they did not believe they could be judged on their achievements unless unfair barriers to their inclusion were removed.

## Discussion

Overall, both the questionnaire responses and the interviews with students highlighted some core themes:

- Amongst non-disabled students, there was a considerable lack of knowledge about the circumstances of disabled students and disabled people generally.
- Social contact between disabled and non-disabled students was not extensive. However, over half of those who had known disabled children at school had friendships with disabled students at college.
- Students strongly supported the need for legislative action to secure the rights of disabled people.
- Students supported the view that early social and educational contact with disabled peers will encourage more understanding and overcome future problems disabled (and non-disabled) people may face.
- Students supported inclusive education in principle, but were less convinced that this was viable for all students, particularly those with a learning difficulty.

It is sometimes suggested that concentration on the issue of physical access conflates the debate about inclusion to the concrete and visible, and that other more complex and challenging barriers to social inclusion may be overlooked. Certainly, access was the foremost barrier and problem identified by students. Disabled students themselves emphasised the difficulties their physical exclusion caused, and the additional problems they had to face in overcoming access problems in the colleges. This affected both their educational careers and their social interaction with other students. It meant non-disabled students had to go to considerable lengths to involve disabled friends in social activities. Whilst all the colleges had gone a long way to improve accessibility, the creation of a fully accessible environment was not yet a reality for all disabled students.

### Inclusion

Most non-disabled students did not identify insurmountable barriers to the inclusion of students with sensory or physical impairments. They had, however, more reservations about the inclusion, in all college programmes, of students with learning difficulties. The existence of discrete units for students with a learning difficulty may well reinforce uncertainty about the feasibility of inclusion of students with learning difficulties in mainstream curricula. Given that the majority of non-disabled students had had little contact with these students, and their widespread belief that physical access was the key barrier to inclusion, their views may well reflect current experience, rather than an extrapolation of that experience to what can be made possible.

### Relationships

The contention that early inclusion in mainstream education facilitates the social inclusion of disabled students was borne out by this study. There was no evidence that inclusion had a negative effect on the development of social relationships. However, this evidence relates to students with a physical or sensory impairment, as there was little or no experience in the student group of early inclusion of students with learning difficulties.

## Models of disability

The perception of disability by most non-disabled students appeared to relate most closely to the 'medical' paradigm. There was some recognition of external factors which constrained the inclusion of disabled people – largely barriers to physical access. For disabled students, perceptions embraced both social and medical models. They believed the social and physical barriers to their full participation should be removed, and that this required action. They also emphasised the personal responsibility of the individual to claim rights and fight for individual recognition. This was articulated as a personal rather than a political challenge, in the sense that disabled students did not perceive themselves as being part of any wider struggle with other groups at risk of exclusion.

The notion of disability as the focus of a social movement is, Shakespeare (1993, p. 263) argues:

> . . . important in the formation of disabled people's own identity, just as it is in breaking down patterns of prejudice and discrimination. In making 'personal troubles' into 'public issues', disabled people are affirming the validity and importance of their own identify, rejecting both the victimising tendencies of society and their own socialisation.

The personal troubles of the young people who took part in this survey had not, in most cases, been elevated to 'public issues'. However, the awareness by disabled students (the large majority of whom were under 19) of the social roots of many of the barriers which impeded then suggests that, for many, this transition might only be a matter of time.

## Reflective questions

Using your own experience(s) of Higher/Further Education, consider:

1    Was there any attempt by the organisation to ascertain the views and attitudes of disabled and non-disabled students about the inclusion (or otherwise) of disabled students?
2    What was the nature and extent of relationships between disabled and non-disabled students?
3    To what extent could it be said that any inclusion facilitated social and task-focused relationships between disabled and non-disabled students?
4    What could/should be done to improve these areas?

## References

Alderson, P. (1995) *Listening to Children: Children, Ethics and Social Research* (Barkingside, Barnardo's).
Berliner, W. (1993) Further needs of the special student. *Observer*, 13 March.
Bradley, J., Dee, L. and Wilenius, F. (1994) *Students with Disabilities and/or Learning Disabilities in Education and in Further Education: A Review of the Research* (Slough, National Foundation for Educational Research).

British Association for Community Child Health and Department of Health (1994) *Disability in Childhood – Report on the Working Group on Definitions of Disability in Childhood* (London, BACCH) (www.bacch.org.uk).

Further Education Funding Council (1994) *Chief Inspector's Report* (Coventry, FEFC).

Minkes, J., Townsley, R., Weston, C. and Williams, C. (1995) Having a voice: involving people with learning disabilities. *British Journal of Learning Disabilities*, 23, pp. 94–7.

Oliver, M. (1992) Changing the social relation of research production. *Disability, Handicap and Society*, 7, p. 2.

Oliver, M. (1996) *Understanding Disability: From Theory to Practice* (Basingstoke, Macmillan).

Reiser, R. and Mason, M. (1992) *Disability Equality in the Classroom: A Human Rights Issue* (London, Disability Equality in Education).

Roberts, H., Smith, S. and Bryce, C. (1995) *Children at Risk? Safety as a Value* (Buckingham, Open University).

Shakespeare, T. (1993) Disabled peoples' self-organisation: a new social movement? *Disability and Society*, 8, 3, pp. 249–64.

Whittaker, J. (1991) Inclusive Education for a more creative and effective further education sector. *Educare* 39 (National Bureau for Students with Disabilities—SKILL).

# CHAPTER 17

# INCLUSIVE EDUCATION IN UNIVERSITIES
## Why it is important and how it might be achieved

T. Nunan, R. George and H. McCausland

*International Journal of Inclusive Education* (2000), 4 (1), 63–88

## Introduction

This chapter addresses two questions: Why is it important that universities aim for inclusive education? How can universities achieve this aim? Our answer to the first question arises from consideration of the type of person – and graduate – an educational institution wishes to promote. This is a fundamental educational (and political) question. For example, the educational writings of Plato, Rousseau, Montessori and Mao Zedong talk of what type of person and what type of society are ideal and link these to questions of how to educate to achieve such ideals. In this chapter we connect the qualities of our graduates with particular views of citizenship and public good and, to achieve these qualities, we focus upon issues of how curriculum in universities should be shaped. The view of civil society behind our prescriptions is one that is best described by the term inclusive – that is, a society built upon ideals of social justice where participation and success are irrespective of 'race', gender, socio-economic status, ethnicity, age and disability so that disadvantage is not reproduced.

Our answer to the second question 'how can universities achieve inclusive education?' is connected with our answer to the first question about the importance of inclusive education. We see curriculum justice as the key to bringing about the qualities that we wish to promote in our graduates. Curriculum justice is achieved through a university's approach to inclusivity in seeking to shape graduate outcomes in ways that aim to build a distinctive and socially responsible (inclusive) society. Graduates are seen not just as beneficiaries of a fairer system of education but as having a responsibility to practise within their professions in more inclusive ways.

Our approach is to put inclusive education into the mainstream of curriculum formation and challenge staff to reshape their curricula, teaching, learning and assessment processes with the values and principles that embody inclusive education. This chapter outlines the first steps in that challenge – a conceptual framework that can be taken up in a staged fashion and influence curriculum practices on an institution-wide basis. It is not intended to trace theory to practice – instead we anticipate ways in which the conceptual framework informs policy development and strategic thinking. To paraphrase Ellyard (1999), the future must be imagined in order to decide how to get there and the conceptual framework is such an imagined future. It is a future in which inclusive education is consistent with the highest traditions of academic excellence and, as a future to aim for, one which regenerates and renews our notions of what it means to be a university.

## What is meant by inclusivity?

The type of person – and graduate – that an educational institution seeks to develop is influenced by decisions made about the ideal balance between the rights and responsibilities of the individual and society. It is the relationship between these two emphases that determines the patterns of key political concepts and values – participation (or exclusion), democracy (or non-representative forms of power), equality (or generation or reproduction of privilege) and emancipation (or disempowerment) – which are given expression within education systems and through their outcomes. For example, an educational system can reproduce existing economic power structures by excluding those who cannot afford to attend; it can bring together future networks which become the economically advantaged elite; it can reproduce non-representational forms of power to advantage the already advantaged.

By contrast it is possible to aim for an education system that strives to bring about greater participation, democracy, equality and emancipation for all. Barnett (1990) argues that the liberal arts provide an education which is fundamental to living in a democratic society and involves the development of a self-reflective and socially critical position (Robbins 1966), while critical perspectives such as those of Habermas (1987) inject a political perspective in arguing that higher education should be concerned with critique of society and commitment to social justice. Such an education system is understood to be in a dialectic relationship with inclusive education. That is, the values and concepts being promoted inform and are informed by the practices of inclusive curriculum.

Two sorts of notions about inclusivity in higher education illustrate the range of assumptions that can underpin the construction of inclusivity and, in turn, the sorts of mechanisms an institution might implement to achieve a particular construction of inclusivity. One notion can be linked with liberal ideals, while the other derives from critical approaches (Wyatt-Smith and Dooley 1997).

The liberal view of inclusivity focuses upon increasing participation and success in higher education, particularly by individuals representing groups within society that have traditionally been excluded on the basis of, for example, gender, socio-economic status, age, disability, 'race' and ethnicity. Activity may focus upon broadening the base of recruitment and selection, affirmative action with respect to particular target groups and provision of support in various forms to enable success. While such approaches might show impressive statistics on improved rates of participation (access), success is still framed according to traditional understandings of achievement. In this view, inclusivity could be seen as broadening access to opportunity for enculturation and reproduction of particular professional knowledge bases and practices. Success is focused upon benefits to the individual. For those who would otherwise not be involved in higher education, the benefits include the social and economic advantages that come through participation in higher education. For those from traditional backgrounds who would have been involved, the benefits include the development of tolerance, sensitivity and empathy within the wider community (Wyatt-Smith and Dooley 1997). Inclusivity framed in this way is largely to do with manipulating the inputs and processes and little to do with challenging outcomes that perpetuate unequal or oppressive social and economic structures and relations. Marginson (1997) would argue that increasing opportunity might not make the sharing of goods any more equitable as those best placed to take up the enhanced opportunities are the already advantaged. The effect of interventions based on this liberal position has been to maintain the status quo of power and privilege with exceptions proving the rule.

There is another more critical set of notions that see inclusivity in educational contexts as concerned with successful participation which generates greater options for all people in education and beyond. This construction of inclusivity has as a focus not just the factors directly affecting access, participation and success but also the criteria for judging success, and by whom and how success is determined. It is not just concerned with representing the full range of views (clearly an untenable position given the limitations of time on a curriculum) but in ensuring that the decisions about what is included are made according to criteria which affirm the basic human values of participation, democracy, equality and emancipation.

This view is not just about the means of achieving equitable outcomes for particular groups – it is also integral to the professional outcomes of courses for all participants. That is, personal benefit (important though it may be) is seen as a less desirable outcome than where all graduates operate in more inclusive ways for the betterment of society. The learning undertaken by students is more than just an apprenticeship into the field or profession – rather, a key outcome is to engage in socially transformative practice.

Connell (1998: 94) raises this reform agenda, noting that:

> The problem is not so much in unequal shares of an educational service, as in the educational relationships embedded in that service which make its effects unequal or oppressive. To reform these relationships in the interests of the least advantaged is to pursue 'curricular justice'. This is not a modest agenda. It involves rethinking teaching methods, the organisation of knowledge, and educational assessment, from new points of view.

## Curriculum justice, scholarship and 'gift' value

A critical view of curriculum focuses upon the relative power of, and relationship between, students and teachers: curriculum justice is about our valuing the social relationship 'lived-out' within the process of education and which carries over into the wider social context. Where curricula reflect a dominant Eurocentric world view, those who are not members of this culture or who resist Eurocentrism are effectively excluded from the educational process and social advantages that come with success (Barnett 1994; Bourdieu *et al.* 1994; Bowser *et al.* 1995; King 1995; Mitchell and Feagin 1995). However, where such social relationships include all participants and provide opportunities for the expression of the capacities of all individuals or of any group we have a situation in which oppression, exploitation and domination are minimized or rejected. The notion that education is a key site for demonstrating and developing such social relationships is central to our argument. It is through the development of such social relationships that students gain an understanding of the need for a balance between their rights and responsibilities as members of society and as individuals – in other words, to develop as citizens as well as professionals (Barnett 1990; Bridges 1993; Reid 1996). It is through this development that students engage with ethical and social dimensions of knowledge and see purpose in their involvement and valuing of social and public good.

We have shown that with this notion of balance comes an irreducible social dimension in any analysis of educational purposes. Within institutions this means an institutional valuing of a theme that has run through university education since its inception: that is, that the social relationships of teaching and learning should also convey components of social or public good that extend beyond the demands of the workplace to the redressing of social inequalities by an 'informed citizenry' (Wyatt-Smith and Dooley 1997). Boyer (1990), for example, uses the concept of 'scholar' and 'scholarship' to promote change in American higher education. Among the marks of being a scholar are demonstrating integrity along with the virtues of honesty, courage, persistence, consideration and humility. One of the forms of scholarship is concerned with application and is about 'scholarly service' where a scholar applies knowledge to consequential problems (Jaspers 1959; Bok 1982; Gardiner 1994) The point here is that Boyer felt the need to revitalize higher education by restating moral dimensions that apply both within institutions, between teachers and learners, and in their relationships with their communities.

Such notions about scholarship as citizenship sit uneasily in the marketplace, where the focus is on the commodification of education and further, the formation of students as commodities for the marketplace (Marginson 1993), rather than education as participation in society (Kenway *et al.* 1993, Richardson 1993, Watkins 1993). Scholarly service for civic or public good can be seen as having 'gift value' where the service is offered as a 'no charge' public service. However, there are pressures upon institutions to recast service as consultancy which has 'exchange value' in the market. The more that governments see universities as self-funded businesses with the potential to generate global income, the more that their products, internal social relations, and values will become oriented to exchange values. Reid (1996) argues that this causes a shift in the focus of debate from the values or worth of education to the price or cost of delivering the educational experience. Service as gift to social good becomes a drain upon income generation and a distorting factor in markets.

So persuasive is this environment that Marginson (1988: 9) contends that 'the Australian university by becoming a corporation, is ceasing to be a university'. This environment is corrosive to the social relationships of curriculum justice which, by their very nature, must include acts based upon 'gift value'.

## The so-called fiscal crisis of the state and market approaches in higher education

The 'fiscal crisis of the state' is shorthand for the retreat from and transformation of the welfare state. The global reorganization of industry, finance and trade – post-Fordist change – created conditions where the tax impost to maintain the welfare state was challenged in a 'revolt of the rich'. The accompanying ideological challenge was that the operation of markets through deregulation, privatization and reducing state intervention would more effectively and efficiently handle the distribution of 'social goods'. Universities in this view, as state or quasi-state institutions, should be transformed in line with these new directions.

In their quest for national competitiveness in global markets and in a rapidly changing technological and social context, governments have seen at least part of the solution in promoting mass higher education and lifelong learning (National Board of Employment Education and Training 1992; Australian Department of Education and Training Higher Education Division 1993; Organisation for Economic Co-operation and Development 1993; Candy *et al.* 1994; Morrison 1995; Reid 1996). These are viewed as critical elements in the development of 'human capital' as a necessary prerequisite to economic wellbeing. They have also argued that this expansion cannot be sustained by taxpayer funds and since individuals benefit from their university education there should be a fee or contribution paid by students towards the costs of education.

The next step in the government response to fiscal crisis is to invoke market forces as a solution (Meek 1995 cited in Reid 1996). Barton and Slee (1999: 5) note that governments have taken up the agenda of the New Right where 'competition as the instrument of selection will include...[and] exclude' according to 'market equilibrium [which] defines social good.' Further, as Rouse and Florian (1997) observe, educational reform and its legislative context has been underpinned by this marketplace philosophy which rejects equity, social progress and altruism, replacing them with academic excellence, choice and competition.

Educational goods are seen to produce private advantage and the provision of the range and quantity of such goods is thus best regulated through a market. Globalization of education has meant that institutions from outside of a national system (or belonging to private interests) have the potential to supply services thereby speeding up the adoption of market approaches. New internal fee-for-places mechanisms add to the market.

The current Australian government has sought to establish 'choice' by cutting funds to institutions in real terms. Institutions are now engaged in cutting or containing costs, competing with other institutions for students and selling their intellectual capital and services to survive. Government has made the political choices about education – and these choices are about operating in advanced capitalism, in a global competitive context of post-Fordist production.

## Universities' responses to market pressures

Coaldrake and Steadman (1998: 63) note that universities have no option but to respond to market pressures – 'the national competition policy agenda is going to force a scaling-up of the sophistication and competition activities across the university sector.' Universities' responses to the market situation include differentiation and selective specialization. Some universities have moved swiftly to protect their position in catering for the elite – 'favouring those clients who will bring the greatest return for the least investment' (Barton 1997: 238). After all, in a market situation it is such groups that can pay or pay more! In strengthening such an elite-focused brand image, these institutions have cast the move from a semi-elite to a semi-mass higher education system as undesirable on the 'self-evident' grounds that more (students) means worse (standards). Such universities have responded by aggressively competing for and recruiting 'quality' students and staff, leaving other institutions with 'poorer' students and staff (in all senses of the word).

This strategy is accompanied by the development of a brand identity based on elite status in the hope that more of the 'right type' of student will seek admission to a 'first class university'. The educational ideals underpinning such brand identity include: a competitive academic curriculum encourages and promotes highest standards of excellence; valuable traditions of leadership in research and scholarship are continued; and service to the community is through the largesse of an elite minority furthering knowledge for the benefit of all.

Other universities have reacted to this seizing of the educational high ground by attempting to emphasize their areas of 'selective excellence' – like the curate's egg, they present themselves as 'good in parts'. That is, they can compete as a 'first class university' but not in all or as many fields as others.

In this current climate joining the competition as an inclusive university is not a popular option. The very notion of inclusive education as a goal for an educational system places an institution in an ambiguous position. This tension is recognized by Rouse and Florian (1997) when they identify the need for institutions to chart their way through either/or opposites of inclusion/exclusion; equity/excellence; producers/consumers; choice/planning; entitlement/differentiation; altruism/self-interest; individuals/groups. Yet, as Corbett (1997: 55) contends, practice is not derived from ideologies which attend bipolar opposites and instead is about messy 'compromises, adjustments and individual preferences'. Interpreting the boundaries and meanings of 'inclusive' and 'exclusive' means dealing with the politics of difference. As Rizvi and Walsh (1998: 9) note:

> Difference is not something that is external to the university; a resource that students bring to university. Rather it is something that is constitutive of social relations within the university. It is constructed and enacted through the practices of curriculum. To view difference as simply an external factor to be taken into account in the construction of curriculum is to treat it in an instrumental manner, to regard it as involving a cultural formation that is somehow external to what goes on within the university. It is to assume that student diversity is mainly relevant to issues of interpersonal relations, and not to the issues of academic content and pedagogies. But to do this is to fail to see how those institutions within which curriculum is constructed may themselves be culturally biased and exclusionary. What is required is a careful analysis of the political dynamics of cultural interactions that form the borders of curriculum planning within which difference acquires significance. Furthermore, universities can no longer assume a position of neutrality in the formation of curricular relations, as somehow being external to the more general processes of intercultural articulation.

At an institutional level our framework for embedding inclusivity within desired outcomes in our graduates illustrates how we seek to address inclusive values in the socially constructed knowledge of our curriculum and the social relations in teaching and learning.

Thus, given the political imperative to operate in a market environment, institutions must come to terms with issues of curriculum construction and intercultural articulation. To focus upon the site (curriculum decision-making) where compromise, adjustment and preference is writ large in choices of content and methodologies is the fundamental way of addressing issues of inclusivity. As this position is underpinned by a view of educational excellence which is relevant for all students, it can be argued that it has market advantage – especially for mass markets driven by economic imperatives.

This is contrasted with the view of excellence which underpins the market responses of differentiation and selective specialization where the notion of excellence suits economic input models of education. These link quality and excellence to resource inputs – people (their entry scores or qualifications) and money. Under such a set of assumptions it follows that dealing with diversity costs more than dealing with homogeneity. That is, with all other things being equal diversity lowers quality and excellence because money is 'wasted' on 'coping' with diversity.

Consequently it is argued that those institutions that manage to deal with diversity are inevitably forced to compromise quality to do so.

## Challenging views of excellence

If a less simplistic view of excellence were chosen, such arguments might not be sustainable. If instead of considering educational inputs we choose to look at what are educational outputs, these notions of excellence might be challenged. If we consider an output view of excellence we start to consider 'fitness for purpose' of our graduates and grapple with more complex and social considerations which can come into judgements about what excellence means. Excellence examined in such a way might mean asking questions about who judges, against what criteria, and whose interests are being served by particular ways of defining excellence.

This immediately challenges any notions of a 'gold standard' for excellence in university education and underlines the fundamentally political nature of defining excellence.

Making excellence problematic and political brings us back to our starting point that education systems contain decisions about the ideal balance between the rights and responsibilities of the individual and society.

This chapter takes the view that the notion of educational excellence cannot be extricated from a social dimension – education is ultimately about the ideal balance between the rights and responsibilities of individuals and of society which are expressed through individual and collective action. To cite Romero (1998: 53): 'excellence is an intellectual, cultural and social construction that not only represents social inequalities through its reflective practices, but as well, arbitrariness as a characteristic of its construction'.

This social dimension of excellence applies whether we are seeking to define excellence in a system or in an individual. Because of this view we contend that that being inclusive is one measure of educational excellence.

Excellence is gauged by the ways in which the curriculum and teaching, learning and assessment convey values of inclusivity. The curriculum presents, through its content and processes, varied opportunities for students to engage with it. Its selection of content and assessment, its use of particular learning styles, its assumptions about what students already know and bring to their studies, its use of language, its covert assumptions about the nature of academic argument and its silences all impact upon how individuals participate in educational experiences. Further, the opportunities for students to hear, affirm or reject the experiences and knowledge of those involved in studying a curriculum contribute to their participation.

Consequently, fundamental 'curriculum justice'–which is based around rethinking teaching methods, the organization of knowledge and educational assessment (what we call inclusive curriculum) – is a component of educational excellence.

## An inclusive curriculum – what does it look like?

A curriculum is a bounded set of information, knowledge, skills and attitudes. It is limited by time (the period of study required for graduation) and scope (what is considered important for graduates). Those responsible for a curriculum continually redefine both its boundaries and the set of information, knowledge, skills and attitudes within the boundaries. We argue that its purpose is generally to reproduce groups that value the information, knowledge, skills and attitudes within the curriculum and that are legitimated by those in power. The processes used to reproduce power often involve change processes that allow those with power to form new power structures to reproduce existing balances of power within a community.

A curriculum is a cultural artefact as it represents a set of choices about what knowledge and values should ultimately be transmitted to preserve the community that holds such values. As a cultural artefact it is a symbol of power and what is left out of a curriculum says much about the values held by those who have less power. Values and ideology are implicit within the curriculum and it is assumed that participants in the curriculum share these.

In a democratic society, a curriculum, under some circumstances, can become a lever for wider social change. That is, the information, knowledge, skills and attitudes contained within it can represent views which are not necessarily those of the groups which hold economic power. Such curricula aim to transform or reshape social values and attitudes about social justice, social harmony, ethical or moral stances or other value positions which are deemed a priori 'good'. Where a curriculum is seen as a social lever it is contested and resisted by those who hold that social engineering, in any form, presents serious challenges to the rights of individuals and, ultimately, democratic systems. Consequently, where a curriculum addresses issues such as racism, equity, multiculturalism, sexism and social class it is open to charges that it is shaped by ideological values. That is, ideology is only contested where it is overt!

## Views of inclusivity – whose prevails on curriculum?

Various groups may claim that they should have their views and values included within a curriculum. Any curriculum represents some balance of stakeholder interests within boundaries of time and resources.

Where a curriculum attempts to minimize exclusion, stakeholders must be prepared to allow the incorporation of ideas and values which may contradict those that they hold. There may be competing claims for legitimacy and the 'owner' of the curriculum must be able to withstand the pressure of particular stakeholders to shape ideas and values according to their sectional interests. The defining characteristic of an inclusive curriculum promotes this pluralism within a rigorous intellectual environment – a climate of critical consideration. It does not exclude ideas and values on the sole basis that they are linked to gender, culture, class, or 'race'. This is not to say that all ideas and values are equal and warrant inclusion in a curriculum but that a richer and more sustaining debate about ideas and values will inform choices which lie behind political concepts and values of participation, democracy, equality and emancipation. When a university declares through its mission that it will strive to be inclusive, it is declaring a political and educational ideal manifest in an inclusive curriculum. This ideal, then, becomes the touchstone against which the university tests and decides on the competing claims of stakeholders.

It is the university that confers the rights and responsibilities of being a graduate. It is the university that determines the curriculum that seeks to develop particular qualities in its graduates. There will be advice sought, stakeholder views expressed and challenged, differing views about the curriculum and whether it will meet requirements of graduates who will be operating into the future, different views about the required skills to be developed and the level of development of such skills and so on. Ultimately, decisions are made about these matters by the processes declared by the university – the governing body of the university is responsible for broad educational directions and strategies that enable the mission of the university to be achieved. When a university declares through its mission that it will strive to be inclusive it is for the university to decide upon how this will be achieved through its courses and evident in the qualities of its graduates. Thus, one approach to improving inclusivity is to focus upon a set of outcomes – the qualities of graduates – and look at ways in which these are aligned with the values that lie behind inclusive education.

## Mainstreaming inclusive education

A university that is committed to inclusive education welcomes diversity in the student population. It accepts that diversity brings with it a greater range of experience, prior learnings and cultural values which, when used within educational settings, can enrich learning outcomes for all concerned; more (students) does not mean worse (standards). It views inclusive education as one measure of educational excellence and accepts the notion that educational outcomes (rather than input measures) are the most appropriate indicators of excellence. At an institutional level it attempts to be inclusive in the ways in which it administers and supports students and – at the level of teaching, learning and assessment – it attempts to make its curricula and delivery processes inclusive. It consciously monitors the extent to which its resources are used by different groups and how its course outcomes vary for those groups. Such an institution has progressive educational strategies that go beyond the narrowing of the curriculum and social stratification engendered by a market agenda. It understands that inclusive education is certain to be contested from both within and without on the grounds that is both unachievable and undesirable and thus the institution seeks to encourage and contribute to debate about the nature of excellence.

## Conclusions

This chapter has sought to describe the current environment in which the higher education sector is itself learning to operate. It argues against narrow and elitist responses to market forces and instead for the importance of inclusivity to build social good as well as individual benefit, to enrich and make transparent curricula, and to recognize the 'gift value' of service to the community. We argue that curricula should focus upon outcomes – on what sort of professionals, citizens and individuals we seek to shape for the benefit of society. We believe that our conceptual frameworks enable us to describe and work towards successive inclusivities – to recognize the developmental and incremental nature of inclusivity. The success of such approaches will rely upon an institution having: a clear and integrated vision; a commitment to choose bravely for the long haul; a commitment to contribute 'value' to the individual, the professions and society; intellectual rigour by making choices about knowledge that are transparent; and, by all these means, the ability to demonstrate the continuing value (not just costs) of universities to society.

Further, we assert that it is important for universities to aim for inclusive education because it is fundamentally in their own interest to do so. The current context in which higher education is operating exerts particular pressures upon universities to 'evolve' and the choice about the directions of responses to such 'evolutionary pressure' will be critical in their long-term effects. We believe that addressing inclusivity is central to remaining an educational institution in an environment where technology and globalization – through creating markets for educational services – are reforming universities as corporations which adopt corporate competitive values. Universities can go only so far down the line of being an enterprise and promoting the values of enterprise as this soon begins to eat away at their social purposes and support. As Marginson (1998: 15) notes: 'It is to court disaster by losing sight of why universities exist, why they are economically and culturally productive, why they command public support, why people use universities and what makes universities better at what they do'. Universities that promote inclusive education have answers to Marginson's questions. They understand that inclusive education makes them, and the society that they serve, more economically and culturally productive because they use and extend the talents of all. They command public support because part of their mission is to support the public good. They are better at what they do because they are 'learning institutions' and people use them because they treat people well and are guided by social justice considerations. And finally, they exist for reasons that go well beyond those economic rationalist views of society and education!

## Reflective questions

1   You (the reader) are likely to have engaged with at least one form of Higher Education. Ask yourself 'How inclusive was my HE institution'?
2   With specific reference to Inclusivity Indicators and Strategies, was there/is there any evidence of these in your own experience of Higher Education courses?
3   Would there be scope for applying Audit Indicators to your own educational setting?

## References

Australian Department of Employment Education and Training Higher Education Division (1993) *National Report on Australia's Higher Education Sector: 21 May 1993* (Canberra: Department of Employment Education and Training Higher Education Division).
Barnett, R. (1990) *The Idea of Higher Education* (Buckingham: Society for Research into Higher Education and Open University Press).
Barnett, R. (1994) *The Limits of Competence: Knowledge, Higher Education and Society* (Buckingham: Society for Research into Higher Education and Open University Press).
Barton, L. (1997) Inclusive education: romantic, subversive or realistic? *International Journal of Inclusive Education*, 1, 231–42.
Barton, L. and Slee, R. (1999) Competition, selection and inclusive education: some observations. *International Journal of Inclusive Education*, 3, 3–12.
Bok, D. (1982) *Beyond the Ivory Tower* (Cambridge: Harvard University Press).
Bourdieu, P., Passeron, J.-C. *et al.* (1994) *Academic Discourse: Linguistic Misunderstanding and Professional Power* (Cambridge: Polity).
Bowser, B., Jones T. *et al.* (eds) (1995) *Towards the Multicultural University* (Westport: Praeger).
Boyer, E. (1990) *Scholarship Reconsidered: Priorities of the Professoriate* (Carnegie Foundation for the Advancement of Teaching).
Bridges, D. (1993) Transferable skills: a philosophical perspective. *Studies in Higher Education*, 18, 1.
Candy, P., Crebert, G. *et al.* (1994) *Developing Lifelong Learners through Undergraduate Education* (Canberra: AGPS).
Coaldrake, P. and Steadman, L. (1998) *On the Brink: Australia's Universities Confronting their Futures* (St Lucia: University of Queensland Press).
Connell, B. (1998) Schools, markets, justice: education in a fractured world. In A. Reid (ed.), *Going Public: Education Policy and Public Education in Australia* (Australian

Curriculum Studies Association in association with the Centre for Study of Public Education at the University of South Australia), 88–96.

Corbett, J. (1997) Include/exclude: redefining the boundaries. *International Journal of Inclusive Education*, 1, 55–64.

Ellyard, P. (1999) Preferred futures [Keynote speech], Pathways to Sustainability – Local Initiatives for Cities and Towns, international conference, Newcastle, Australia [http://www.portstephens.infohunt.nsw.gov.au/pathway/speakers/ellyard.htm].

Gardiner, L. (1994) *Redesigning Higher Education: Producing Dramatic Gains in Student Learning* (Washington, DC: ASHE-ERIC Higher Education).

Habermas, J. (1987) *Towards a Rational Society* (Cambridge: Polity).

Jaspers, K. (1959) *The Idea of a University* (London: Peter Owen).

Kenway, J. and Bigum, C. *et al.* (1993) Marketing education in the 1990s: an introductory essay. *Australian Universities Review*, 26, 2–6.

King, W.M. (1995) the triumphs of tribalism. In B. Bowser, T. Jones and G.A. Young (eds), *Towards the Multicultural University* (Westport: Praeger).

Marginson, S. (1993) *Education and Public Policy in Australia* (Cambridge: Cambridge University Press).

Marginson, S. (1997) *Educating Australia: Government, Economy and Citizen Since 1960* (Cambridge: Cambridge University Press).

Marginson, S. (1998) Nation-building universities in a global environment. University of South Australia Public Lecture Series – The Role of Universities in Australia in 2010, accessed 15 September 1998 [http://www.unisa.edu.au/newsinfo/lecture/Marginson_lecture.htm].

Marchese, T. (1998) Not-so-distant competitors: how new providers are remaking the post-secondary marketplace. American Association for Higher Education, May Bulletin, accessed 15 September 1998 [http://www.aahe.org/].

Mitchell, B.L. and Feagin, J.R. (1995) America's racial-ethnic cultures: opposition within a mythical melting pot. In B. Bowser, T. Jones and G.A. Young (eds). *Towards the Multicultural University* (Westport: Praeger).

Morrison, T.R. (1995) Global transformation and the search for a new educational design. *International Journal of Lifelong Education*, 14, 188–213.

National Board of Employment Education and Training (1992) *The Quality of Higher Education: Discussion Papers* (Canberra: AGPS).

Organization for Economic Co-operation and Development (1993) [Proceedings of the conference] The Transition from Elite to Mass Higher Education/DEET, Higher Education Division/OECD (Sydney: AGPS).

Reid, I. (1996) *Higher Education or Education for Hire?: Language and Values in Australian Universities* (Rockhampton: Central Queensland University Press).

Richardson, C. (1993) Higher education as a commodity. *Australian Universities Review*, 36, 7–8.

Rizvi, F. and Walsh, L. (1998) Difference, globalisation and the internationalization of curriculum. *Australian Universities Review* 41, 7–11.

Robbins, L. (1996) *The University in the Modern World* (London: Macmillan).

Romero, M.M.R. (1998) Educational change and discourse communities: representing change in postmodern times. *Curriculum studies*, 6, 47–68.

Rouse, M. and Florian, L. (1997) Inclusive education in the market place. *International Journal of Inclusive Education* 1, 323–36.

Watkins, P. (1993) Centralised decentralisation: Sloanism, market quality and higher education. *Australian Universities Review*, 36, 9–15.

Wyatt-Smith, C. and Dooley, K. (1997) Shaping Australian policy on cultural understanding. *International Journal of Inclusive Education*, 1, 267–82.

# ANNOTATED LIST OF FURTHER READING

(Includes items retrieved and considered promising but eventually excluded from the above)

Ainscow, M. (1999). *Understanding the Development of Inclusive Schools*. London and New York: RoutledgeFalmer.

Allan, J. (1999). *Actively Seeking Inclusion: Insiders, Outsiders and Deciders*. London and New York: RoutledgeFalmer.

Archer, L. (2003). Social class and higher education. In: Archer, L., Hutchings, M. and Ross, A. (eds), *Higher Education and Social Class: Issues of Exclusion and Inclusion*. London and New York: RoutledegeFalmer. (pp. 5–20)
(A clear exposition of classical and modern conceptions of social class and issues of measurement, social capital and multiple class identities, in relation to access to higher education.)

Beveridge, S. (1999). Concepts of special educational need. In: *Special Educational Needs in Schools* (2nd edn). London and New York: RoutledgeFalmer. (pp. 1–15)
(A useful review of historical conceptualisations, including issues of interactivity, constructionism and continuity.)

Booth, T., Nes, K. and Stromstad, M. (eds) (2003). *Developing Inclusive Teacher Education*. London and New York: RoutledegeFalmer.

Broadhead, P. and Cuckle, P. (2002). Starting with learning: new approaches to development and improvement planning in primary schools. *Research Papers in Education*, 17 (3), pp. 305–22.
(This paper focuses on all involved children and the use of different development targets and their impact on improved teaching and learning.)

Clark, C., Dyson, A., Millward, A. and Robson, S. (1999). Inclusive education and schools as organizations. *International Journal of Inclusive Education*, 3 (1), 37–51.
(Establishes another 'tool in the box' for analysing' the inclusive school' and states the need to apply inclusive practice far more widely than just the SEN debate.)

Clegg, S. and McNulty, K. (2002). Partnership working in delivering social inclusion: organizational and gender dynamics. *Journal of Education Policy*, 17 (5), 587–601.
(Excellent extended description of social inclusion issues in the United Kingdom. Investigates the 'Partnership process' and how the skills associated with feminine leadership are gaining in recognition, with men also adopting them.)

Cole, T. (1998). Understanding challenging behaviour: Prerequisites to inclusion. In: Tilstone, C., Florian, L., and Rose, R. (eds), *Promoting Inclusive Practice*. London and New York: RoutledegeFalmer. (pp. 113–27)
(Reviews substantial research on inclusion, then offers a review of very different conceptualisations of problematic pupil behaviour in school, critiques each and explores the implications for action of each.)

Department for Education and Skills. *Inclusion: A Catalogue of Resources to Support Individual Learning Needs*. http://inclusion.ngfl.gov.uk. London: DfES.

Dorries, B. and Haller, B. (2001). The news of inclusive education: A narrative analysis. *Disability and Society*, 16 (6), 871–91.
(Very interesting paper focusing on the media coverage of a specific autistic youngster in the United States and the family's legal battle to have their son educated in a regular classroom. Specific themes are extracted and commented upon.)

Dyson, A. (2000). Questioning, understanding and supporting the inclusive school. In: H. Daniels (ed.), *Special Education Re-formed: Beyond Rhetoric?* London and New York: Falmer Press. (pp. 85–100)
(Discusses the practical difficulties of inclusion in terms of methods, problem solving and politics, and endemic resistance. Proposes a model of 'critical support'.)

Evidence for Policy and Practice Information and Co-ordinating Centre (2002). *A Systematic Review of the Effectiveness of School-level Actions for Promoting Participation by all Students.* London: EPPI-Centre, Social Science Research Unit, Institute of Education, University of London (http://eppi.ioe.ac.uk).

Farrell, P. and Ainscow, M. (2002). *Making Special Education Inclusive.* London: David Fulton Publishers.

Florian, L. and Rouse, M. (2001). Achieving high standards and the inclusion of pupils with special educational needs. *Cambridge Journal of Education*, 31 (3), 399–412.
(Considers the tension between raising standards in an educational context dominated by league tables comparing schools, and the inclusion of pupils with special needs. Research in five secondary schools leads the authors to conclude that achieving both goals is possible simultaneously.)

Francis, B. (2000). Gender and achievement: A summary of debates. In: *Boys, Girls and Achievement: Addressing the Classroom Issues.* London and New York: RoutledgeFalmer. (pp. 4–12)
(Gives a historical perspective of change over the last 30 years, from a feminist perspective. A useful starter for onward debate.)

Gilroy, D. E. and Miles, T. R. (1996). The dyslexic's strengths and weaknesses. In: *Dyslexia at College* (2nd edn). London and New York: RoutledgeFalmer. (pp. 1–9) also Appendix 6 by F. Zinovieff, pp. 220–28.
(A brief, simple and balanced description of the positive and negative aspects of dyslexia in college, followed by a report by a dyslexic student of her travails in college.)

Gross, J. and White, A. (2003). *Special Educational Needs and School Improvement.* London: David Fulton Publishers.
(A practical guide.)

Hastings, R. P. and Oakford, S. (2003). Student teachers' attitudes towards the inclusion of children with special needs. *Educational Psychology*, 23 (1), 87–94.
(Introduces a new measure of attitudes towards inclusion, the Impact of Inclusion Questionnaire (IIQ) 'found to have good reliability' . . . 'needs more exploration of psychometric properties'. Results indicate that student teachers are more concerned about the impact of children with Emotional Behavioural Difficulties rather than children with intellectual difficulties.)

Hayes, B. (2002). Community, cohesion and inclusive education. *Educational and Child Psychology*, 19 (4), 75–90.
(In the context of community cohesion and participation, discusses the domains of social capital as a framework for intervention, connecting with the development of performance indicators for inclusive practice and the role of external consultants.)

Her Majesty's Inspectorate of Education (Scotland) (2002). *Count us in: Achieving Inclusion in Scottish schools.* Edinburgh: HMIE. www.hmie.gov.uk/documents/publication/cui.pdf

Higgins, N. and Ballard, K. (2000). Like everybody else? What seven New Zealand adults learned about blindness from the education system. *International Journal of Inclusive Education*, 4 (2), 163–78.
(A very interesting paper that demonstrates themes of perceived inclusion and exclusion of seven blind adults who were all educated in mainstream settings but do not believe that they were 'included'.)

Inclusion Press Online www.inclusion.com (a Canadian resource site).

Jackson, S. (2000). Promoting the educational achievement of looked-after children. In: T. Cox (ed.), *Combating Educational Disadvantage: Meeting the Needs of Vulnerable Children.* London and New York: Falmer Press. (pp. 65–80)
(Reviews 'the problem' in the context of a discussion of resilience and risk factors and a report of research on high achievers who were looked after. Considers the impact of legislation and recent interventions.)

Kugelmass, J. W. (2001). Collaboration and compromise in creating and sustaining an inclusive school. *International Journal of Inclusive Education*, 5 (1), 47–65.

(An excellent example of the power of collaboration in developing an inclusive school. Provides 'how tos'. Two very illuminative figures on pp. 54 and 55 illustrate how collaboration supports diversity in inclusion.)

Mittler, P. (2000). *Working Towards Inclusive Education*. London: David Fulton Publishers.

Mukherjee, S., Lightfoot, J. and Sloper, P. (2000). The inclusion of pupils with a chronic health condition in mainstream school: what does it mean for teachers? *Educational Research*, 42 (1), 59–72.

(Focuses on the young person's view point; how their education and success is perceived to be dependent on teachers' knowledge, understanding of their condition, and time to meet their subsequent needs. A good advice document, could be a basis for school policy writing.)

Ofsted and the Audit Commission (2002). *LEA Strategy for the Inclusion of Pupils with Special Education Needs*. London: OFSTED. www.ofsted.gov.uk/publications/docs/2675.pdf

Peters, S. (2002). Inclusive education in accelerated and professional development schools: A case-based study of two school reform efforts in the USA. *International Journal of Inclusive Education*, 6 (4), 287–308.

(Focuses on two urban schools with large numbers of 'at risk, disadvantaged, minority and SEN' students; some examples of peer-assisted learning and accelerated learning and an overall climate of collaboration and enquiry; stresses the need for continual focus on research and development to inform training to meet the needs of all students. Particular emphasis on flexibility, high expectations, balance of academic and social needs, relevance of curriculum to student lives, importance of peers as role models and collaborative learning.)

Potts, P. (2002). *Inclusion in the City: Selection, School and Community*. London and New York: RoutledgeFalmer.

Purdue, K., Ballard, K. and Macarthur, J. (2001). Exclusion and inclusion in New Zealand early childhood education: Disability, discourses and contexts. *International Journal of Early Years Education*, 9 (1), 38–9.

(An interesting introduction; including an overview of early childhood education in New Zealand and extensive research based on oral and written statements. Findings range from experiences of being seen as 'different' and belonging elsewhere, to experiences of belonging in ordinary early childhood settings.)

Social Exclusion Unit. www.socialexclusionunit.gov.uk (United Kingdom government site).

Tett, L., Munn, P., Kay, H., Martin, I., Martin, J. and Ranson, S. (2001). Schools, community education and collaborative practice. In: S. Riddell and L. Tett, *Education, Social Justice and Inter-agency Working: Joined-up or Fractured Policy?* London and New York: RoutledgeFalmer. (pp. 105–23)

(Discusses full-service schools, community participation in decision-making, with a useful analysis of the various benefits and disadvantages of inter-agency collaboration, with helpful figures. Discusses barriers to change.)

Tilstone, C. and Rose, R. (eds) (2003). *Strategies to Promote Inclusive Practice*. London and New York: RoutledgeFalmer.

Vaughan, M. (2002). An index for inclusion. *European Journal of Special Needs Education*, 17 (2), 197–201.

(Describes a practical tool for the development of increasingly inclusive practice using a school improvement model. Demonstrates how some schools have linked the Index to school development planning.)

Wearmouth, J. (ed.) (2001). *Special Education Provision in the Context of Inclusion Policy and Practice in Schools*. London: David Fulton Publishers.

Westwood, P. (2003). Teaching children self-management and self-regulation. In: *Commonsense Methods for Children with Special Educational Needs: Strategies for the Regular Classroom* (4th edn). London and New York: RoutledgeFalmer. (pp. 55–64)

(Brief and relatively lightly referenced, but succinct and well founded and by no means only craft knowledge and common sense.)

Wolger, J. (1998). Managing change. In: Tilstone, C., Florian, L. and Rose, R. (eds), *Promoting Inclusive Practice*. London and New York: RoutledgeFalmer. (pp. 78–91).

(Touches on school effectiveness research and issues of organisation in large systems, emphasising the role of school development plans, leadership, planning and staff training.)

# International Journal of Inclusive Education

## EDITOR
**Roger Slee,** *McGill University, Canada*

The *International Journal of Inclusive Education* provides a strategic forum for international and multi-disciplinary dialogue on inclusive education for all educators and educational policy-makers concerned with the form and nature of schools, universities and technical colleges.

Papers published are original, refereed, multi-disciplinary research into pedagogies, curricula, organizational structures, policy-making, administration and cultures to include all students in education.

The journal extends beyond enrollment to successful participation which generates greater options for all people in education and beyond.

**Find out how to access this journal online by visiting
www.tandf.co.uk/journals/online.asp**

**Download a free online sample at:
www.tandf.co.uk/journals/onlinesamples.asp**

## SUBSCRIPTION RATES
*2004 – Volume 8 (4 issues)*
Print ISSN 1360-3116
Online ISSN 1464-5173
Institutional rate: US$350; £214
(with access to the online version)
Personal rate: US$174; £105 (print only)

Taylor & Francis
Taylor & Francis Group

**Please contact Customer Services at either:**

Taylor & Francis Ltd, Rankine Road, Basingstoke, Hants RG24 8PR, UK
**Tel:** +44 (0)1256 813002   **Fax:** +44 (0)1256 330245   **Email:** enquiry@tandf.co.uk
**Website:** www.tandf.co.uk

Taylor & Francis Inc, 325 Chestnut Street, 8th Floor, Philadelphia, PA 19106, USA
**Tel:** +1 215 6258900 **Fax:** +1 215 6258914   **Email:** info@taylorandfrancis.com
**Website:** www.taylorandfrancis.com